Your Official America Online® Internet Guide

4th Edition

Your Official America Online® Internet Guide

4th Edition

by David Peal

AOLPress

Dulles, VA

Your Official America Online® Internet Guide, 4th Edition

Published by

AOL Press

An imprint of IDG Books Worldwide, Inc.

An International Data Group Company

919 E. Hillsdale Blvd., Suite 400

Foster City, CA 94404

www.aol.com (America Online Web site)

Library of Congress Control Number: 00-107558

ISBN: 0-7645-3552-8

Printed in the United States of America

10 9 8 7 6 5 4 3 2 1

4B/RW/RQ/QR/IN

Distributed in the United States by IDG Books Worldwide, Inc. and America Online, Inc.

For general information on IDG Books Worldwide's books in the U.S., please call our Consumer Customer Service department at 800-762-2974. For reseller information, including discounts and premium sales, please call our Reseller Customer Service department at 800-434-3422.

 is a trademark
of America Online, Inc.

 is a registered trademark or trademark under exclusive license to IDG Books Worldwide, Inc. from International Data Group, Inc. in the United States and/or other countries.

Welcome to AOL Press™

AOL Press books provide timely guides to getting the most out of your online life. AOL Press was formed as part of the AOL family to create a complete series of official references for using America Online as well as the entire Internet — all designed to help you enjoy a fun, easy, and rewarding online experience.

AOL Press is an exciting partnership between two companies at the forefront of the knowledge and communications revolution — AOL and IDG Books Worldwide, Inc. AOL is committed to quality, ease of use, and value, and IDG Books excels at helping people understand technology.

To meet these high standards, all our books are authored by experts with the full participation of and exhaustive review by AOL's own development, technical, managerial, and marketing staff. Together, AOL and IDG Books have implemented an ambitious publishing program to develop new publications that serve every aspect of your online life.

We hope you enjoy reading this AOL Press title and find it useful. We welcome your feedback at AOL Keyword: **Contact Shop Direct** so we can keep providing information the way you want it.

AOLPress

About the Author

David Peal teaches in the Educational Technology Leadership MA program at George Washington University in Washington, DC. As the former editorial manager of AOL's Internet Connection, he developed forums about the Internet and helped create AOL's first comprehensive online source of Internet help. In addition to this book, David has written other books for AOL: *Student's Guide to the Internet* (1998), *Picture This* (1999), and *Your Official America Online Guide to Pictures Online* (2000). He wrote *Access the Internet* (1994-97), edited the Lycos Small Business Web Resource Guide (1997), and developed one of the first newsletters devoted to the commercial use of the Internet (1994-95). He was a finalists judge for the education category in the 2000 Global Information Infrastructure (GII) awards.

Credits

America Online

Technical Editors
Ann Burkhart
Jim Callahan
John Crotty
Kerstin Crutchfield
Kristie Cunningham
Caroline Curtin
Keith Fleming
Todd Forest
Marta Grutka
Pam Irvine
Sandra Jackson
Jeff Kimball
Jane Lennon
Debra Llavoy
Mary-Sara Ortutay
Dan Pacheco
Mark Pilipczuk
Lisa Pittman
Bruce Stimpson
Ginny Wydler

Cover Design

DKG Design, Inc.

IDG Books Worldwide

Senior Project Editor:
Nicole Haims

Acquisitions Editor:
Kathy Yankton

Copy Editors:
Rebecca Huehls
Paula Lowell
Beth Parlon

Proof Editor:
Jill Mazurczyk

Technical Editor:
Lee Musick

Permissions Editors:
Carmen Krikorian
Laura Moss

Publishing Director:
Andy Cummings

Editorial Manager:
Leah Cameron

Media Development Manager:
Laura Carpenter

Editorial Assistant:
Seth Kerney

Project Coordinator
Emily Wichlinski

Layout and Graphics
LeAndra Johnson
Brian Torwelle
Erin Zeltner

Proofreaders
Laura Albert
Vickie Broyles
Joel K. Draper
Susan Moritz
Angel Perez
Carl Pierce
Marianne Santy
Charles Spencer

Indexer
Lori Lathrop

Special Help:
Rebecca Senninger

Author's Acknowledgments

Many people at IDG Books WorldWide provided the support required to revise this long book in a very short period, beginning with Walter Bruce and Andy Cummings, associate publisher and publishing director respectively. Twice in a short period I have had the good fortune to work with Nicole Haims, senior project editor, who ably took charge of a book project involving two big companies, one complex manuscript, and a large team. Leah Cameron, editorial manager, oversaw the many levels of editorial work, and I have now had a second chance to work with talented technical editor Lee Musick.

Rima Regas and Tyler Regas — writers, technical gurus, and genial neighbors — revised several chapters and provided technical advice throughout the project.

At AOL, John Dyn once again oversaw a complex effort made much simpler through his sharp understanding of the ultimate goals of this project. I also want to thank Kathy Harper, editorial director of AOL Press, and Marta Anne Grutka of AOL's Corporate Communications staff, who graciously fielded many detailed questions. Behind the scenes, Mario Fragoso, in AOL customer support, helped me work through some difficult software questions, and the AOL Plus Support Staff patiently helped me get up to speed with DSL and the world of broadband. Others who helped at AOL: Mark Goldstein, DSL product manager; Adam Bartlett, of the AOL Anywhere team; Dan Shilling, in marketing communications; and Stephanie Diamond, product manager for AOL's voice-recognition program.

At home, I am happy to report that scooters, quarters, and *Goblets of Fire* took precedence over deadlines and hardware meltdowns. Once again, special thanks to my wife and anchorwoman Carol Weiss. I wrote the book with kids in mind, especially the two kids to whom the book is dedicated.

Dedication

For Gabriel and Ella

Contents at a Glance

Foreword xxiii

Introduction 1

Part I: From AOL to the Internet 9
Chapter 1: What Is the Internet? 11
Chapter 2: I'm on AOL. Where's the Internet? 25
Chapter 3: Making AOL Work Your Way 45
Chapter 4: AOL for the Whole Family 73

Part II: Discovering the World Wide Web 99
Chapter 5: Using the World Wide Web to Simplify Your Life 101
Chapter 6: Behind the Wheel: Using AOL's Web Browser 123
Chapter 7: All-Purpose Vehicle: Netscape Navigator 153
Chapter 8: Finding Your Way: Internet Searching Made Easy with AOL .. 169
Chapter 9: From Breadth to Depth: Search Engines and Specialized Searches 187

Part III: Communicating on AOL and the Internet 209
Chapter 10: You've Got Mail: Handling the E-Mail You Receive 211
Chapter 11: Sending Mail 239
Chapter 12: Live Communication: From Instant Messages to Internet Chats 263
Chapter 13: Joining Focused Communities: Mailing Lists 287
Chapter 14: Global Bulletin Boards: Newsgroups 313

Part IV: Extending Your Internet Connection 345
Chapter 15: From the Internet to You: Downloading Software 347
Chapter 16: Internet Tools that Extend Your Reach 371
Chapter 17: Internet Everywhere: New Ways to Access AOL 389
Chapter 18: Did You Know You Can ...on AOL? 409

Index 429

Table of Contents

Foreword xxiii

Introduction 1

    What's New in AOL 1

        Enhanced E-Mail 1

        AOL Expands Its Web Presence 2

        Improved Ease of Use 2

        High-Speed Internet Access and Content 3

    How This Book Is Organized 3

        Part I: From AOL to the Internet 3

        Part II: Discovering the World Wide Web 4

        Part III: Communicating on AOL and the Internet 5

        Part IV: Extending Your Internet Connection 5

    Using This Book 6

Part I: From AOL to the Internet   9

Chapter 1: What Is the Internet? 11

    The Net, At Last 13

    AOL and the Internet: How Are They Related? 14

    New in AOL 6.0 15

    A Way to Think of the Internet 18

        Internet Destinations 20

        Internet Tools 20

        Internet Communities 21

        The Internet as a Network of Networks 21

Chapter 2: I'm on AOL. Where's the Internet? 25

    AOL and the Web: A Blurring Boundary 26

    An AOL Road Map 27

        AOL's Red Carpet: The Welcome Screen 30

    About AOL Keywords 31

        Channeling Your Energy 32

        What's on AOL's Menus 33

AOL 6.0's New Toolbar 34

Where Do They Keep the Tools Around Here? 35

AOL Roadside Assistance for Internet Travelers 36

Help! Where Am I? 37

Teach Yourself Step-by-Step, in Pictures 39

Take an Online Class to Learn Basic Skills 39

Use the AOL Message Boards to Ask Internet Questions 40

NetHelp: Web-Based Internet Help 41

Staying Informed with an Electronic Newsletter 42

Getting Help If You Can't Get Online 42

Buying Computer Gear Online 43

Chapter 3: Making AOL Work Your Way **45**

Customizing Your AOL Experience 47

Creating Your Own Online Newspaper: the AOL Anywhere Service 48

Taking Charge of Your Schedule:

The My Calendar Service 51

Keeping Track of Your Favorite Places 54

Managing Your Favorite Places 57

Using the Same Favorite Places on Several Computers 59

Selecting Your AOL Favorites: My Places 60

Customizing Contact Info: Your Buddy List and Address Book 61

Setting Up Your Buddy List 61

Creating a Member Profile 63

Organizing Your Address Book 64

Understanding Your AOL Account 65

Choosing Screen Names and Passwords 65

Updating Your Billing Information 67

Customizing Your Internet Connection 67

Signing on to AOL over a Network 67

Locations: Where You Are

When You're Online 69

Using AOL as Your Default

Internet Software 70

Chapter 4: AOL for the Whole Family **73**

    Online Safety for the Whole Family 75

    Maintaining Your Family's Online Safety 75

        Using Parental Controls 77

        Assigning a Screen Name to an Age Bracket 79

        Fine-Tuning with Custom Controls 80

            Setting Mail Controls 81

            Setting Download Controls 82

            Setting Web Controls 82

            Setting Newsgroup Controls 83

            Online Timer 84

    AOL@School 85

    Doing Family-Friendly Web Searches 86

    Discovering the World's Largest Reference Library 88

        Encyclopedias 88

        Columbia Encyclopedia 88

        Encyclopedia Mythica 89

        Information Please 90

        Presidents on the Net 90

        Technology Encyclopedia:Whatis.com 91

        When You Need the Right Word 91

        Acronyms 91

        Bartlett's Familiar Quotations 92

        Web of Online Dictionaries 93

        The World in Numbers 94

        CIA World Factbook 94

        Fedstats 95

        Online Newspapers, Magazines, and Books 96

    Onward to College and Life 97

Part II: Discovering the World Wide Web   99

Chapter 5: Using the World Wide Web to Simplify Your Life 101

Starting Out on the Web 103

Financial Planning: What You Have, Where You're Going 105

Planning Your Finances 105

Banking Online 106

Need New Wheels? 107

Looking for that Dream House? Do the Groundwork Online 109

Getting Ahead: Jobs and Careers 110

Stop Working So Hard: Having Fun Online 111

Shopping Online 112

Shop@AOL, Now Open for Business *112*

Shop@AOL, Shop Smart *113*

Buying Computers and Computer Gear *114*

Buying Books Online *116*

Buying CDs Online *117*

It's Showtime: Movies Online 117

From House to Home 118

For Gourmands 119

For Travelers 119

Going Once, Going Twice: Online Auctions 120

Chapter 6: Behind the Wheel: Using AOL's Web Browser 123

Ten Long Years of Web History in a Minute 125

Why You Need a Browser to Surf the Internet 125

Your AOL Browser: A Tool for Using Other Tools 126

Electronic Mail 126

Newsgroups 126

FTP 127

Web Pages and Their Elements 127

The AOL Browser in Action 133

Telling Your Browser Where to Go:

The Address Box 134

There Must Be Some Mistake: Error Messages 134

Telling the Browser How to Get There: Navigation Buttons 135

Your Compass: The Status Bar 137

Seize the Page: Right-Click! 138

Right-Clicking Text *138*

Right-Clicking a Graphic *140*

Making the AOL Browser Work Your Way **140**

How the Browser Keeps Track of Where You've Been 141

Following Your History *141*

Managing Your Temporary Internet Files (Cache) *141*

Changing How Things Look (Colors and Fonts) 143

Plugging into Multimedia **146**

Getting Plug-Ins 147

RealPlayer Brings Radio, TV, and Video to the Web 147

RealJukebox Brings Music to the Web 147

Animating the Web with Shockwave and Flash 148

Other Video Formats: MPG, AVI, QuickTime 149

Sounds of Yore: WAV, AU, MIDI 150

Chapter 7: All-Purpose Vehicle: Netscape Navigator **153**

Installing Netscape 6 . . . . **155**

Getting to Know Netscape 6 . . . . **156**

Using the Menu Bar **158**

Using My Sidebar **159**

Adding and Deleting Panels
from My Sidebar 161

Customizing Content in My Sidebar 162

Browsing the Web with Netscape 6 . . . . **163**

Using the Netscape 6 Taskbar and Status Bar **164**

Using Netscape 6's Bookmarks **165**

Adding Bookmarks 165

Managing Bookmarks 166

**Chapter 8: Finding Your Way: Internet Searching
Made Easy with AOL** **169**

Why Is Searching the Web Such a Pain? **171**

The AOL Search Solution **172**

Understanding the Difference between Browsing and Searching 172

Doing a Sample Search: Labrador Retrievers 175

Interpreting Your Results 176

Extending Your Search 177

Refining Your Search 179

Refining Your Search with Power Operators 180

AOL's White Pages, Yellow Pages, and E-Mail Finder 182

Finding Residential Addresses (White Pages) 183

Finding Business Addresses (Yellow Pages) 183

Finding E-Mail Addresses 183

Getting Maps and Directions: MapQuest 184

Using the AOL People Directory 184

Chapter 9: From Breadth to Depth: Search Engines
and Specialized Searches 187

What to Look for in a Search Engine 189

AltaVista 190

Google 191

Lycos 194

Northern Light 195

Doing Many Searches at Once 196

Tips for Asking Good Questions 197

Special-Purpose Search Collections 198

Digital Librarian 199

The WWW Virtual Library (VLIB) 199

Argus Clearinghouse:

Librarians Rate the Net 200

Finding Authoritative Resources 202

Health: Specialized Resources 202

Law: Specialized Resources 203

From Libraries on the Web to Digital Libraries 204

Library Catalogs on the Web 204

Digital Libraries 205

Part III: Communicating on AOL and the Internet 209

Chapter 10: You've Got Mail: Handling the E-Mail You Receive . . 211

A Word about E-Mail Addresses 213
   Finding Out Someone's E-Mail Address 215
   Getting E-Mail Help 215
Doing Mail on AOL 216
Sizing Up Your Messages Before Reading Them 218
Reading Your Mail 220
Managing Your Mail 221
   Replying to a Message 221
   Forwarding a Message 223
   Saving a Message as a Text File 223
   Printing Messages 223
   Deleting Messages 224
Got Files? 224
   Downloading Attached Files 225
   Using Downloaded Files 226
Using and Managing Your Filing Cabinet 226
   Moving Messages to Your Filing Cabinet 229
   Getting Your Mail Automatically 230
AOL Anywhere: New Ways To Do Mail 231
   AOL Mail on the Web 232
   AOL Mail for Handhelds 234
   Using AOL Mail on a Palm Handheld 235
You've Got Junk Mail 236

Chapter 11: Sending Mail 239

Who's the Message For? 241
What's the Message About? (Subject Line) 242
Playing Nice: Mail Netiquette 243
   Keep Your Voice Down 243
   Avoid Needless Provocation 243
   Fight Fires When They Do Break Out 244
   Quote Pithily in Thy Replies 244
   Signal Your Feelings 244
   Rewrite Again and Again 245

Talking Back 245

Just Say No to E-Mail 245

Make It Easy on Your Reader 246

Sending Your Message on Its Way **246**

Sending Mail: Preferences 246

After the Message Is Out the Door 248

Unsending a Message 249

Address Book **249**

Adding a Name to the Address Book 250

Creating a Group (Mailing List) 252

Attaching One or More Files **253**

Embellishing Messages **254**

Emphasizing Text 254

Adding Links, Text Files, and Images to Your Messages 256

Adding a Link to a Message *256*

Inserting an Image *257*

Inserting a Background Picture *258*

Inserting a Text File into a Message *258*

Inserting HTML *259*

Caffeinated Stationery 259

Closing with a Signature **259**

**Chapter 12: Live Communication: From Instant
Messages to Internet Chats** **263**

Communicating Live on AOL **265**

Getting Started with Instant Messages **266**

Customizing Your IM Experience 268

Setting Your IM Privacy Preferences 268

Using the AOL Instant Messenger Service **270**

Downloading, Installing, and Running the

AOL Instant Messenger Service 271

Adding Buddies to Your Buddy List 273

Making New Buddies 274

Helping Potential New Buddies Find You 275

Sounds Like Fun 276

Protecting Your Privacy on AIM 277

Sending Messages with AIM 278
   Chatting with Your E-Mail Buddies 278
   Creating and Joining AIM Chats 279
   Exchanging Files with AIM 280
   Changing Your Screen Name 280
   Formatting Your Screen Name 282
Using AIM When You're
Away from Your PC 282
Using AIM's Stock and News Tickers 284
Setting Your AIM Preferences 285

Chapter 13: Joining Focused Communities: Mailing Lists 287

Mailing Lists and the Web 289
Understanding the Difference between Discussion Lists
and Newsletters 291
   Discussion Lists 291
   Electronic Newsletters 293
      Subscribing to AOL Newsletters 296
      A Sampler of AOL Newsletters 297
Finding Lists to Join 299
   Liszt 299
   Publicly Accessible Mailing Lists (PAML) 300
   Listserv 301
Using Listserv Lists 301
   Joining Lists (Listserv) 302
   Sending Messages (Listserv) 304
   Making the List Work Your Way (Listserv) 305
Leaving a List (Listserv) 306
Creating Your Own Mailing List 306
Newsletters to Help You
Keep up with the Net 308
Loathsome Lists and What to Do about Them 310

Chapter 14: Global Bulletin Boards: Newsgroups 313

Newsgroups: The Untamed Frontier 315
Newsgroups on AOL 315
How Newsgroups are Organized 317

Adding Newsgroups to Your Favorites 322

Searching for Newsgroups on AOL 323

Searching for Newsgroup Postings on Deja 324

Ready to Read 326

    Marking Messages as Unread or Read 328

    Saving Newsgroup Messages 328

Sending Messages 328

    Replying to a Newsgroup Message 329

    Composing a New Message 329

    Deleting Your Posts 330

Playing Nice 330

    Flaming Hurts 331

    Lurk Before Posting 331

    Post Appropriately 332

A Few Good Newsgroups 332

Setting Newsgroup Preferences 334

    Setting Global Newsgroup Preferences 334

        Newsgroup-Viewing Preferences (Viewing Tab) 334

        Posting Preferences (Posting Tab) 335

        Filtering Out Garbage (Filtering Tab) 336

    Setting Preferences for an Individual Newsgroup 337

FAQs: Essential Reading 338

Messages with Files 339

Using Automatic AOL for Your Newsgroups 340

Message Boards on the Web 341

Part IV: Extending Your Internet Connection   345

Chapter 15: From the Internet to You: Downloading Software . . 347

Getting Software from the Web 349

Getting Software from AOL 353

Getting Software and Other Files Using FTP on AOL 353

The AOL Browser 354

AOL Keyword: **My FTP Space** 355

   Uploading a File to My FTP Space 356

   Managing My FTP Space 358

   AOL's Built-in FTP Program 359

Downloading a File at AOL Keyword: FTP 359

Using Third-party FTP Programs 361

Understanding File Types 361

General Files 361

Graphics Files 362

Sound Files 362

Video Files 363

Handling File Formats in Windows 363

Finding FTP Files 365

Chapter 16: Internet Tools that Extend Your Reach **371**

Software for the Asking 373

Choosing the Right Software 374

Finding Internet Software 375

Awesome Internet Software 376

Compressing and Decompressing

Mac and Windows Files: Aladdin Expander and WinZip 377

Making Accessible Web Sites: Bobby 378

Communications Software on Steroids: ICQ 378

Avoiding Viruses: McAfee and Norton 380

Keeping Kids Safe: NetNanny 381

Logging on to Remote Computers: NetTerm 382

Software for Playing and Making MP3s 383

   Making Music Files: Real JukeBox and MusicMatch 383

   Playing Music Files: Spinner and Winamp 385

   Downloading and Uploading Files: WS_FTP 387

Chapter 17: Internet Everywhere: New Ways to Access AOL **389**

Introducing High-Speed Internet Access 391

Essential Definitions 392

Awesome DSL 393

   Getting AOL Plus 394

   Installing AOL Plus 395

   Securing Your AOL Plus Connection 396

Cable: The Familiar Broadband Alternative 397

   Cable's Benefits 398

   Signing on to AOL with Your Cable Connection 399

AOL's High-Speed Satellite Access 399

Choosing the Right High-Speed Connection 400

AOL Anywhere: Through the

Air and on TV 401

   Installing and Using AOL Mail with PDAs 402

   Using AOL Mail for Wireless Phones 405

   AOL in the Living Room: AOLTV 407

Chapter 18: Did You Know You Can . . . on AOL? **409**

   Watching Movies 411

   Listening to Your Favorite Music

   at All Hours 413

   Creating Digital Pictures 415

   Reading Books 417

   Reading Your E-Mail Anywhere 419

   Sending a Fax over the Internet 420

   Using the Phone 420

      Receiving Voice Mail over the Net 421

      Using the Net to Talk on the Phone 421

   Making Payments Online 422

   Creating Web Pages: AOL Hometown 423

   Creating a Community: Groups@AOL 425

Index **429**

Foreword

Andy Grove, the Chairman of Intel, has said that soon, all businesses will be Internet businesses. What he meant was that all businesses — big and small — will be using the Internet to manage their businesses and make them more efficient, productive, and responsive to customers' needs.

What's true of business is already becoming true of life. Soon all living will be Internet living, as all of us use the new medium to make our daily lives better.

That will be especially true as we enter the second Internet revolution, in which the medium will spill beyond the PC to touch our lives via television, mobile devices, and appliances around the home — putting the ability to shop, communicate, get news and information, choose entertainment, and manage health and finances at our fingertips, anywhere and all the time.

At the center of this second Internet revolution will be AOL — the defining company of the Internet century. It will bring together many of the interactive and media brands that people trust for the best in news, information, and services.

And AOL will provide a powerful platform for reaching the Internet, especially as our new 6.0 version makes it easier to search the service and the Web, compare products and prices, share digital photos, download music, and capitalize on the power of broadband services.

Cyberspace is a big place, but David Peal knows his way around it — not to mention AOL — and he has selected the best of the Web when it comes to managing your busy daily life. He'll show you what's out there, how to get there, and how to make the maximum use of it to help you and your family. David Peal is the former editorial manager for the Internet Connection Channel on AOL, and the author of previous editions of this book, as well as *Your Official America Online Guide to Pictures Online* and *Access the Internet!*

It's time to get into life in the Internet century — and I hope you enjoy what in essence is a guide to our future!

Steve Case

Chairman and CEO, America Online, Inc.

Introduction

Once hard to grasp, the Internet is now at your fingertips, with new devices designed to bring you e-mail in the kitchen and at the playground. Once sluggish, the Net is now speedy, thanks to fast browsers and new forms of high-speed access. Once tricky to navigate, using the Net is now about as difficult to use as ordering a pizza. Once designed for readers, the Net is now versatile enough for music lovers and movie goers to enjoy as well. Once the world's scruffiest and worst organized library, the Net is now the most convenient place to read the classics, watch old movies, find phone numbers, and look up last night's scores and today's news and weather. And it's all coming together on America Online.

The fourth edition of *Your America Online Internet Guide*, heavily revised for AOL 6.0, offers a guide to the Net's many possibilities, all of which are made available through AOL 6.0.

What's New in AOL

New versions of software create a need for new editions of computer books. In the case of the *Internet Guide* the release of AOL 6.0 has prompted this revision. The many changes in AOL's service and software, together with the countless changes on the Internet itself, can't be described in this or that chapter; they permeate every page. The most significant changes to AOL are described in the next few pages.

Enhanced E-Mail

In some ways e-mail has replaced the postal service for many of AOL's 25 million or so members, who send well over 100 million messages a day. A cluster of changes makes for real improvement in how and where you can use e-mail. Here's a list of improvements you'll discover:

▶ You can now read AOL Mail on the Web, on a Palm or PocketPC handheld data assistant, and on some wireless phones. You'll find that reading and sending on your desktop computer is easier than it's ever been, and now, you can send and receive mail away from your desktop.

▶ Your mailboxes and your Filing Cabinet are now sortable, making it much easier to find and manage e-mail messages. You can also create folders to hold related messages.

▶ The AOL Address Book now holds more information, in a more useful format. Use it online to store e-mail addresses and offline to store addresses and a great deal of personal data. It's now synchronized across your copies of AOL on different machines, so you'll have access to *all* contact information wherever you are. Your Buddy List® — which keeps track of your online buddies — is also synchronized across your various copies of AOL.

AOL Expands Its Web Presence

AOL has vastly expanded its presence on the World Wide Web:

▶ AOL's new Channel lineup organizes a vast range of useful information to support every aspect of your daily life. See Chapter 5.

▶ Shop@AOL is not only a big online mall, but its features (which are tailor-made for your convenience) set it apart from all real-world malls. You can search for products across stores; you can use the AOL-only Quick Check service to zip through the checkout line; and you have several levels of customer service, backed up by AOL's Guarantee. Also find out about AOL's Shopping Assistant. See Chapter 5.

▶ AOL's local-information resources key you into what's going on in your community. With Moviefone you get movie reviews, theaters, showtimes, and the ability to buy movie tickets; with MapQuest, you can get driving directions and find out about traffic jams; with Digital City you can plan trips, evenings out, and nights out. See Chapter 5.

▶ The Web-based "My Calendar"sm service (which I discuss in Chapter 3) manages your entire schedule (work, school, and play) — and just like your address book, you can access the calendar both online and offline.

▶ AOL Search provides a comprehensive tool for searching AOL's information resources, as well as the Web's. Plus you can find other resources like the White Pages and newsgroups.

Improved Ease of Use

AOL is as easy to use as ever, but AOL 6.0 takes usability yet another step. The reorganized *interface* (what you see when you sign on to AOL) brings the most useful and the most-often used features up to the Welcome Screen the instant you log on. The revamped AOL toolbar is now brighter and easier to read. The toolbar groups and arranges useful features, functions, and online destinations and now has two layers of buttons. The bigger buttons (top row) provide menus that put a broad range of online destinations and functions at your fingertips. The smaller buttons perform essential tasks like taking you directly to your AOL Mailbox so that you can read your e-mail.

Usability also means that *you* decide how you want things to work. The Settings and Favorites menus give you considerable scope to set your preferences. On the Welcome Screen, you can now create ten of your own favorite destinations — double the number you can create with AOL 5.0. I discuss customizing AOL in Chapter 3.

High-Speed Internet Access and Content

AOL now supports high-speed Internet access. First, consider the new connectivity services AOL offers in conjunction with other companies. In the near future, look for AOL to offer its own high-speed cable service; for now you can use AOL 5.0 with a cable modem. In the works as this book went to press is a high-speed satellite service called DirecPC. I discuss high-speed access in detail in Chapter 17.

High-speed access alone means little without the cool content that you can enjoy best (or only) over a fast connection. The AOL Plus content offering includes all sorts of *broadband* music and movie content, together with partners like SonicNet, MTV Online, Rollingstone.com, Launch.com, and major television networks like Fox, CBS, CNET, and CNN.

How This Book Is Organized

If you're new to AOL 6.0 or even experienced with earlier versions of the AOL software, you may want to skim the first three chapters to become completely familiar with the new features and possibilities of AOL 6.0. Beyond that, feel free to read chapters in any order; I do not assume that you want to read the book front to back! The four parts make it easy to locate what you're looking for — when you need it.

Part I: From AOL to the Internet

In the first part, I try to answer some basic questions about AOL, the Internet, and AOL's Internet tools and services. For example, if you want to know

▶ What the Internet is, and what drives it and you're interested in finding out how the Net and AOL are related, Chapter 1 provides the big picture you need to understand where you are when you are online.

▶ How you can find the AOL services and tools you need to make full use of the Internet, Chapter 2 introduces you to those AOL features that allow you to use the Internet.

▶ How you can customize AOL to take control of your online travels, Chapter 3 shows how the AOL services can be adjusted to work for you, putting you in control of as much of your online experience as possible. Find out all about the "AOL Anywhere"sm service, which brings AOL and the Net to you wherever you are, no matter what technology you use to get online.

▶ How your whole family can enjoy the Internet, Chapter 4 introduces AOL's helpful tools for making the Net safe and fun for everyone. It also introduces some of the Web-based resources that make the Internet indispensable for families. And in general, this book tries to serve the needs of all AOL members, including kids and seniors.

Part II: Discovering the World Wide Web

The Web is all the rage these days. Part II explores the Web's tools, the Web's most useful destinations, and the Web's diverse tools for *finding* specific information.

▶ Chapter 5 identifies some of the essential Web destinations in your day-to-day life. This chapter is full of useful destinations for people planning a job change, buying a new car, shopping for a house, taking a trip, or planning a meal.

▶ Chapter 6 switches from destinations to tools, showing how to use AOL's browser to effortlessly enjoy the entire Web and take advantage of the many new multimedia features that bring you sounds and video, as well as text and graphics.

▶ Chapter 7 introduces the Netscape Navigator 6 browser. This free software opens new opportunities for exploring the Web.

▶ Chapters 8 and 9 cover the huge subject of searching AOL, the Web, and the Net at large for just about anything worth searching for. Chapter 8 focuses on AOL Search, AOL's comprehensive search tool for finding resources on AOL as well as on the Web, and for looking beyond the Web when necessary. In Chapter 9, I discuss some of the Internet services that bring you the most reliable, authoritative, and specialized information available online.

Part III: Communicating on AOL and the Internet

The Internet's real strength lies in its many opportunities and tools for bringing people together. AOL has contributed much in this area, with software such as the "AOL Instant Messenger"sm service. Part III covers communication, tool by tool,

▶ Chapters 10 and 11 introduce electronic mail, which some consider the most powerful Internet tool. In Chapter 10 you'll get a very thorough introduction to reading and managing your mail, including use of AOL Mail on handheld devices and the Web. Chapter 11 is about writing mail, a bigger topic than you may imagine. As easy as it is to send and receive mail, spend some time with these chapters to find out how much you can do with mail.

▶ Chapter 12 introduces *live online communication*. Unlike mail messages, instant messages are exchanged with other individuals or groups in real time: you and other folks see each others' words onscreen as soon as you type them; you then respond to each other. With messaging services you take part in a new kind of conversation, which can be intense or informal, or both at the same time! This chapter introduces the indispensable AOL tool geared exclusively for AOL members (Buddy List) and the fuller-featured AOL-Internet tool (AOL Instant Messenger service) that allows you to exchange messages live with anyone online, whether they are AOL members or not.

▶ Chapter 13 provides what you need in order to find, join, create, and participate in mail-based communities called *mailing lists*. These communities provide a framework for acquiring info from and sharing info with other people. You can also find out more about AOL's new Web-based support for newsletters.

▶ Like mailing lists, *newsgroups* plug you into communities of interest and passion. They differ from lists in mechanics and organization, but they also deliver the community-based knowledge that makes the Net an unparalleled learning environment.

Part IV: Extending Your Internet Connection

As much as you can do through AOL's Internet tools, you can extend your connection through other tools, faster connections, and new forms of content. As a result the Net is coming alive as a place that supports basic activities like placing phone calls, transferring money, and reading books. All these tools and activities are available through AOL.

▶ Chapter 15 shows how to extend your Internet connection by downloading software from the Internet. The chapter shows how to download from the Web and through something called FTP.

▶ Chapter 16 profiles Internet software, much of it free, that you can readily downloaded through AOL. With this software you will find there is nothing you cannot do on AOL and the Internet.

▶ Chapter 17 introduces new ways of connecting. First, learn about the basic types of broadband (high-speed) connection: phone, cable, and wireless. Then, learn about the new devices you can use to connect to AOL and the Net: AOLTV, AOL for hand-held computers, AOL Mobile Services for Web-enabled phones, and a look at the AOL of the future — a new generation of Internet appliances that will make your AOL experience even more convenient are on the horizon.

▶ Chapter 18 profiles some of the important online activities supported by AOL and the Internet, including reading books, listening to music, creating digital pictures, building Web pages, and creating new communities.

Using AOL Keywords and Web Addresses

Keywords are AOL's shortcut to nearly everything on the AOL service. They are indicated in this book in this way: AOL Keyword: **AOL Search**. The boldface indicates what you are to type. Keywords are not case sensitive, so you can type **aol search**. Keywords work only when you are online. Looking for a keyword? Start at AOL Keyword: **Keyword**. Throughout your travels on AOL, keywords are indicated (when they're available) in an AOL window's bottom-right corner.

I've indicated the address of Web sites using strikethrough type, as follows: aolmail.aol.com. I've left out the *http://* part because on AOL you don't need it.

You can jump to a keyword or Web address by typing either into the text box in the center of the AOL toolbar, at the top of your AOL 6.0 window, and then clicking the Go button.

A special box for jumping to keywords, but not Web address, is available by pressing Ctrl+K (Windows) or Ô+K (Mac), typing into the Keyword window, and clicking the Go button.

Using This Book

Windows and Macintosh programs have much in common with AOL. Basic AOL tasks are grouped in a horizontal *menu bar* consisting of five menus lined up horizontally at the top of the AOL window: File, Edit, Window, Sign On, and Help. Below the menu bar, AOL has its own set of brightly colored options called the *toolbar*. The AOL toolbar itself has menus. A small downward-pointing arrow indicates the presence of a toolbar menu. You can read more about menus and toolbars in Chapter 2.

How do you use menus? Throughout the book, I show menubar and toolbar selections using the ⇨ symbol. For example:

▶ On the menu bar, Edit⇨Dictionary means to click on AOL's Edit menu and then roll the mouse down the menu and release when you get to the Dictionary menu item.

▶ On the AOL toolbar, Settings⇨Preferences⇨WWW tells you to click Settings on the AOL toolbar and roll the mouse down to Preferences. In the window that comes up, click the WWW button.

The ⇨ symbol takes you to buttons to click as well as to menu items to select. I also use ⇨ for other programs I discuss in this book, and for other paths from one place to another.

In the margins, you find many short comments that emphasize certain points, provide supplementary information, show you useful shortcuts, and give you cross-references:

Use the Tip icon to get a handy piece of advice.

A Note gives you a simple piece of information you should be aware of.

Use the Caution icon to find out about problems or dangers you should be aware of.

This icon highlights features new to AOL 6.0.

The Definition icon explains a new or unfamiliar term.

Use this icon to find the Internet resources I discuss throughout the book.

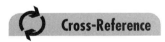

Use Cross-Reference to find more information about a topic I discuss in the book.

Chapter 1
What is the Internet?

Chapter 2
I'm on AOL. Where's the Internet?

Chapter 3
Making AOL Work Your Way

Chapter 4
AOL for the Whole Family

Chapter 1

What Is the Internet?

IN THIS CHAPTER

The Internet starts to deliver on its promise

What's new in AOL 6.0

How AOL and the Internet are related

How the Web and the Internet are related

How big is the Internet?

Since the previous edition of the *AOL Internet Guide,* the number of Web pages has soared past a billion, and information devices like handheld computers and wireless cell phones can be seen and heard on every street corner. Often missed at the start of the Internet century, however, is a much quieter change. The Internet is starting to deliver on its promise.

The Net, At Last

Here is a very small sampling of what you can do on the Internet with AOL 6.0. Information on other activities — doing homework, financing a house, listening to music, creating communities, creating and sharing digital pictures, downloading software, and so on — can be found throughout this book.

▶ **Shopping.** Shop@AOL (AOL Keyword: **Shopping**) had just launched when the third edition of this book came out in late 1999. Since its launch, online shopping has become simpler, quicker, and less expensive than real-world shopping, in part because Shop@AOL offers more than a collection of stores. (This supermall now features more than 300 stores.) You can search store offerings across the entire mall, and when you find something you like, AOL stands behind its merchants with its own secure technologies, customer service, and money-back guarantee.

▶ **Reading.** Very quickly, traditional publishers have decided that electronic book publishing matters. Electronic publishing would matter without them, but eBooks are more likely to go mainstream with their involvement in creating standards and publishing content. The publishing revolution is only beginning, but you can already find and read all sorts of writing — old, new, academic, technical, children's, mainstream, and independent — through special readers and secure Web sites, as you can see in Chapter 18. The "new medium" of the Internet has become a book-lover's paradise and the best place to search for and buy books.

▶ **Learning.** Thanks to high-speed Internet access and improved multimedia technologies (audio and video that actually work), learning is now moving from the classroom to the community. The Internet is bringing together students, teachers, experts, and widely dispersed electronic learning materials. Online projects can help an existing curriculum and enhance learning in many subjects from elementary school to grad school. Hundreds of colleges and universities already offer distance courses and even degree-granting programs entirely through the Internet. As a result, lifelong learning at home and training-on-demand at work have

Note

The *Net* is standard shorthand for the Internet, a global network of information services and human communities (a fuller definition is provided later in this chapter). The *Web* is short for the World Wide Web, the visual part of the Net, where you click links to move effortlessly from one place to another. Part II is devoted to the World Wide Web.

Definition

Multimedia refers to digital creations such as music videos, which combine images, sounds, and video in an integrated whole. For more about high-speed access, use AOL Keyword: **High Speed**.

Feature

Shop@AOL also has a new Shopping Assistant that enables you to shop with confidence. You can use the Shopping Assistant to find out which of AOL's partners carries an item and has it in stock; you can also compare prices and find out a vendor's rating. See Chapter 5 for more on Shop@AOL.

Cross-Reference

Chapter 9 explores the world of digital books. Time Warner Trade Publishing has announced an electronic-publishing venture called iPublish, which you can read about in Chapter 18.

Cross-Reference

AOL@School brings together some of the best Web content for the benefit of parents, teachers, and kids in all grades and subjects. Chapters 8 and 9 are of special interest to anyone who uses AOL and the Net to do research or simply to find out something straight-forward like next week's train schedule.

Find It Online

For full-length movies, including film classics and independent files, you can find much to watch at Atomfilms (www.atom.com), Ifilm (www.ifilm.com), and the American Film Institute (afionline.org), among many others. Chapter 18 provides a guide to some of the many new online theaters.

become a routine experience for millions. AOL provides the tools to use these services and also provides its own opportunities for learning, as you'll see throughout this book.

▶ **Hanging out.** With music and movies on the Net, even doing nothing has become easier. In your real life, AOL delivers, too. MovieFone provides complete movie listings, reviews, and ticketing services, while Digital Cities helps you find something to do anywhere, anytime in your city (or favorite city). If you'd still rather be watching TV after a hard day's work, AOLTV adds a new dimension to the viewing experience with flexible programming and interactive services such as e-mail, chat, and Web access. Even without AOLTV, AOL enhances TV-watching with schedules, reviews, chat, Web sites, and other goodies discussed in Chapter 5.

AOL and the Internet: How Are They Related?

AOL is an easy-to-use network of content and community, much of which only AOL members can access. AOL is also a place *from* which its members can access the entire Internet, including the Net's countless information services and communities. AOL's closely integrated Internet tools and services — such as the built-in Web browser, channels, and Shop@AOL — add many layers of value to your Internet experience.

How does AOL improve your Internet experience?

▶ You get full access to the Internet at no extra cost.

▶ AOL offers a well-integrated set of Internet tools, including a World Wide Web browser, a mail reader, integrated FTP (file transfer tools), a reader that helps you take part in online discussion groups (called *newsgroups*), plus security features that protect you and your family from junk e-mail and offensive Web sites. These and other tools are thoroughly covered in this book.

▶ With AOL, you can run any third-party Internet software, including other browsers, file-download programs, and safety filters to keep kids out of danger on the Net. Anything *not* in AOL can be added *to* AOL, usually for free, as you see in Chapter 16.

▶ AOL gives you information about the Internet, some of it available only to AOL members. And you get guidance in using AOL's tools and services to maximum benefit.

The Web as Part of the Internet

Many people mistakenly equate the World Wide Web with the Internet, even though the Internet had to be invented (back in the late 1960s) to make the Web possible. The Web was first conceived in 1989 but took some time to catch on — it didn't really start becoming popular until 1993 and 1994.

Basically, the Web is a system of sites that use *hyperlinks* (clickable text or graphics) to transport browsers around the Internet. The Web's mission has always been both to make diverse networked information readily available and to make it easy to contribute to the Net. Web browsers can, in fact, do the work of many Internet tools, such as handling electronic mail, newsgroups, and file transfers. Tim Berners-Lee, the Web's inventor, shares his early vision for the Web and his ideas for its further development in his book, *Weaving the Web* (HarperSan Francisco, 1999).

 Cross-Reference

See Chapter 17 for more about AOLTV. Note: AOLTV was just rolling out as this book went to press.

 Note

I'll be using *e-mail* and *mail* interchangeably.

 Find It Online

Want to know more about the Internet's technical foundations? At the excellent online technical encyclopedia, Whatis.com, you can find a tutorial called "How the Internet Works" (www.whatis.com/tour. htm).

New in AOL 6.0

Some of the changes in AOL 6.0 lie in improved performance of existing features, such as the enhancement of the Web-browsing and mail-reading tools. Other changes involve greater integration between AOL and its broad range of Internet tools and services, such as the new Invitations service and the changes made to the My Calendar service. You also have new ways of accessing and experiencing AOL, as with the AOL Anywhere service and AOL Plus. Here, in brief, are the major changes you can now enjoy on AOL and in the AOL 6.0 software:

▶ **AOL Anywhere.** Introduced with AOL 6.0, AOL Anywhere offers you full access to all of AOL's features — whether you're using AOL to connect to the Internet or not. Whether you're at work or at home, or using a pager, cell phone, or PDA *(personal digital assistant)* you can still connect to AOL — and the Internet — and have all the options and features you have when you sign on to AOL using your regular AOL connection. Just click the AOL Anywhere button on the AOL toolbar, use AOL Keyword: **Anywhere,** or type `aol.com` into your browser. I discuss AOL Anywhere in detail in Chapter 17.

▶ **AOL Plus.** If you have a high-speed Internet connection, you can enjoy AOL Plus when you log on to AOL. Here's how AOL Plus jump-starts your AOL experience. Whenever you you visit an AOL channel or area with special mulitmedia features, an AOL Plus tower appears in the lower-right corner of your screen. As you (See Figure 1-1) visit different AOL areas AOL's channels and links, the tower provides links to these areas' multmedia features. AOL Plus updates its links to match what you're looking at. For example, if you click the Entertainment Channel, you may be able to see live film footage of a TV show you like, hear CD-quality sound of your favorite musical group, see cool photos of the hottest stars, and more. Just click the link in the tower and you're hooked in to the best Internet-technology has to offer. I go into more detail about AOL Plus in Chapter 17.

Figure 1-1. AOL Plus Radio plays non-stop radio while you're online. The "tower" (tall window) on the right changes as you move about AOL, highlighting music, video, and other cool content specially design for a high-speed connection.

▶ **Browser.** Microsoft's integrated Web browser has performance enhancements and a few interface changes, outlined in Chapter 6. You'll appreciate the speed when you want to experience multimedia content like Launch (Figure 1-2). At the same time, AOL is launching Netscape 6.0, the latest version of the Internet classic (AOL Keyword: **Netscape**). With these two browsers you can enjoy a better experience of the latest Web content.

Figure 1-2. Launch.com: popular music, music videos, and more.

▶ **E-Mail.** AOL has updated and refined its electronic mail services.

• On the AOL service, mail is now sortable by type, date, sender, and subject. You can use this new feature to manage and find messages!

• Stored mail in your Filing Cabinet is now sortable, too, and you can add and name folders to store related messages, which is a tremendous way to bring some order to your life online.

• When you're not using the AOL software, you can still read your AOL Mail on the Web, a Palm-compatible handheld, or PocketPC.

• New in 6.0, AOL synchronizes your address books across copies of the AOL software on different computers. This means you can now access the same address book from any computer, a very convenient service as you begin to use AOL everywhere.

Tip

The experience of reading your mail away from your desktop computer can be liberating. Expect broader access to AOL content and services through non-desktop computers in the future. In some areas, you can now use AOL over a television set, and you can already read your mail and use key Web content through certain wireless cell phones (see Chapters 10 and 11 on e-mail and Chapter 17 on the AOL Anywhere service).

Cross-Reference

The main e-mail chapters in this book are Chapters 10 and 11. In addition, you can read about AOL Instant Messenger in Chapter 12.

Throughout the book, I also note some of the smaller changes AOL has made, such as improved toolbar organization and consolidated navigational features.

Use Parental Controls to set limits on the type and now the amount of a child's online access. See Chapter 4 for more on this important feature.

In this book, *tool* refers mostly to software that helps you carry out a task more effectively. Using the Internet requires a variety of tools. Some Internet tools help you quickly find specific *information*. Other tools enable you to meet people. Some tools, like the AOL browser, let you carry out many tasks, such as reading e-mail and downloading files. And a new set of tools included with AOL 6.0, called players and plugins, enable you to experience video and music content.

- In the new "You've Got Pictures" area, you can effortlessly store and share digital pictures.

▶ **Groups@AOL.** This new Web-based service enables any AOL member to create a private community that has its own discussion boards, mailing lists, instant messaging, and space to store shared digital pictures. Chapter 18 introduces Groups.

▶ **My Calendar.** Your personal calendar provides all sorts of options for keeping appointments and remembering important dates. Available both offline and online, the My Calendar service contains closer ties to other Web services such as AOL's Moviefone and Digital City, so you can find movies and other events, get tickets and details, and quickly click to add the events to your calendar. You can add items and important dates to your calendar with greater ease. With all that's possible online, you'll come to need your calendar to keep track of your life, online and off.

▶ **Online Timer.** The Parental Controls settings now feature an online timer that enables parents to set how long kids are online. Parents can use the online timer to prevent children from accessing the Internet at certain times or spending an excessive number of hours online.

▶ **Printing Center.** AOL 6.0 sports a new Printing Center (available from the menu bar), where help, project ideas, and printer supplies are all available.

A Way to Think of the Internet

The Internet has been compared to a fast-growing, hopelessly disorganized library. The comparison does not go very far, because, unlike a standard library, the Net enables you to contribute your own creations, as well as read others'. With AOL's tools, you can build your own Web pages, share pictures with your friends and family, and create online communities with Groups@AOL. In addition, while libraries contain mostly printed materials and tapes, the Net offers an overwhelming variety of music, film, interactive games, simulations, calculators, searchable encyclopedias, and more newspapers and magazines than any library in the world. As for books, the Net is only just becoming the global digital library envisioned since its beginning.

So much for what the Net is not. So, what is it?

The Net encompasses a vast set of places to visit and things to do, plus a set of tools that you use to visit these destinations and do those things. More than raw information, the Internet provides a home for thousands of communities. For some people, *community* signifies a group of people with similar interests, such as a shared profession, hobby, or parenting concern. For many, *community* means nothing more than the pleasures of socializing. A vast network of networks (millions of computers wired together, which you fortunately never have to think about) facilitate the world of information services and human communities.

Internet factoids

For current collections of statistics on Internet usage, CyberAtlas (`www.cyberatlas.com`) is the best place to start.

▶ According to ACNielsen, nearly two-thirds (64 percent) of U.S. residents 12 or older have used the Internet this year, and 31 percent of them go online every day.

▶ Also according to ACNielsen, nearly half of the people who use the Web have purchased something online.

▶ More than 25 million children in the U.S. (40 percent of children aged 2–17) access the Internet. This number is three times the number of children who went online in 1997, according to a report by Grunwald Associates.

▶ Fewer than half of U.S. households with average incomes of less than $15,000 will have entered the Internet population by 2005.

▶ According to *Computer Industry Almanac,* by the year 2002, 490 million people around the world will have Internet access.

▶ By 2002, U.S. residents will make up one-third of all Internet users.

AOL now offers a solution to the challenge of finding an obscure destination in the vast Net cosmos. AOL Search (AOL Keyword: **Search**) is a large catalog of hand-selected Web sites. It saves you the nuisance of sifting through useless sites in search of what you want. AOL Search also provides a single starting place where you can search other information resources, including online Yellow and White pages, AOL's electronic bulletin boards (message boards), and Internet discussion groups. Chapter 8 is devoted to AOL Search.

Internet Destinations

What draws tens of millions of new people to the Internet every year? Primarily, it's the vast amount of information resources — Web sites and other online destinations. A *destination* is anyplace online where you find entertainment, shopping, information, and occasionally knowledge. The fancy new-media term for a destination is *content*. The Internet is becoming the pre-eminent way to learn about AIDS in Africa (Figure 1-3), ancient civilizations, inkjet technology, and just about everything else. It's also the place for indispensable facts without intrinsic worth, such as weather forecasts, driving directions, airfares, and so much more. And it's the place for intrinsically interesting destinations without a shred of redeeming worth, such as hilarious humor sites like The Onion (www.theonion.com).

Figure 1-3. Why wait for the networks to sift through, select, and show you breaking news stories? This RealVideo clip on BBC Online was shown shortly after Nelson Mandela addressed the recent World AIDS Conference in South Africa.

Internet Tools

How do you get to all these destinations, all this content? Internet tools enable you to reach across computers and networks to access specific information and to communicate with individuals and groups. Tools help you find files to download and manage the process of making a Web page. A tool such as AOL's Web browser (Chapter 6) lets you read the newspaper in any place in the world that *has* an online newspaper. AOL's e-mail reader (Chapter 10) puts you in touch with friends and colleagues. That's just the start. Much of this book is devoted to the four sets of Internet tools available on AOL: the built-in browser, as well as the Netscape browser (Chapters 5 through 9); the e-mail reader and the related tools for writing and managing messages (Chapters 10 and 11); bulletin boards on AOL and the Web (Chapter 14); and the various tools for uploading and downloading files (Chapter 15).

Because of simpler tools with richer features, doing things on the Net has become much easier from year to year. Once a private sandbox for academics, the Internet has become a playground for children throughout the developed world.

Internet Communities

Consider the Net more of a pub or coffee bar than a library, a place where talking — chatting, at least — is encouraged. Using AOL, you can create your own communities, such as mailing lists, interactive Web pages, and Groups. (Chapter 18 covers Groups@AOL.) These communities differ from real-world ones in their strongly voluntary character and the high degree of motivation among their participants.

The distinction between destinations and communities can be blurry. Online communities can become destinations where parents, experts, kids, and others congregate to discuss what's going on in a sphere of their life. And communities usually create brand-new content to serve their needs as well as others'.

How do you join communities? You can find out in Part III, which focuses on Internet tools that make online communities possible, including e-mail, mailing lists, newsgroups, live conversation, and chat.

The Internet as a Network of Networks

Ultimately, the Net is a *physical network of networks* consisting of widely diverse computers that share a set of computer languages (called protocols). Protocols enable individual

Use AOL Keyword: **Communities** to find out about AOL's rich community life.

For reasons of space, I won't go into the fascinating history of the Internet, but you can find a good general history of the early days in *Where Wizards Stay Up Late: The Origins of the Internet*, by Katie Hafner and Matthew Lyon (Touchstone Books, 1998). My favorite online place to get an overview of Internet history is the Internet Society's All About the Internet page (www.isoc.org/internet/history), with its many timelines, interviews, statistics, classic papers, and profiles of the Net's founders.

computers in a *network* of computers to support simultane-
ous streams of information flowing around the world almost
at the speed of light. Think of the Internet — with its constant
flow of uncoordinated activity, vast stores of content, increasingly efficient ways of retrieving knowledge and providing
services, and seemingly infinite ability to store and make new
content available — as a developing brain, adding neurons
faster than it sheds them.

A Global Community? Not yet

As a community, the Net is not quite as global as the media
would have you believe. The U.S., Germany, Japan, U.K., and
Canada make up more than half of the Net's population.
Most people in the U.S. get initial access to the Net over traditional telephone lines. High-speed data networks string
together the major computers on the Internet *backbone*.
But according to a recent United Nations Development
Program, more than half of the world's population lives
several hours from a telephone. Novel forms of access
(such as wireless) won't necessarily make the Internet
more broadly available, however. In addition to a mere connection, Internet *use* requires literacy, minimal computer
skills, and the fulfillment of basic health needs. As a result,
millions in the U.S. and billions abroad remain uncon-
nected. Among AOL's programs to address these issues is
PowerUp (`www.powerup.org`), which seeks to bridge the
digital divide in the United States.

Where to Go from Here

The Net isn't difficult to understand, and it's actually pretty
simple to use. There's just so much of it! This book tries to
make the experience of accessing and using the Internet manageable, useful, and fun. Where you go from here depends on
your background and what you want to do.

▶ Start with Chapter 2 for a summary of the basics of
   AOL 6.0. Chapter 2 also shows you where you can find
   AOL's Internet tools and services.

▶ Chapter 3 shows many ways to customize AOL's Internet tools and services to work the way you and your family want them to.

▶ Part II explores the World Wide Web in depth.

▶ Part III introduces a broad range of personal communication tools, such as electronic mail and instant messaging services.

▶ Part IV shows how to use software and hardware to extend your Internet connection as far as you want to take it.

Chapter 2

I'm on AOL. Where's the Internet?

IN THIS CHAPTER

Finding your way around AOL 6.0

Using the AOL Welcome Screen, Channel menu, toolbar, and navigation bar

Where are the Internet tools?

Where to get Internet help on AOL

Ready to go? This chapter takes you on a tour of AOL, starting with the familiar sights you see every time you use AOL: the Welcome Screen, navigation bar, toolbar, menus, and other key features. Start with this chapter to learn about AOL's Internet tools, services, and help resources.

AOL and the Web: A Blurring Boundary

Since its beginnings, AOL has been a *proprietary* service, meaning that all information is available in a uniquely easy-to-use format to AOL members only. Easy-to-use software and a friendly environment, combined with community-building tools such as electronic mail, instant messages, and chat rooms, made AOL a huge success — the largest online community in the world. AOL has helped bring ease-of-use to the

Internet, where it attempts to provide the best online experience while providing the easiest access to the broadest range of Internet tools and destinations.

That's why you can find more and more AOL tools and resources available in Web format. For example:

▶ Your communication resources have taken on a Web format. For example, you can insert links to Web sites or to Favorite Places into e-mail messages, message-board postings, and Instant Messages. AOL 6.0's e-mail supports HTML, which means you can insert links into messages going to people not on AOL and receive linked messages from them. (Read all about AOL Mail in Chapter 11.)

▶ Groups@AOL (AOL Keyword: **Groups**), a new community-building service on AOL, helps AOL members create communities of AOL members and Internet users. These communities have a "home" on the Web outfitted with many communications tools such as e-mail, private message boards, and the AOL Instant Messenger^{sm} service.

▶ The process of conducting an online search now has a Web-only interface and combines AOL and Web searching. Read about AOL Search in Chapter 8.

Expect to see more of this trend. AOL continues to improve its members-only tools, taking advantage of the best new Internet technologies, to help members find the best Internet communities and destinations.

An AOL Road Map

If you're familiar with using a Web browser, you'll recognize one aspect of the AOL interface right away — the navigation buttons (Figure 2-1). These buttons help you get around both AOL and the Web.

Channel menu   Navigation bar   Menu bar   Address box   Search box   AOL toolbar

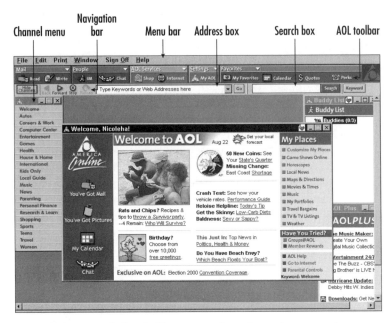

Figure 2-1. AOL 6.0 looks a lot like AOL 5.0: The toolbar and navigation bar give you access to all of AOL and the Internet.

Cross-Reference

The Back, Forward, Stop, and Reload buttons are especially useful when you're exploring the Web (more about that in Chapter 6).

Find It Online

The easiest way to access the Internet is to click the Internet button on the AOL 6.0 toolbar.

Cross-Reference

Chapter 3 is devoted to the many personal preferences available to you when you use AOL 6.0.

The AOL toolbar simplifies access to AOL content, Internet tools, and other online destinations. You can use it to set your preferences and tweak AOL to your liking.

In the navigation bar's Address box, you can enter either a Web address or an AOL keyword. Clicking Go is the same as pressing Enter.

Your PC at a Glance

If you want a compact overview of your hardware setup, shown in the following figure, you can do so from the Start Menu: Select Programs⇨America Online⇨AOL System Information. A dialog box like the one in the following figure appears.

An on-screen gauge offers plenty of useful information at a glance. You can see your AOL and Windows version numbers, your browser (MSIE) version number, your current monitor resolution, the amount of free space on your hard drive (*very* useful), and more. Every time you install new software you're likely to need some of these handy facts. In addition, the AOL Status tab has a log of your recent online activity, including all AOL messages displayed during your travels online. The Utilities tab gives you a quick way to clear your browser's cache — the folder where browsers keep the information they use to keep track of where you've been.

Usually a cache improves performance by keeping data nearby where it's easy to retrieve. Beyond a certain point, however, a large cache can actually impede performance. Like a vacuum cleaner with a full bag, the cache needs emptying now and then. (See Chapter 6 for more about this technical-sounding but useful feature.)

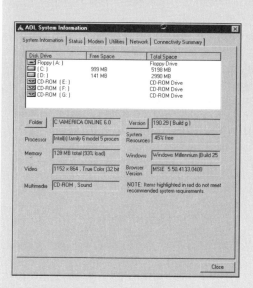

Definition

Sometimes you may see a Web address referred to as a URL, or *Universal Resource Locator.* Basically, the URL identifies the exact location of a Web document, also called a *page.* Chapter 6 has more to say on the subject of URLs and pages.

Tip

The improved Welcome Screen, shown in Figure 2-2, is always available when you're signed on to AOL. Closing the Welcome Screen *minimizes* it without really making it go away. You can always view it again by selecting it from the Window menu at the top of the AOL window.

Cross-Reference

Chapter 3 is devoted to customizing AOL.

Cross-Reference

For a complete reference on the "You've Got Pictures," service see my book *The America Online Guide to Pictures Online,* available at AOL Keyword: **Book Shop.**

AOL's Red Carpet: The Welcome Screen

The Welcome Screen, shown in Figure 2-2, has had a facelift in AOL 6.0, with the addition of the ability to make it more dynamic with timely, relevant information to use in your everyday life and an expanded My Places. Some Welcome Screen features are consolidated and reorganized; some are expanded; all are easier to customize. What better launch pad to AOL or the Internet could you ask for? Here's a minitour of what you see:

▶ AOL's 20 Channels are listed in the new Channels menu (shown in Figure 2-1). Click the Hide Channels button on the toolbar to hide this menu from view.

▶ Underneath the famous You've Got Mail button is a new button for AOL's "You've Got Pictures" service. With AOL 6.0, "You've Got Pictures" provides unlimited online space for you to store digital images. Through this AOL service, you can also take rolls of film to a participating photo developer (see Chapter 10 for more info) and receive both digital *and* paper images. The digital images go directly to your AOL screen name. You can put them on your Web page, include them with e-mail messages, or print them out for use in photo albums. You can also add any digital image to your online storage space for use in e-mail, albums, Web pages, and projects of every sort. When your photos are ready for you, a familiar voice says, "You've Got Pictures!" when you sign on.

▶ The My Calendar service (revamped for AOL 6.0) is a tool for keeping track of plans, schedules, deadlines, upcoming events, your local weather, and all the diverse goings-on that never quite fit into a paper calendar. You can use the calendar offline or online, and you can even use the My Calendar service to buy tickets and coordinate outings with friends (for details, see Chapter 3).

Your mail   Your digital pictures   Your online (and offline) calendar   Hot features   Your favorite online places

Definition

Figure 2-2. The AOL 6.0 Welcome Screen.

Familiar features on the Welcome Screen include a handy Go to Internet link in the lower-right corner. You can also find a handy link to AOL's Parental Controls in the lower-right corner of the Welcome Screen. Down the middle of the Welcome Screen are links to AOL's new areas, live events, and special promotions, as well as to breaking news stories of general interest. These links change throughout the day and night.

On AOL or on the Web, a *link* is a bit of text (sometimes a picture) that takes you to related information when you click it *once* with your mouse. Although text links *usually* appear underlined and in a different color, other links aren't at all evident. You'll know a link when your mouse pointer turns into a pointing hand when you pass it over a word or image. (Chapter 6 has the full story.)

Cross-Reference

Parental Controls are covered in depth in Chapter 4.

About AOL Keywords . . .

Throughout this book, you will be seeing references to keywords. An AOL *keyword* is a word or phrase that takes you directly to a specific area of AOL (sometimes a Web site) when you type it into the toolbar's Search box or Keyword window (Ctrl+K).

To use an AOL keyword, simply type it into the Address box (see Figure 2-3) and then click Go. For example, type **Health** and click Go (shown in the next section in Figure 2-4).

Find It Online

When you visit a "Keywordable" area of the AOL dominion, you can find the area's keyword in small letters in the lower-right corner of a window or screen (Figure 2-4 shows an example). When you want to visit the area again, enter the keyword and you're magically transported. For a complete list of Keywords, go to AOL Keyword: **Keyword**.

Figure 2-3. The AOL Address box. Enter AOL keywords in this box and then click Go.

If you're an AOL old-timer (or just like to type), you can still use the keyboard shortcut Ctrl+K and type your AOL keywords in the Keyword window.

Chapter 8 goes into AOL Search in depth.

Notice the Search box to the right of the Address box? You use it when you need to find specific online information. Type a search term such as **Millennium bug** or **Maui vacation** in the Search box and click Search. This way, you'll be using AOL Search to search AOL *and* the Internet.

Channeling Your Energy

AOL orders its online world into 20 *channels* (21 if you count the Welcome Screen). The channels include reference information, communities, and shopping districts, all arranged as large, familiar categories. The Health Channel (AOL Keyword: **Health**), shown in Figure 2-4, is an example. This channel has message boards, an online pharmacy (Planet Rx), online magazines, polls, chat, access to doctors, a myriad of connections to hand-selected Web sites, text articles available only on AOL, and a great deal more.

AOL keywords always appear in the lower-right corner of a screen

Figure 2-4. AOL's Health Channel — for advice, support, and reliable information.

Each AOL channel takes you to hand-picked Web sites directly related to the channel's theme. The Computer Center Channel, in particular, offers massive resources for using specific Internet tools, building Web pages, buying Internet software, and learning programming. And that's just for openers.

What's on AOL's Menus

AOL 6.0 not only has new menus — it also has a new look and structure. The toolbar, the navigation bar, and the Welcome Screen provide the dashboard for your life online. The File and Edit menus give you control of files you either create within AOL or access through AOL. The Window menu lets you keep track of open windows and prevents the clutter caused by too many open windows. Sign Off is the menu to use to switch screen names while you are online (as well as to sign off). Help is (exactly as you'd expect) the menu to use when you want help using AOL. Help is available offline, too, when you are not signed on to AOL.

Tucked away in these menus are some important features:

▶ From the File menu you get access to AOL's Picture Finder for managing the digital pictures you get from the Internet or use in your Web pages. The Picture Gallery provides simple, effective image-editing features and is available when you're offline.

▶ Edit⇨Dictionary and Edit⇨Thesaurus provide a handy searchable dictionary and thesaurus, but they're available only when you're signed on to AOL.

▶ Edit⇨Find in Top Window is for finding a specific item in a list. You can use this feature to go through new messages (in your electronic mailbox), old messages (in your Filing Cabinet), a specific message board posting, or even to look up a specific word on a Web page.

▶ Edit⇨Capture Pictures lets you control your scanner or videoconference camera (if you have one) from AOL. This tool is available whether you're online or offline. You can use it to scan an image, capture a photo, or view what's in the AOL Picture Gallery.

▶ Window⇨Add Top Window to Favorite Places. By clicking the heart in the upper-right corner of any window, you can add to your Favorite Places folder. If a window fills the AOL screen (when it's *maximized*), the heart is not viewable; in this case, use this Window menu command or press Ctrl-+.

Definition

A *menu* is simply a list of choices. To make a selection, click the menu's name and hold down the mouse button as you move the cursor through the menu options. When your mouse highlights the option you want, release the button. The menu option takes you to an online destination (as when you select Edit⇨Dictionary) or does something (as when you select File⇨Print).

Cross-Reference

The File menu also has options that take you to AOL features such as the Download Manager (Chapter 16), "You've Got Pictures" (Chapter 10), Music Player (Chapter 6), and Voice Recognition (Chapter 18).

Tip

The Find command (Ctrl-F) is one of the most useful features on AOL because it works in so many different contexts.

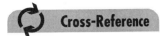

Cross-Reference

Favorite Places can be Web pages, AOL areas, e-mail messages, nearly any place, in fact, that your heart desires (see Chapter 3).

▶ Sign Off⇨Switch Screen Names lets you switch from one screen name to another within an account *without signing off AOL*.

AOL 6.0's New Toolbar

The toolbar in AOL 6.0 (Refer to Figure 2-1) looks much like the one introduced in AOL 5.0; it continues the colorful theme of the previous version. Some menu items have changed to buttons (which may seem a little confusing if you're used to the old system), but you'll soon find that this improved toolbar makes more sense and works more easily. Figure 2-5 shows the menu items available when you click the AOL Services button on the new toolbar.

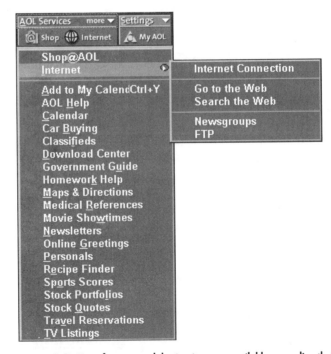

Figure 2-5. More features and destinations are available more directly in the AOL 6.0 toolbar.

Cross-Reference

Chapter 3 covers setting your AOL and Internet preferences (Settings⇨Preferences) and shows you how to modify the toolbar itself (using a link in the Preferences box).

AOL divides the toolbar into five areas. Large and small buttons provide access to important features or destinations.

▶ **Mail.** This button gives you access to your e-mail filing cabinet; control preferences; new, old, saved, and deleted messages, and the Automatic AOL service.

- ▶ **People.** Use this button to get to Chat areas, the Groups@AOL service, and more.
- ▶ **AOL Services.** Use this button to access a great diversity of online destinations, available through the navigation bar, channels, links, and through AOL Search.
- ▶ **Settings.** Use this button to customize the way online tools and services work (Chapter 3 is devoted to customizing AOL).
- ▶ **Favorites.** This button is your fast track to Favorite Places.

Move your mouse over a big button, and you'll see the word *more* light up on-screen. Click to see a menu and perhaps submenus (refer to Figure 2-6). Likewise, when you pass your mouse over a button such as IM (Instant Message), it glows, meaning you can click. Such toolbar buttons work only when you are online.

With a single click you can read and write e-mail, send an instant message, and find great deals in the Shop@AOL area.

Where Do They Keep the Tools Around Here?

AOL comes with a full set of Internet tools. On AOL you can use any Internet tools you want, as long as they work on your Mac or Windows operating system, of course. You can also easily use different types of tools at the same time and use AOL's tools with third-party tools. All AOL tools are available from the new AOL Services menu by selecting Internet⤳ Internet Connection (see Figure 2-6).

Find It Online

The Internet Connection and its Internet Extras (home to the major Net tools) are available at AOL Keyword: **Internet**.

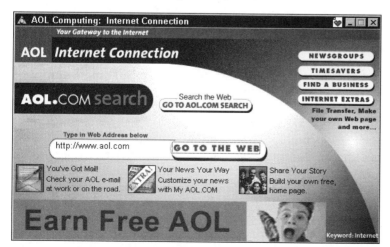

Figure 2-6. The Net's tools at your fingertips.

Cross-Reference

In later chapters, especially Chapter 16, you find out about third-party tools that you can use on AOL. Chapters 11 and 12 focus on AOL's e-mail.

Cross-Reference

All of Part II is devoted to the Web.

What follows is a list of some of the tools you need to use the different parts of the Internet. All of the following tools are built right into your AOL software (on your computer) or are directly available from AOL:

▸ **E-Mail.** For sending and receiving messages or files to anyone on AOL or the Internet. Just click the Read or Write buttons on the AOL toolbar to read your mail or write a message, respectively.

▸ **A Web browser.** For searching for and viewing any of the billion-plus pages of entertainment, information, and sundry lunacy on the World Wide Web. A browser opens whenever you click a Web link in a document, on your Windows desktop, or elsewhere. AOL 6.0 comes with a version of the Microsoft Internet Explorer 5.5 browser.

▸ **Newsgroups,** available at AOL Keyword: **Newsgroups**. For taking part in tens of thousands of discussion groups (sometimes called bulletin boards) to which anyone with Internet access can post and read. Newsgroups are also available from the new AOL Services menu. Open the menu and select Internet⇨ Newsgroups.

▸ **An FTP program,** available at AOL Keyword: **FTP**. For downloading and uploading files, which is indispensable in creating a Web site of your own. FTP is also available from the new AOL Services menu. Open the window and select Internet⇨FTP.

AOL Roadside Assistance for Internet Travelers

AOL provides complete outfitting services for your Internet adventures, including training, help, tips, all the gear you need, and round-the-clock troubleshooting. Even if you already know your way around, Net technology changes fast and new destinations emerge frequently; it's wise to read up on AOL's resources for getting help and staying up-to-date. Here's an overview to help you find and use AOL's excellent help resources.

Help! Where Am I?

As you'll notice right away, Help resources come in all sorts of formats, so you can choose the one that matches your needs and the way you like to learn. Some resources help you learn to use certain AOL and Internet tools; others help you deepen your knowledge or do some troubleshooting. Use these resources (and this book) whenever you need help.

Refer to Table 2-1 for help in finding the answers to virtually any question about the Internet.

Table 2-1. *Some Places on AOL to Find Assistance*

Help Resource	Do This	What's There
AOL & Computer Basics	Type AOL Keyword: **Basics**	List box takes you to classes on graphics editing, HTML, e-mail, and more; buttons take you to schedules and transcripts
AOL & World Wide Web Help	Type AOL Keyword: **NetHelp**	Similar to NetHelp on the Web, but provided on AOL itself. Comprehensive help for AOL and the Net; NetHelp is a part of Help
AOL NetHelp	Type `aol.com/nethelp/home.html`	The closest you'll find to a comprehensive source of Internet Web-based information about AOL and the Internet
Computing channel message boards	Type AOL Keyword: **Computing Communities**	Includes Net-related message boards like Building Home Pages, Virus Protection, and Networking & Telecom
Computing help (general)	Type AOL Keyword: **Get Help Now**	Thorough advice for using PC and Windows; links to computer vendors (AOL Keyword: **Companies**) and related help resources

continued

Note

Gopher is an Internet tool that had its heyday in 1993-94. It provided access to information by clickable links, as in the Web, but graphics had to be displayed using a separate program, and the links were simple menus, without context. The major Gopher sites have disappeared or been converted into Web sites. If you ever stumble across Gopher resources, you can use the Web browser to browse their easy-to-use numbered menus. Make a note of the experience and tell your grandchildren.

Find It Online

If you want to know *about* the big-I Internet — the companies, personalities, policies, and trends — go to AOL Keyword: **Internet Pros.** Among other things, you can find out about new products and Internet-related jobs of all sorts.

Tip

You can use AOL Keyword: **Customer Service** to find an array of AOL Help features.

2

I'm on AOL. Where's the Internet?

Table 2-1. *Some Places on AOL to Find Assistance (continued)*

Help Resource	Do This	What's There
Kids Only Help	Type AOL Keyword: **KO Help**	Comprehensive help resources for children with Kids Only (restricted Internet access.) Articles can be printed and saved for convenient access online or offline
Mail Center	Click the Mail Center's Help button	All the resources and help you need to write, read, and manage your e-mail on AOL (see Chapters 11 and 12)
Members Helping Members	Type AOL Keyword: **MHM**	Message boards about a range of Internet and AOL topics
Member Services	Type AOL Keyword: **Help**	Near-comprehensive AOL and Internet help
Newsgroups	Click Newsgroups on the toolbar; then click Set Preferences	Specify how to order newsgroups, what to filter, where the headers go, and so on (see Chapter 13)
Plain, old help	Choose AOL Help from the Help menu or type AOL Keyword: **Member Services**	Generic, task-oriented procedures for setting up AOL, signing on, using AOL, using the browser, and so on
Visual Help	Type AOL Keyword: **Visual Help**	Beginners' message boards; AOL Slideshows; visual help in sending e-mail, downloading from the Web, using chat, and so on

Teach Yourself Step-by-Step, in Pictures

A newer resource on AOL serves the needs of what teachers like to call "visual learners" (Figure 2-7). Also at AOL Keyword: **Visual Help** you will find more than two dozen simple, annotated graphical introductions to basic AOL tasks, a few Internet tasks, and downloading files from the Web. Bear in mind that a tutorial provides a single set of steps and can't capture every particular context or need.

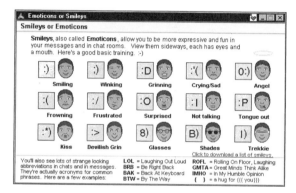

Figure 2-7. At AOL Keyword: **Visual Help**, you get illustrated overviews of basic Internet tasks. This one translates Smileys — cartoons made of keyboard characters — that clearly signal emotions.

Take an Online Class to Learn Basic Skills

Chat put AOL on the map, and over time chat rooms have come to serve many purposes. AOL Keyword: **Basics** provides a growing list of chat-based classes led by knowledgeable AOL members. Many classes are AOL-focused, some are Net-focused, and some cover both worlds. For each topic, information is available in several forms; you can learn the way you like. For example, click AOL 101 or Build a Web Page in the List of Classes, and you find a collection of related information, including chat transcripts and message boards for the topic (see Figure 2-8).

Find It Online

Use the Computer Center Channel's Online Learning link to find a variety of classes and tutorials.

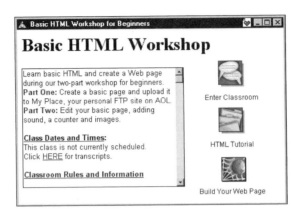

Figure 2-8. Learn from someone who's been around; if you miss the chat, read the transcript.

Use the AOL Message Boards to Ask Internet Questions

Chat, message boards, e-mail, and now AOL Hometown (Web pages) form the backbone of AOL's community life. Message boards provide public bulletin boards in which you can explore specific topics. Chat is all here-and-now, interactive only as long as the typing goes on; message-board postings are available over longer periods. Message boards are always interactive — just at a more leisurely pace.

Message boards give AOL members the chance to ask each other's advice when they get stuck with some tricky question about which printer to buy or how to handle a malfunctioning scanner. Other members can strut their stuff, share similar experiences, and provide links to AOL and Internet resources.

The Computing channel has the most (and perhaps best) Internet-related message boards on AOL. Go to AOL Keyword: **Computing Communities** to see a list of available boards, some of which focus largely on the Net and the Web. (Figure 2-9, for example, shows one on Building Home Pages).

Find It Online

The Computing channel focuses on PCs and Windows. At the channel's AOL Keyword: **Help Desk** you can acquire Windows 95/98 basics such as copying files, creating folders, and formatting disks.

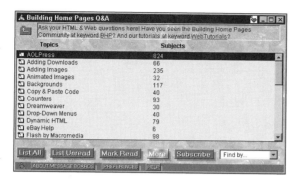

Figure 2-9. A message board at AOL Keyword: **Computing Communities**, available only on AOL.

NetHelp: Web-Based Internet Help

AOL's first comprehensive Internet help resource (NetHelp) went live in late 1996; I was lucky to have been part of that effort. Today, NetHelp is available on the Web at the following address: `aol.com/nethelp`. Each topic leads to a list of subtopics that help you zero in on specific information.

The most comprehensive online help resource for AOL and the Internet can be found at AOL Keyword: **Help**, shown in Figure 2-10. On AOL itself, AOL Keyword: **Nethelp** takes you to the same help window as AOL Keyword: **Help**, with one small difference — the list of items on the left is scrolled down to the Internet tools section. The assistance offered in the Internet section is organized by tool (WWW, Newsgroups, etc.).

To get around, single-click a tool from the list on the left to see a list of text articles on the subject. Click an article to read it in the right-hand panel (see Figure 2-10).

Start at AOL Keyword: **Help** if you have any questions about installing AOL, connecting to the service, downloading AOL files, and staying safe online.

Here's how to visit a Web address: type a Web address such as **www.idgbooks. com** into the AOL Address box and then click the Go button or press Enter. Note that you don't have to type the *http://* part.

An old tradition on AOL is for members to help each other. At AOL Keyword: **MHM** (members helping members), or at AOL Keyword: **Help Community**, you'll find general help-related message boards and a list of frequently asked questions — with answers!

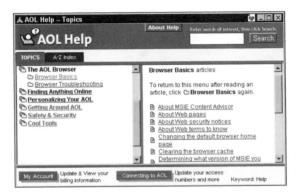

Figure 2-10. AOL Member Services has comprehensive help resources. Keep clicking until you find what you need.

Staying Informed with an Electronic Newsletter

Cross-Reference

Chapter 13 goes into mailing lists in depth and introduces newsletters of vital interest to cybernauts such as yourself.

Many AOL channels and areas have their own weekly electronic newsletters (e-mail messages, really), most delivered directly to your Online Mailbox (see Chapter 11 on managing your mail). These newsletters contain editorials, AOL news, schedules, and other tidbits of interest to people who frequent a particular area or channel. AOL Keyword: **Newsletters** lists AOL newsletters by channel, allows you to subscribe by clicking a button, and usually provides archives of back issues.

AOL 6.0 allows you to receive and read newsletters from your Online Mailbox in a new Web-like format (otherwise known as HTML) that makes your reading experience brighter and a lot more fun and interactive.

The new service gives you access to newsletters in over 150 categories of interest. If you are using AOL 6.0, you won't have to use Interest Profiles any longer to keep up with online areas of interest, but if you use earlier AOL versions you may want to use both AOL Keyword: **Interest Profile** and AOL Keyword: **Newsletters**.

Getting Help If You Can't Get Online

If you can't get online at all (or if you'd like to know what you're doing *before* exploring the online world), AOL provides complete general help for performing essential online tasks and using basic tools. When you're offline, you can access these topics from the Help menu (select Offline Help). When you're online, you can still get to the same help topics by using the appropriate option on the Help menu.

The fine-grained info is formatted in standard Windows fashion, with short sets of steps to follow, definitions of technical terms, and links to related information. As with all Windows-style help, the absence of context and examples makes the material a bit dry but useful enough for people who know exactly what they are looking for and have some experience with Windows applications, such as AOL.

Buying Computer Gear Online

AOL has joined with CNET — the creator of computer-related television programs and one of the largest sites on the Web — to create a series of consumers' guides. You can find these in the Computing channel's main window. When you're ready to purchase software or hardware, visit one of the many online vendors at Shop@AOL.

Cross-Reference

More about CNET and its many services for computer buyers can be found in Chapter 5.

Where to Go from Here

This chapter presented the information you need for using AOL as a base for exploring the Internet. The new AOL 6.0 incorporates Internet features just about everywhere. Changes in the software (and on AOL's computers) provide a richer — and simpler — experience of the Internet.

AOL offers Internet-related help resources in text and pictures, available offline and online (on AOL and on the Web). Where to go from here?

▶ Chapter 3 shows how to define your preferences and customize how AOL and its Internet tools work for you.

▶ Chapter 4 explores the family perspective on AOL, including the many ways AOL provides a safer online experience.

▶ Beyond that, you can go in any direction you want, depending on what you want to do online. For most people, the key online activities include browsing the Web (Chapter 6), searching the Web (Chapters 8 and 9), and using e-mail (Chapters 11 and 12).

▶ For a complete guide to AOL and the resources available on AOL at AOL Keyword: **Book Shop**, see Dave Marx and Jennifer Watson's *Official America Online Tour Guide*, 6th Edition.

Chapter 3

Making AOL Work Your Way

IN THIS CHAPTER

Creating a personalized newspaper: The "AOL Anywhere"ˢᵐ service

Taking charge of your schedule: The "My Calendar"ˢᵐ service

Keeping track of your favorite online destinations: Favorite Places

Keeping in touch with your online friends: Buddy List

Keeping tabs on your friends, wherever they are: Address Book

Customizing your Internet account

Whenever you're on the Internet, remember that you're only using software. More precisely, you're using one or more software tools for navigating, searching, and contributing to the Net. Most of this software is provided to you by AOL. Some software products were created by AOL and made available to anyone on the Internet, including Netscape Navigator and AOL Instant Messenger. Some Net software was created by independent programmers or third-party companies for general use, and as such is readily available to AOL members. AOL brings all these tools to you, free.

AOL itself is software — a large, feature-packed application that comes in versions for the Windows and Macintosh operating systems. Think of AOL as a tool that makes other tools available and simplifies their use — Internet tools in particular. Other Internet service providers offer a few special-purpose tools, such as a Web browser and e-mail reader. AOL takes things a step further by integrating more tools and making them easy to use. AOL also provides a diverse mix of helpful resources, opportunities to socialize, and recommendations of online destinations.

Customizing Your AOL Experience

Customizing AOL means two things: you can adjust the settings of specific tools and services, such as electronic mail, so that they accommodate your preferences; you can use AOL to receive and create the content you want. This chapter focuses on important ways of customizing AOL and Internet *content* to meet your needs:

▶ The AOL Anywhere service (formerly My News), your customizable newspaper on the Web

▶ The My Calendar service, your online and offline guide to all the events, appointments, and goings-on in your life

▶ Favorite Places, the single place to keep track of diverse destinations on AOL and the Internet

In addition I introduce two general AOL features that can personalize your online experience:

▶ Your Buddy List and Address Book keep track of all your friends and acquaintances, online and offline.

▶ Your AOL account and Internet connection can be modified in ways that many AOL members are not familiar with. When you travel, for example, you can create special *locations* set to dial local access numbers.

Preferences for AOL's specific tools are discussed in Chapter 6 (browser preferences) and Chapters 10 and 11 (key mail preferences). AOL 6.0 lets you set almost all your online preferences at the My AOL Preferences window; use AOL Keyword: **Preferences** (Setting⇨Preferences). This window is shown in Figure 3-1. The window is arranged in three columns:

Note

Many of AOL's customization features can be found on the toolbar's Settings menu. You can benefit from exploring AOL thoroughly early in your online adventures, in the same way you would want to identify the main features on the dashboard of a new car.

3

Making AOL Work Your Way

▶ **Account Controls.** Use the Password control to have your computer remember your password so that you don't have to type it in every time you sign on. The Privacy controls let you set your instant message privacy controls, which are further discussed in Chapter 12.

▶ **Communications.** These controls relate to your use of electronic mail on AOL, and you can read about them in Chapters 10 and 11.

▶ **Organization.** These tools help you keep track of e-mail messages and newsgroups postings (in your Filing Cabinet) and downloaded file (Downloading preferences). Click Internet Properties (WWW) for your AOL browser preferences.

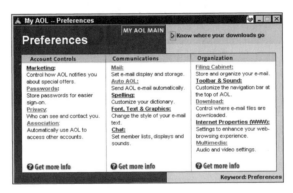

Figure 3-1. Use the My AOL Preferences window to adjust AOL's major tools.

Tip

Use the AOL Anywhere service to serve as your Web-based hub. You can access many functions of the AOL service from any computer connected to the Internet. Some of those functions include your Sports ticker (which you can set up in the Sports Channel); your own portfolio (which you can set up in the Personal Finance Channel); and your Calendar (available at AOL Keyword: **Calendar**).

Creating Your Own Online Newspaper: the AOL Anywhere Service

Think of the AOL Anywhere service as your own, customizable newspaper on the Web. Figure 3-2 shows my own page, which I'm always tweaking; you can modify yours as often as you want, from your desktop computer. Unlike a typical paper newspaper, which may be full of articles and ads that don't interest you, with AOL Anywhere you only get the stories and departments you want (with no ads), on a single, fully customizable Web page. From the new AOL 6.0 toolbar, simply click

AOL Anywhere to start customizing your page. You can add content and rearrange sections at any time. Here are some tips for creating your own page:

> ▶ To add content to your page, click Personalize My Page. In the box that appears, put check boxes next to the content you want to include in your page. At the bottom of the box, use My AOL Settings to indicate how often you content *refreshed*, or updated on-screen. News, stock portfolios, and sports scores are the kinds of items you may want to refresh as frequently as possible.

> ▶ Having chosen your content, you can arrange it in any way on the page. For example:

> > • To add content to a specific column (right or left), scroll to the bottom of the page, use the Add Content drop-down list.

> > • To move a content window from one place to another, click the long gray box just below the window's Personalize window and drag the content window to another location on the page. Move the box slowly. When you see Reposition Here, you can drop the window by releasing the mouse.

> ▶ To customize the information *within* a content window, click the window's Personalize button. If content can be personalized, select Customize. ***Note:*** Some windows, such as AOL Search and the Recipe Finder, *cannot* be customized.

> ▶ Some windows you may want to customize include Weather and News. For News you can choose to read international news, stock news, entertainment news, football news, and more than two dozen other types of news.

You can access your personal AOL Anywhere news page, with portfolios, weather, the news you want, and other features you've customized and personalized, even when you are not logged on to the Internet using AOL. All you need is an Internet connection and browser. Just log on to `aol.com`. If you subscribe to a wireless phone service, such as Sprint PCS or AT&T Wireless, you can also access your personalized page by phone.

Definition

Content refers to specific newspaper-like features, such as News, Sports, Weather, Portfolio, and your Horoscope.

Tip

Use the My Profile button to provide enough information about yourself (such as birth date and zip code) to have your weather forecast, movie schedule, and horoscope automatically generated.

Tip

If you add AOL Search to your AOL Anywhere customizable newspaper page, you can conduct AOL searches anytime, and anyplace. The AOL Search box takes up only a small amount of space (see Figure 3-2).

Tip

You can click Personalize at any time to add and drop content.

3

Making AOL Work Your Way

Tip

The world's flow of news, weather, business, and other information never ceases. To have AOL update the information you're receiving, click Personalize My Page and choose a refresh frequency.

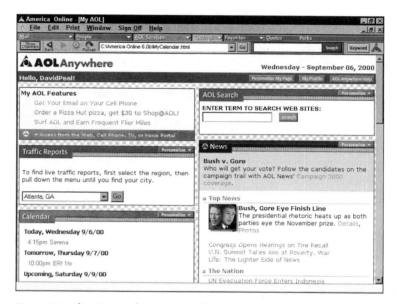

Figure 3-2. The AOL Anywhere service is like your own personalized Web page, with custom-news stories, traffic reports, local weather forecasts, and other goodies.

Getting News by E-Mail

AOL's News Profile area provides a way of getting your news by e-mail. Use AOL Keyword: **News Profiles**. A *profile* consists of

▶ A set of words that capture your interest (such as *oil, Texas, politics*)

▶ A selection of news sources you want to scan for stories containing those words

You can also specify words that must be present in the stories. You can create up to five news profiles for each screen name on your account, and each screen name can receive up to 50 e-mail messages a day from sources that include

▶ The Associated Press

▶ PR Wire

▶ Reuters

▶ Business Wire

Because you receive the news stories via e-mail, you can access them using any Internet connection, whether you're using AOL to log on or not. To find out about using the AOL service and the Web to access your AOL Mail, see Chapter 10. You can find out about using a *personal digital* assistant (PDA) such as a Palm in Chapters 10 and 17. Read more about using a wireless phone and AOLTV to access your AOL mail in Chapter 17.

Taking Charge of Your Schedule: The My Calendar Service

The My Calendar service makes your schedule available in the place where you may be spending the most time nowadays (online and at the PC). With this simple but comprehensive calendar (see Figure 3-3), you can keep track of all your appointments, meetings, dates, business lunches, birthdays, anniversaries, favorite TV shows, classes, and the other events in your life. My Calendar is available from the Welcome Screen, from the AOL 6.0 toolbar, and at AOL Keyword: **Calendar**. You can access the My Calendar service offline by opening the AOL software and clicking the My Calendar icon on the toolbar. No one has access to your calendar but you.

 Feature

New to AOL 6.0, the My Calendar service lets you use and add appointments to your calendar whether you're offline or online. You can even access it directly on the Web, without being signed onto AOL, at `calendar.aol.com`.

3

Making AOL Work Your Way

Tip

Starting at Moviefone (profiled in Chapter 5), you can add a movie, together with theater and time details, to your calendar.

Daily appointments   Find AOL events   See other months   Add appointment

Figure 3-3. The My Calendar service helps you keep track of meetings, anniversaries, and all the events in your life.

Tip

Don't spend all your time online.

To find events to add to your calendar, click the Event Directory tab. Click Movies, Cultural Events, Music, Special Events, or another link, for detailed events listings. To add the times and places of events to your calendar automatically, click the check boxes by the particular events, and then click Add (see Figure 3-4). For different kinds of events, you can get related information — synopses, trailers, and reviews, for example. Or, for a museum exhibit, get ticket information, dates for the show, directions to the museum, and hours. Spend some time exploring the Event Directory to appreciate how much there is to do in your community, then use the My Calendar service to start taking advantage of it all.

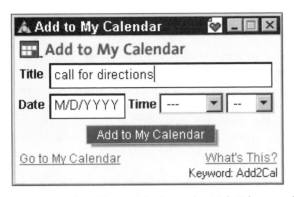

Figure 3-4. The Add to My Calendar window (Ctrl+Y) lets you add appointment times and details to My Calendar, whether you're offline or online.

To add an appointment, meeting, or other personal event

1. Display the calendar's Month view (such as, August).
2. Click in the event date in your calendar (such as, August 23).
3. Type in a name for the appointment (like *Dinner with Andre*). Now click elsewhere on the calendar.

To edit the just-added appointment, click the text you just added (it reads *Dinner with Andre* in this case). The Appointment Details box appears, where you can provide the event's time and other details. Click OK to save this information to your calendar. In the future, click this new link to jog your memory or add further details about the appointment.

You can view the calendar in many ways — unlike the old drugstore calendars. The monthly view, shown in Figure 3-3, provides the most convenient overview of your schedule. The daily view gives hour-by-hour details. The daily view gives you a monthly calendar (without all the appointment details), which comes in vary handy for any kind of planning. From either the monthly or daily view, you can scroll to the next month or day by clicking the left- and right-pointing triangles flanking the date.

Tip

In My Calendar's daily view, you can maintain an ongoing schedule hour by hour. Consider printing out a day's appointments and carrying it around on busy days.

3

Making AOL Work Your Way

You can view, edit, and visit your Favorite Places by choosing Favorites⇨Favorite Places.

Keeping Track of Your Favorite Places

One of the most useful ways of personalizing your online experience is to keep your own record of your favorite online destinations, in order to share them with others and to return to those places yourself. Your Favorite Places folder, available from the new AOL 6.0 Favorites menu, lets you keep a list of your favorite online destinations whether they are on AOL or the Internet.

A Favorite Places consists of a name (which you use to indicate where you want to go) and an Internet address or AOL Keyword (which AOL uses to take you there). With Favorite Places, you never have to remember obscure addresses or even simple AOL Keywords!

You can use Favorite Places as a hot list of your favorite Web sites, but you can add much more than Web sites to your Favorite Places folder:

Not only can you store different kinds of items in your Favorite Places folder, but you can also create folders to hold related content. I keep a folder of the information and resources I use for each of my work projects, for example. I also keep folders and subfolders just for this book so I won't forget to include the valuable resources I keep stumbling across.

▶ E-mail messages (for example, important job-related or personal messages)

▶ Both newsgroups and individual newsgroup postings (see Chapter 14)

▶ Favorite AOL or Web message boards

▶ FTP sites you frequent

▶ AOL areas and windows within them

▶ AOL channels

▶ Individual Web pages obscurely tucked away in some large site

Using Favorite Places is a breeze. To add any page, message, site, or AOL area to your Favorite Places folder:

1. Click the small heart in the window's upper right-hand corner, shown in Figure 3-5.

Not all AOL areas have the Favorite Places heart, which means you cannot add them to your Favorite Places folder. Everything on the Web should be Favorite Place-able.

Favorite Places heart

Figure 3-5. Whenever you see a heart in a window's upper right-hand corner, click it to add the destination to your Favorite Places folder.

The Favorite Places heart is not visible if a window is maximized (made as large as possible by clicking the square in the window's upper right-hand corner). In this case, you can still add the maximized window to your Favorite Places folder, in one of three ways:

- Reduce the window size (click the little picture of overlapping squares in the upper-right corner), and then click the heart.
- Hold down the Ctrl key and press the plus key on the number keypad.
- Choose Window⇨Add Top Window to Favorite Places.

2. A window like the one in Figure 3-6 pops up offering you some choices. To save the link in your Favorite Places folder, click Add to Favorites.

Tip

Be sure to use the plus key on the number keypad; the +/= key on the keyboard does not work.

Tip

You can even insert a link to individual e-mail messages and message-board postings.

3

Making AOL Work Your Way

Figure 3-6. Store your favorites in the Favorite Places folder, or share them right away by inserting a live link to the destination into an e-mail message or instant message.

Tip

The Favorites menu on the AOL 6.0 toolbar shows the first 20 items and folders in your Favorite Places folder. You can arrange the folders in your Favorite Places folder (Figure 3-8) so that the most often used items are among the first 20 in the Favorite Places folder and displayed on the toolbar menu.

To view your Favorite Places, choose Favorites⇨Favorite Places. Figure 3-7 shows my folder; yours will differ, depending on the favorites you choose.

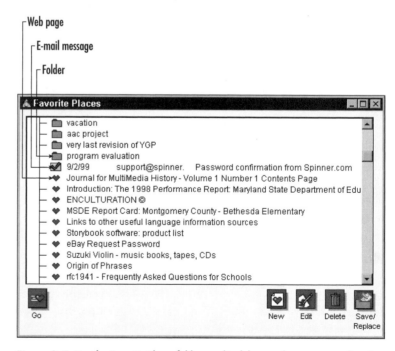

Figure 3-7. Use the Favorite Places folder to edit, delete, and rename your favorite AOL areas, message boards, and Web sites.

On the AOL toolbar, the Favorites menu displays the first 20 items in your Favorite Places folder. As you can see in Figure 3-8, the first items consist of folders, each consisting of individual Favorite Places. Note that in the figure, as on-screen, the folders in the menu (with the arrows) correspond to the folders in the folder (with the folder icons). These Favorite Places folders, which you'll see how to create in the next section, have little black triangles to their right. Move your mouse over a folder's name to see a drop-down list of items in the folder. The drop-down list also displays the first 20 items. In both the Favorites menu and the individual drop-down lists, if you can't see your entire list, click More Favorites... (at the bottom of either list) to bring up the standard AOL Favorite Places folder.

Favorites menu　　　　　　　Favorite Places folder

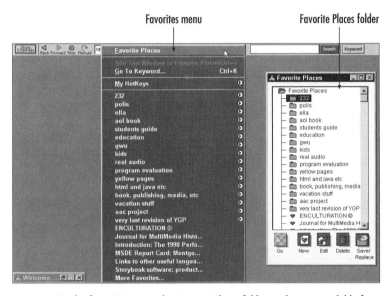

Figure 3-8. The first 20 items in the Favorite Places folder (right) are available from the AOL 6.0 Favorites menu (left).

Managing Your Favorite Places

In no time, all sorts of links can crowd your Favorite Places folder. Favorites become unrecognizable after a year or two. Here are a few tips for organizing them. Like all tips, they are completely useless unless you try them out!

Tip

You can move folders up and down within the Favorite Places folder. Just click a folder and drag it up or down. You can also move items around within a folder, or drop them into a folder. Again, just click and drag.

3

Making AOL Work Your Way

▶ **Creating New Folders.** Click the New button, and when the Add New Folder/Favorite Place box pops up, choose New Folder. Type in a name for the folder, choosing a name that makes sense to you. Click OK.

To drag an item into your new folder (or any folder), simply click and drag the item into the folder. You can move folders into folders, and you can move both folders and items up and down the main list or the list of items in a folder. Try it and see!

▶ **Deleting Old Items and Folders.** Select any no-longer-favored item or folder and click the Delete button. Shift-click to select and delete more than one item or folder (listed one after the other) or Ctrl-click to select and delete items that aren't next to each other in your list.

▶ **Finding Lost Favorites.** If you want to keep all your favorites, you can find and retrieve specific items using AOL's search feature. With the Favorite Places folder open, press Ctrl+F. Type in a word to search for, and click Find. You can make your searches case sensitive by clicking the Match case box. (A *case-sensitive* search for *TCP/IP* would find *TCP/IP*, but not *tcp/ip*.) You can only search within one folder at a time.

▶ **Ordering Items within a Folder.** Favorite Places is not without endearing quirkiness. When you add an e-mail message to your Favorite Places folder, the message is automatically placed at the *top* of the list. When you add an AOL area or Web page, this new favorite goes to the *bottom* of the list. If you have several subfolders at the top of your favorites list, you can't drag an item *above* those folders in the list — instead, the item falls in a folder! Plop, gone. To get around this problem, save any e-mail message to a Favorite Place by clicking the heart in the Read Mail window. You can now move an item or folder above the message. When you're done, you can delete the message.

▶ **Adding Favorite Places.** You can add a Favorite Place from scratch by clicking New, choosing New Favorite Place, and supplying a name and a URL (online address). The name is what shows in the folder, while the URL tells AOL how to get to actual destination.

▶ **Editing a Favorite Place.** Sooner or later you *will* want to edit a Favorite Place. Just select it and click Edit to bring up the window shown in Figure 3-9. I use this feature all the time to provide titles that make sense to me. I also change a URL when a Favorite Place's URL itself changes. E-mail message titles can't be edited, which is unfortunate because message names are usually long and don't identify a message's content.

Figure 3-9. Edit your Favorite Places to give them meaningful names and update their URLs if they change.

Using the Same Favorite Places on Several Computers

If you use one screen name on many computers, you will soon discover that all your Favorite Places folders differ. AOL 5.0 and 6.0 let you keep them up-to-date and synchronized. Here's how:

1. From the copy of the AOL software with the most up-to-date Favorite Places folder, open Favorite Places and click the Save/Replace button in the lower right-hand corner (refer to Figure 3-7).

2. In the Save and Replace window, select *Save the Favorite Places for your current screen name* (if it's not already selected), and click OK.

3. Save your Favorite Places on a floppy (usually the A: drive).

4. Remove the disk and put it in the other computer's floppy drive.

5. Open the Favorite Places folder on the other computer. Click the Save/Replace button. In the Save and Replace window, select Replace the Favorite Places for Your Current Screen Name. Follow the onscreen prompts.

Note

Each screen name on a master account has its own set of Favorite Places, and each of these screen names can be used on any number of computers.

3

Making AOL Work Your Way

Tip

You can now use the same Favorite Places folder on different computers, such as that laptop you use only when you're on the road and the desktop computer you use the rest of the time.

Note

Choices, choices. Yes, AOL provides three ways of keeping track of favorite online destinations. Favorite Places takes you to any type of online resources on AOL or the Web. Hot Keys take you to AOL or Internet destinations, but only ten of them. My Places takes you to ten AOL destinations.

Feature

Although the My Places feature was around in 5.0, you can now customize up to ten My Place spots, turning the Welcome Screen into your own navigational service. Your choices are currently limited to sites chosen by AOL.

Instant Access to Your Favorites

Here's an old and little-known way to customize AOL. People who love keyboard equivalents, and the millions of people who cannot use a mouse because of a disability, will appreciate this tip. My Hot Keys lets you assign up to ten simple keystrokes to your favorite destinations on AOL and on the Web. To create shortcuts, choose Favorites⇨ My Hot Keys⇨Edit My Hot Keys.

Notice that each horizontal row in the Edit My Hot Keys window has two boxes. In the first box of any row, type a name you want to use to remember the area or site, for example, *Amazon*. I set up Amazon in the top row of my Hot Keys by simply typing over the existing selection. In the second box in the horizontal row, type a keyword for an AOL area or a Web address (URL) for a Web site: www.amazon.com in this case. The actual shortcut Keys are preselected by AOL; Ctrl+1 in this case. Click Save Changes when you're done.

To visit a shortcut, you must be online. Hold down the Ctrl key and press a number from 0 to 9, corresponding to the keystroke assigned to your shortcut (for example, Ctrl+1, for Amazon). Remembering all ten keystrokes may be difficult, so you may want to use a small number of keystrokes to take you quickly to your favorite Web search sites, bookstores, encyclopedias, and so on.

Selecting Your AOL Favorites: My Places

With My Places you can choose up to ten general AOL resources that you want at your fingertips, right on the Welcome Screen. Remember that the Welcome Screen is always available when you're signed on. If you don't see it, select Window⇨Welcome Screen.

To customize My Places from the Welcome screen:

1. Click the Customize My Places link in the top-right corner of the Welcome Screen.

2. Click the Choose New Place button. The menu that pops up corresponds to AOL's channel listings. You see categories such as Entertainment and Sports.

3. Click a menu item (Figure 3-10). Continue making selections for the rest of the My Places categories, but remember that you don't have to use them all. Click Save
Changes when you're done.

The Welcome Screen displays your selections right away and
whenever you sign on. You can change them at any time.

You can also customize My
Places at AOL Keyword: **My
AOL**. Click the My Places
link under the Daily tab.

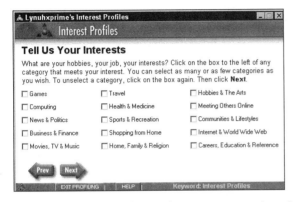

Figure 3-10. My Places puts your favorite AOL sites on the Welcome Screen for
ready access whenever you are on AOL.

Customizing Contact Info: Your Buddy List and Address Book

Net newcomers do not always realize that the Internet contains not only valuable information, but incredibly diverse human perspectives, as well. AOL provides many tools for both
keeping up with your online friends and meeting new people
online.

Setting Up Your Buddy List

With your Buddy List, you can instantly find out who among
your friends and colleagues is currently online. If a buddy is
online, you can send that person an instant message (for a
one-to-one live conversation) or create a chat room — a useful
way for a group to discuss a joint project, plan a party, or have
a party. Figure 3-10 shows my list of buddies, grouped into
convenient categories such as work and family.

To smooth your relations, both
online and offline, AOL provides a free reminder service
(AOL Keyword: **Reminder**).
The service ensures that you
won't forget appointments,
birthdays, and the like (hence
it makes sense to use the service in conjunction with the
My Calendar service). Click
Create Your Reminder, and
indicate what you want to
remember. You'll receive an
automatic e-mail messages
several days before the event.
The service includes a calendar with the dates of each
major holiday in the current
year.

3

Making AOL Work Your Way

Tip

If you want your Buddy List to show up automatically when you sign onto AOL, click the Setup button, which is shown in Figure 3-11. Click the Buddy List tab, and then put a check in the appropriate box on the Buddy List tab. If your Buddy List is ever not visible, use AOL Keyword: **Buddyview** to bring it to light.

Cross-Reference

AOL's own Instant Messenger service, which you use to talk to people who are on the Internet, has refined the Buddy List idea considerably. You can read all about it in Chapter 12.

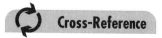

Tip

In editing your Buddy List, you can add your AOL Instant Messenger (AIM) friends to your Buddy List. You must first find out their AIM screen names. If you're online and have an online buddy, you can exchange messages, but (1) your friend must have the free AOL Instant Messenger service and (2) you will receive the messages in AOL's IM window, not in the AIM window. Chapter 12 has all the details.

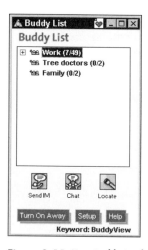

Figure 3-11. Your Buddy List lets you know who's online right now and who's not, so you can carry on an electronic conversation with one or more of them.

To add a buddy to your List:

1. With your Buddy List (Figure 3-11) displayed, click Setup.
2. From the Buddy List Setup window (Figure 3-12), click Add Buddy.
3. In the little Add Buddy window, type in a screen name and click Save. Close the Setup window unless you are adding more buddies or groups.

Creating a group is an almost identical process, except in Step 2 click Add Group and then in the little window type in a group name (click Save). Three groups shown in Figure 3-12: Work, Tree Doctors, and Family; each consists of individual buddies.

How do you add a buddy to group? You have a choice. From the Buddy List Setup window, select a group before clicking the Add Buddy button. Or, simply click and drag an existing buddy from one group to another.

Figure 3-12. Set up your Buddy List to work the way you want.

At any time, you can add and remove your Buddy List groups or add and remove individuals to or from any group. Simply display your Buddy List, click the Setup button and make any changes you want. In AOL 6.0, you can now sort buddies in a group by simply clicking and dragging buddy names up and down in the list of buddies.

Spend some time familiarizing yourself with Privacy Preferences, which give you the ability to block or allow Instant Messages from specific people. Instant Messages are invaluable, but some people abuse them. Use AOL Keyword: **Notify AOL** to report such abuses or click the Notify AOL button right in the IM window.

Buddy Lists let you know who's online. If someone is online, his or her screen name appears in the appropriate group. A plus sign before a group name indicates a closed folder; click the plus sign to open the folder.

A ratio after a group name (such as 7/49 in Figure 3-13) indicates how many buddies are online out of the total number of buddies in the group. Double-click an online buddy to bring up the Instant Message window, which you can read all about in Chapter 12.

Cross-Reference

The Buddy List Preferences window is available from the Buddy List: click Setup, and then click Preferences. The window has three tabs, including Privacy. Chapter 12 contains the details about Privacy preferences, which you can set when you set up your Buddy List.

3

Making AOL Work Your Way

Creating a Member Profile

In adding people to your Buddy List, the AOL People Directory can be a useful place to find screen names. In AOL 6.0, you can access the directory by choosing People Directory from the People menu. You can search the directory by name, location, hobby, birthday, language, country, and so on. Most often, of course, you'll know a screen name from experience or from an IM or e-mail message from the person.

Note

Non-AOL members on the Internet do not have access to your personal information. With AOL Instant Messenger (AIM), however, you can create a personal profile that can be made available to anyone on AOL or the Internet who uses AIM, which is free. Chapter 12 has the details.

Note

New in AOL 6.0, you can use the Address Book anywhere, with any copy of AOL 6.0, and you don't have to copy your Address Book to a disk or otherwise lug it around. Your Buddy List and your Address Book are stored on AOL's computers. By contrast, your Favorite Places are kept on your hard drive. If you use AOL on several computers (and thus several hard drives), you need to synchronize your Favorite Places manually, as explained earlier in this chapter.

Cross-Reference

I give more details about the Address Book in Chapter 11.

To make your personal information available to and searchable by anyone in the AOL community, choose Settings⇨My Directory Listing. Fill in any or all of the boxes with quotes, the type of computer you have, your city, and so on, and then click Update. This information can be retrieved by anyone on AOL, so avoid personal or compromising information. Children should never provide a last name or any contact information, and children should be at least 13 years old to create a profile of any kind.

Organizing Your Address Book

Your Address Book, shown in Figure 3-13, lets you keep a list of the people to whom you regularly send e-mail, so you never have to remember their e-mail addresses or keep track of multiple addresses for one person. Chapter 11 provides details on using the Address Book, which keeps track of people with either an AOL screen name or an Internet mail address. For now, note that the Address Book on AOL 6.0 allows you to keep all sorts of information about people, including contact information, birthdays, and so on. Chapter 13 shows how to create a mailing list using the Address Book so you can send a single message to several people at the same time.

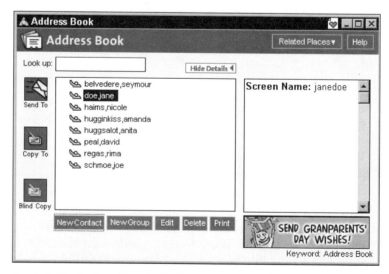

Figure 3-13. The AOL Address Book helps you keep detailed contact information for any of your buddies: address, phone, fax, cell, e-mail, spouse's name, birthday, and more.

Understanding Your AOL Account

Your account information consists of your screen name (it's how others recognize and communicate with you), your password (known only by you), and your billing information (known only by you and AOL). You can customize and update screen names, passwords, Mail Controls, Parental Controls, and Preferences using AOL Keyword: **My AOL**. Just click the Controls tab and then click the appropriate link.

Choosing Screen Names and Passwords

What is a screen name? Your screen name is your e-mail address on AOL; friends from the Internet sending you an e-mail start with your screen name and add `aol.com` to the end. Your screen name shows up in other people's Buddy List (if they've added you, of course); if they see your name in their Buddy List, they are able to send you an instant message.

Here are some guidelines to bear in mind in selecting a screen name:

▶ Every account can have up to seven screen names, including the screen name used to establish the account and provide billing information.

▶ You need a screen name when you sign on to AOL, but your AOL software automatically remembers the screen names on your account, so all you have to do is select from a list on the Sign On screen.

▶ The first character of a screen name is capitalized automatically. Letters that you capitalize *after* the first character appear as capitals in the screen name.

To create a screen name, go to AOL Keyword: **Names** and click Create a Screen Name. Use this keyword to delete screen names, too. Any screen name you want to use must be unique on AOL. If the name you prefer is not unique, AOL offers you a name that may include a string of numbers tacked on to the end of the name you wanted. Keep trying for a name of your own choosing, perhaps by opting for more characters. Sixteen characters give you the scope for creativity but long screen names can tax your friends' memory. Remember, screen names are mostly for others — so that they can communicate with you.

Tip

One way to customize your online experience is to create new screen names. Consider screen names for work, home, or for receiving certain kinds of mail, such as the mail you get from News Profile or from mailing lists, which I discuss in Chapter 13.

Cross-Reference

You can read all about screen names in Chapter 10.

Tip

You can now create as many as seven screen names for each master account. Each screen name can be between 3 and 16 characters, as opposed to 10 characters in the older versions of AOL.

Note

To use Parental Controls (see Chapter 5), a parent must first set up a screen name for a child, because the controls apply to screen names.

Caution

Using offensive words as screen names can lead to account termination.

Note

To add an icon to your toolbar, your screen resolution must be set to 800 x 600 pixels or higher so that enough room is on the toolbar. To change your screen resolution, go to the Windows desktop. Right click and select Properties. In the Display Properties window, click Settings and, in the Screen Area section, drag the needle right or left until you're at 800 x 600 (or higher). Click OK.

Tip

AOL now stores a copy of all screen names for your account on its computers. When you add a new computer to your account, your screen names are automatically downloaded and appear in the AOL Sign On window. You still have to enter the passwords, though, which only you know, but these too can be stored. At Settings⇨ Preferences⇨Passwords you can have your computer remember your password (or any password for a master account) so that it need not be entered into the Sign On window.

Customizing the AOL Toolbar

You can customize AOL's toolbar, which is introduced in the last chapter, to display only words instead of words and icons, freeing up some space and reducing visual distraction. You can also opt to put your toolbar at the bottom of the screen.

▶ Choose Settings⇨Preferences, and click Toolbar and Sound.

▶ Click Text Only and then click OK.

You can add an item to the toolbar, in place of either Calendar or Help.

1. Display the item you want to include on your toolbar for immediate access (a specific Web site, for example). The item must have a Favorite Places heart in the upper right-hand corner.

2. Right click the toolbar item that is less important to you (Calendar or Help), and select Remove from Toolbar.

3. Drag the Favorite Places heart from the window to the toolbar. AOL then prompts you to choose a label and icon, so you can identify the new button.

Your calender is always available through the AOL Anywhere service on the Web (`calender.aol.com`) and at AOL Keyword: **Calender.**

Every screen name has its own password, and passwords can be changed at any time (the only thing you can do to a screen name, by contrast, is delete it). Changing passwords adds security to your account by preventing others from accessing it. To change a password, sign on to AOL using the screen name whose password you want to change, and go to AOL Keyword: **Password.** Follow the instructions, and remember to make your passwords difficult to figure out: Don't use familiar names or dates, use at least three characters, and try alternating numbers and letters.

Updating Your Billing Information

Billing, too, involves personal information, but in this case you share information only with AOL. When you initially became an AOL member, you provided an address, chose a billing method and price plan, and supplied some additional information. At any time, you can update all that information by going to AOL Keyword: **Billing**. There, you can also view your current bill and payment info, change your contact information and payment method, and sign up for cost-effective longer-term plans.

To modify your contact or billing information, visit AOL Keyword: **Change**.

Customizing Your Internet Connection

On AOL you can choose the content you want, as you've seen with AOL 's many services, including AOL Anywhere, My Calendar, and Favorite Places, as well as with your Address Book and Buddy List. Did you know that with AOL your Internet connection itself can be customized? In the next few pages I look at *networking*, the main alternative to modems, and at *locations*, the way to use AOL when you're not at home and not using a modem. You will need to know a little about both networking and locations to use a high-speed cable modem. In Chapter 17, I look in more detail at high-speed, non-desktop, and wireless connections. The upshot is that AOL is becoming available everywhere. These alternatives allow you to use AOL on your own terms, wherever you happen to be.

Signing on to AOL over a Network

The modem has been a popular access method since AOL's beginnings in 1985. Since the mid-1990s, accessing AOL over a network has grown in popularity. Network access means one of several things:

► Accessing AOL through your local area network (LAN) at work. Ask your systems administrator if you have questions about your work connection.

► Accessing AOL through your Internet service provider (ISP).

► Accessing AOL through a cable Internet connection. You can do this if your cable provider offers Internet services and if you have an account and the proper

Definition

Location is AOL's blanket term for the bundle of connection details describing how you access AOL (and hence the Internet): by modem or by network; you give each location a name to make all these details easy to access. The term *location* has more meaning for modem access, because, with modems, a location is a group of access numbers in a real place — the single area code (or adjacent area codes) that you can use when you're traveling. With networks, a location is a connection *type*, not a place from which you connect.

equipment, including a splitter, a modem, and a network card.

▶ Accessing AOL over a DSL connection. DSL is a high-speed Internet connection delivered over existing telephone wires.

If you use any of these connections, consider using the Bring Your Own Access billing plan, which gives you full access to AOL's content but not to AOL's physical network, which is used primarily by folks with modems. AOL Keyword: **Billing** reviews your billing options.

To run AOL over a network connection, you must first create something called an ISP/LAN *location*, as follows.

1. From the Sign On screen (or Goodbye screen if you've signed off AOL without closing the AOL application), click the Setup button to bring up the AOL Setup window (Figure 3-14).

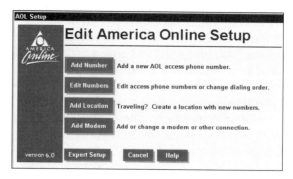

Figure 3-14. Use the Add Location button to create a new location so that you can use a network or ISP to access AOL. By switching locations in the Sign On/Goodbye Screen, you can alternate between a modem and a network connection.

2. Click the Add Location button to bring up the Add Location window (Figure 3-15).

3. In the Add Location window

   • Give your connection a Name, which you can later select from the Sign On window's Location box to use the new location.

   • Ignore the Try to Connect option.

   • Under Select a Connection Using One of These Available Devices, select TCP/IP: LAN or ISP (Internet service provider).

4. Click Next and complete setup, following the onscreen instructions.

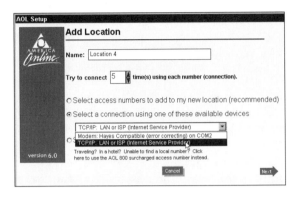

Figure 3-15. Create a location, so you can use your ISP, cable modem, DSL, or other network connection.

Now, to sign onto a network:

1. Establish the ISP, network, or cable connection.

2. Open the AOL software.

3. After choosing the correct screen name and password, select the new ISP/LAN location and click Sign On.

Locations: Where You Are When You're Online

You can access AOL when you're on the road, using a modem, but you'll need to provide AOL with a different access number (phone number to use in order to dial in). Sure, you could dial your ordinary Pittsburgh access numbers while visiting San Francisco, but do you want to pay the long-distance phone charges? Probably not. Instead, you simply create a new location, taking advantage of AOL's nationwide network of access numbers.

The following example shows how to create a new location for an upcoming visit to San Francisco, in the 415 area code:

1. On the Sign On (or Goodbye) screen, click Setup.

2. In the AOL Setup window, select Add Location.

3. Follow these steps:

3

Making AOL Work Your Way

You can have AOL automatically attempt to dial each access number in a location up to 25 times!

- In the Add Location box (shown in Figure 3-14) give the new location a name (such as **San Francisco**).
- For the Try to Connect option, indicate how many times you want each number to be dialed. The default setting is 5.
- Under Select a Connection Using One of These Available Devices select Modem from the drop-down list.
- Click Next.

4. In the Search for AOL Access Numbers window, type (in this example) **415** into the Area Code box.

5. From the list of phone numbers, select at least two local access numbers, following the onscreen instructions.

   In choosing access numbers, consider whether any of the numbers carry a toll charge, as many calls do within larger area codes. Sometimes adjacent area codes will be listed along with the area code you chose. Search for 415 in San Francisco, and you'll pull up a couple of 510 numbers in the East Bay.

   After you have selected all of the numbers you think you might need or use, click Next. Now you will be able to modify the numbers as needed, depending on what features your phone line has. The two most common options are accessing an outside line by dialing 9 and turning off call-waiting by dialing *70.

   Click Next and follow the instructions to confirm your numbers and complete setup.

To add to your choices: you can put a link to a favorite Web site right on the Windows desktop. Here's how: open the page in AOL, right-click, select Create Shortcut. Click OK. Use this trick to make the AOL Anywhere and My Calendar services even easier to access!

Using AOL as Your Default Internet Software

Another important choice relates to whether you want AOL 6.0 to serve as your *default Internet application* when you use the Web, e-mail, and newsgroups. You can choose this option while installing AOL 6.0, and you can change your mind at any point thereafter.

Many applications let you embed Internet links in documents. Microsoft Word and the other Microsoft Office applications, for example, let you link directly to Web sites. What happens when you click a link such as this — a link *not* within AOL or a window opened within AOL? Such links are popping up everywhere, even on your desktop.

Here's how the default Internet option works.

If you're online

▶ *and AOL is your default Internet application,* the AOL software opens automatically and displays the page in the AOL browser.

▶ *and AOL is not your default application,* the Microsoft Internet Explorer browser opens and displays the page.

If you're offline

▶ *and AOL is your default Internet application,* AOL opens, signs on automatically (you must type in your password, if you have not had it automatically stored), and then displays the page.

▶ *and AOL is not your default Internet application,* the Microsoft Internet Explorer browser opens, but does nothing unless you're on a network.

To make AOL your default Internet application, make sure that you're online and follow these steps:

1. Go to the toolbar and choose Settings⇨Preferences. You can also use AOL Keyword: **Preferences**.

2. Click the Association link. Read the instructions and click OK to make AOL your Internet application. In practice, that means that whenever you try to visit a Web site or open the browser, AOL automatically opens and acts as your default Internet application even if your connection to the Internet is through an ISP, LAN, or cable modem.

Where to Go from Here

AOL 6.0 greatly extends the ways in which you can customize AOL. This chapter has focused the many ways you can customize AOL and Internet *content,* including the AOL tools that simplify your access to your favorite online people and places.

▶ Tool preferences are discussed in the chapters dealing with various tools, such as Chapter 6, which covers the AOL Web browser, and Chapters 10 and 11, the chapters on electronic mail. For more about the Address Book in particular, see Chapter 11, and for more about the Buddy List, see Chapter 12.

▶ AOL's Help menu is available whether you're online or offline.

▶ For more about AOL Plus, a new kind of content on AOL, see Chapter 17.

Chapter 4

AOL for the Whole Family

IN THIS CHAPTER

Securing your children's safety on the Internet

Working with Parental Controls

Exploring AOL@School

Doing safe Web searches

Discovering some of the world's reference resources

Using the Net to plan every aspect of going to college

The Net mirrors the real world. Sometimes the Net distorts, illuminates, and amplifies the real world, too. Just as you need to think of your family's safety and security when you're offline, so should you when you're online. Many parents and teachers worry about online safety issues when children use the Net, but don't let this concern overwhelm you. The low incidence of online crime simply does not justify avoidance of the Internet altogether. This chapter looks at both sides of the picture, giving you information about

► Simple tools for keeping kids safe
► Rich and readily accessible educational resources

Online Safety for the Whole Family

AOL takes online safety very seriously and offers you several options to help you maintain the level of security that is just right for you and your family. AOL's core Internet tools and services were designed with safety in mind:

- ▶ **Parental Controls** were designed to help you keep your kids safe on both AOL and the Internet, regardless of the tool they are using. Use these controls to keep your children from accessing adult areas of the Internet. You can also use Parental Controls to keep kids from inappropriate Web sites to restrict the e-mail and other messages they can send and receive. Use AOL Keyword: **Parental Controls**.

- ▶ **AOL@School** is the latest service AOL has created to offer the kind of online resources students of all ages (and their parents and teachers) want to explore. This area brings together a large and well-selected set of Web sites on every school subject for students at every grade level. AOL Keyword: **AOL@School.** For an AOL-only kids channel, check out Kids Only, available at that keyword or from the new Channels menu.

- ▶ **AOL's Web browser** enables parents and students to tap some of the world's great reference resources, more than a dozen of which are profiled in this chapter. Parental Controls apply to this browser, which is integrated into the AOL service, but not with any freestanding browser such as Netscape Navigator or Microsoft Internet Explorer.

Maintaining Your Family's Online Safety

With 200–300 million people on the Internet, you can appreciate that not all of these people are trustworthy — just as you can imagine that not everyone you encounter in the offline world is a nice guy. Just as a thief may want the contents of your wallet, so an online criminal may want your password, your address, or your credit card. Some Internet crooks operate by sending unsolicited e-mail messages to thousands of people or through instant messages, while others send

Note

If you ever receive e-mail or an instant message from someone claiming to be an "AOL employee" requesting your password, don't fall for it. The only person in the world who knows your password is you. No one from AOL will ever ask you for your password. Use AOL Keyword: **Notify AOL** to report anyone who asks for your password.

Tip

To find out more about protecting your computer from viruses, use AOL Keyword: **Virus**.

4

AOL for the Whole Family

AOL Keyword: **Neighbor-hood Watch** takes you to AOL's online safety areas. To understand the risks and your choices, follow the links from this area.

Make sure your kids know that if they are ever bothered online they should report the incident immediately at AOL Keyword: **Kids Pager**. The incident will be followed up immediately by AOL staff.

virus-infected files attached to e-mail messages; these viruses can harm your system if you download and open them.

With a little practice, recognizing potential fraud is pretty easy. AOL provides tools to keep unwanted and unsavory types at bay and pursues the worst offenders in court. Not only that, but AOL also provides practical advice online that can help you keep your family safe.

If anyone *ever* asks for your password or is otherwise unpleasant, use AOL Keyword: **Notify AOL**. There, you'll find options for reporting obscene screen names, unwanted password solicitations, and other violations of AOL's Terms of Service (AOL Keyword: **TOS**). Everyone who uses AOL must follow these guidelines.

Online Safety Tips

Online safety requires a bit of effort on everyone's part. If you are a parent, teach your children to follow these simple guidelines:

- ▶ Never give out information that provides your address, phone number, or other personal information.

- ▶ Never provide your password to anyone online. If anyone asks for it for any reason, even if it sounds legitimate or if the person claims to work for AOL, immediately report the request to AOL Keyword: **Notify AOL** or **Kids Pager**.

- ▶ Never open files to e-mail messages sent by someone you don't know. Even if the subject line seems friendly or makes you curious, remember that the attachment could contain a virus, a small program that can harm computers.

- ▶ Report inappropriate comments using AOL Keyword: **Notify AOL**.

- ▶ Tell your parents if something happens online that makes you uncomfortable.

▶ Get to know the best of the Net, starting with a place like 700 Great Sites for Kids (www.ala.org/parentspage/greatsites/amazing.html) or a long-time favorite, Kathy Shrock's Guide for Educators (school.discovery.com/schrockguide/). Baltimore's E-quarium shown in the following figure exemplifies the ALA's selected sites.

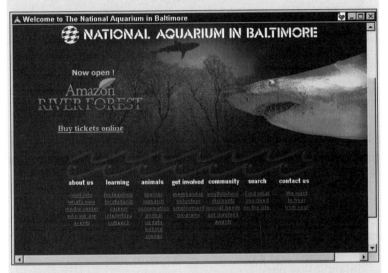

Use the computer together as a family. Surf the Web with your children, perhaps they will teach you a thing or two. And you can be sure that they're not doing anything inappropriate.

Direct children's attention to the kind of resources they can use for homework, family activities, games, and projects. I provide specific suggestions later in this chapter.

Using Parental Controls

The first thing you should do if you're concerned about your children's online safety is to use AOL's Parental Controls, shown in Figure 4-1 (AOL Keyword: **Parental Controls**). Parental Controls help you customize your family's access to AOL and Internet features and content.

You can access Parental Controls from many places on AOL:

▶ Use the button on AOL's Welcome Screen.
▶ Select Parental Controls from the AOL 6.0 Settings menu.
▶ Use AOL Keyword: **Parental Controls**.

Know what your kids are doing online. Find out what sites they're visiting (see Chapter 6 on the AOL browser's history trail). Check out the e-mail your children send and receive by learning to use the Filing Cabinet, as explained in Chapter 11. Do online activities together, such as genealogy and homework projects.

4

AOL for the Whole Family

Tip

In Parental Controls, click Getting Started & Common Questions for an overview of the controls' purpose and operation. Also, watch the slideshow to get an overview.

Tip

It's hard to make this point too strongly: Keep a record of your kids' screen names and passwords in a safe place. You'll collect many passwords as you start to use Web services and buy products online. Write them all down someplace. Or keep them in a special computer file that you regularly print out and back up.

Note

To set up controls for any one of your children, you must first create a screen name for him or her. Use AOL Keyword: **Screen Names** to create and delete screen names; create a password for each new screen name.

▶ Use AOL Keyword: **Neighborhood Watch**. Neighborhood Watch pulls together AOL's safety information in one place, including Parental Controls. You may want to store Neighborhood Watch in your Favorite Places folder for ready access from the Favorites menu. (See Chapter 3 on Favorite Places.)

Figure 4-1. Parental Controls main window.

You can apply Parental Controls to all or some of the screen names on your AOL account and customize the controls for each screen name individually. There are two steps in setting Parental Controls, each of which is explained in greater detail in the next few pages.

1. Assign a screen name to one of the age brackets defined below. Each age bracket is defined by a set of specific controls regulating access to various Internet and AOL tools and services.

2. Fine-tune the custom controls available for each major tool or service. This step is optional, but I recommend it.

Internet Safety Sites

The following list of Web sites can help you better understand potential risks and the appropriate safety measures:

GetNetWise	www.getnetwise.com
Online Safety	www.aol.com/info/ onlinesafety.html
Safe Surfing	www.safesurfin.com

Site Seeing on the Internet	`www.ftc.gov/bcp/conline/pubs/online/sitesee`
Family PC's Kids' Safety & Parental Safety Clearinghouse	`www.zdnet.com/familypc/content/kidsafety/index.html`
Safe Kids	`www.safekids.com`. includes a review of Internet filtering software (`www.safekids.com/filters.htm`)
Safeteens.com	`www.worldvillage.com/wv/school/html/control.htm`
National Center for Missing and Exploited Children	`www.missingkids.com`

Assigning a Screen Name to an Age Bracket

Setting up a new, billed AOL account automatically puts the master account holder in the 18+, or general bracket, which entitles that person to unlimited access to AOL. Only the master account holder can create new screen names and set up Parental Controls for those screen names.

To assign an existing screen name to an age bracket, click Set Parental Controls Now at the Parental Controls window. (Refer to Figure 4-1.) Use the Set Parental Controls window (shown in Figure 4-2) to assign screen names to one of several age brackets.

1. Select the screen name from the drop-down list.
2. Choose from one of these four options and click the appropriate button at the bottom of the window.
   - **Kids Only** restricts younger children to the Kids Only channel. A Kids Only account user cannot send or receive instant messages (IMs), cannot enter member-created chat rooms, cannot use premium services such as games (billed on an hourly basis),

Tip

Avoid giving children screen names that indicate their real names, gender, or contact information.

Note

This procedure applies to existing screen names. If you're creating a new screen name, you are first asked whether the screen name is for a child. If you say Yes, you'll be presented with a long, informative document regarding AOL's safety policies and measures. Click OK when you're done, and you'll be walked through the process of choosing a screen name, choosing a password for that name, and assigning the name to one of the four age brackets.

Note

The choice between young and mature is a judgment call that depends more on maturity than age. The choice also depends on an adult's readiness to monitor a child's online use.

but *can* send and receive text-based e-mail (no pictures, inserted or attached, in other words).

- Parents of teenagers may want to select the **Young Teen** (ages 13–15) or **Mature Teen** (ages 16–17) bracket. These levels of access provide more freedom than the Kids Only level, but still prevent access to certain Web sites. Young Teens may visit some chat rooms. However, they may not visit member-created rooms or private rooms. Teens can use Web sites that are appropriate for their respective age groups, but they do not have access to Internet newsgroups that contain file attachments and premium (fee-based) gaming services.

- The 18+ bracket provides unrestricted access to all features on AOL and the Internet.

Tip

Any screen name assigned to the 18+ category can be designated as a master account holder using the Custom Controls area of Parental Controls. That way, more than one adult can set Parental Controls for screen names on the account.

Click an age category   Choose a screen name   Scroll additional options

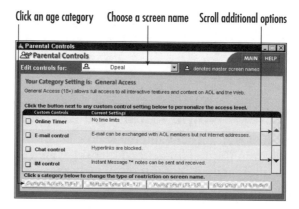

Figure 4-2. Click one of these four age restrictions for each screen name you set up on your account.

Fine-Tuning with Custom Controls

Custom controls let you define more precise settings for the individual tools and services covered by Parental Controls. To set custom controls, Use AOL Keyword: **Parental Controls** and click the Set Parental Controls link. (See Figure 4-1). Select the screen name for which you want to set controls and then click the up and down arrows to select a control to set. To adjust any control, you can click the little square to the left of the control's name (Figure 4-2).

You can fine-tune nine controls:

- ▶ Online Timer
- ▶ E-mail control
- ▶ Chat control
- ▶ IM control
- ▶ Web control
- ▶ Additional master (to give a screen name the authority to set Parental Controls)
- ▶ Download
- ▶ Newsgroup
- ▶ Premium Services

The Mail, Download, Web, Newsgroups, and Online Timer controls directly affect a child's access to the Internet, so I focus on them in the following sections. For information about Instant Message controls, see Chapter 12.

Setting Mail Controls

Many consider e-mail *the* essential Internet application. Unfortunately, its abuse is in some ways a measure of its huge popularity. Unsolicited mail can contain annoying or fraudulent offers or attempt to lure children to offensive Web sites. Or children could receive unwanted file attachments from strangers. As annoying as junk mail can be, on AOL you have the power to ignore it — and to control it. AOL itself does a good job of keeping unwanted mail away from members' mailboxes. Figure 4-3 shows the AOL Mail Controls window.

Tip

To find out more about curbing junk mail, also called *spam*, use AOL Keyword: **Junk Mail**.

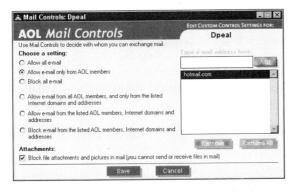

Figure 4-3. Use the Mail Controls window to specify what you want to receive and what you don't want to receive, and from whom.

▶ The 1st, 2nd, and 3rd options have a blanket effect; permitting all e-mail, permitting all *AOL* e-mail, and blocking all e-mail, respectively.

▶ The 4th, 5th, and 6th options let you accept or deny messages from specific AOL or Internet (or both) addresses. A *domain,* for example, is *aol.com* (see Chapter 9). An address is *getrichfaster2001@aol.com.* In the list on the right, you type the addresses (or domains) from which you want or don't want to get mail.

▶ For any of the six options under Mail Controls, you can block e-mail that contains file attachments or inserted pictures, both of which I discuss in Chapter 10. Why block pictures? File attachments can contain viruses, and pictures inserted in e-mail can take a long time to download or may contain content you find offensive.

Setting Download Controls

This control sets limits on the kinds of files kids can download. You and your family should be careful about downloadable files for all of the same reasons you should be careful about files and photos attached to e-mail messages — they may contain viruses or material you don't want to see, and they can clog up your hard drive!

You can set two controls for each screen name. You can choose if a child may download files

▶ From AOL's software libraries.

▶ From the Internet's FTP (or *File Transfer Protocol*) sites. FTP is a tool for moving files from one Internet computer to another.

AOL's software libraries are unlikely to represent any threat, but the same is not true for the Net's FTP archives (see Chapter 17). A good reason to block either kind of download is to prevent kids from cluttering up the hard drive or downloading games or pictures of which you disapprove, of music that may be copyrighted.

Setting Web Controls

Web controls appear to duplicate Parental Controls in that they offer a set of four levels of access:

Caution

Parental Controls do not apply to third-party (non-AOL) software, such as FTP programs and stand-alone Web browsers, including Microsoft Internet Explorer.

> ▶ Access to sites appropriate for ages 12 years and under
>
> ▶ Access to sites appropriate for ages 13 to 15
>
> ▶ Block explicitly mature Web content, but give access to all other Web sites (recommended for ages 16 to 17)
>
> ▶ Access to all Web sites (recommended for adults only)

Why set the Web Controls separately from setting the age bracket, which automatically sets Web controls? Because you may want to consider giving a child broader Web access while keeping e-mail, downloading, and other controls at a lower level of access. Why broaden Web access? The Web offers extraordinarily rich educational resources, as you'll see later in this chapter. The Kids Only age bracket, for example, offers no Web access.

Setting Newsgroup Controls

A newsgroup is an Internet discussion group focused on a specific subject. It's a publicly accessible, electronic bulletin board to which you can send a message or file and at which you can read messages and download files.

You don't have to look hard for quality, highly specialized newsgroups on subjects of narrow professional interest. If you're convinced of the value of specific newsgroups, you need to do some research before adding them to a child's Favorite Places folder.

Newsgroup controls offer many choices:

> ▶ The effect of **blocking all newsgroups** is clear. Why block them all? Over the years, inappropriate postings have flooded many newsgroups. If you're unfamiliar with this venue, determining which groups are appropriate for kids may be difficult.
>
> ▶ **Blocking adult-oriented newsgroups** from the Add Newsgroup list means that a youngster can't browse AOL's listing of "adult" newsgroups that are blocked to kids' and teens' screen names.
>
> ▶ **Blocking expert add of newsgroups** prevents access to newsgroups whose specific names kids happen to know. (A newsgroup name like this: `rec.cars.antique`).

Cross-Reference

See Chapter 13 for more information about newsgroups.

Tip

At AOL Keyword: **Newsgroups** you can set specific newsgroup preferences that enable you to filter out junk postings. Chapter 13 has the details.

Note

You indicate newsgroup controls with check boxes, which means you can combine Newsgroups options to provide specific access controls.

4

AOL for the Whole Family

Definition

A *binary* is a fancy name for a computer file. Images, word-processing files (with all the fancy formatting), and sound files are all binaries. *Text* (sometimes called ASCII text) is for you to read; binary is for a computer program to read and then display, run, or play.

▶ **Blocking the download of binaries** prohibits the downloading and viewing of inappropriate images. Parents concerned about their children obtaining and storing large music files on their computer hard drives may want to block the downloading of binary files. MP3 music files, for example, typically run to more than a megabyte. In addition, many music files available on the Internet may violate copyright laws.

▶ **Blocking newsgroups with certain words in their names** lets you selectively prevent access to newsgroups with suggestive words in their titles.

▶ **Block specific newsgroups** (last box in window) lets you prevent a child from hanging out in certain newsgroups that, in your opinion, have no value or are dangerous for any reason. You must, of course, know the full names of these newsgroups to use this control.

Online Timer

If you're like me, your concerns about your kids' access to the Internet isn't restricted to the sites and areas they visit online. Many parents express concern that their kids will spend more time online than playing, reading, and hanging out with family and friends. Also, if the account is being charged on an hourly basis, some parents worry that the amount of time their kids spend online will run up the bill.

You can limit the time kids spend online with AOL's new Online Timer control. To get there from AOL Keyword: **Parental Controls**, you can click Set Parental Controls.

Setting the timer is like setting any control. Start at the window shown in Figure 4-4. Select a screen name and then click the small square to the left of the Online Timer control. A simple process lets you specify the total number of hours per day, plus the specific times, during which a screen name may use AOL. You can set weekdays and weekends separately. And you can set a custom amount of time for each day of the week.

Figure 4-4 shows a child set up to use AOL for up to an hour a day and only during the 7–8 PM time slot.

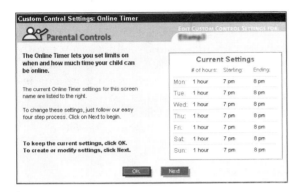

Figure 4-4. Use the Online Timer to limit the amount of time kids can spend online.

When the child's time runs out, the AOL connection is simply terminated. Parents can find out how much time has been used by signing on to the children's accounts and going to AOL Keyword: **Online Timer**.

AOL@School

Obsessing about online safety can easily detract from the more rewarding effort of discovering family-friendly destinations. A new service called AOL@School, shown in Figure 4-5, gives students, parents, and teachers a single, safe Web destination filled with learning resources that don't necessarily feel educational.

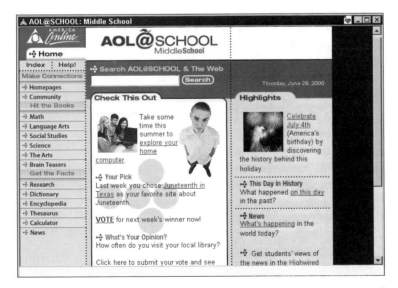

Figure 4-5. AOL@School: Many floors, a diverse student body, and no cafeteria smell.

Use AOL Keyword: **Online Timer** to find out more about this feature and to set it up.

AOL@School brings together Web sites useful in plumbing the depths of most topics kids encounter throughout their school years. In the rest of this chapter, you can read about some outstanding reference works that can be found and searched online.

AOL@School can be found on both AOL at AOL Keyword: **AOL@School** and the Web at www.school.aol.com. Teachers can order a CD providing free access to e-mail, chat, and other tools by calling 1-888-708-0719. You can also find great resources at AOL Keyword: **Homework Help**.

4

AOL for the Whole Family

The Net has a great number of *homework helper* Web sites, such as Studyweb.com (`www.studyweb.com`). These vast collections of Web sites, usually organized by subject, vary greatly in quality, scope, and reliability. AOL@School, a new service, is addressed to the needs of teachers, as well as students and imposes real standards of the selection and presentation of educational resources. Surprisingly, AOL@School has less of a commercial feel than many homework helpers, therefore promising resources of more consistently high quality.

At AOL@School, sites are selected by the American Association of School Administrators according to stringent criteria. They're well annotated (described) and organized. Behind the site are other leading educational organizations such as the National School Board Association and the National Education Association.

So, who can use the site?

▶ **Students** can use AOL@School as an online reading room to support both day-to-day homework and longer-term projects. The information, links, and services are arranged by grade level, from primary school through high school. Each grade level is organized by curriculum area, such as social studies and science, and each curricular area highlights carefully selected Web sites. For kids doing homework, AOL@School provides an encyclopedia, dictionary, and thesaurus.

▶ **Parents, teachers, and PTA members** can use AOL@School to build Web pages for their school or program. These pages are hosted at `Myschoolonline.com`, a service of the Family Education Network. Teachers can learn about new technologies, browse lesson plans, and learn of upcoming training sessions and conferences. They can even purchase supplies, books, and software online.

Doing Family-Friendly Web Searches

How can young people learn to integrate the Internet into their learning without being exposed to inappropriate images, neo-Nazism, and other unsavory stuff on the Web? Many schools and parents are grappling with the issue by teaching kids how to recognize and analyze the difference between opinion and fact. The Internet industry has grappled with the problem in many ways:

- ▶ By controlling what children can retrieve from the general-purpose engines and filtering out apparently offensive sites.
- ▶ By creating handpicked directories of kid-appropriate sites.
- ▶ By devising technologies for offline browsing, such as WebWhacker, a product from Blue Squirrel (`www.bluesquirrel.com`). In the controlled offline environment, parents and teachers can focus on content.

Here are a couple of kid-friendly search sites:

- ▶ AOL's Kids Only Search is available from the AOL Search opening page (AOL Keyword: **Kids Search**).
- ▶ Searchopolis (`www.searchopolis.com`) is a full-blown kids search community, with its own directory.
- ▶ Three of the general-purpose search engines discussed in Chapter 9 let parents filter search results by merely clicking a link. The service is called Family Filter in AltaVista, SafeSearch in Google, and Search Scrub in Lycos.
- ▶ Information Please for Kids, which I profile in a few pages and show in Figure 4-6, has a wide variety of destinations for kids. Focusing on homework, the service provides many opportunities for fun, too (`kids.infoplease.com`).
- ▶ NetNanny, which I profile in Chapter 17, provides additional software protection. You can use Parental Controls (which I discuss earlier in this chapter) to protect children while they're using the AOL software and the AOL browser. NetNanny keeps children safe if they use other Internet software or browsers, such as Netscape Navigator or Microsoft Internet Explorer, which are not subject to Parental Controls.

Cross-Reference

For more about AOL Search, skip to Chapter 8.

Figure 4-6. InfoPlease for Kids: Quick access to facts.

For any reference resource you discover out there, make sure to find out what organization or person is behind it and how long it's been in activity. Testimonials, impressive print publications from the same source, and credible editorial boards all add legitimacy to an online reference.

This chapter is not comprehensive, and if you need additional reference materials, you can explore the **Internet Public Library** (www.ipl.org) and **refdesk.com** (www.refdesk.com).

Discovering the World's Largest Reference Library

Reference books seem right at home on the Internet: their content can change quickly; they must be searched in order to be used effectively; and they don't have to be read more than a paragraph or a couple of pages at a time. The next few pages look at reliable, credible, and long-standing sources of reliable facts.

Encyclopedias

Many of the authoritative print encyclopedias, like the *Columbia Encyclopedia*, are available online, and you can also find Net-only resources, such as the Encyclopedia Mythica. The next few pages sample the Web's great encyclopedias. Look for many new encyclopedias in the years ahead, especially on special subjects that call for international cooperation.

Columbia Encyclopedia
http://www.bartleby.com/65

Start with the *Columbia Encyclopedia* for approximately 50,000 up-to-date, authoritative, and compact encyclopedia entries. Browsable by letter and searchable by the keywords of interest to you, the *Columbia Encyclopedia* counts as one of the most reliable general-purpose online encyclopedias.

A search for a complicated subject, like *Richard Nixon*, brings up a list of articles about the former president with links to all the entries in which he is mentioned (Watergate, Spiro Agnew, Gerald Ford, Vietnam, and so on). The textual entries are dense with cross-references to other entries, which makes the encyclopedia an outstanding tool for exploring relationships and not just digging up isolated facts.

Encyclopedia Mythica

`www.pantheon.org/mythica/`

At a certain age, some kids become fascinated with mythology. They may identify with those not-quite-human figures who do cool things and exemplify human traits worth emulating or avoiding. The award-winning Encyclopedia Mythica covers the mythologies of Haiti, Persia, Japan, Norway, India, and Greece, among many other cultures, with definitions of almost 6,000 gods, goddessess, and assorted supernatural beings. The encyclopedia's mastermind, M.F. Lindemans, modestly notes that his work is not exhaustive. However, you may not feel deprived to find, for Haiti, a mere 66 articles on Voodoo, the country's religious folk cult.

The site, shown in Figure 4-7, is fully searchable if your needs are specific and if you can spell what you're looking for. For general interest or deeper study, select Explore on the main page for a list of the major mythologies (Greek, Hindu, and so on). An A–Z index gives direct access to the encyclopedia's individual entries.

Students cramming for exams should not overlook the genealogies showing the principle lineages in Greek and Norse mythology. Younger children may enjoy having folktales read to them, especially the dozens of fairy tales collectively known as the Arabian Nights.

Find It Online

The complete Encyclopedia Britannica (`www.eb.com`) is available online, but for a fee. From the same publisher, the free Britannica Internet Guide (`www.brittanica.com`) presents focused pieces on special topics, incorporating the full text of relevant Encyclopedia Britannica articles plus numerous links to related Web content.

Tip

For any paper that students need to write, encyclopedias can be a great place to start. After reading the relevant encyclopedia entries, students can sharpen their focus by asking more specific questions and doing more precise queries. Use the local library and Web search tools discussed in Chapters 8 and 9 to gather and synthesize a variety of materials.

4

AOL for the Whole Family

Find It Online

Infoplease for Kids (www.infoplease.com/kids) offers a brightly designed homework center that includes an atlas, learning games, and in-depth features.

Tip

Reference resources, online and off, can often be more effective when used together than alone, since no one resource can answer all questions. Plus, some encyclopedias have different perspectives and strengths. For example, a student can get quick facts at InfoPlease or InfoPlease for Kids and then turn to the Columbia Encyclopedia or AOL@ School for context and analysis.

Find It Online

Presidents on the Net is a subsite of the Internet Public Library (www.ipl.org). When the library has closed and that report is due tomorrow, the Internet Public Library is always open.

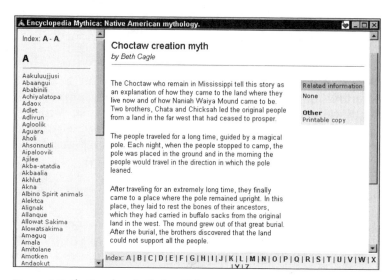

Figure 4-7. The Encyclopedia Mythica Web site.

Information Please
www.infoplease.com

Information Please (refer to Figure 4-6) attempts to be an all-encompassing reference work. The online version is part of the Family Education Network, an organization that participates in AOL@School.

Information Please offers a variety of fact-finding resources, including dictionaries, encyclopedias, and assorted almanacs (mini-encyclopedias that present general information on just about every subject). Plus, Information Please has actual articles arranged for quick reading and recall, including a timeline of world history, a list of the best-selling children's books, and the highest-circulation newspapers in the world.

Presidents on the Net
www.ipl.org/ref/POTUS

A subsite of the Internet Public Library (www.ipl.org), Presidents on the Net brings together factual information about every U.S. President. Go directly to a president's profile or browse the alphabetic Index to Subjects and Topics. For example, if you need to learn about the Teapot-Dome scandal but aren't sure whose presidency it sullied, you can click the letter T in the *Subjects and Topics* index at the bottom of the main page to find out. (It was Warren Harding. For the scandal itself, check out the site!)

You can find out facts about each president, such as date of birth, career, family, election results, dates in office, cabinet, and (most important, for those school papers) major events. Most significant are the links to online historical documents for the presidency in question (for example, the full text of John Kennedy's moving "City on the Hill" speech). For many presidencies, the profile includes links to other sites. Profiles of the most recent presidents include sound and video documents.

Technology Encyclopedia: Whatis.com
www.whatis.com

This user-friendly guide provides encyclopedic depth in its coverage of computer technologies. The encyclopedia is not comprehensive, but the depth of treatment for each entry makes the site indispensable, especially with the carefully selected links to supplementary information. You can access the entries in two ways. You can browse the alphabetical listings in the top right of the opening page. Or if you want to see clusters of entries about big topics, such as Using the Internet, Creating a Web Site, and Graphic Design, you can click a topic on the left side of the page. Learning Paths, in particular, provides quick access to the entries dealing with basic concepts.

When You Need the Right Word

When you need to look up a word, you can't turn to a better place than the Internet. At least, there's no place more convenient if you have a PC and AOL. This section is a sample of what is available. The Web of Online Dictionaries (see below) is on its way to its goal of providing a single comprehensive set of links to the world's online dictionaries.

Acronyms
http://www.acronymfinder.com

An *acronym* is the shorthand for a longer phrase. Instead of International Business Machines, most people say IBM. The problem with acryonyms is that you, as a listener or reader, often have no idea what a writer or speaker is talking about

Note

DSL stands for (among a dozen other things) a Digital Subscriber Line, the kind of broadband access AOL offers at AOL Keyword: **AOLPlus**. XML refers to the Extensible Markup Language. Did you know that NATO is the acronym for both the North American Treaty Organization and the National Association of Theater Owners? Or that PLATO stands for Programmed Logic for Automated Teaching Operations, an early experiment in educational technology?

 **Find It Online**

A few of the other classics available at Bartleby's (www.bartleby.com): *Roget's II: Thesaurus,* Fowler's *King's English,* Strunk's *Elements of Style,* and *Gray's Anatomy.* Bartleby's is indispensable for readers of all ages.

when using an acronym, such as ADA. (It stands for the landmark Americans with Disabilities Act of 1990, but also for Another Darned Acronym, the American Dairy Association, and the American Dental Association.

With the Acronym Finder (AF), you too can use acronyms that no one else can understand. The AF is one of several such Internet services. Type in an acronym (like **NATO**), and the AF searches for and displays the corresponding phrase. Next time you're stumped by a newspaper article on a DSL connection or XML as the future of HTML, don't pass up the opportunity to learn something new. This particular database contains approximately 150,000 acronyms and abbreviations.

Bartlett's Familiar Quotations
http://www.bartleby.com/99/

John Bartlett's *Familiar Quotations,* a collection of more than 9,000 great quotations, was first published in 1901. The original edition has been available on the Web for several years and is now part of a top-quality commercial reference site called Bartleby.com (www.bartleby.com), shown in Figure 4-8. At the Bartleby.com site, you can also use a searchable version of the American Heritage Dictionary and the complete 2000 Columbia Encyclopedia, profiled earlier.

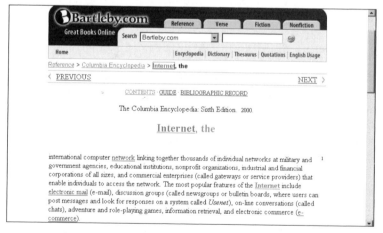

Figure 4-8. You can use Bartleby.com to find useful information, definitions, and quotations.

This user-friendly collection arranges authors both alphabetically and chronologically. Clicking on any author's name in either listing brings up a page with all of that author's collected quotes. You can search for quotes at Bartlett's opening page using any word, including an author's name. Results from searches include a hyperlink from the author to a list of his or her famous quotes.

Web of Online Dictionaries

`www.yourdictionary.com`

The Web of Online Dictionaries (Figure 4-9), created by Bucknell English professor Robert Beard, brings together in one place thousands of dictionaries in over 200 languages. If you must write, like to read, want to travel, just love words, or otherwise need to look anything up in any language, Mr. Beard has created a destination in which to spend all the time you can afford.

Good organization prevents the site from becoming a hodgepodge. Where to start? You can browse the Web of Online Dictionaries by language. For many languages, grammars are available. For English, specialty lexicons are available on dozens of subjects including agriculture and medicine.

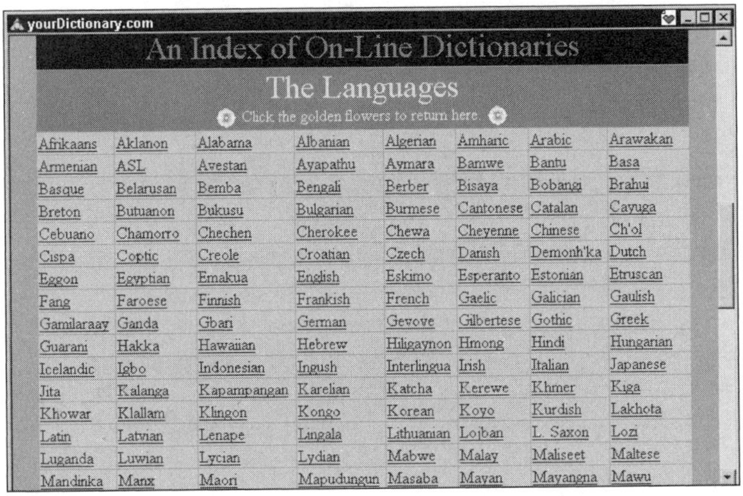

Figure 4-9. Web of Online Dictionaries: Look up a word and come home with a hundred.

Every member of the family can find something useful. The Etymology Of First Names dictionary can help parents decide on a suitably unique name for that baby-to-be. Everyone can find something fun, including word games, word quizzes, and the chance to see your name in hieroglyphics. Students in every grade can readily find a searchable dictionary.

Your Daily Coordinates: Time, Weather, History

For **U.S. weather** in-depth — satellite photos, weather predictions, photos of historical weather disasters, fire weather forecasts, current weather, and forecasts up to 10 days out — tune your browser to the official home of the National Weather Service (www.noaa.gov/wx.html).

For time to the second, anywhere in the 50 states, set your watches at NIST's **Official Time** site (www.time.gov). Select a time zone, and a Web-embedded software clock downloads to your computer where it runs until you get bored with clock-watching and browse somewhere else. Initially set to correspond to an atomic clock, the clock is accurate to within 2.5 seconds

From its vast dusty holdings, the Library of Congress is constructing a place of multimedia wonders. **Today in History**, for example, offers pictures and documents from the Library's ambitious American Memory project (lcweb2.loc.gov/ ammem/today/today.html).

Note

Ever wonder why much of the world isn't wired? Uganda had a population of 22 million in 1990, but only 61,000 telephones!

The World in Numbers

The profiles of the two resources below give only the merest hint of the enormous wealth of statistical data available on the Web. You can find information, including official and archival data, on every subject from current Internet censuses to state-by-state slave demographics in the pre-Civil War South.

CIA World Factbook

http://www.odci.gov/cia/publications/factbook/

The factual information in this classic online reference resource is always a year or so out of date because the print publication is not simultaneously published on the Web.

However, for about a decade now, savvy teachers and travelers have known the CIA World Factbook to be a thorough and reliable source of data on every country in the world. (The 266 countries include independent states, dependencies, and governments not recognized by the U.S.) For each country, you can find dozens of facts and statistics, including information about climate, geography, and political structure.

Fedstats
www.fedstats.gov/

More than 70 agencies in the U.S. government gather statistics of public interest. This interagency Web site collects these numbers and reports and then arranges them in useful ways. You can find specific data by doing direct searches, browsing a state's data, and exploring categories such as earnings, health, and housing.

Fedstats' Kids Page

www.fedstats.gov/kids.html

Many U.S. government agencies do an amazingly good job of educating students about their official scope and their areas of responsibility, usually without sounding too pedantic. A game at the CIA Homepage for Kids, for example, gives students a chance to break a code. The Environmental Protection Agency's Explorer Center does some multimedia teaching about recycling, water, and other subjects. Young kids can have fun with the EPA's Planet Protectors Coloring Book. Parents of daughters over 7 or 8 can learn about the Center for Substance Abuse Prevention's Girl Power site. Parents whose kids have the collecting bug can learn about the U.S. Mint's kids' site, show on the following figure, has all sorts of information about state quarters. Dozens of similar resources are available and are worth the trouble of checking out!

(Continued)

Find It Online

For global population statistics and policies, a useful place to start is the Population Reference Bureau (www.prb.org/).

Cross-Reference

AOL's Government Guide (AOL Keyword: **Government Guide**), part of AOL Search, provides an easily browsable arrangement of the U.S. government's information storehouses. It's public, so it's yours. I was happy to discover here the official After School (www.after-school.gov) site, with information about federal programs, plus links to Web sites for latchkey kids. The U.S. government is developing a comparable federal megasite called FirstGov (www.firstgov.gov).

Tip

Of special interest for students is Fedstats' Contacts link on the main page, which helps you find the federal staff members who serve as public contacts on specific issues. This option may be a last resort if you are unable to find the statistics you need.

IPL's collection of online newspapers: `www .ipl.org/reading/news/`.

IPL's collection of online magazines: `www. ipl.org/reading/serials/`.

IPL's collection of online books: `www.ipl.org/ reading/ books/`.

Cross-Reference

For more about digital libraries, see Chapter 9. For more about eBooks, see Chapter 18.

Find It Online

An excellent source of information about every stage of the college-application process can be found at College Admissions (`collegeapps. about. com/`). On AOL, visit AOL Keyword: **College** for a great deal of information related to the eventful process of attending college.

(Continued)

Online Newspapers, Magazines, and Books

`www.ipl.org/reading/`

A classic Internet resource, the Internet Public Library (IPL) is organized by the student's age and, within age, by subject (Dewey-Decimal style). IPL brings together almost 30,000 links. The beauty of the site lies in the quality of the selections, their clear organization, and the easily navigable interface. I like the way students of different ages are directed to special places within this huge site. Students of all ages can count on finding valuable, in-depth information. IPL's Reading Room contains online books, magazines, and newspapers.

There's nothing like reading a local newspaper to get a good first-take of a new place — what the weather is like, what the important issues are, and what everyday life is like. The Internet Public Library's Online Newspapers area brings this immediacy to a global audience. The IPL provides a useful way to get the local information you need without relying on the little snippets that manage to pass through the heavily filtered cable and network news. Even more interesting, students can do research about their own community, or the U.S. as a whole, by reading foreign newspapers. What did people in Bangladesh and Vietnam, for example, think of the recent presidential scandals? Reading different online newspapers about the same story can provide a reality check and, for students, a powerful form of learning.

Like online newspapers, online magazines (serial publications) are available in great number and wide variety in the IPL Reading Room, which has more than 3,000 online magazines. Here you find online versions of print publications like *Wired*, plus Net-only e-zines like *HotWired*. Browse the topical hierarchy to find publications of interest.

IPL's 12,000-item collection of Online Texts (Books) is arranged both alphabetically by author and title and in the Dewey system (students can transfer their search skills back and forth between the Web and their school or public library). The books tend to be older titles, including hundreds of classics and works of great authors whose copyright has lapsed. They're available here in text-only form.

Onward to College and Life

The Web gives older students the tools to do deeper research on more things — not to mention the new possibilities of publishing research on the Web and doing cooperative research with students in other locales. The Web's support of learning goes further and deeper. High-school students and their parents can now plan every step of the road to college on the Web. Web-based services now support every aspect of the college-application process — taking SATs, choosing a college, applying, getting financial aid, moving in, and understanding the distance-education process.

Where to Go from Here

This chapter provides only the hint indication of the positive, educational, useful, and fun resources on the Net. Invariably, you (or your kids or parents) will have information needs not covered in this chapter.

▶ To get a thorough introduction to searching the Internet for anything you want to know or do, turn to Chapters 8 and 9.

▶ For a compact set of links to a vast amount of reference material, visit Refdesk.com (www.refdesk.com).

▶ Part of the attraction of the Net, for kids and parents alike, is the seemingly endless number of places devoted to fun and games. For every serious reference work or collection of books available on the Internet, you can find several fun destinations where kids can safely spend time, have fun, improve hand-eye coordination, and perhaps learn a thing or two. One place to start is AOL Keyword: **Kids Search** (click Fun Sites). Another is MaMaMedia (www.mamamedia.com).

Chapter 5
Using the World Wide Web to Simplify Your Life

Chapter 6
Behind the Wheel: Using AOL's Web Browser

Chapter 7
All-Purpose Vehicle: Netscape Navigator

Chapter 8
Finding Your Way: Internet Searching
Made Easy with AOL

Chapter 9
From Breadth to Depth: Search Engines
and Specialized Searches

USING THE WORLD WIDE
WEB TO SIMPLIFY YOUR LIFE

Chapter 5

Using the World Wide Web to Simplify Your Life

IN THIS CHAPTER

The essential Web

Getting the information you need

Planning your future

Making important purchase decisions

Kicking back after work — books, movies, gardens, travel, and all those nights at home

Finding the right computer gear

Taking part in online auctions

The World Wide Web can support, simplify, and reduce the time and cost involved in making essential decisions and conducting daily activities. Consider AOL's Web-based My Calendar service, for example. It can help you keep track of your appointments, stay organized, and find public events in any community. Other Web tools can help you find a job, book a vacation, find out which check just bounced, plan your retirement, and make the best use of your computer hardware. Sometimes characterized as a carnival or flea market, the World Wide Web in fact serves as a source of the hard information you need to navigate the days and years ahead, and then to decide what movie to see tonight. This chapter samples useful sites. Chapter 6 helps you get comfortable with every aspect of the AOL browser, the software you use to visit the Web.

Starting Out on the Web

The more you use the Web, the more starting points you'll find. You may read about a Web site, copy down its address, and type it into the AOL Address box. Or, if you're on the trail of highly specific facts, you may want to conduct a search of the Internet. (Chapters 8 and 9 cover all your search options on AOL.) You just want to explore a new subject or find out about new movies, current stock prices, or your congresswoman's voting record. AOL has simplified the Web and Internet experience by focusing on content. AOL's channels bring all that content together.

How Do I Get to a Web Page?

This book is chock-full of Web addresses. How do you get from AOL to a Web site mentioned in this book or to another Web site of your choice?

- ▶ **By clicking links on AOL.** AOL's Welcome Screen, the first window that comes up when you sign on, takes you to some of the hottest sites on the Web. Every AOL channel (available from the new Channels menu on the left side of the AOL 6.0 toolbar) contains selected links on the channels' specific themes. All you have to do is click the highlighted (underlined) text. Every channel window takes you to AOL areas containing links to great content on both AOL and the Web. Both the Welcome Screen and the Channels menu are covered in Chapter 2.

- ▶ **By clicking links on the Web.** Web pages consist of *content* and *links* to content. Links are other people's selections of places to go. They often consist of underlined text or colored text; sometimes pictures are links, too. Click a link to visit the linked-to Web site.

- ▶ **By typing in a specific Web address.** This is how you go to a place on the Web that *you* choose. A Web address looks like `www.governmentguide.com`. (This particular Web address belongs to a large directory of U.S. government services, created by AOL.) Type a

(Continued)

Definition

Content is the fancy term for information you find at an online destination — anything of interest to you, whether it's a plane schedule or movie review. A *link*, short for hyperlink, is anything you click with your mouse in order to jump to additional content. On the Web, the basic unit of content is the *page*, and every page has a unique Web address. An organized collection of pages (like the AOL Web site) is a *site*. For more about pages, sites, addresses, and content, see Chapter 6.

(Continued)

> Web address into AOL's Address box and click Go. From the new page, you can proceed by either clicking links or typing addresses.
>
> This whole world of content, links, and pages is what makes the Web the Web.

Start with AOL's 20 channels when you want the latest news and information in an area of personal or professional interest. AOL's Channel menu, shown in Figure 5-1, shows the AOL channel line-up. Channel themes have been redefined for AOL 6.0, and many have a sharper focus. You can find several new channels — even a new channel devoted to autos (see a later section, "Need New Wheels?") has been added.

Channel menu　　Main Sports Channel window　　Click Full Coverage to see a page like this

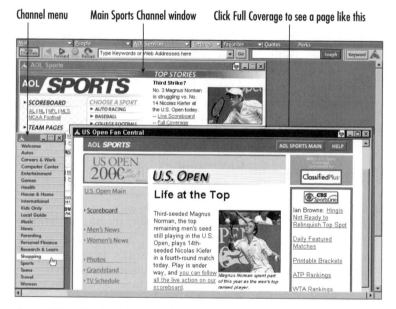

Figure 5-1. AOL's Channel menu takes you to the 20 communities devoted to big topics such as Sports.

Each channel points you to the best AOL and Web content and communities on current events and larger themes. Note the the Channels menu can be clicked and dragged to any location on the AOL window.

Financial Planning: What You Have, Where You're Going

Many people would create a financial plan if it didn't seem both intimidating and discouraging. Online, the process has become much simpler even if the underlying reality can still be daunting! Think of financial planning this way: When you have a financial plan, the reality can seem more manageable. Creating such a plan online is simpler than doing it offline.

In creating a plan, you need to think about where you are now financially, where you want to be in the future, what investments you need, and how much money to have on hand — whether at retirement or when a child goes off to college.

Planning Your Finances

AOL's Personal Finance Channel gives you access to dozens of Web-based calculators for doing everything from saving the right amount of money to figuring out the mortgage you can afford. Planning to retire? From the Personal Finance channel on AOL, you can click directly to valuable planning guides and calculators to help you save, invest, and spend.

Like all other channels, you can search the Personal Finance Channel for information available through both AOL and the Web. The search process takes advantage of AOL Search, AOL's comprehensive online search solution, fully described in Chapter 8. Each channel also has an A – Z site index.

To use one of the many online fill-in-the blank calculators, you need to provide enough information for the Web-based tools to run some quick calculations. The calculators are quick, mistake-free, and easy to use. Many of the most useful financial-planning calculators are available by clicking the Planning button in the Personal Finance Channel's main window.

The Debt Reduction Planner (shown in Figure 5-2) is directly available at `quicken.aol.com/saving/debt`, and lets you review your debts, savings, and income in order to generate a plan to reduce debt.

 Cross-Reference

Chapter 8 covers AOL Search (AOL Keyword: **Search**), a highly selective catalog of almost two million Web sites. This directory is a major volunteer effort that is creating the Web's largest collection of annotated, rated, and organized Web sites.

 **Definition**

You can think of an AOL *channel* as the central place from which to find both AOL and Internet information about a subject. Only AOL members can access these channels.

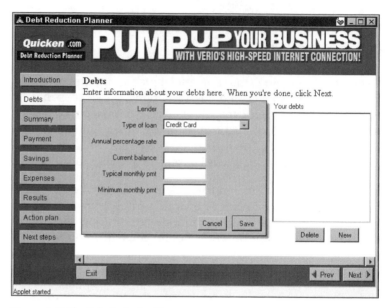

Figure 5-2. The Debt Reduction Planner.

Find It Online

At AOL Keyword: **Banking**, use the drop-down list of states to find links to those banks that have online Web services in your state. Most banks require you to provide your unique check or card number along with your personal identification number if you want to review balances, transfer money, or track checks.

Want to see how you're doing? The Quicken.com Financial Health Checkup helps you with daily activities like managing money, investing, finessing taxes, paying for college, and planning for retirement.

Banking Online

Home banking once required special software and a lot of patience; it never got people very excited — before the Web, that is. Now, banks are making more and more services available through the Web, and banks seem to offer everything — except, of course, the ability to use your PC as an ATM. My bank, for example, provides access to balances and allows transfers between accounts. I can tell which checks have cleared and which have bounced.

From AOL's Personal Finance Channel, you can now check your bank account balance and make transfers between accounts. Just visit AOL Keyword: **Banking** for links to most major U.S. banks. A new feature called called My Account Manager, available from the main Personal Finance Channel window, lets you keep track of banking and investment accounts in a single Web-based window. Like many Web sites linked from AOL, this one has its own AOL Keyword: **My Account Manager**.

Many people go an extra step and download their banking data to Quicken, the personal-finance PC software. Other banks allow (for a fee) online bill-paying and loan applications. Bank of America, for example, provides insurance quotes online and helps you choose the best checking plan for your needs. Such services make choosing a new bank easier in many circumstances, such as when you move to a new city or state.

Need New Wheels?

In the few times that I've had to buy a car, I have usually felt at a disadvantage in not knowing which model to buy, who's offering the best price, what the car will cost in long-term maintenance, and so on. For many people, intimidation in the showroom comes from not knowing what your adversary (the salesperson) seems to know. Shopping for used cars is worse: You have fewer choices; knowing what a car has been through and what it's worth is difficult. And it's much harder to know whom to trust.

Surprise! AOL and the Web can make life easier for you as a car purchaser as well, whether you want a used, new, leased, or rental vehicle. When you use the Autos Channel, you have tools and information to do your research — so you can walk into that showroom with confidence based on fresh information. Soon enough, the showroom will be electronic, but it's not entirely there yet. Figure 5-3 shows an online form to make short work of hard car-buying choices.

The Autos Channel, like the other channels, brings essential features to the opening channel window. For example, you can search for makes and models of both new and used cars from the main channel window. The results of your auto-related searches are displayed in a Web-based window that puts a wealth of information at your fingertips. All you have to do is click the links that interest you. Web-based decision guides and dealer locators are also available from the main Autos Channel window.

Cross-Reference

Chapter 18 profiles a payment service called Paypal.com, which allows individuals to pay each other sums of money, using an online bank as a secure intermediary. Such services, together with bill-paying services, can be expected to grow dramatically in the next years.

Cross-Reference

eBay now has a special section where you can buy and sell used vehicles online. See "Going Once, Going Twice," later in this chapter. The Web address is www. ebaymotors.com.

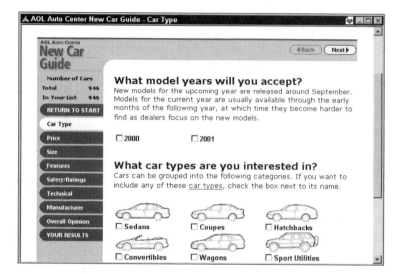

Figure 5-3. Simplify the car-buying process with a decision-making guide.

AOL's new Decision Guides, created in cooperation with Personalogic, help you choose big-ticket items and make lifestyle choices (relating to education, careers, who to vote for, and so on). AOL Keyword: **Personalogic** takes you to all the guides currently available on AOL.

For a soup-to-nuts auto site, try AutoWeb.com (`www.autoweb.com`), which provides detailed specs on all new cars.

The classic place for used car info is the Kelley Blue Book (`www.kbb.com`). Kelley has its share of new-car info, too.

In the Autos Channel, you can carry out tasks essential to the car-buying process:

▶ Use decision guides, which ask you a series of questions, give you boxes to check or buttons to click, and then match your answers with car features in their databases. The result is a list of likely cars for you to compare or investigate one at a time, in-depth. You can save your information for later use.

▶ Get the specs and pricing for any new car you've got your eye on, with details on price, dealer incentives, size, customer complaint ratings, performance statistics, crash tests, closest competing autos, optional features, and more.

▶ Plug numbers into the calculators to find out what monthly payment you can expect, at what rate, and for how long.

▶ Link to and use AOL's Digital Cities (AOL Keyword: **Digital City**) for your city. Browse dealers' hot deals and look through the classifieds. Wherever you find classifieds, of course, you can sell as well as buy, if you're trading up for example. Digital Cities, plus Your Town (devoted to smaller communities), are now available from the AOL 6.0 Channels menu; just click Local.

▶ Get competitive bids on insurance. Link to a handful of reliable Web sites that provide background information, including Consumer Reports and Quicken.com.

▶ Use the Dealer Locator to identify a place where you can close the deal you researched online. Search more than 11,000 dealers with a presence on your Digital City.

▶ Read the latest car reviews in the online versions of *Road and Track*, *Car and Driver*, and other magazines for auto enthusiasts.

▶ Find out how to change your car's oil, flush the radiator, jump start an ailing battery, and install snow chains. You can even learn what's under the hood to avoid intimidation at the service station.

Looking for that Dream House? Do the Groundwork Online

A late-1990's TV commercial showed two suburban neighbors comparing the cool stuff they bought on the Web. One showed off an antique Pez dispenser, the other an old house; both items were bought on the Web. The comparison contains a bit of hype and more than a touch of suburban one-upmanship. But you can do your house shopping from AOL and save money in the process.

A house is something too personal and too expensive to buy without seeing it, poking around the basement, checking out the work required, and so on. What you *can* do on the Web is learn about the house-buying process, compare mortgage rates, prequalify for a loan, investigate second mortgages or refinancing, estimate your monthly payments, and compare offers. In early 1999, I was able to refinance with a national, online broker (now known as `www.iown.com`) at a rate better than anything offered in my area. The real-world tasks were whittled down to several overnight-express deliveries, a brief visit by an appraiser, and a quick trip to a lawyer.

The next best thing to opening the window or inspecting the basement of a house is to see a picture of the house. Realtor.com (`www.realtor.com`) brings you the descriptions, prices, and pictures of more than a million houses. Both Realtor.com and AOL Keyword: **Realtor** also link you with housing and finance markets and provide the resources for you to teach yourself about the entire process of buying a house.

Find It Online

At AOL Keyword: **ClassifiedPlus**, you can search more than a million ads and post your own in a marketplace that spans the AOL, Compuserve, Digital City, and Netscape online communities. To narrow your search to the classifieds for your area, start at AOL Keyword: **Digital City** (or just **DC**), find your city, and look for a Classifieds link. AOL's Digital City currently reaches more than 60 metropolitan areas in the U.S., and Digital City's new Your Town service reaches even further, to more than 200 small towns.

Tip

Any major expense is likely to involve at least two kinds of decision making: choosing among the available products, vendors, and features, and then figuring out how to finance the product you decide on. The Web can help you make both types of decisions.

If you're serious about that new house, make sure you spend time using the many thoughtful services and inventive calculators available at Homefair.com (www.homefair.com), one of the longest-lasting business services on the Web. Using a site like Homefair.com (shown in Figure 5-4), you can plan the entire process. Choose a community based on schools, low crime rate, taxes, and climate; find affordable and agreeable homes in the community where you want to live; choose a mortgage and mortgager; and find a job in your new community. Buying one house is usually coupled with selling another one, and you can start the selling process here, too.

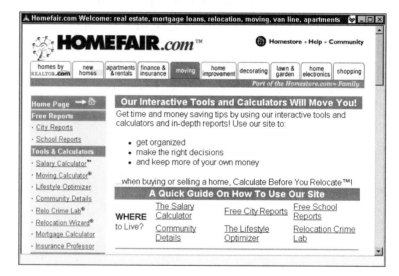

Figure 5-4. HomeFair.com helps you find the right house in the right place.

Getting Ahead: Jobs and Careers

Right up there with planning for the future is finding a job, or a new job, *now*; a regular income may be all that stands between you and the future you want.

The place to start is your own community, if that's where you want to work. Digital City (AOL Keyword: **Digital City** or **DC**) offers more than 120,000 classified job listings that you can search or browse. For your city or the city where you want to work, DC also offers listings of employment agencies.

In the Careers & Work (formerly, Workplace) Channel, a prominent Job Search button takes you to Monster.com's well-established Web service that brings together job seekers and employers. Currently, you can search almost 400,000 openings. Using the service (which is free, of course) is quite simple:

1. Type in your city or select your state (or both).
2. Select the kind of work you are seeking from the Select a Profession drop-down list.
3. If you want, in the Optional Keywords text box you can type a word or two to narrow your search.
4. Click Search.

In the resulting list of matching jobs, you may be surprised to find local jobs that actually appeal to you. Pay attention to the date for any opening. Not all online listings are up-to-date, but even older listings can indicate which companies are looking for what kind of skills.

As you may be coming to expect, all sorts of essential services are a click away when you're doing a search. From the channel's opening window, you can do research on companies and make your resume available online. Don't know what you want to do? Use the channel's Career Finder. Already gainfully employed, but frustrated by workplace constraints and politics? Look into the possibilities of starting your own business.

Don't miss the links to online executive search agencies, interview tips, resume-writing advice, and on and on. Every little bit counts when you're looking for that perfect job, and every bit of the process is online — even, in some cases, the interview itself.

Stop Working So Hard: Having Fun Online

The Information Age drives everyone harder and gives many of us cause to grumble about sleeping less, working harder, putting in more hours, and thus not spending enough time with family and friends. Not all the sages of the information economy appreciate the long-term toll on "productivity"

Find It Online

People looking for employment with the federal government might want to start at the Office of Personnel Mangement's useful, searchable USAJobs (`http://www.usajobs.opm.gov/`).

Find It Online

AOL Keyword: **Workplace** (the AOL Careers & Work Channel) has direct links to many job-hunting services on AOL and the Web.

Find It Online

In doing research about a company for which you want to work, start with the company's Web site. In addition to its product line and organizational structure, you can learn about its culture and image.

caused by hectic, nonstop working. Why not use AOL's information age services to make the most of your free time? Here are some ways you can enhance traditional leisure-time activities, including shopping, traveling, reading, and cooking. Chapter 18 explores some of the newer, purely online pastimes.

Shopping Online

Each holiday season brings record-breaking news of online shopping as millions discover the nearly effortless pleasures of choosing the gifts they want for loved ones and, of course, themselves. The convenience doesn't stop at the saved time, the point-and-click ease, or the ability to search for just the right gift. Often, the choice is broader and the prices lower.

Shop@AOL, Now Open for Business

With a plan, a job, a car, and a place to live, you can start enjoying the Web as a place to shop and have fun.

The first serious Internet stores in the mid-90s had the good idea of joining together to form malls, so that, like real-world malls, they could share overhead, generate traffic, and provide something for everyone, including a place to eat. The first such malls lacked anchor tenants and failed to attract foot traffic, much less real business. Today, just about every large retailer does substantial business on the Web, and thousands of smaller ones are getting into the act. Every business school, it seems, introduces its students to the benefits of electronic commerce. Not surprisingly, many stores are joining to form mega-malls on the Internet.

NEW   **Feature**

In AOL 6.0, a new toolbar button, under AOL Services, takes you directly to Shop@AOL's starting point on AOL.

Shop@AOL (AOL Keyword: **Shopping**) brings together online vendors in a one-stop shopping experience that real stores cannot match. When people shop at real stores, they must cope with the long distances between stores, the confusing maze of displays, and difficulty finding the simplest items. At Shop@AOL on the Web, you shop at your own pace in stores with a real-world presence (like J.C. Penney and Banana Republic) as well as in stores that exist only online (like NetMarket and eToys). Shop@AOL takes you to an AOL-only window where you can start your shopping trip.

AOL's online emporium — with more than 300 vendors —
never feels like a big mall. When you use Shop@AOL to shop
for a computer, software, books, or anything else, AOL provides a full range of customer support at every point:

▶ While you're looking for products and choosing among
   brands and vendors

▶ During transactions

▶ After you receive the products you've ordered

Even though no one has figured out how to offer an online
food court, shopping at AOL beats visiting your local mall in
many ways.

Shop@AOL, Shop Smart

When you buy online, AOL's Shopping Assistant (shown in
Figure 5-5) and other customer service features can simplify
your experience in many ways. The Shopping Assistant is a
small toolbar that appears at the top of your AOL browser
window when you visit any Shop@AOL vendor. (Click Shop
on the AOL 6.0 toolbar to go to Shop@AOL.) The Shopping
Assistant offers a handy set of shopping services.

Tip

Use AOL's Reminder service
(AOL Keyword: **Reminder**)
to remember to shop for
birthdays and anniversaries.

Find It Online

AOL Quick Checkout is an
option on the new, AOL 6.0
Settings menu.

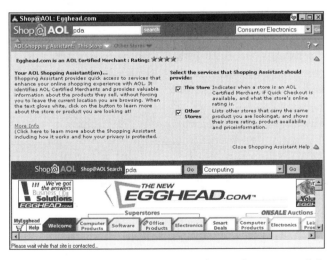

Figure 5-5. Use the AOL Shopping Assistant for complete support to help you find
products, see what's in stock, and compare prices.

▶ Use the Search box to search all Shop@AOL merchants for a specific item. Type in the name of a product type (such as a personal digital assistant, or *PDA*) or brand (such as *Palm*), and click Go. To search entire categories of products, choose a category from the drop-down list on the right, and click Go.

▶ Use the check boxes (refer to Figure 5-5) to get information about vendors. First, find out whether the vendor you are visiting is an AOL Certified Merchant. (If it is, the return policies are backed up by AOL's money-back guarantee.) Then, if you're doing a Shop@AOL search for a specific product, find out which vendors have the item in stock and how much they charge for it. Merchants are being continuously rated by individual members and are given a rating, with favorite vendors getting five stars. You can always view all merchant ratings at `onlinestoreratings.com`.

During a transaction, AOL provides the Quick Checkout service. This service allows you to enter credit-card information just once and then reuse that stored information later for quick shopping at Shop@AOL. Use AOL Keyword: **Quick Checkout**. Only AOL members can use Quick Checkout.

Keep in mind that

▶ Merchants must meet AOL's stringent standards for customer service, customer privacy, professional packaging, and product delivery.

▶ AOL provides its own round-the-clock customer services, available by e-mail, chat, phone, and message board. At AOL Keyword: **Shopping**, click Customer Service. All your options are spelled out in one place, and you will also find a list of phone numbers for all your questions about Quick Checkout and Shop@AOL gift certificates.

Buying Computers and Computer Gear

Your computer hardware and software have a direct impact on what you can do online. Buying anything computer related, however, can be about as intimidating as buying a car. For starters, the jargon and terminology used to sell this stuff can be confusing. At *bricks-and-mortar* (or real-world) stores, salespeople often encourage shoppers to buy the latest features without clarifying why they need them and what they do.

AOL's Computer Center Channel, together with CNET (AOL Keyword: **CNET**), the Web megasite produced by the CNET cable TV, greatly simplify the process of getting background information, matching your needs to current products, and making informed decisions. The following list briefly describes some of the help available through the AOL Computer Center Channel and CNET:

▶ **Decision Guides:** Decisions can be especially tricky when you're trying to match many features and brands with your needs and budget. AOL's Decision Maker guides come to your aid. From AOL's Computing Channel, you can currently find decision-making guides for help in selecting a computer, laptop, scanner, printer, or handheld computer. Each guide walks you through a series of questions that help the guide match your preferences with the many items in its database.

▶ **Product Reviews:** After you identify a few products of possible interest, you can get background information and product reviews at AOL Keyword: **CNET**. From the opening page, click hardware or software and then browse to the product or type of product (or a vendor or price range). Use the Search box to go right to the product about which you want information. However you get the information about your product, you can then do comparison pricing to find out which online vendor has the lowest price (the list of vendors is large but not comprehensive).

▶ **Online Help and Support:** Need help using all that new computer gear? From AOL's Computing Channel, click Get Help Now (AOL Keyword: **GetHelpNow**) for live help from experts, message boards (where you can ask other people questions), a new-user computer guide, and a technical dictionary. AOL also offers support through online lessons. At AOL Keyword: **Online Classrooms** or **Help Community**, you can take free classes on AOL, HTML, PaintShop, and office productivity applications. For a fee, you can take computing lessons from Learn2.com (AOL Keyword: **Learn2**).

Tip

When you're using Shop@AOL to shop for popular brands, use the Shopping Assistant to compare AOL's merchants for prices and item availability. If you're in the market for an expensive, obscure, or out-of-print book, consider doing some comparison shopping. You can search for the online store with the lowest price for a wide range of consumer items, including books. Remember, however, that price is only one component of customer satisfaction: always try to find out about product availability, the return policy, customer services, and transaction security in dealing with a lesser-known store. Two sites that compare the prices of just books are AddALL (www.addall.com) and BestBookBuys (www.bestbookbuys.com).

Cross-Reference

Chapter 9 has more to say about digital libraries, and Chapter 18 introduces the new world of eBooks.

Buying Books Online

Online media have invigorated every aspect of the book business. New stores have sprung up to compete with existing stores. Older independent bookstores are joining online cooperatives to stave off both aggressive brick-and-mortar superstores and new online-only superstores. Publishers are learning how to publish books in a secure, electronic online format, bringing existing books and new titles to a broader audience at a lower price.

New media's biggest boost to traditional book publishing has been as a distribution medium — simplifying the process of helping people buy the books they want to read. Shop@AOL offers easy access to popular booksellers, including Barnes and Noble (AOL Keyword: **BN**) and Amazon.com, to make book searching and buying as convenient as possible for AOL members You have access to a vast and convenient selection of books, often without sales tax. In addition to books, both stores offer movies, CDs, DVDs, and other items. Amazon now sells consumer electronics; Barnes & Noble sells electronic books, among other items.

Is It Safe to Buy Things Online?

Yes. AOL Keyword: **AOL Guarantee** includes a limit on customer liability for fraud, a money-back guarantee, and several layers of customer support.

Consider also that the browser, which is based on Microsoft's industry-standard technology, scrambles data so that it can't be intercepted or tampered en route without automatically invalidating the transaction. Also, most sites that you buy from are *secure*. This means that the site must provide your browser with a *digital certificate*, which proves that the site is legitimate (as certified by a trusted third party) before you send confidential information such as your credit card number.

Buying CDs Online

Like books, CDs lend themselves to online sales. Online shoppers can search for a specific CD in a fraction of the time they normally take to find a store that has their CD in stock, drive there, find a parking place, stand in line, and so on. Online CD stores can readily ship CDs anywhere. To top it off, most CD vendors let you listen to snippets from an audio CD before buying it, just so you're sure the CD has the particular Dan Bern or Bob Dylan tune you really want. The only problem is, the snippets are never long enough; they often serve as teasers.

CDNow (AOL Keyword: **CDNOW**) is AOL's official music store. At Shop@AOL, you can also buy CDs at Columbia House and Tower Records.

It's Showtime: Movies Online

AOL's Moviefone (AOL Keyword: **Movie**), whose quirky ads you may have seen at the movies before a feature film starts, has become a comprehensive, interactive source of movie intelligence. Much of the information is very practical: where new movies are playing in your area, what kids' movies are playing in your area, when the show times are, what reviewers think of the movies, what normal people think of the movies, and so on. Plus, you can order tickets online *without paying a service charge.*

You can search for local movies by Zip code or title. If a movie you want to see is not playing in your Zip code, Moviefone looks further afield. Figure 5-6 shows the kind of information you get about movies. The information you get from a movie search includes a plot synopsis, a rating, critics' comments, *moviegoers'* comments, show times, nearby locations, directions to the theater, *and* the chance to add the movie's name, place, and time to the My Calendar service with just one click.

Tip

AOL's Media Player, new in AOL 6.0, makes hearing music snippets at places like CDNow easier and faster. AOL comes with the RealPlayer, too, which automatically plays RealAudio files, such as those used by most CD vendors.

Note

If you have a new computer with a CD-R, a CD-RW, or a DVD drive, you should be able to play your audio CDs in that drive.

Cross-Reference

This chapter looks at ways to find out about the old-fashioned movies that you watch in a movie theater. Chapter 18 has a section on movies that you can view online.

Find It Online

For information about local theater, dance, opera, and concerts of all sorts, visit AOL Keyword: **CultureFinder**, which is also available on the Web at www.culturefinder.com. CultureFinder currently tracks well over 300,000 events in over 1,500 cities and publishes an e-mail newsletter on local cultural events. CultureFinder has its own chat and message boards on AOL.

Find It Online

HouseNet (www.housenet.com) grew out of an online forum formerly available only on AOL and now open to the entire Web. Today, the attractive and easily browsable Web site offers gardening, design, roofing, and every manner of fix-it advice. Click the House & Home Channel from the Channel menu.

Find It Online

If you're not the do-it-yourself type and need a contractor, Digital City offers a searchable guide at aol.digitalcity.com/homeimprovement.

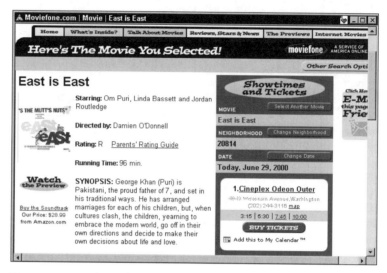

Figure 5-6. Moviefone: why get movie info in the newspapers when you get the information *you* want, faster, online?

Another place to get movie information available through AOL is the Local Guide Channel. Local Guides cover larger metropolitan areas (Digital Cities) as well as smaller communities (Your Town). For every community, an enormous range of information is available, including info about movies (of course), concerts, restaurants, classifieds, personals, weather, garage sales, local news, and much more.

From House to Home

Now that you've paid the mortgage or rent, you can use the Net to make your house into a place where you want to live. Start with the House & Home Channel for comprehensive guidance in planning and carrying out those major projects. Much of the information comes from the Better Homes and Gardens Home Improvement Encyclopedia, which includes all the wiring, masonry, carpentry, painting, and other information you need to plan or price. Handy estimators (fill-in-the-blank calculators) help you figure out the amount of wallpaper or paint for those home projects.

In the Gardening department, get advice about planting herbs, planning borders, choosing ground cover, caring for indoor plants, and more. Link to Shop@AOL stores like Gardenworks.com (part of 1-800-flowers.com) to browse for bulbs, seeds, tools, books, cut flowers, and the like.

For Gourmands

Everything food-related has found a home on AOL or the Web, and you can find much of it at the AOL Keyword: **Food**. Or, select Recipes from the new AOL 6.0 AOL Services menu. AOL's new Recipe Finder is a Web-based search tool that was created by the same folks who make the Decision Guides you use when buying a car or digital camera. In the Recipe Finder search box, type a pertinent word or two (**lobster** or **cobbler**, for example) and click Search. A page of results comes up after a few seconds. Click the links of any recipes that interest you.

For Travelers

Sometimes, planning vacations can be the least enjoyable part of the process. Doing it online can cut the time and cost. At AOL Keyword: **Travel**, you can start by booking your plane, lodging, and car rental, courtesy of the Web's leading travel agency, Travelocity.

If you know where you're going and how to get there, Frommer's Destination Guides (AOL Keyword: **Destinations**) help you create a Custom Mini-Guide — see Figure 5-7. All you do is indicate where you're going and what kind of information you need. Your custom guide will include the hard information you requested, plus the names and addresses of any local organizations at your destination where you might turn for further assistance.

Find It Online

Where to go? For help selecting a cruise or choosing a national park to hike, you'll find decision-making tools on the Travel Channel or at AOL Keyword: **Travel**. The tools are similar to the ones you'd use to buy a new car, computer, or digital camera. AOL Keyword: **Personalogic** brings together all of AOL's Decision Guides.

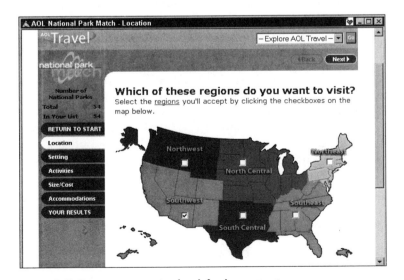

Figure 5-7. Discover a new national park for that next outing.

Note

eBay is adamant about the responsibilities of buyers and sellers. This publicly traded company doesn't sell goods, but provides the services through which buyers and sellers can contract with each other. If you take part, as buyer or seller, study all the online information available at eBay.

Tip

A new payment service called PayPal (www.paypal.com) simplifies auction payments. The popular Web service is free to both buyers and sellers, but some services will cost you money.

Tip

eBay provides full information about how to post pictures of the things you want to sell online. The simplest way is to use a digital picture from "You've Got Pictures" (AOL Keyword: **Pictures**), download it to your hard drive, and upload it to My Place (AOL Keyword: **My FTP Place**). See Chapter 15 to get all the information you need on uploading. The Web address for your uploaded picture will look like this: hometown.aol.com/myscreenname/mypenny.jpg

Going Once, Going Twice: Online Auctions

Online auctions bring together millions of people who need something with people who have that certain something. The idea is simple. Say that you have an 1891 Indian Head penny in mint condition. It can be valuable because you like it, because others want it, or because it's rare or in particularly good condition — maybe even for all three reasons.

How do you find a buyer, provide details about your penny (including a picture), handle bids, and ensure payment? Online auction sites provide the basic services that bring together buyers and sellers. Only a very few auction sites attract the numbers of people required to create true markets for just about anything. The biggest of these is eBay (AOL Keyword: **Ebay**), with more than 4,000 categories of items, 450,000 new items, and about 4 million bids on auctions every day.

At eBay, you can search for anything at any time, using the search box on the opening page. To either bid or put something up for bid, you must register and become an eBay member, which means you must provide contact information and a credit card number. Registration is free — you don't pay eBay any money if you bid on and win an auction, but you do pay fees when you list an item for auction.

Searching is quick and powerful. You can browse eBay's categories (you will be surprised by how much is being sold) or search for a specific object across categories. A nine-year-old in my neighborhood regularly searches eBay for old coins — with adult assistance and approval, of course.

You can limit your search to a region and a city if you want to meet the seller, see the item, and explore additional trading opportunities. For any item, you get a text description of the object, optionally a picture of the object, information about the seller's reliability as reported by other buyers, and bidding history for the object, plus payment and shipping options. Using eBay is much less complicated than it seems.

Advice for Buyers and Sellers

If you're selling: Provide clear and explicit information about the thing you are selling and include a picture whenever possible. Don't change the item's description subsequently or misrepresent it: The winning bidder could use any such discrepancies to void the transaction. You must accept the winning bid, a bid that either meets your minimum or exceeds all other bids. Bids are usually entertained for a fixed amount of time, which you choose (3–10 days). If you want, you can end the auction early, but remember that many bids are submitted toward the end of the bidding process. Make sure that you understand any fees involved. eBay charges a variety of fees for specific services, all described in detail when you register to sell something.

If you're buying: Check the seller's ratings (what other buyers thought of doing business with that person). Acknowledge your responsibility to pay for any bid you win, at the terms requested by the seller. Make sure you know what you are buying, from whom you're buying, and how you will pay for the item just in case you win the bid.

Where to Go from Here

In a matter of years, the Internet has become the place to start when pricing a computer, booking a cruise, finding an address, buying a house, and doing a hundred other things.

▶ To shop for almost anything, click the AOL 6.0 toolbar's Shop button.

▶ For details about using the AOL Web browser, see Chapter 6.

▶ For an introduction to the new Netscape Navigator browser, see Chapter 7.

C H A P T E R

6

BEHIND THE WHEEL: USING AOL'S WEB BROWSER

Chapter 6

Behind the Wheel: Using AOL's Web Browser

IN THIS CHAPTER

What is the Web?

What is a browser?

Understanding your browser's controls

Understanding the elements of a Web page

Navigating the Web with the AOL browser

Customizing the AOL browsers

Multimedia madness: music, video, and animation

The World Wide Web, or *Web* as most call it, has become a part of daily life for tens of millions of people. One can hardly believe that a young English physicist conceived the Web only a decade ago. As Internet tools go, the Web is wonderfully simple. So simple, in fact, that Chapters 4 and 5 can get you started right away; if you type or use a mouse, you know everything required to get started with those chapters. This chapter has everything you need to use AOL's Web browser — the software that fully integrates your AOL experience, bringing the entire Web to your doorstep.

Ten Long Years of Web History in a Minute

In the future, historians may consider the year 1989 as the end of the 20th century: The Berlin Wall fell, closed societies started opening borders and minds, and the World Wide Web was invented.

For decades, innovative scientists had seen the need for tools to access the rapidly growing body of scientific knowledge. Faced with the growth of electronically networked knowledge, Tim Berners-Lee, a young English physicist studying in Geneva, developed an ingeniously simple way of linking documents across computer networks. In 1989, he came up with the broad outlines of such a web of knowledge. Mr. Berners-Lee developed both the first Web browser and HTML, the computer language used by Web browsers.

The Web is not the same as the Internet. The Internet consists of many types of information that you access with different tools, such as e-mail and newsgroup readers. The Web was originally a way of accessing and linking research papers, data files, and messages using a single tool. However, the Web quickly became a way of publishing new information. Since 1989, the types of information published on the Web have come to include not just text (words) but also media (and multimedia) of every sort: animation, graphics, animated graphics, video, sounds, and more.

Why You Need a Browser to Surf the Internet

When you type a Web address into the browser software on your computer, the browser asks a computer (called a server) on the Internet to send a copy of the Web page you requested to your computer. The server then turns the requested page into little packets of data, which the browser puts back together again so that you can experience the page. Web browsers:

- ▶ Make the Net visual (and aural and animated and alive)
- ▶ Simplify Net navigation (all you have to do is click with your mouse to move from document to document)

Tip

Tim Berners-Lee tells the inside story of the Web's concepts and development in *Weaving the Web* (HarperSan Francisco, 1999).

Definition

The Web and the Internet are not the same thing. The *Internet* is a worldwide network of computers that simplifies the exchange of different kinds of information between different kinds of widely dispersed computing devices. The *World Wide Web* is a collection of online destinations created and linked together using a very simple computer language called HTML, short for HyperText Markup Language.

6

Behind the Wheel: Using
AOL's Web Browser

A medium carries information of a specific physical format, such as video, sound, text, and graphics. The information is the content; the medium is the channel that delivers the content to you. When more than one media is used to share information (such as text, graphics, and sound used together), the format is referred to as *multimedia*.

Cross-Reference

See the "What You Need to Know about Web Addresses" box later in this chapter.

Note

AOL's built-in browser is based on Microsoft Internet Explorer (MSIE). One thing to get used to about the Internet: You can usually do anything about six different ways. You can, for instance, use the AOL browser and the stand-alone version of the MSIE browser at the same time. When you're online, MSIE is always available by clicking the Internet Explorer icon on your Windows desktop. This book does not go into detail about the MSIE browser.

▶ Opens publishing on the Net to anyone

The basic unit of the World Wide Web is the *page,* a document you view with a browser. Click a link on one page, and the browser downloads and displays another page, including formatted text, graphics, animation, musical accompaniment, and all the glitz and wonder people expect on the Web.

Your AOL Browser: A Tool for Using Other Tools

When the first browsers were being developed in the early 1990s, most multimedia formats hadn't been invented. The browser remains an amazing all-purpose tool, but today's purposes differ from the original purposes. Still, major browsers remain true to their origins by supporting electronic mail, newsgroups, and FTP.

Electronic Mail

AOL's browser supports e-mail in two main ways. First, you can actually read and manage your AOL Mail directly on the Web at (aolmail.aol.com). Chapter 10 shows you how.

Second, you can click what is called a Mail to link on a Web page. This kind of link enables people who are reading a page to send an e-mail message to someone responsible for the site. Mail to links are a good way to ask questions about a site or provide feedback.

If you click a Mail to link, and AOL is set up as your default Internet application (see Chapter 3), your Write Mail opens. If AOL is not your default Internet application, clicking such a link opens up the Microsoft Outlook program, which most computers include. (If you don't have an account with a non-AOL Internet provider, you won't be able to use Outlook.)

Newsgroups

Click one of the Web's News links and you bring up AOL's newsgroup reader with the newsgroup's messages ready for you to browse. In other words, you don't read messages inside the browser, as you can with a News search engine such as Deja.com, discussed in Chapter 14. AOL must be your default

Internet application to read newsgroups in the AOL News-groups window. Use the Address box to enter such addresses from scratch to immediately start reading a newsgroup.

FTP

FTP stands for *File Transfer Protocol* and that's exactly what it is: a way to move files across the Internet. For now, think of FTP as a way of accessing part of someone else's hard drive — at the other end of a very big network. FTP sites show you only file names, so you must know exactly what you're looking for. In Chapter 15, I discuss searching FTP sites for specific files. If you know the address of the FTP site you want to visit, simply type it into the Address box (`ftp://ftp.aol.com/` is an example of an FTP address). You can use the AOL browser to download files from the site.

Tip

Some Web sites let you click a link to send e-mail to some-one at the site. To find out the actual e-mail address, move your mouse cursor over the link and look in the status bar at the bottom of the browser window. Or if you're comfort-able with such things, right-click, choose View Source, and look for the embedded mail address.

Cross-Reference

For all you need to know about AOL e-mail, see Chapters 10–11.

Creating Your Own Web Pages

Over the years, creating Web pages has become incredibly popular. At AOL Hometown, AOL provides tools for quickly creating and sharing Web pages. If you prefer to do things from scratch, all you need is a word processor to make a page. Microsoft Office applications let you create a Web page by simply saving just about any Word, Excel, PowerPoint, Publish, or other Office document as an HTML document — a Web page, in other words. (HTML is the language used to create Web pages.)

For information about creating Web pages, see *Your Official America Online Guide to Creating Cool Web Pages,* 2nd edition, by Edward Willett (IDG Books Worldwide, Inc.).

Web Pages and Their Elements

As you explore the World Wide Web, you'll see an amazing variety of Web pages, ranging from pages with simple text to multimedia creations featuring animation, video, 3D effects, and interactive games. Think of multimedia as a combination of physical page elements, each conveying some sort of infor-mation to you.

Tip

If you know the exact name of a newsgroup, you can go directly to the newsgroup by typing its name into the Address box and clicking Go. For example, type in **news:rec.toys.cars**. Notice you don't need the forward slashes (//) after the colon.

In the next few pages, I outline some of the page elements you can expect to run across when you browse the Web. AOL's Entertainment Asylum, whose opening page is shown in Figure 6-1, uses many of the elements that are available today. The AOL browser knows what to do and how to display these things. Knowing what you're looking at can be an enormous help if you're trying to learn to make pages yourself or if you just want to know what's going on. Here's a list of commonly used Web page elements and media:

Link   Words Picture

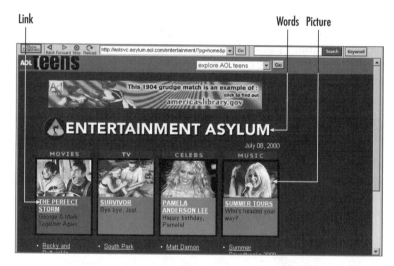

Figure 6-1. Entertainment Asylum, the brainchild of AOL's Ted Leonsis, has grown into a super-site for superstars. It uses many of the available Web tricks and tools.

Tip

You can get started with digital pictures at AOL Keyword: **You've Got Pictures**. Using your film camera, you can develop film as usual and fill out a form requesting that the photo retailer post digital pictures directly to your AOL screen name. When you sign on to AOL, you'll hear "You've Got Pictures" as well as the famous "You've Got Mail." You can also upload pictures from a scanner or a digital camera. Check out my recent book, *Your Official America Online Guide to Pictures Online* (IDG Books Worldwide, Inc.).

▶ **Words** (sometimes called *text*) constitute the basic page element because they can convey large amounts of complex information. While words and graphics are often contrasted, the important point to remember on today's Web is that everything is visual, including the text. Good Web designers can vary font type, color, and size; play with the length of a line of text; create graphics files consisting of words; and use style sheets to create elegant color, type, and link designs.

▶ **Pictures**, or graphics, enrich words on the Web and provide intrinsic interest. Kids expect illustrations, scientists expect diagrams, sports fans expect to see action shots, and so on. With digital cameras and scanners, plus easy-to-use software like MGI PhotoSuite, Web builders of every level can easily add pictures to their pages.

Graphics include photographs (digital pictures) and clipart, as well as less noticeable things like bullets (in a list) and buttons (which you click to do something on a Web page). Graphics have made the Web compelling. The latest version of HTML enables designers to position graphics at precise places on a page. When they are also used as links, a graphical image map can both clarify a site's organization and simplify navigation from place to place within the site.

▶ **Links**, or *hyperlinks,* are the glue that connect the Web (see Figure 6-2). You can call a Web page from within another Web page by including a link. Links make documents available with a single click. Click a link such as `The Perfect Storm` (see Figure 6-1) to get more information about the book, the movie, and the characters. You may be able to see a picture, watch a video clip from the film, or see a virtual reality simulation of a storm at sea. What a link does all depends on the connections that the author or designer wants to create.

Links can be either words or pictures (or parts of pictures). Links in text are usually highlighted in a different color and underlined; links in pictures can sometimes be harder to find. Clicking a link can take you to another part of that same page, another page on the same Web site, or anywhere on the Web.

Tip

As page design becomes more sophisticated, you may have a hard time knowning what you can click. To identify a link, move your mouse pointer over different elements in a Web page. If the pointer changes from an arrow to a pointing finger, you've found a link. Click and release the mouse. Also, text that is blue and underlined is usually a giveaway that something is a link, but more designers are resorting to other sorts of visual cues.

Learning HTML...from the Web	
Resource	**Comments**
ABCs of Creating Your First Student Web Page	A simply designed and *long* page created for students of Women's literature at the University of Texas, with enough information about the basic tags for students to create their own course-related pages. http://www.cwrl.utexas.edu/~gsiesing/314/siesing/webhandouts/
Barebones Guide to HTML	Strictly a reference guide to HTML 3.2, *translated into almost 20 languages*, including Russian, Danish, and Chinese. Tags are usefully grouped into functional categories such as "lists," "forms," and "tables." Includes an HTML FAQ. http://werbach.com/barebones/
A Beginner's Guide to HTML	Originally written by Marc Andreessen, a creator of Mosaic and founder of Netscape. One of the best designed of the HTML sites, it requires use of a Java-capable browser. A PDF (Adobe Acrobat) version of the tutorial is available, as is a single long document (print it out and it's all you need!). This is the guide to which GWU sends students for advice in creating student pages.

Figure 6-2. This Web page (`members.aol.com/davidpeal/recommend.htm`) includes plain text and links (the underlined bits of text) to list and annotate Web resources for learning HTML.

▶ **Tables** are used by Web designers to display text or pictures (or anything) in neat rows and columns. You'll probably be most aware of tables of text. In fact, even pages that don't appear to have tables may be full of them. Until recently, tables helped designers organize text and graphics on a Web page by controlling margins and line lengths. Now, HTML is getting much more sophisticated, and the current browsers (like AOL's) give page designers much more control over how a page looks. Today, designers have control, just as they do in real-world publishing.

▶ **Forms** turn static Web pages into interactive ones. Good examples of forms include the acronym finders and dictionaries discussed in Chapter 4 and the search sites profiled in Chapter 9. You type words into a box, press Enter, and your words go out to the Internet, where databases are searched. You'll get an answer to your question or a message explaining that your search was unsuccessful. Among other things, people use forms on Web sites to participate in online polls, request regular e-mail newsletters from the site, and order jelly beans at online stores.

▶ **Frames** allow more than one Web page to be displayed at the same time, in different windows in your browser. Netscape invented frames and made them hugely popular on the Web. When a page has thick borders and scrollbars affecting different parts of a page, you know you're looking at frames, but sometimes their use is less obvious. A navigation page, or table of contents, that is always visible in part of a page, while everything else changes, is a typical use of frames. Links to all the other pages on the site show in one frame, and the actual content shows up in a second, larger frame.

▶ **Video.** Many sites today use video. Chapter 18 profiles some entertainment sites that use video. You'll encounter two main kinds of video out there: streaming and non-streaming.

 • **Non-streaming video** is the old-fashioned way and has become less and less common. You click a link to download the clip. When the movie has completely downloaded, you can play it in a stand-alone video player. Both Windows and AOL have integrated players. Often, the player, or *helper*

Definition

Interactivity has many meanings. At its simplest, Web interactivity means that a Web page doesn't just present information but has buttons and fill-in-the blank boxes for you to express preferences and add information (as when you use AOL Anywhere's customization features to create a custom newspaper, covered in Chapter 3). At the other extreme, interactivity means that people can communicate with each other over the Web, as in Web-based message boards (Chapter 14) and Groups@AOL (Chapter 18).

application as it used to be called, plays the clip automatically. You can read more about players later in this chapter.

- **Streaming video**, on the other hand, is delivered a little bit at a time and is stored on your PC. Streaming video starts playing before you've received the entire clip. Because you don't have to download the entire clip before it starts playing, streaming video starts playing faster. However, it tends to be low-quality and may sputter or stop altogether due to dreaded "Net congestion." Even with high-speed access such as a cable modem or DSL connection, streaming video is sometimes low-quality, because it's heavily compressed. Later in this chapter, you can read more about the most popular streaming-video plug-in, RealPlayer, shown in Figure 6-3.

Note

Over a modem connection, even the best quality streaming video is still jerky because an adequate frame rate (number of frames displayed per second) is hard to come by, owing to network congestion, modem speed, and display technology: yet another reason to consider a high-speed connection (see Chapters 17 and 18).

6

Behind the Wheel: Using
AOL's Web Browser

Figure 6-3. Jazz pianist Chick Corea on RealPlayer.

Definition

(For geeks only) *Java* is a programming language that takes considerable effort to master, and designers use Java to embed separate, small programs in a Web page. Examples of Java include AOL's Quick Buddy (Chapter 12) and Easy Designer (AOL's Web-page builder, AOL Keyword: **AOL Hometown**). Unrelated to Java except in name, *JavaScript* is a simple text-based scripting language that Web designers use to create clocks, games, drop-down menus, visually enhanced links, and other effects.

▶ **Java** is a programming language that is used to write little programs called applets. Applets are little programs that run from a Web browser and enable you to view and use games, mortgage calculators, Web-based chat programs, scrolling news windows, and so on. Java programs aren't dependent on any specific hardware, such as a PC or Macintosh; they can run on any computer with any Java-ready browser, such as AOL's browser. For a wonderful example of how Java can be used, go to `prominence.com/java/poetry` to create your own refrigerator poetry — just drag the words around with your mouse until you've completed your very own poetic masterpiece.

Definition

HTML (the hypertext markup language) works behind the scenes to make a Web page look how it looks and do what it does.

▶ **JavaScript** is a scripting language added to HTML to enhance a Web page. A common use of JavaScript is to make the kind of pull-down menus that take you to a Web page as soon as you have scrolled down a list of items, and then clicked and released your mouse. Another common usage is the *rollover*: If you move your mouse arrow over a link, for example, *and* the link changes color, increases in size, appears highlighted, or displays an image. In Figure 6-4, a classic card game that develops memory in young children employs JavaScript.

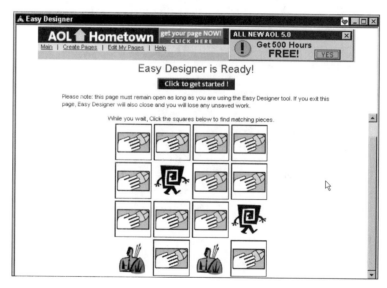

Figure 6-4. A JavaScript game to keep you entertained while Easy Designer (AOL's Web-page tool) loads.

What You Need to Know about Web Addresses

Cross-Reference

Chapter 10 goes into domains in more depth.

In your Web travels, you will quickly start encountering Web addresses, or *URLs*. A URL (short for Universal Resource Locator) identifies every document on the Internet. A Web address such as `http://www.aol.com` has several parts.

▶ The **protocol** indicates how you (your computer, really) want to receive a Web page or other kind of data. The best-known protocol is `http://`, the protocol used to transfer Web pages from Internet computers to your browser. A protocol is a language, but one spoken only by computers to help them send different types of resources back and forth.

▶ The **Internet computer** (server) is where the information is stored, plus that computer's **domain**. In `www.idgbooks.com` the computer is called `www` and the domain is called `idgbooks.com`.

▶ The **specific page** you want to use. You'll either see a specific file name, such as beach.htm or baby.html. Or when the URL doesn't explicitly contain a file name, as in `www.idgbooks.com`, the default is index.htm or something similar. A page can have either HTM or HTML as a file extension. Chapter 15 goes into file extensions in detail.

When you display a page, its URL appears in the AOL Address box. Sometimes these URLs appear with a URL vastly more complex than what you originally typed. The reason for this is that a great number of Web sites keep track of the visitors who use their pages. For example, on-line storse track you so that they can keep track of your purchases as you move from item to item.

The AOL Browser in Action

To see the browser in action, just open any Web page. To do so, type a Web address — for instance, **www.idgbooks.com** — into the Address box and click Go (or press Enter). After you've typed the address, you can go to the site by clicking the Internet button on the AOL 6.0 Toolbar.

Cross-Reference

Chapter 5 explores the essentials of accessing Web sites, and Chapter 8 is all about AOL Search, AOL's comprehensive Web-based search service.

Web pages often display so much information that you need to maximize the browser by clicking the 2nd of the three boxes in the browser window's upper right-hand corner. To see even more, minimize the AOL toolbar. Choose Settings⇨ Preferences. Click Toolbar. In the Toolbar & Sounds Preferences window, find the Toolbar Appearance window and click Text Only. Click Save.

Web addresses begin with `http://`, which tells the computers that you want to use a specific Web page. The AOL browser assumes that you're looking for a Web page, so you don't have to type **http://**. Just type the latter part of the site's address, such as **www.aol.com**.

The AOL browser is an ordinary window with buttons in the upper right-hand corner to make the window smaller or larger and to close it. Like any window, you can click on the browser's title bar to drag it around the screen as you see fit. To resize it, click any border and drag it into a new position. What goes on inside the browser is subject to the AOL's navigation buttons, shown in Figure 6-5, grouped at the left end of the navigation toolbar, to the left of the AOL Address box.

Telling Your Browser Where to Go: The Address Box

The Address box is just a box in which you type the address of the page you want to visit. After you type the address, press Enter. Ever since AOL 4.0, you've been able to enter either an AOL Keyword or Internet address into the box. (Old-timers on AOL will appreciate the continued presence of the Keyword button on the toolbar.)

New for AOL 6.0, you can put either a search descriptor or keyword into the new Search box (to the immediate left of the big blue Search button) and use AOL Search to look for stuff on AOL or the Net. Chapter 7 has the details.

There Must Be Some Mistake: Error Messages

You used to get errors all the time when trying to access Web sites. Now, both the number and seriousness of errors have gone down. An *error* is anything that can prevent you from viewing a Web page that you're trying to access. A better definition of an error is anything that causes an error message to appear.

Causes of error messages vary:

▶ You have mistyped the URL.

▶ The page no longer exists.

▶ The page just isn't downloading. It may be in high demand, or the server may be creaky. Try again later, as in five seconds later. Net traffic varies by the second.

▶ The page is password protected, is accessible only to the Webmaster, or can be viewed only by members of some organization.

Here are some solutions:

- ▶ Check your spelling. If it's any consolation, finding a single erroneous character can drive anyone nuts. URLs can't have any spaces, by the way, and the capitalization of folder and file names can matter.

- ▶ Maybe you just got the address all wrong. Go to AOL Keyword: **AOL Search** and do a search for the Web address, using the company or organization's name!

- ▶ Maybe you have the right site, but the wrong page. In this case you might try *going up* one directory, and then another directory until you find a working a page. To go up, delete the URL's last-named folder or file name. For example, you would change the (fictitious) Web page

  `www.aol.com/Africa/travel/killimanjaro.html`

  to

  `www.aol.com/Africa/travel`

  If that doesn't work, go to

  `www.aol.com/Africa`

  and finally to

  `www.aol.com`

  and do a site search.

The good news is that the AOL browser displays a message letting you know why you couldn't access a page and what to do about it. Another bit of news: more and more sites are posting friendly error messages that indicate, for example, when the server address is correct but the page requested is incorrect (such as when a page maintained by a college student disappears because the student has graduated).

For a simple explanation of various error messages, go to the NetHelp Web site (`www.aol.com/nethelp`) and click Internet Error Messages.

Telling the Browser How to Get There: Navigation Buttons

The navigation buttons, shown in Figure 6-5, work quite simply. These buttons keep track of AOL screens as well as Web pages, and the trail backward and forward extends to 25 different online places.

Forward

Back Stop ┌ Reload   Address box

Figure 6-5. At least one of the four navigation buttons is usually grayed out (not usable) in a particular circumstance.

▶ **Back.** This button takes you back to the last page or AOL area you've viewed. You can continue clicking this button to backtrack through all the pages you've seen in the current *session* (a fancy way of saying as long as you've been signed on) or longer. You can find out how to set your preferences for the Previous button in the section, "Making the AOL Browser Work Your Way," in this chapter. Keyboard alternative: Alt+left arrow.

▶ **Forward.** After you've backed up, if you want to move forward again through the pages you've viewed, click the Next button. Note that the Next button is active only if you've already used the Previous button. Keyboard alternative: Alt+right arrow.

▶ **Stop.** If a page is taking a long time to arrive in your browser or you change your mind about viewing a page before it's finished loading, click the Stop button. If some of the page has already loaded, you see a partial page. Use the Previous button to return to the last complete page that you viewed. Keyboard alternative: Esc.

Tip

Some pages have their own, built-in navigational buttons showing arrows or words like *Next*. For navigation within a Web site, use the site's own controls to avoid confusion.

Note

Buttons are grayed out and indistinct if they are unavailable at a particular page.

The History of Browsers

A reasonable point to start the history of browsers is in the early 1990s. A college student at the University of Illinois named Marc Andreessen, with a small group influenced by the work of Berners-Lee and others, developed a browser called Mosaic, which could display images as well as text. In 1994, Andreessen helped create both Netscape (the company) and Netscape Navigator (the browser).

Software giant Microsoft got its start in the browser business by licensing browser software based on Mosaic, and Microsoft aggressively and successfully caught up with Netscape in the browser business. Setting a precedent for software companies (and following an Internet tradition), the two companies *gave away* the software. The heated competition of these two companies, in combination with the Web's popularity and freely available browsers, led to the dramatic improvement in browser's capabilities — what they can do and display. Now anyone can create and communicate on the Web, and anyone can also find an astonishing number of facts and perspectives on, well, everything. The browser is becoming the software through which we do just about everything, on our own computers as well as on the Internet.

AOL members have benefited from the white-hot browser wars of the mid-1990s. The AOL browser is based on Microsoft's Internet Explorer (MSIE) browser, and AOL now owns the Netscape browser, the subject of Chapter 7.

Tip

If downloading a page from the Web seems to take all morning, the page may have encountered some Net turbulence along the way. Refreshing it can sometimes do the trick.

▶ **Reload.** This button reloads the current page. If you're viewing a page that is constantly updated with fresh information, using the Refresh button insures you're seeing the latest version of the page and not one that your browser has stored when you viewed it previously.

Your Compass: The Status Bar

At the bottom of the browser window, the status bar tells you what's going on as you're downloading a Web page. Move your mouse arrow over a Web link until the arrow turns into a finger and the status bar shows the page's Web address. Click the link, and the status bar shows you each step of the process (see Figure 6-6):

▶ Whether you've successfully connected with the computer where the page is sitting

▶ Which items (text and graphics files) are being downloaded from the server to your browser

▶ How much of the page has been transferred (using a blue bar meter in the lower-right corner)

Keeping an eye on the status bar may not ease your frustration when the browser seems to be taking forever to download a page, but at least the status bar will show you what the browser is trying to do! If it's not doing anything, you may want to click the Stop button and then the Refresh button.

The status bar tells you the browser is in the middle of downloading a page. After the requested page arrives, the word Done appears on the far left of the status bar.

What the browser is doing   How much of the page has downloaded

[4 items remaining] Downloading picture

Figure 6-6. The status bar keeps tabs on whatever task you've asked the browser to do.

Seize the Page: Right-Click!

If you're familiar with computers, you probably already know that your computer mouse actually has two buttons: the left button that you're accustomed to using and the right button, which offers additional menu options in most software programs. AOL's browser is no exception.

Right-clicking anywhere on a Web page in the AOL browser offers you many useful ways of using the page. You can capture information about it — or directly from it. The options offered to you when you right-click change somewhat depending on where you click on a page, particularly whether you click text or a picture.

Right-Clicking Text

Right-clicking text or a part of the page where no picture is displayed opens another menu. How do you tell whether what you are clicking is the background? One easy way to tell is when one of the options available is "Save Background As." If you see "Save Picture As," you have right-clicked on a graphic.

The menu groups together related commands. From top to bottom, those commands are:

You can open several AOL browsers at the same time. Back and Forward and other commands apply only to the active browser.

▶ **Back, Forward.** These work the same as the Previous and Next buttons on the AOL browser's navigation bar. Unlike the AOL navigation bar, these choices apply only to Web pages you've visited in this browser, not to AOL areas you've visited.

▶ **Save Background As** saves the background image (if there is one) to your hard drive under a name you can select.

▶ **Select All** highlights everything on the Web page; right-clicking after all these items have been high-lighted brings up an additional menu which includes the option to **Copy** the highlighted items to the

Clipboard. The **Paste** command is usually not active because you cannot paste material to a page you're viewing on the Web.

▶ **Create Shortcut** creates a shortcut to this Web page on your desktop; to visit the page again (assuming you're online), all you have to do is click that shortcut. This is a great way to set up a link to a valuable Web site. It can function as a second home page — a sort of Web beach cottage. When you click the desktop shortcut, either the AOL browser or Microsoft Internet Explorer opens, depending on which you define as your default Internet application (see Chapter 3).

▶ **Add to Favorites** adds the page to the list of favorite sites maintained by the MSIE browser. Be aware that this list is not the same as Favorite Places on AOL; this list is available from the Start menu's Favorites list. Favorite Places are available only when you're using AOL. Both systems have benefits, but using both is a sure way to lose track of your favorite Web sites. The advantage of AOL's Favorite Places is that it can hold any kind of information, not just Web pages.

▶ **View Source** displays the HTML skeleton of the page (usually Notepad). This is a tremendous way to learn the ins and outs of HTML and find out how certain effects were achieved. Using View Source is also a tremendous way to troubleshoot for problems with your own page.

▶ **Print** sends the current page to your default printer. Pressing Ctrl+P does exactly the same thing.

▶ **Refresh** reloads the page, which, in the case of pages that change frequently, ensures you're looking at the latest version, not the earlier version that your browser stored in its *cache* (something discussed later in this chapter in "How the Browser Keeps Track of Where You've Been").

▶ **Properties** provide you with basic information about the page, such as its address, size, and when it was created and last modified. The Properties box tells you which particular page, deep in a site's architecture, you're viewing. Sometimes, on AOL, a Web page is displayed as an AOL Keyword but doesn't show a URL. To get the URL and explore the site, you can copy the

Tip

You can select part of a Web page by highlighting that part with your mouse. To copy, right-click and select Copy. Then, go the the place where you want to put the highlighted stuff, right-click, and select Paste. This is a fast way of snagging quotes, addresses, and product information from a Web page. For just about everything else, you're pretty close to copyright infringement whenever you take other people's words and use them for your own purposes. AOL Keyword: **Copyright** has sobering information on this hot subject.

6

**Behind the Wheel: Using
AOL's Web Browser**

URL from the Properties box (Ctrl+C), and paste it in the Address box (Ctrl+V). Note that the Web address in the Properties box can be highlighted and copied, even though it looks like it can't!

Right-Clicking a Graphic

Right-clicking a picture or link in a Web page brings up a different menu:

> ▶ **Open Link** opens the page or file that the object links to in the current browser window if the link is a hyperlink. The page you're currently browsing is replaced.

> ▶ **Open Link in New Window** opens the linked-to page in an entirely new browser so that the current page is still displayed.

> ▶ **Save Target As** saves the page or file that the link points to onto your hard drive (do this if you're doing some serious study of others' pages or to troubleshoot your own page if you don't have the original file handy). Note that this saves only a page's HTML, not any of the embedded graphics or linked-to pages.

> ▶ **Print Target** prints the page or file that the link points to even if you don't visit the place.

> ▶ **Save Picture As** saves the picture to your hard drive. Watch out for those copyright infringements.

> ▶ **Set as Wallpaper** makes the picture your desktop wallpaper (remember, most people see their wallpaper for about a minute a day).

> ▶ **Copy** a picture to the Clipboard. From the Clipboard, you can paste a picture into other programs.

> ▶ **Copy Shortcut. Right-click a link** to copy the picture's URL to the Clipboard for use in other programs.

> ▶ **Add to Favorites** puts a link to a picture in your list of Favorites. Again, this is not the same as Favorite Places.

Tip

To save a copy of a page or entire site, make sure the browser window is active (to make it active just click it), go to File, and select Save As. A seemingly normal Save As dialog box appears with one exception: You have four options for saving the document. The more interesting ones are "Web Page, complete" and "Web Archive, single file." If you choose "Web Page, complete," the page and all of its associated graphics and other elements download, and the graphics and other things are stored in a folder next to the page. If you choose "Web Archive, single file," a single, neat and tidy file contains everything.

Making the AOL Browser Work Your Way

You have many ways to tweak AOL's browser so that it works the way you like. Sometimes you can set your preferences within AOL; sometimes you need to tinker with the underlying

Microsoft browser. In either case, the process is simple. The things you might want to adjust include:

▶ The maintenance of your history and temporary files

▶ The accessibility of pages

How the Browser Keeps Track of Where You've Been

Your browser keeps track of the sites you've visited so that you can find them again in a hurry. The idea is that if you've visited a site once, you probably want to go back again. Sometimes remembering a Web address (or 20) can be difficult to do, which is why the AOL browser helps you keep track of pages you have visited (see Figure 6-7).

Following Your History

Figure 6-7. AOL's browser lets you easily revisit sites you've visited recently by checking your history trail.

AOL keeps track of the past 25 places you've visited. This includes windows you open on AOL, pages you view on the Web, and pages you view within a Web site. You can view this list, your *history trail,* by clicking the down-arrow to the right of the Address box (Figure 6-7).

Thanks to the history trail, you can use the Previous and Next buttons (those big arrows on the toolbar) to backtrack and retrace your steps and jump to any place you've recently visited.

Managing Your Temporary Internet Files (Cache)

You may notice that when you do return to some sites, they load (display) very quickly. That's because your browser has stored them in its *cache,* a cubby hole on your hard drive

Caution

You may want to save or share something that you discover online, but remember that copyright laws protect just about everything that is not marked public domain, freely distribute, or something similar. In this way, the Web is no different from books, on television, and in other forms of media. To find out more, use AOL Keyword: **Copyright.**

Tip

You can have AOL clear your history trail whenever you sign off AOL. Use AOL Keyword: **Preferences** and click Toolbar. You can choose to clear the history trail right now, when you sign off, or when you switch screen names without signing off.

where your browser squirrels away frequently used files from Web sites. So, if a site uses lots of graphical doo-dads like bullets, icons, buttons, and background images, the browser has to download them only once. When you visit a page again, your browser uses the cached images instead of the images out on some Internet computer. These cached items are sometimes called *Temporary Internet files.*

All those stored files take up disk space, and if hard-drive space is at a premium, you may want to get rid of cached items or at least limit the amount of space devoted to this heap of page parts.

Fetching files from the cache on your hard drive is much faster than downloading them from some distant Internet computer. However, cached pages can get out of date because Web pages change over time. When you revisit a site on the Internet, you will want to avoid seeing an old version stored on your hard drive. You need to make sure your browser visits the actual page and updates its cache from time to time, as explained below.

The following maintenance procedure can help your browser run faster. First, you'll need to open up the Internet Properties box shown in Figure 6-8. From the desktop, right-click the Internet Explorer icon and choose Properties.

Do not get confused by the title *Internet Properties* that appears at the top of the Internet Options dialog box. They are one and the same, and the Internet Properties title only appears in the title bar. It is called Internet Options everywhere else.

▶ **To delete your temporary files**, stay in the General tab of the Internet Options box. In the Temporary Internet Files section, click Delete Files. You'll be asked to confirm your desire to remove all cached files.

▶ **To change the way your browser deals with temporary files**, click Settings. This opens the Settings dialog box in Figure 6-8.

At the top of the dialog box, select how often you want the browser to check for updated versions of pages stored on your hard-drive. Always updating removes the value of having a cache altogether. If you select Automatically, the page is checked only if you visited it in a previous session, not if you visited it in the current session. Choosing Never puts you at risk of having many out-of-date (but quickly available) cached files. Something in between is a good idea.

Click to adjust additional Internet properties.   ┌Click to adjust how cached pages are stored.

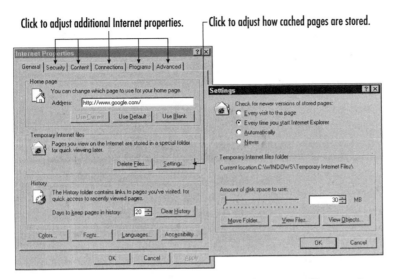

Figure 6-8. Customize the way your browser deals with temporary files using the Settings box.

▶ **To specify how much disk space you want to use for storing temporary Internet files**, use the Settings box. Pages are more likely to be stored on your hard drive, and those pages load quicker if you allow the browser to use more disk space.

Changing How Things Look (Colors and Fonts)

In the AOL browser, you can easily specify what colors and fonts appear. Based on the options you choose, your browser can display text larger or more legibly. These features have more than cosmetic value, but can make pages more accessible, especially to the millions of people with a visual impairment.

Click the Colors button in the Internet Options dialog box to open the Colors box. The choices in this box determine what colors you see in your browser if the page's designer hasn't specified the colors. You can set text color, background color, and link color. If you have trouble seeing, for instance, increase the size of the text and sharpen the contrast between the text and background color.

Tip

Consider how up-to-date the pages that you frequent need to be. If you're reading the *Odyssey* or Shakespeare's plays online, you may not want the cache refreshed; the pages never change. But if you're a day trader, you may not want to cache anything, because your data must always be fresh.

Note

HTML supports three kinds of links: Links that haven't been clicked *(unvisited)*, links that have been clicked *(visited)*, and links on the fence. Links on the fence are links that you"ve moved your mouse over but haven't yet clicked. *(Hovering* is the preferred, albeit menacing, term.) You can set the color of each type of link using the Accessibility settings.

The Web Is for Everyone

Sometimes, the value of a feature may not be evident to everyone, because the feature was created for a specific group of users. Take the ability to customize font colors and sizes. A text's readability depends on letter shape, text size, the spacing between letters, line length, and the color contrast between the text and the background. Millions of people, especially people who are visually impaired, need to adjust the size and colors of text and backgrounds to make browsing possible.

Microsoft has been in the forefront of companies who support the needs of the disabled. The WWW Consortium (consisting of all major vendors, including Microsoft) recently issued a set of guidelines for designing Web pages so that the broadest possible audience can access pages. Go to www.w3.org/WAI for more information about the consortium. The consortium's director, Tim Berners-Lee (the same guy who invented the Web), summarizes why the W3 Consortium is creating accessibility standards: "The power of the Web is in its universality." Browser accessibility features like Colors & Fonts make the Web that much more universal.

Among vendors, Microsoft has aggressively introduced accessibility features in its Windows operating systems. With AOL 6.0, America Online introduces voice recognition features (File⇨Voice Recognition) that make it easier for the visually impaired to use e-mail and chat. You muse configure this option when you install AOL 6.0 using a CD-ROM.

You can change the colors that a page's designer has specified, too, by clicking the Accessibility button in the Internet Options box's General tab (see Figure 6-9). The Ignore Colors Specified on Web Pages option ensures that all pages display the colors you specify in the Colors box.

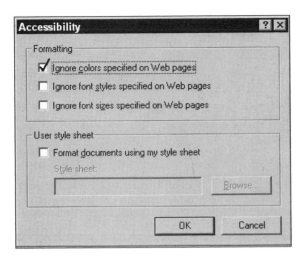

Figure 6-9. In the Accessibility dialog box, you can tell your browser to override designers' garish and unreadable designs.

Note the other two options at the top of the Accessibility box: Ignore Font Styles Specified on Web Pages and Ignore Font Sizes Specified on Web Pages. If you choose one of these, Web pages display only the font you specify using the Fonts button at the bottom of the Internet Options dialog box. Click the Fonts button to see the box in Figure 6-10 where you choose a legible typeface.

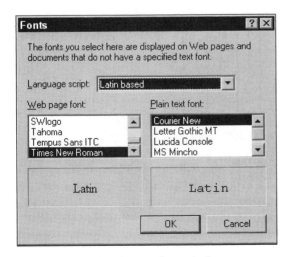

Figure 6-10. Explorer lets you choose the font you want to use for displaying text on pages.

Plugging into Multimedia

The most recent versions of Microsoft Internet Explorer and Netscape Navigator can handle any multimedia fireworks the Web has to offer. Browsing the Internet is far better than it was five years ago when multimedia was slow and required annoying additional programs.

The good news is that the latest browsers can handle some very exciting sounds, video, and animation through the use of *plug-ins,* small programs designed to automatically open and play files. When you install a plug-in, Windows 95/98 learns that whenever it sees a certain type of file, the browser should fire up the plug-in and play the file.

You used to need a special program to do multimedia. You'd download the sound or audio or video file and then open a helper application to play it. Now, plug-ins integrate multimedia effects — either directly into the page or by automatically launching an unobtrusive and often very cool player. Real-Player, which is considered the Web's most popular plug-in, plays a video in a small window. (The video of Chick Corea in Figure 6-3 is an example.) Figure 6-11 shows AOL's Media Player, which is a wonderful tool for listening to MP3 music files as well as your CD audio disks.

Figure 6-11. The AOL Media Player plays high-quality music and gives you control over what you're hearing.

Getting Plug-Ins

How do you get plug-ins? The most important ones, including
RealPlayer, Shockwave, and Flash, are included with AOL 6.0;
you don't have to do a thing. Any content not supported by a
plug-in usually plays in either AOL's player or Microsoft's new
Media Player. If you encounter a file for which you don't already have a plug-in, you'll probably be asked if you'd like to
download the plug-in right away and be provided with a link
to do so. Plug-ins are downloaded and installed in the right
place for you.

Plug-ins evolve continually, and the improvement from year to
year is remarkable. Plus, they're almost always free. Most, like
Apple's QuickTime, provide a means to get updates. Some, like
QuickTime RealAudio, have commercial versions that have
more features than the free versions. If you don't update your
plug-ins regularly, you might miss out on the latest features
and improvements and even find your plug-in unable to handle
some files. Luckily, most plug-ins let you know when a newer
version is required and download and install it.

RealPlayer Brings Radio, TV, and Video to the Web

RealAudio made streaming sound hugely popular in the past
few years. Sound and player quality have improved enormously
in that time. A product called RealPlayer plays both audio and
video.

Entire sites and mailing lists are devoted to RealAudio.
Hundreds of radio stations, including some Net-only stations,
make music and talk available in this format. When you shop
at CDNOW on the Web, for example, you can often sample
a CD by listening to RealAudio snippets. Follow the news on
BBC Online, and you'll enjoy RealVideo as well as RealAudio.

RealJukebox Brings Music to the Web

Just as RealPlayer is optimized for accessing and managing
streaming media, RealNetworks designed RealJukebox specifi-
cally to handle music — MP3 in particular. In other words,
RealPlayer doesn't do MP3s very well, though it plays them,
and RealJukebox doesn't do video at all. Chapter 16 tells you
more about managing music and creating your own MP3 files
with RealJukebox.

 Note

A word about how AOL
plays different files on the
Web. AOL has its own small
helper application to play
MIDI and AU sound files. For
WAV sound files, AOL calls
up the Microsoft Windows
Media Player. (WAV files are
not streaming files, which
means a program plays them
only after they are completely
downloaded.) For just about
everything else, special
plug-ins are required, but
you got the most important
ones when you installed
AOL in the first place.

 Find It Online

RealNetworks (the maker
of RealPlayer) has created an
enormous collection of radio,
TV, and entertainment links
that make use of its player.
Visit its home page (www.
real.com). Currently, the
media directory is at the bottom of this page.

In Figure 6-12, RealJukebox is playing a CD while at the same time copying the same music files to your PC, so you can listen to the music in the future without the CD. For more information about RealJukebox, start at `www.real.com`.

Figure 6-12. RealJukebox.

Animating the Web with Shockwave and Flash

Macromedia's Shockwave adds strong imagery, movement, and animation to a Web site without making you download gigantic files and play them on some dinky helper application. Figure 6-13 shows a Shockwave application snagged from Macromedia's Shockwave page.

Find It Online

For cool pages that include games, animated shorts, dynamic comic books, and music with visual accompaniment, start at `www.shockwave.com`.

Shocked pages bring you games, Dilbert cartoons, physics experiments, and simulations of every sort (like how hard you'll hit a truck at 30, 50, and 70 miles per hour when the truck breaks suddenly). Macromedia's Flash is used to make simple, elegant animations that download quickly. The educational applications of Shockwave simulations are endless.

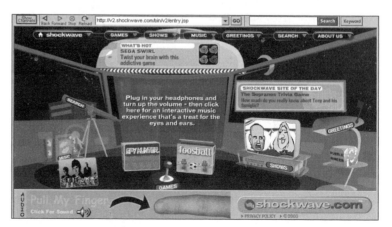

Figure 6-13. A Shocked (Shockwave) game from `www.shockwave.com`.

Publishing *Real* Documents on the Web with PDF

Plug-ins are meant to help browsers read and display any kind of formatted information including spreadsheets, images, and complex Word documents. When your AOL browser downloads a page posted on the Web with a DOC file extension (a plain old Microsoft Word document, in other words), the document displays fully formatted, with a Word toolbar at the top, inside the AOL browser. Adobe's PDF (short for Portable Document Format) gives publishers a way of distributing documents in their word-processed form, complete with page numbers and complex formatting — no HTML required! When you use a PDF file, you can print selected pages in longer documents, a kind of selectivity unavailable for a Web page, which printers see as one long page. Academic papers are available in this form, as are thousands of government documents. To view them, you need Adobe Acrobat Reader, which is free from www.adobe.com.

To publish PDF files, you need a commercial product from Adobe called Adobe Acrobat Writer (now up to Version 4.0). To use this useful product, print a word-processed document to a file (instead of to a printer) and then upload the file to AOL using My FTP Space, as described in Chapter 15. From there, anyone can view your document.

Other Video Formats: MPG, AVI, QuickTime

AVI and QuickTime are the standard video formats for Windows and Apple computers respectively, but you'll also find a sophisticated QuickTime player for Windows. The QuickTime player offers the same features and the ability to display many types of files, including ordinary graphics (PICT, a Mac graphics file) and sound (MIDI). Figure 6-14 shows a QuickTime movie in Internet Explorer. Windows' built-in Media Player can handle both AVI and the older MPG format, which is now available in a streaming version.

Figure 6-14. QuickTime player, showing one of the many movie trailers (clips) available at Apple's Web site.

Note

The QuickTime-software download is conspicuously short because you're just downloading a download utility; the files need to be downloaded!

You can download QuickTime at Apple's Web site for free (www.apple.com). The free version is quite powerful and can handle a wide range of video and audio formats from all platforms, including Windows, Unix, and Mac. Paying for the Pro version gets rid of the annoying pop-up window asking if you'd like to upgrade. It also gives you access to a greater range of powerful tools and the ability to save videos and sounds.

Sounds of Yore: WAV, AU, MIDI

MP3 may be the most popular format for music on the Web, but a huge reservoir of sound in older formats is scattered over thousands of FTP sites (see Chapter 15). WAV and AU files are digital recordings of actual sounds, while MIDI files play electronically simulated music. (WAV is the default sound format used by Windows, and the preferred format for the famous "You've Got Mail" message!) Winamp, RealPlayer, and Windows Media Player all play WAV and AU files. Although WAV and AU files capture the fidelity of an original, they tend to be quite large and play for a short time. MIDI files, as digital creations that merely simulate music, are smaller and play much longer. Huge MIDI archives contain specific types of music, like the Classical MIDI Archives at www.prs.net/midi.html.

Where to Go from Here

The Internet may seem intimidating the first several times you venture out, but after a while and with some practice, you'll be comfortable in your roomy new home. To help, here are two indispensible Web sites with loads of help and assistance:

▶ CNET is probably the largest Web site on the Internet (It even has its own AOL Keyword: **CNET**). Its large Help center (`www.help.com/`) includes sections on browsers and Web building. CNET lives and breathes computers, and the people at CNET really know how to help newcomers to the Web.

▶ When you're done at CNET, cruise on over to AOL Keyword: **Computing** (AOL's Computing channel) for a huge amount of information about the Web. CNET and AOL are partners in creating the Computing channel.

▶ Help is always available, online and off, from the AOL Help menu. Online, click the toolbar's Help button.

▶ Chapter 7 is all about Netscape Navigator.

Chapter 7

All-Purpose Vehicle: Netscape Navigator

IN THIS CHAPTER

Using Netscape 6 with AOL

Installing Netscape 6

Getting to know Netscape 6

Using the sidebar

Creating and managing bookmarks

Netscape 6 has been a long time coming. Now that it is here, it offers a new look and a number of enhancements compared with previous versions of this classic Internet software — the first popular graphical World Wide Web browser. First of all, you may ask why would you want to use Netscape at all when you have a simple and unobtrusive browser built right into AOL?

▶ **You can save time.** Say you're doing something time-consuming (such as downloading 5MB of software) with your AOL browser. If you have a second browser, you can continue surfing and searching the Internet without interfering with your download.

▶ **You get a prettier picture.** Some sites look best when viewed by a particular browser — that's just how they were designed. Usually, you see a message right off the bat that says `Page best viewed with` *such-and-such* `browser, version` *so-and-so*. For pages made for Netscape, you'll want to have the Netscape browser handy.

▶ **You already know how it works.** You may want to use Netscape simply because you're familiar with it. If you use Netscape at work or school, for instance, you may find that using Netscape at home is more convenient.

▶ **You just like some of Netscape's features.** The new version, Netscape 6, has a reputation for fully supporting Internet standards. If you have an Internet e-mail account, for example, Netscape 6 gives you access to it, as well as to AOL Mail on the Web (`aolmail.aol.com`).

Tip

AOL's Internet connection allows you to run several Internet applications at the same time. To do so, simply sign on to AOL and open one or more Internet applications, such as Netscape Navigator. You can run two or more different browsers at the same time. Chapter 16 profiles several Internet programs and shows where and how to download such software.

Installing Netscape 6

You can download Netscape from the Netscape home page (AOL Keyword: **Netscape** or `home.netscape.com`), as follows:

1. Look for the prominent Download button, and click it. The Download button looks like an arrow that's pointing down. You are taken to the page where you can start downloading Netscape 6.

2. Respond to the on screen questions about which version of the software to download and which operating system you use. In general, you'll want to use the latest version. Follow the other on screen instructions.

3. After you answer all the questions, the Download Now button appears. Click it!

   A dialog box appears and asks if you'd like to run the program from its current location or save it to disk.

Note

Because this chapter was written using prerelease software, you may notice some differences between the steps and links described here and what you see when you download the software. However, the overall process is the same. Use AOL Keyword: **Netscape** if you have questions.

Note

At this point in the process, you have only downloaded an installation program called Smart Download, not the program files. After you retrieve Smart Download, that program runs automatically and downloads the larger Netscape files. It's worth noting that Netscape is a smaller and faster program than comparable browsers (for example, MSIE). Nonetheless, if you download all of Netscape's utilities and plug-ins, you will probably be online long enough to run the risk of getting disconnected for one reason or another. If this happens, Smart Download remembers where it stops and resumes at that point, rather than making you download everything again.

Tip

Selecting a Complete installation is best, unless you have little room to spare on your hard drive. In this case, select the Navigator (browser-only) option.

4. Elect to *Save* the program on your computer, and then click OK. Be sure to remember where you save the Setup file on your computer.

   A dialog box briefly appears on screen, indicating that the download is taking place. After an extremely short period of time, the download finishes, and the dialog box disappears.

5. Locate the Netscape Setup file and double-click it.

   A dialog box appears, welcoming you to Netscape 6 and asking you to exit all running applications. Close those applications and click Next.

6. Agree to the License Agreement by clicking the Accept button.

7. Now you're asked to select an installation type. The choices are Typical, Complete, Navigator, and Custom. Make a choice and click Next.

8. Click through the next few dialog boxes and the download to complete the installation.

Getting to Know Netscape 6

You can start Netscape 6 in three ways. In each case, you must first be signed on to AOL.

▶ From the Start menu, choose Programs⇨Netscape 6⇨ Netscape 6.

▶ From the desktop, click the Netscape 6 shortcut icon, which was created during the installation.

▶ You can also drag the Netscape 6 icon from your desktop to your Windows taskbar, which is ordinarily at the bottom of your Windows display. Dragging from the desktop, by the way, doesn't remove the icon from the desktop. You wind up, instead, with two icons, one on the desktop and the other on the taskbar. Click either icon to start Netscape 6.

After a moment, Netscape appears, and you can begin to explore the Internet. Here is some information to help you understand the interface elements before you try Netscape for the first time. (See Figure 7-1.)

Status bar   Taskbar   Toolbar

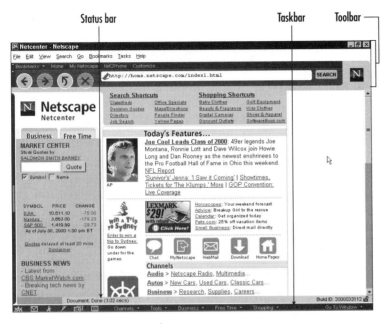

Figure 7-1. The Netscape 6 interface.

The Netscape 6 interface consists of four main parts:

▶ At the top of the screen, you have the **toolbar**, which includes the Menu bar, the Address bar, and the Personal Choice bar.

▶ On the side of the screen, **My Sidebar** allows you to get customized information without using the browser window.

▶ The **browser window**, which shows you all your options and takes you to any Web address you choose, takes up the main part of the screen.

▶ At the bottom of the screen, you have the Netscape **taskbar**, which includes preset channels and tasks to simplify your online experience.

I discuss these areas of the interface in the following sections.

7

All-Purpose Vehicle:
Netscape Navigator

Note

Netscape 6 is a stand-alone browser, meaning it is a full application with its own complete set of tools and features. Recommended online destinations are built right into its bookmarks, toolbar, and taskbar.

Tip

You control the menus on the Personal Choice toolbar, which comes with some core customizable features: bookmarks, your preferred home page, and My Netscape (your version of Netscape's NetCenter). A *bookmark* is one of your favorite Web sites; a *home page* is the page to which you want Netscape to open.

Tip

If you come across a Web page that's in a language you don't understand, use one of Netscape 6's coolest new tools to translate it. With the foreign-language page displayed, choose View⇨ Translate. Just follow the simple instructions to get a usable word-by-word translation.

Using the Menu Bar

The more you know about the software on your computer, the more control you have when you need to get something done. After all, computers are no smarter than a speck of dust until someone comes along and tells them what to do. With that in mind, the Netscape people organized the most commonly used controls, on the toolbar so that you can easily see and use them.

Netscape presents the toolbar's controls in three rows — the Menu bar, the Address bar, and the Personal Choice bar — as shown in Figure 7-2. You may notice that several of the features are similar not just to Windows applications but also to the AOL browser interface, which I discuss in Chapter 6.

Figure 7-2. The Netscape 6 toolbar.

Here are the contents of the Menu bar, from left to right:

▶ The **File** menu opens new windows and allows you to save files, edit a Web page in Netscape's Web-page editor (called *Composer*), and print a displayed page. File⇨ Open can be used to take you to a Web page (HTML file) located on your hard drive, whereas File⇨New opens a new browser window.

▶ The **Edit** menu is mainly for editing text. Here, also, is the home of your Preferences, which give you the ability to customize many Netscape features.

▶ The **View** menu lets you see the HTML (Web code) used on a page. This feature is indispensable for people who are designing their own Web pages and want to see how someone made a particular page or achieved a particular effect. From this menu, you also get two important usability features: the ability to present a page's text as smaller or larger.

▶ The **Search** menu provides handy access to various kinds of searches. For example, you can search for a Web page, a word *within* a displayed page, your Netscape address book, and the Internet White and Yellow Pages.

▶ The **Go** menu gives you access to the key navigational actions of going Back, Forward, and Home. Like the AOL Window menu, the Netscape Go menu includes a list of open pages and recently visited pages for quick backtracking.

▶ The **Bookmarks** menu allows you to add, manage, and visit bookmarks (favorite Web pages). See "Managing Bookmarks," later in this chapter.

▶ Use the **Tasks** menu to carry out Internet-related activities in Netscape 6, such as creating a Web page (using Composer), using AOL Instant Messenger (Instant Messenger), editing your online calendar, and simply browsing the Web (Navigator).

▶ Fortunately, the **Help** menu can bail you out when you have a question or problem about Netscape's myriad features. If a technical support person asks you which version of Netscape you're using, you can find out by choosing Help⇨About Netscape 6. Unlike AOL's Help menu, Netscape's is available only when you are online.

The Address bar, with its navigation buttons, is discussed later in this chapter in "Browsing the Web with Netscape 6."

Use *keyboard shortcuts* for commonly used navigational features. To go back a page, press Ctrl+[and, likewise, to move forward (after having gone backward), press Ctrl+]. Such keyboard equivalents appear on the menus to the right of the name of the options.

Choosing File⇨Edit Page is useful if you want to view your *own* page and edit the HTML.

Using My Sidebar

New to Netscape 6 is an information-packed features called My Sidebar, which is essentially a pull-out window located on the left side of the Netscape browser window (see Figure 7-3). If you don't see the sidebar, check to see if the sidebar is selected by choosing View⇨Sidebar. If the sidebar is selected and you still don't see it, click the sliding door's handle and drag the handle to the right.

The sidebar includes numerous panels, which you can use to display news, sports scores, weather, your online Buddy List for the AOL Instant Messenger service, and pretty much anything you can think of.

Tip

The sidebar is organized in what is called a tabbed interface: Each sidebar panel is shaped like a manila folder with a clickable tab at the top. Click the tab (with the panel's name, such as *CNN.com* or *Search*) to display a panel's contents. The layering of the panels allows many panels to fit into a single sidebar and creates an extremely efficient, compact interface.

Definition

A *bookmark* is the name and Web address of a favorite page that you add using the Bookmarks menu (similar to AOL 6's Favorites menu). While using Netscape, you can quickly revisit a favorite page by selecting the page's bookmark.

Netscape 6 comes with a set of preselected panels, which currently include

▶ **CNN.com.** Yes, *the* CNN. The sidebar panel lists headlines about events in the U.S. and around the world. If you miss the 1930s, you can watch videos — the equivalent of newsreels.

▶ **What's Related.** As you're browsing, open this panel to see a list of pages related to the page that you're viewing.

▶ **Search.** Start here if you want to look for something on the Web and you're using Netscape 6. Type the word or words that you're looking for in the space at the top and click Search. (Separate words with a space or comma.) The results appear as a list in the panel. Click any promising link to view a page in the big browser window to the right. (See Figure 7-3.)

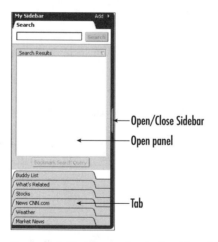

Figure 7-3. The What's Related tab on My Sidebar shows pages that relate to the page being viewed, Netscape's NetCenter.

▶ **Buddy List.** The AOL Instant Messenger service has been a huge hit, and it is fully integrated in Netscape Navigator. Not only can you use AIM directly from Netscape's Tasks menu, but you can view, edit, and use your AIM Buddy List from the sidebar. To use AIM on

Netscape, you must register and select an AIM screen name and a password. Once registered, your Buddy List appears in your sidebar. Double-click any of your buddies on the list to summon up a Netscape version of AOL Instant Messenger, with familiar features (see Chapter 12) but a slightly different look.

▶ **Stocks.** This panel displays any stocks you have entered into a personal stock portfolio. If you've never modified your portfolio, then you'll get the default. To create your own portfolio, click My Portfolio to bring up a window in the browser. Follow the on-screen instructions to add information about your stocks and funds.

▶ **News.** Click this panel to see headlines from Reuters.

Adding and Deleting Panels from My Sidebar

In addition to the news and other panels included with Netscape 6, you can add and also remove panels from your sidebar. Note that removing a panel merely means to remove it from view, not to physically delete it. Here's how to add and delete sidebar panels:

1. Open Netscape 6.

   If your sidebar isn't showing, click the small light-blue handle on the left side of the Netscape 6 window (refer to Figure 7-3). My Sidebar slides into view. You can also drag that blue tab to the left and right to resize your sidebar.

2. On the sidebar's top right is an Add button; click this button from the drop-down menu, select Customize Sidebar to view the Customize Sidebar window, shown in Figure 7-4.

   • You can select panels from a list of Netscape panels on the left.

   • On the right is a list of current panels.

Tip

You can also type words to search by using the Address box and then clicking the Search button. If you don't enter a proper Web address, your words are submitted to Netscape Search (a version of AOL Search).

Cross-Reference

With the AOL Instant Messenger service (AIM), you can use your existing AOL screen name and password. Chapter 12 is devoted to AIM.

Note

Two things to note about the AIM Buddy List that you see in Netscape: It's based on the AOL, not the AIM, Buddy List. If you separately install the AIM software, you can create an AIM-only Buddy List, but in Netscape, you'll be using your AOL Buddy List (Chapter 3). Secondly, Netscape lets you keep Address Cards with a great deal of contact information about everyone in your Buddy List, a feature not available on AOL's Buddy List.

Figure 7-4. Customize your sidebar to show the content you want.

Note

The little page icons with the blue ribbons represent pages that can be used within panels. The folders with the ribbons are folders *containing* panels. Only the default panels and a few others are actually located on your computer. The rest are on the Internet. Therefore, when you click a folder and nothing happens, wait. You'll likely be rewarded with a panel list after a few seconds.

3. You're ready to add or remove panels.

- To add a panel to your sidebar, click the panel you want from the list on the left. When the panel is highlighted, click Add. If you want to know what's inside a panel, click it and then click the Preview button at the bottom of the window. Another window displays the contents that would appear in your sidebar. Close the window when you're done.

- To remove a panel from the My Sidebar display, click it once in the right panel and click the Remove button.

4. After you're done adding and removing panels, click OK.

If you're interested in changing the order of panels in your sidebar, select a panel listed on the right and click the up or down arrow to position it where you want.

Customizing Content in My Sidebar

You can also customize the content of some panels. For example, you can build a News panel that shows local and national news, the weather, and more.

To find out if you can customize a panel, follow these steps:

1. Click the Add button and then choose Customize Sidebar. The Customize Sidebar dialog box opens (refer to Figure 7-4).

2. Click an active panel from the list on the right.

If the Customize Panel button lights up and becomes clickable, then you can modify the panel's content. Modifying content usually means just checking the types of content you want and unchecking the content you don't want.

Browsing the Web with Netscape 6

The browser window — the most important area in Netscape 6 — is simple to use. Shown in Figure 7-1, the browser window is simply the place where you view Web pages. A page on Netscape is no different from a page on AOL's browser. However, some pages look different on different browsers because each browser may have its own way of interpreting the pages' HTML (code).

Other essential tools are the *Address bar* and the *Address box*. To visit a page, type its Web address (such as `www.aol.com`) into the Address box (known in Netscape as the *Location field*; see Figure 7-5) and click Enter. As with AOL, you can leave off the `http://` part of the address.

The Address bar contains buttons that let you move around in the Browser window. The buttons, also available from the Go menu, are also shown in Figure 7-5. Just as in the AOL browser, you use these navigational buttons to go backward and forward among pages recently visited. The Address box, to the right of the navigation buttons, does just what the similar box does in AOL: It gives you a place to type in a new Web page to visit (which will then be your current page). Click Search after typing an address.

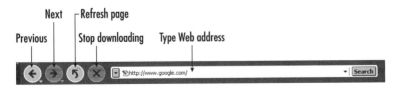

Figure 7-5. The Address bar and Address box are key elements to your Web-surfing experience.

Caution

Although developed by AOL and accessible when you are signed on to AOL, Netscape 6 is an independent program that is *not* subject to AOL's Parental Controls (Chapter 4). Netscape 6 has no equivalent of AOL's Online Timer, either, also discussed in Chapter 4. To restrict the sites children can access or the amount of time children spend online with Netscape, parents must use third-party security software such as NetNanny, which I discuss in Chapter 16.

Note

If you've ever used Netscape browsers, you'll find yourself right at home using Netscape 6. If you have not, you won't find it complicated in the least, because Netscape has whittled down the collection of buttons to the four most important ones.

Tip

If you use AOL with a BYOA (Bring Your Own Access) account and have Internet e-mail (at work, for example), you can set up Netscape 6 to read your non-AOL mail. You need to know the addresses of your POP3 and SMPT mail servers, which you can usually get from your Internet service provider or Web service administrator. Start by choosing Tasks⇨ Mail or by clicking the Mail icon on the taskbar. If you have AOL mail only, you can use Netscape to access AOL Mail on the Web (`aolmail.aol.com`) as explained in Chapter 11.

Note

You cannot customize taskbar menu options.

Cross-Reference

The AOL Instant Messenger service is the focus of Chapter 12.

Cross-Reference

For more about the customizable AOL calendar and newspaper, see Chapter 3.

Using the Netscape 6 Taskbar and Status Bar

The taskbar, shown in Figure 7-6, gives you quick access to a broad range of activities and online destinations. Unlike the options in your sidebar or Personal Choice toolbar, you cannot customize these selections. The status bar has a more limited function: primarily to provide a visual indicator of a page's status as it downloads to your computer.

Here are some of the features worth noting on the taskbar:

▶ AOL Instant Messenger (AIM) is always a click away. If you have already registered and created a Buddy List, you can immediately start using AIM. Just click the Running Man icon.

▶ My Netscape will be familiar to you if you have used My AOL (now called AOL Anywhere); it's Netscape's custom newspaper.

▶ Your Netscape Calendar is no different from the My Calendar service on AOL. In fact, edits are saved and synchronized across your calendars, and you can use the calendar offline as well as online.

▶ Netscape's channels are very similar to AOL's channels, discussed in Chapter 5.

▶ Shop@Netscape, is nearly identical to Shop@AOL.

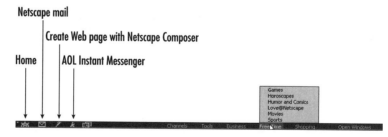

Figure 7-6. The Netscape 6 Taskbar with the Channels menu highlighted to show the array of online destinations.

Using Netscape 6's Bookmarks

Bookmarks are Netscape's convenient way of helping you keep track of your favorite places to visit on the Internet. Instead of typing in a keyword, you double-click a bookmark to visit a favorite.

Adding Bookmarks

To add a bookmark follow these steps:

1. One way or another, display a page you like enough to bookmark:

    * Type a Web address of a site you'd like to visit again in the Netscape Address box. For example, you can go to NewbieNET by entering its Web address, www.newbie.com, in the Address box and then pressing Enter.

    * You can, of course, also view a page by linking to it from somewhere else.

2. Choose Bookmarks⇨Add Current Page, or simply press Ctrl+D. This places the bookmark at the bottom of a list of bookmarks available from the same menu. If you bookmark the example site, NewbieNET Ask! Someone Knows! appears on the menu.

All your bookmarks are readily available from Bookmarks on the Menu bar (see Figure 7-7).

Cross-Reference

AOL's channels provide a hub of practical information; Chapter 5 looks at channels and also introduces Shop@AOL.

Tip

In the Bookmarks window, you can drag any bookmark (favorite Web site) into the Personal Toolbar folder. It then appears as a link on the Personal Choice toolbar to the right of the Customize link (refer to Figure 7-2).

Tip

You don't have to bookmark a site's home page, and you can bookmark more than one page within a given site. Bookmarks work best when you select the specific pages with the information you want.

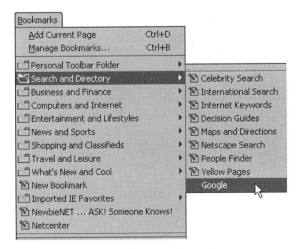

Figure 7-7. The Bookmarks menu: Select a favorite page to visit it.

7

All-Purpose Vehicle:
Netscape Navigator

Managing Bookmarks

One long list of individually added bookmarks can become a tangle of unfindable favorites. That's why you need to know about Netscape's folders. When you *manage* your bookmarks, just as when you manage favorite places on AOL, you're simply creating folders for related bookmarks (sports sites, for example), and dragging your bookmarks into those folders.

To add a folder to manage your bookmarks:

The easiest way to delete bookmarks and folders is to select them and press the Delete key.

1. Choose Bookmarks⇨Manage Bookmarks.

   In the Bookmarks window (shown in Figure 7-8), you will see a list of existing folders and their contents (more folders and individual bookmarks). I recommend leaving the existing folders and bookmarks as they are and adding your own folders to manage your personal bookmarks.

   Go to the place in the bookmark list where you want to add a new folder, and select the item, merely to indicate *where* you want the folder.

2. Choose File⇨New⇨New Folder.

   A small folder appears just after the item selected in Step 1.

3. To give the folder a name, select it. Then choose Edit⇨ Properties, and change the name from New Folder to something else.

To place a bookmark into a folder, in the Bookmarks window, simply drag the bookmark until your pointer (still holding the bookmark) is directly above the folder into which you want to move it, and then let go. In Figure 7-8 for example, NewbieNET is being dragged to the Computers and Internet folder.

You can also create folders inside folders. Practice creating folders and subfolders, giving them names, and dragging bookmarks into them. You can appreciate Netscape's Bookmark feature only when you have added dozens of bookmarks and begun to lose track of them. If you get lost even with perfectly organized bookmarks, use the search bookmarks feature. In the Bookmarks window, choose Edit⇨Search for Bookmarks.

Drag bookmark here to have it appear in your Personal Choice toolbar

Folder   Bookmarks

Manage Bookmarks

File Edit View Tasks Help

Name	URL	Custom ...	Description	Last Visit	Added On	Last Mo...
▾ ☐ Personal Toolbar Folder					8/8/00 1...	
🗐 Customize...	...e.netscape.com/bookmark/6_0b1/cust...			7/30/00 ...	7/30/00 ...	
▸ 🗐 Search and Directory					7/30/00 ...	
▸ 🗐 Business and Finance						
▸ 🗐 Computers and Internet						
▸ 🗐 Entertainment and Lifestyles					7/30/00 ...	
▸ 🗐 News and Sports					8/8/00 1...	
▸ 🗐 Shopping and Classifieds					7/30/00 ...	
▸ 🗐 Travel and Leisure					7/30/00 ...	
▸ 🗐 What's New and Cool						
🗐 New Bookmark				7/30/00 ...		
▸ 🗐 Imported IE Favorites						
NewbieNET ... ASK! Someone Knows!	http://www.newbie.com/			7/30/00 ...	7/30/00 ...	7/30/00 ...
🗐 Netcenter	http://home.netscape.com/index1.html			7/31/00 ...	7/30/00 ...	7/30/00 ...

http://www.newbie.com/

Figure 7-8. Create a new folder in Netscape 6's Bookmarks window. You can use the mouse arrow to click and drag folders and individual bookmarks anywhere in the window.

A New Home

So, you want your browser to start at someplace quieter than the insanely busy Netscape home page? In your wanderings, you may have found a different and perfectly worthy starting point such as the AOL Anywhere service, My Netscape, AOL Search, or something entirely different. With that new page displayed, here's how to change your preferences
so that Netscape opens to a different page:

1. Choose Edit⇨Preferences.

   The Preferences window is separated into two areas. On the left side, you select the *kind* of option to set, and on the right, you make the actual selection.

   If the Navigator item on the left is not already selected, click it. Home page options appear on the right.

   (Continued)

Definition

A *separator* (File⇨New Separator) is a horizontal line that provides a visual cue that folders above and below the line are unrelated or otherwise separated. A separator is a useful way to bring some more order to your bookmarks.

7

**All-Purpose Vehicle:
Netscape Navigator**

(Continued)

2. In the Navigator Starts With section, you have three generic choices: opening the browser to a blank page, a home page (which requires Step 3), or the page displayed when you quit Netscape the last time.

Make a selection. If you select Home Page, you must complete the Home Page section.

3. In the Home Page section, click Use Current Page. If the home page you want isn't currently displayed and you happen to know its address, type its address in the box.

4. Click OK at the bottom of the window.

Now, every time you start Netscape 6 or click the Home button on the Address bar, you'll return to your newly selected page.

Definition

A *home page* is the page at which your browser opens when you begin using the Internet. In other contexts, a *home page* is a Web site's opening page.

Where to Go from Here

This chapter covers the core functions of Netscape 6 — browsing, searching, using the sidebars, and managing bookmarks. This chapter did *not* look at Netscape Composer (the Web page editor built into the browser) or the specifics of reading mail and newsgroups in Netscape.

▶ If you can't find the answer to a question about Netscape 6 in this chapter, use the Help menu. At the Netscape Web site, you can find a great deal of information (home.netscape.com/browsers/6).

▶ If you're technically inclined, you can find out more about the Mozilla project (upon which Netscape 6 is based) and download new versions of the software (www.mozilla.org).

FINDING YOUR WAY:
INTERNET SEARCHING
MADE EASY WITH AOL

Chapter 8

Finding Your Way: Internet Searching Made Easy with AOL

IN THIS CHAPTER

Why searching the Web can be difficult

AOL Search: AOL's one-stop solution to Web browsing and searching

Understanding when to browse and when to search

Using AOL Search for non-Web searches

Finding street addresses, businesses, and e-mail addresses

Everything electronic is searchable these days. You can search files on your computer, words in your files, public libraries, online bookstores, online dictionaries, and the holdings of the Library of Congress. And of course, you can search the Web.

This chapter introduces AOL Search, which is AOL's comprehensive solution to searching for people and information online. AOL Search focuses on a highly selective directory of the Web's best sites. It also conducts a broader search of hundreds of millions of Web pages. AOL Search provides, in one place, tools for searching the Web, searching AOL, and searching non-Web content such as White and Yellow Page listings, newsgroup postings, and AOL message boards.

Why Is Searching the Web Such a Pain?

When you search the Web with one of the many standard search engines, you're first confronted by the sheer number of the world's Web pages — well over a billion and growing. The following list describes some of the challenges you face when searching online:

▶ **Gaining access to the entire Web.** No single tool can possibly keep track of all Web pages, so even the best search engine may fail to turn up important information resources for you.

▶ **Using the correct language and correct search terms.** Web pages come in many languages; many of them are probably unfamiliar to you and therefore not easily searchable by you. Even within the universe of English-language pages, predicting the search word that can help you find what you want can be difficult. For example, the following terms all stand for World War I: *Great War, World War One, WWI,* and the "*War to end all wars*." Which to use? A search engine often provides no alternative to trial and error.

▶ **Finding up-to-date information.** The average page is on the Web only for a month or two, making even (or especially) the largest databases of Web pages out-of-date from the get-go. Some pages, including all the on-line versions of news services, change daily. Tuesday's front page of BBC Online differs from Wednesday's; last week's big story and multimedia coverage may no longer be available today.

▶ **Finding relevant information.** This final challenge is familiar to just about everyone because it's been mocked in magazine ads and TV commercials — many of the pages returned by a general Web search are completely irrelevant to what you want. Why? The search engine has no real idea about the context of your question.

 **Cross-Reference**

In Chapter 9, you find out how to use other search tools to do *specialized searches.* Subsequent chapters include searches for mailing lists (Chapter 13), newsgroups (Chapter 14), and files (Chapter 15).

 Note

More than 75 percent of people on the Web use a search engine, according to the Search Engine Watch (www. searchenginewatch. com). It's not hard to see why. The uses for searching arise from everyday situations like looking for a friend's address, thinking about next summer's vacation, or trying to find a good recipe for cobbler.

Definition

A *search engine* is a list of data about millions of Web pages. This information is automatically collected by software that zips around the world's Web servers (computers) collecting information about every accessible Web page, including: its Web address (URL), title, date last updated, size, words used, and any information provided by the page designer about the page's content. In a search engine, you type in a word or words, for example **auction**, that tell the engine what you want to find out. The search engine finds the word and then shows you a list of pages containing the word *auction,* plus links to those pages. Click a link to visit a page! Simple . . . when it works.

The AOL Search Solution

Unlike most search engines, with hundreds of millions of pages and many inherent weaknesses, AOL Search provides a hand-selected and carefully organized *directory* of Web sites. The directory's goal is not to collect *all* pages but to collect the *best* ones, a subjective choice requiring the efforts of tens of thousands of volunteer editors. Instead of searching an engine, you search a directory. The directory organizes its sites into meaningful categories that correspond to the way you are likely to think of subjects.

The AOL Search directory does not pretend to replace a search engine, which has more sites and hence a better chance to representing more perspectives on any subject and also of turning up obscure facts. If the AOL Search directory does not deliver what you are looking for the first time, AOL Search makes it effortless to

▶ Extend your search to a broader Web search, using the Inktomi search engine.

▶ Search non-Web resources, such as encyclopedias, the Yellow Pages and White Pages, AOL message boards, newsgroups, and other electronic resources that I discuss later in this chapter.

Understanding the Difference between Browsing and Searching

To grasp the distinction between searching and browsing, think of a book. To get the main idea in a reference or other non-fiction book, many people start with the Table of Contents and then flip to chapters that look useful. In planning a garden, for example, you may want to read a chapter on annuals found while browsing a gardening book's table of contents. To retrieve a specific fact — like which end of a bulb goes up — you look in the book's index for specific entries and flip back and forth until you find an answer.

These two major techniques, *browsing* from the table of contents and *searching* from the index, correspond to the techniques of using a Web *directory* and using a Web *search engine.* What really sets AOL Search apart is the clean integration of a computer-generated *search* engine and a human-created *browsable* directory. The search engine helps you when you are searching for specific facts, and the directory helps when you're browsing and trying to find out what's available about a subject.

▶ For a general overview of a subject — choosing an insurance plan or learning about mountain bikes, for example — browsing a directory arranged by subject can be the place to start. You start with general categories and click your way to the information you want. You move from category to subcategory to site. Or search the directory to zero in on sites scattered across several categories.

▶ For highly specific data or information, a search engine can be the best place to do your search. Unlike browsing, you must translate your needs by typing in a few specific words. Then begin your search. Pages containing your requested words are returned to you in a list of links.

Figure 8-1 shows the opening page for AOL Search and points out important searching options. To get started searching, try one of the following:

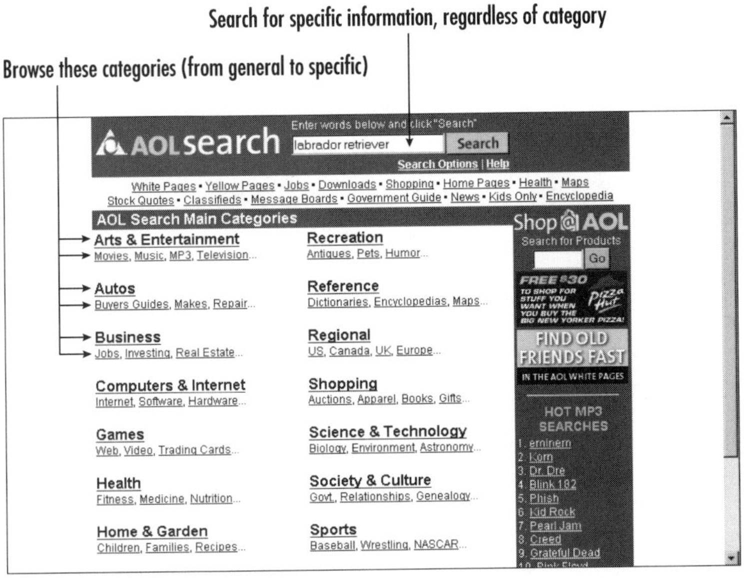

Search for specific information, regardless of category

Browse these categories (from general to specific)

Figure 8-1. AOL Search combines the very best features of a topical directory with the flexibility of precise searching. In this figure, I'm doing a search for **Labrador retrievers**.

The text box on the navigation bar — to the left of the Go button — is for AOL keywords. Any term you enter in this box that is not a keyword is automatically fed into AOL Search.

▶ Use AOL Keyword: **Search**.

▶ Click the Search button on the AOL navigation bar.

▶ From the AOL navigation bar, type a word or words in the AOL search box, shown in Figure 8-1, and click Search.

▶ From the new AOL Services menu, select Internet⇨ Search the Web.

▶ From AOL.COM, there's both a Search button taking you to AOL Search and a search box that runs a search as if you were at AOL Search; your results appear on AOL Search, where they can be refined or pursued.

▶ While using AOL Instant Messenger, type in some search terms where it says Search the Web and click Go.

AOL Search begins with a large directory of (currently) more than 1.5 million sites. This huge effort of creating the directory grew from the Open Directory project (www.dmoz.org), which currently has a vast army of volunteer editors sifting through the Web. Figure 8-2 shows the Open Directory.

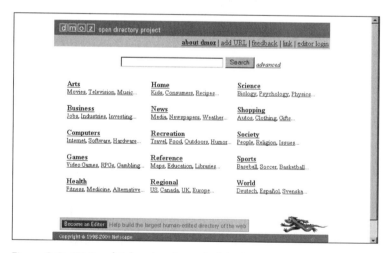

Figure 8-2. AOL Search is based on the work of the Open Directory Project, which you can learn about and use at dmoz.org.

Doing a Sample Search: Labrador Retrievers

This section shows a sample search for information about Labrador retrievers. From the AOL Search navigation box (see Figure 8-1), type in **labrador retriever** and click Search. Notice that it is not necessary to capitalize the *l* in *Labrador*. The results are shown in Figure 8-3.

Note

The Open Directory is used by other Internet search sites, including AltaVista, Google, Hotbot, Lycos, and Dogpile. Some use their own name for the directory, but they're all based on the same content. Approximately 28,000 editors have selected and cataloged more 2 million Web sites in Open Directory's 300,000 categories. Now the standard Web catalog, the Open Directory, is used by search vendors such as Google, Ask Jeeves, and Lycos.

Click to see results of a broader Web search   Click to see next group of matches

Find related news articles and music

Find related pages   Number of matching sites

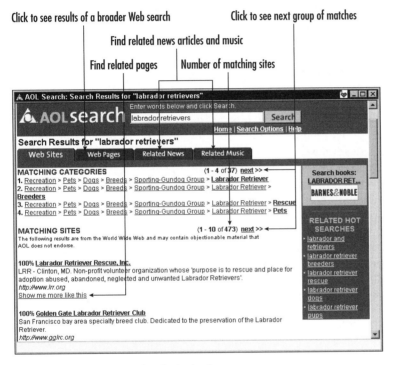

Figure 8-3. Using AOL Search to find Labrador retrievers.

A *query* tells the computer what you want to find out. Concretely, a query consists of the word or words you type into a search box. The art lies in translating your complex information needs into a few words likely to retrieve useful information. The more words in your query, the more refined your search and hence the more likely it will succeed. If you use too many words, however, your search slows down and the results become too narrow. The more specific the words, the better. A search for **training labrador retrievers** instead of **labrador retriever** cuts the number of Web sites returned in half.

Note

Search engines tend to turn up more results than directory-browsing. However, the average quality of pages turned up through such searches tends to be lower, too.

Note

For more information on wording and refining queries, read "Tips for Asking Good Questions" in Chapter 9.

8

Finding Your Way: Internet
Searching Made Easy with AOL

Interpreting Your Results

The purpose of conducting a search is to discover Web sites that meet a specific information need. AOL Search begins with a set of Web sites screened for quality, which is why your search results are likely to be useful for your purposes.

Web pages that an AOL Search returns, such as those in Figure 8-3, are organized primarily in two tabs: Web Sites (from the AOL Search directory) and Web Pages (from the Inktomi general-purpose search engine). Click a tab to see one of the lists. Web Sites are likely to be more relevant to you, while Web Pages cast a larger net; you'll have to sort through the catch on your own.

Look closer at that search for information about Labrador retrievers in Figure 8-3. In the Web Sites tab (which is what is displayed after your query), you can see that the search turns up almost 500 Web sites, all drawn from AOL Search's selective directory of hand-picked sites. In the Web Pages tab, whose contents are not shown in Figure 8-3, the search turned up ten times as many Web pages! The smaller number in Web Sites indicates that AOL Search's directory is smaller (but also choicer) than any engine. The higher number in Web Pages shows what a search engine can do when turned loose in the Web universe. AOL Search, by the way, uses the Inktomi search engine for its broader searches.

Regardless of whether you're reviewing Web Sites or Web Pages, you interpret results in a similar way. Figure 8-4 shows a sample site returned in that search for sites about Labs.

> **Caution**
>
> Whether you're using the Web Sites (directory) tab or Web Pages (non-directory) tab, Web sites contain content over which AOL has no control. Such content can be objectionable, so parents should keep an eye on kids' use of AOL Search tools. Parental Controls, discussed in Chapter 4, provide a simple tool for restricting Web access according to a child's maturity.

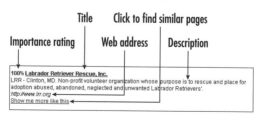

Figure 8-4. Understanding what you found.

Every matching Web site entry has five important components, each of which can be valuable in your search:

▶ The percentage measures the page's importance (or relevancy); it is AOL Search's estimate of the site's value to you. The ratings go from most valuable (100%) to least valuable (0%).

▶ The usually plain-English title of the page is a link to the actual Web page, for example: *Labrador Retriever Information Center*. Click the link to visit the site.

▶ A description of the page or site, if the Web page creator provides one (by using something called the Meta tag). Many pages have no description.

▶ The Web address (URL) of the linked page, which you may find useful if you print the AOL Search results for reference and need to keep track of the URLs.

▶ Show me more like this (a clickable link). If there's a page in AOL Search that is especially good, click this link to find more such pages.

AOL Search shows ten returns per page. At the top of the page is a Next link. Click it to see the next ten returns.

Extending Your Search

From the list of pages matching your query (in this case, pages containing the words *labrador retriever*), you can proceed in many directions.

▶ On the Web, you may want to refine your query by adding or removing words, turning them into phrases (as explained in the next section), and changing their spellings. For fun, you can re-run similar queries done by other AOL Search users.

▶ You can also focus your search on resources *other than the Web*. What sets AOL Search apart is its ability to search AOL resources. Any simple AOL Search query automatically looks through AOL as well as Web resources; the AOL resources are listed first. Beyond that, you can refine a search by focusing on specific AOL resources such as news archives and message boards. Finally, you can search newsgroups: non-AOL, non-Web resources that can yield detailed information plus take you straight to the *people* who have the information you may be seeking.

Tip

Don't worry about the specific numbers in the importance (relevancy) rating. Statistics cannot help you establish with precision the value of any particular resource. After all, the engine doesn't know what you have in mind, only what you type in the query box. In general, the higher the result in the list of all results returned (and the higher the percentage), the more likely the site will be of value to you.

Tip

From the bottom of the page showing the results of any search (see Figure 8-5), you find a long list of Additional Search Resources. These services look through directories for information that you use daily, such as e-mail addresses, White Page and Yellow Page listings, movie times, classifieds, and more.

8

Finding Your Way: Internet Searching Made Easy with AOL

After you decide what direction you want to take your Web search, you can take advantage of the many search options that are available from AOL. For example, you can

▶ **Check out the results of related queries asked by other AOL Search users.** Look in the Related Hot Searches box on the right side of the page (Figure 8-3). Some of these may narrow the search in useful ways. Click any relevant-looking query and click it to run it again.

▶ **Use News Search.** Using the News Search link is the same as clicking the Related News tab at the top of the Search Results page. News Search takes your query and looks for news articles about the subject. These articles are drawn from the major news feeds and archived at AOL.

▶ **Use Web Search.** Clicking the Web Pages tab at the top of the page shows the results of a broader, unfiltered search for Web pages about Labrador retrievers.

▶ **View Personal Home Pages.** Searches AOL Hometown for AOL members' pages containing the words Labrador retrievers. See Chapter 18 for more on AOL Hometown.

▶ **Look at Message Boards.** Searches AOL's message boards for mentions of Labrador retrievers.

▶ **Check Encyclopedias.** Searches the Web-based Compton's Encyclopedia for multimedia articles on the subject of Labrador retrievers.

▶ **Look at Newsgroup postings.** Searches Deja for Internet discussion groups (newsgroups) that either focus on Labrador retrievers or contain (for some reason) many individual postings about them.

▶ **View Health Web sites.** Search Oxygen Media's health-related Web sites, such as Thrive Online, for current health information, in this case on the off chance that a health article might mention Labs.

▶ **View Kids Only sites.** Search AOL Search for Kids. As it turns out, 76 pages came back on Labrador retrievers. Many of these pages are suitable for kids doing research about dogs.

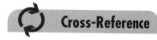

Cross-Reference

See Chapter 14 for more about newsgroups and message boards. Both work like public bulletin boards to which people can post a message and respond to others' messages. While message boards are open only to AOL members, newsgroups belong to the entire Internet.

Cross-Reference

Newsgroups and the standard newsgroup search service, Deja.com, are discussed in Chapter 14.

Click one of these links to search different resources.

Click one of these links to search another service.

Figure 8-5. Scroll down to the bottom of AOL Search and run the same query through one of these resources. Or click a link to do a new search of a different resource.

Refining Your Search

You can refine your query if you are not getting quite the results you want. Usually, refining a query means making the relation between your search words more precise.

The Search Options page gives you a way to construct precise queries without worrying about those pesky ANDs and ORs (the dreaded *Boolean operators*) that once plagued Web searchers. From AOL Search's home page, click the Search Options link to bring up the Advanced Search page shown in Figure 8-6. Don't be put off by the word *advanced;* using this page helps you quickly put together complex searches that can yield better results.

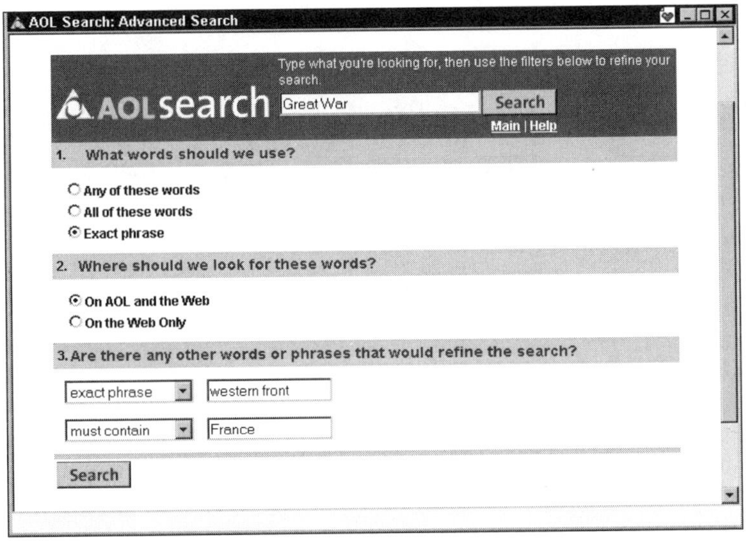

Figure 8-6. Powerful queries without fuss.

Definition

A *phrase* is a series of words in a specific order that together have a specific meaning. *Great War*, for example, has a specific meaning (the Great War of 1914–1918, also known as World War I). When not joined as a phrase, however, the words retrieve many sites irrelevant to the World War I researcher. That is, many wars have been called *great*, and the words *war* and *great* can appear on the same page even if they have nothing to do with each other or with World War I. AOL Search is usually pretty good about assuming that words entered in a certain order should appear in that order on returned pages: *Labrador retrievers* (in the example developed earlier) was not enclosed in quotes yet worked just fine. However, if you don't like the results you're getting, try using phrases instead of single words. Doing so may help to yield better results.

Find It Online

For help using AOL Search's power features, go to AOL Keyword: **Search**, click Help, and then click Search Tips.

To use the Advanced Search fill-in-the-blank form, you first type in your search terms (query) in the text box at the top. Before clicking Search, stop to reflect on your other choices on this page. This powerful form helps you refine your query by specifying

▶ **How to weight the words in a query.** You can look for any or all of the words, or all of the words in order — a phrase. A *phrase* is simply a string of words you're looking for, in a specific order. If you're looking for references to the song *Danny Boy,* for example, you want AOL Search to consider *danny boy* an exact phrase; otherwise it could retrieve pages containing mentions of either (or both), like *Danny* Devito and *Boy* Scouts.

▶ **Where the words must appear — on AOL and the Web, or on the Web only.** AOL's resources are reliably family-friendly; the Web's resources are broader but also more uneven and less family-friendly. The Web's coverage exceeds AOL's (and the Library of Congress's for that matter).

▶ **Which additional words you want to add to further refine your search.** Here you specify any other words that must be included on pages — or not included. These additional search terms can help you both zero-in on specific information and rule out similar-sounding information.

Refining Your Search with Power Operators

If you're seeking very specific information, AOL Search offers additional precision when you use operators with your search terms. Table 8-1 shows a list of operators that can help you further refine your searches.

Table 8-1. *Search Operators*

Operator	Is Used to	Explanation/ Example
"search term goes here"	Search for words in a specific order	Place the phrase in quotation marks, as in "the house that Jack built"
ADJ	Search for words in a specific order	The query (**tony OR anthony**) **ADJ blair** returns Web pages that contain **tony blair** or **anthony blair**
NEAR	Search for words close to each other	The query **lakers near/5 shaquille** looks for pages having **lakers** and **shaquille** within five words of each other
?	Search for any single character	The query **?dsl** finds Web pages containing the acronyms **ADSL** or **HDSL**
*	Search for a series of characters	The query **gin*** finds Web pages containing **ginger ale** and **gingivitis**.

For What It's Worth: Evaluating Web Sites

What makes a site good? Reasons to visit a Web site vary, and so do criteria for evaluating sites. If you're looking for a site about ancient Thrace or for the lowest airfare to Honolulu, you have different criteria for judging the page containing the information you want. If you're doing genealogical research, the site with the most accurate and abundant information about your family wins, hands down. Graphics and design rarely make one site's content better than another site's — except in the case of sites about graphic design.

(Continued)

Definition

A Boolean *operator* is a word used in a query to define the relative importance of the actual search terms or the relationship between them. AND, OR, and NOT are common operators.

Tip

When you do a search, your original query appears at the top of each results page. You can narrow a search by adding words and phrases; it helps to make each word and phrase as specific as possible, for example **Labrador retriever** instead of **dog**. To broaden a search, insert OR (the lowercase *or* is fine) as in *tanks or Great War;* a page gets returned if it has *tanks* or if it has *Great War,* but the word and phrase need not be used on the same page.

Definition

A *wildcard* is a character that stands for another character or characters. You can use wildcards in searches to represent unknown characters in your search. Note that wildcards cannot be used in phrases because phrases look for exact matches of words within the quotation marks.

8

Finding Your Way: Internet Searching Made Easy with AOL

Find It Online

See Hope Tillman, *Evaluating Quality on the Net,* 2000 (www.tiac.net/users/ hope/findqual.html).

(Continued)

Hope Tillman, a librarian and Web authority, suggests asking the following kinds of questions in evaluating a site:

▶ Does the site define its own purpose? Can you quickly assess its scope, so you know whether it may serve your purposes?

▶ Who is the authority behind the site? Authority is sometimes a subjective matter, obviously, but do *you* trust the source? *Is* a source identified?

▶ How up-to-date is the information: How frequently is it updated? When was it last updated?

▶ Does the format (use of pictures, video, or other kinds of multimedia), make sense for the information presented?

AOL's White Pages, Yellow Pages, and E-Mail Finder

Why search for someone's street address or your drugstore's phone number using the old-fashioned White Pages or Yellow Pages? On the Web the same information is always available, so you need not hunt for those heavy books with torn pages. White Pages and Yellow Pages on the Net are simple electronic databases of millions of names. As in familiar phone books, White Pages provide listings of individuals, while Yellow Pages provide listings of businesses. Unlike the phone books, the Web gives access to addresses for entire *countries,* not just your city or county or country. Online listings are updated more often than paper listings — approximately four times a year.

At AOL Search (Figure 8-1), you can find links to the White and Yellow Pages at the top of the opening page. From any page of Search Results (while using AOL Search), these same choices are at the bottom of the page (see Figure 8-5). In either case, these resources help you find real world and e-mail addresses.

Finding Residential Addresses (White Pages)

To do a White Pages search for someone's street address or phone number, click White Pages from the top or bottom of any page in AOL Search. The only piece of information you must provide is a last name, but any additional information improves your chances of uncovering that address.

A simple search yields the same information as flipping through the White Pages book: name, address, phone number. On the Web, you also find additional links, such as driving directions to the person's house, a neighborhood map, and local pharmacies and pizzerias. You can also send that person a message or an online or paper greeting card. No paper White Pages goes that far!

Finding Business Addresses (Yellow Pages)

AOL's Yellow Page service works like AOL's White Pages but goes further in the online benefits it offers. While White Pages are alphabetized by name, business information is also searchable by business category (insurance, pets, and so on). Online, you can search for a category of businesses (like Pet Supplies or Pet Training) or for a business with a specific name.

With the online Yellow Pages, you can precisely screen businesses by location. Click Distance Search to specify the distance (in miles) within which a business must be located. Detailed Search and Canada Search give you additional ways to make your searches more precise and easier to review.

Finding E-Mail Addresses

AOL's E-mail Finder can be found at AOL Keyword: **Email finder**. The E-Mail Finder is *not* based on publicly available databases. Instead, the service works by collecting e-mail addresses from Internet service providers and from voluntary submissions from people who want to ensure that current addresses are available for them. When you do find e-mail addresses, you may be finding old as well as new addresses. The database has no way of knowing which are current — unless individuals take the trouble to submit updated information. In the catch-as-catch-can world of e-mail indexing, you may have less luck finding someone's e-mail address than in searching for the same person's real address. As with the White Pages, you can modify or hide your own e-mail address; just click Revise E-mail Listing.

Find It Online

The AOL White Pages, AOL Yellow Pages, and AOL People Directory are all available from AOL 6.0's People menu. All these options its own keyword (**White pages, Yellow pages, People Directory**, respectively).

Find It Online

Approximately ten national directories are available from the Country drop-down list when you use the AOL White Pages. For even more choices, scroll down a bit for the link to AOL's International Directories, for another 50 countries' business listings.

Tip

You can update or remove information about your own listing on the AOL White Pages. Full instructions are available from the opening page. Just click the Help or Updates to the AOL White Pages link.

AOL Keyword: **MapQuest** supplies local traffic cams, national and city maps of any area of the world, integrated information from Digital City (AOL's comprehensive local events guides), and driving directions between any two addresses in the U.S. and Canada.

Tip

MapQuest forms one piece of a trio of local-information services coordinated by AOL. Together with Digital City and Moviefone, MapQuest provides comprehensive maps and directions. Find a restaurant at Digital City or purchase a movie ticket through Moviefone, and MapQuest provides the driving directions. There's more. My Calendar (Chapter 3) helps you keep track of all those dinners and movies, and the AOL Reminder service ensures that you look at your Calendar.

Note

The Member Directory is now called the People Directory.

Getting Maps and Directions: MapQuest

When you find an address with the AOL White Pages, click the More Information link to get a new page that shows links to all sorts of services near that location. From that page, click Driving Directions to get turn-by-turn directions from your street address to the address you are seeking. Likewise, for any business you find using the Yellow Pages, you get a map, driving directions, and the ability to choose the fastest route.

If you're into maps or want more than driving directions, check out MapQuest (AOL Keyword: **MapQuest**). Created by an Internet pioneer in interactive mapping services, MapQuest is now owned by AOL and closely integrated with AOL's local-information services, MovieFone and Digital City. You can find driving directions between addresses and zoomable maps of addresses at MapQuest. Especially useful for those local commutes are MapQuest's traffic reports and traffic cameras (Webcams), which are updated every few minutes (see Figure 8-7). The MapQuest map store stocks gadgetry such as devices to help you get instructions while driving and hundreds of old-fashioned maps of virtually every place on earth.

Using the AOL People Directory

The Internet White Pages are based on publicly available address listings, much like (often the same as) your phone book's listings. Since AOL has 25 million members (give or take) chances are that someone you're seeking is on AOL. To find out, go to AOL Keyword: **People Directory** and do a search. You can search this directory only when you are signed onto AOL. The People Directory contains profiles only of those members who choose to create them.

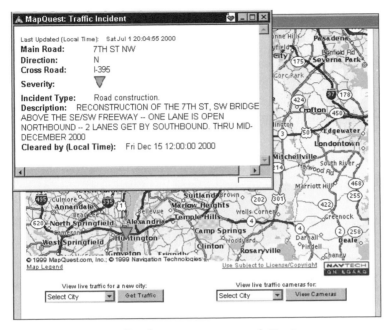

Figure 8-7. Get local traffic information at AOL Keyword: **MapQuest**.

As an AOL member, you can make available your profile, with anything you want to share about your hobbies, computers, job, marital status, favorite quotes, and so on at AOL Keyword: **People Directory**, click My Profile to create or modify your own profile.

Caution

Minors should not provide personal or contact information without parental knowledge.

Where to Go from Here

AOL Search offers a strong solution to the built-in problems of searching the Web. Starting with a hand-picked, well-organized directory of choice Web sites, courtesy of the Open Directory Project, AOL Search gives you the choice of browsing or searching the directory. You can also extend your search to the larger, messier universe of Web pages. Finally, you can search other online resources including AOL message boards, Internet newsgroup postings, the White and Yellow pages, encyclopedias, news archives, and more.

8

Finding Your Way: Internet
Searching Made Easy with AOL

▶ The next chapter introduces some of the non-AOL tools you can use to do special-purpose Internet (not just Web) research. All these tools are available through AOL, of course.

▶ Searching for mailing lists and newsgroups is handled in more detail in Chapters 13 and 14, respectively.

▶ Searching for files to download? See Chapter 16.

Chapter 9

From Breadth to Depth: Search Engines and Specialized Searches

IN THIS CHAPTER

Other search engines and when to use them

How to ask a good question

Family-friendly searching

Using several search engines at the same time

Directories of specialized resources

Authoritative directories (Virtual Library, Argus)

In-depth searching (examples: Health and Law)

Searching libraries and creating digital libraries

Chapter 8 explored the many options available at AOL Search, the place to start your search for just about anything you can find online. AOL gives you the tools to find Web sites, street addresses, e-mail addresses, online White and Yellow Pages, newsgroup postings, and maps of all sorts. Despite such a staggering amount of information to sift through, in so many formats and languages, you may need a back-up tool for those times when your needs are highly specialized or when you must have authoritative, reliable results from a specialized search engine. This chapter was designed to help you in exactly those situations. After looking at a few of the other general search engines, this chapter takes a hard look at special-purpose directories and search engines.

What to Look for in a Search Engine

Some people scoff that the Internet has more search engines than things to search. The variety is wide enough to be confusing. Fact is, you do have enough choice on the Internet to find the search tool for any specific purpose. Look for the following when deciding which search engine to use to supplement your AOL Search:

Note

You can find just about anything you need with AOL Search, but Internet search engines can be wonderful supplements to AOL Search.

▶ **Size.** Size is relative. A site *about* searching, like Search Engine Watch (www.searchenginewatch.com), provides some benchmarks and numbers. Size must be qualified in at least one way: Most search engines include a large number of non-working (*dead*) links.

▶ **Intelligent searches.** Some engines process data in ways that improve your chances of getting the results you expect. Google, for example, measures a site's value in terms of its usefulness as measured by the number of links to that site. Other engines put the power in your hands, letting you create queries of great complexity.

▶ **Special services that enhance the usability of the sites they return.** Some sites returned by a search can't be used in their current form. To help you work with foreign-language sites, for example, AltaVista provides useful translation services. Many search engines also offer filtering services that make both queries and results more family friendly, improving the usability of sites for certain audiences.

▶ **The availability of non-Web search options.** Lycos, for example, offers excellent multimedia and FTP search services.

The following sections introduce you to additional Internet search engines.

AltaVista

AltaVista (www.altavista.com) has always featured a large, fast index. As I wrote this book, AltaVista was neck and neck with Inktomi, the search engine used by AOL Search when you choose to extend a search. Both have lists of around 300 to 500 million Web pages. In addition, AOL Search and AltaVista use the same directory of Web sites, based on the Open Directory Project (see Chapter 8).

So why use AltaVista? Two special features distinguish this respected search engine from others on the Net:

▶ **Media search.** From AltaVista's opening page, click one of the media tabs (Images, MP3/Audio, or Video) to do a search for content of a certain format, such as MPG movies, MP3 music files, black-and-white photos, or streaming video. Each tab takes you to a special page with its own tools, popular downloads, message boards, and technical information.

▶ **International search.** In AltaVista, you can search for pages written in other languages. To do so, select a language from the drop-down list to the right of the Search button on the opening page. You can also click Language Settings for two additional options: entering your search terms in non-Western (like Chinese or Hebrew) alphabets; searching for more than one Western language (such as Italian, French, and Spanish). You can find complete instructions on the Language Settings page. Complementing its international search, look for AltaVista's translation tools, shown in Figure 9-1, available at world.altavista.com. Use these tools to translate your queries (and anything else) to and from half a dozen languages. Also, check out the multilingual international onscreen keyboard, or take a look at AltaVista's sister sites all over the world!

Search for sites in other countries.

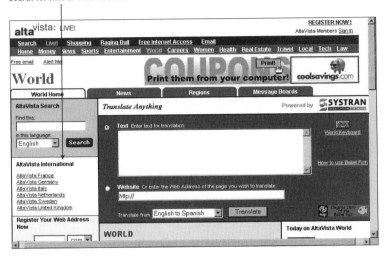

Figure 9-1. AltaVista has wonderful foreign-language features, such as Translate Anything. It also has built-in Web filters, and provides tools for searching for images, sounds, and video.

Google

As search engines crawl the Web looking for Web pages, most collect pages more or less indiscriminately. Google (www.google.com) has a different approach, and it works. When you do a search using Google, the results consist of pages that *other* pages link to; the more pages linking to a page, the higher it will appear in the results page. The premise is that the most useful pages are the pages that other people consider useful.

Google also looks for pages that serve as *hubs* — the most popular pages from which people visit related pages. The approach makes sense because it's based on the actual browsing habits of millions of people. Forget the technology, however; what counts is whether Google can be remarkably accurate. Figure 9-2 shows the results of a Google search for information about Babe Ruth and baseball.

Definition

A *google* is the number 1 followed by 100 zeroes. Google.com now claims to have indexed a billion Web pages, half of which are "partially" indexed.

Tip

Notice the funky I'm Feeling Lucky button? Click it to go directly to the first item that Google would return in response to your query. That's how confident the folks at Google are.

Figure 9-2. Google helps you identify the pages that others visit and link to. Here are the results from a search for baseball *"Babe Ruth."*

You don't have to use Boolean phrases when you conduct a search on Google. AND is assumed.

When Google shows you re-sults of a search, it places the words it used to match pages to your query in bold. This shows how your search terms are actually used on the page. If you enter two words in your query and they're next to each other or used in the correct context, you'll know at a glance whether the page might be useful (see Figure 9-2).

With Google, you use quotes to indicate exact phrases, but you don't have to use *and*, *or*, plus signs, or any other Boolean annoyances. In fact Google always assumes that you're using *and*. When you look for pages with the words *baseball "Babe Ruth,"* you want to see pages with the word *baseball* and the phrase *Babe Ruth*. When you get results, click the link to see a list of pages linking to this page.

Like AltaVista, a Google search can be restricted to pages in one or more languages. In addition, Google's messages and help pages can also be displayed in a different language. Look for the Language Options link on the Google opening page.

A great feature that distinguishes Google is the ability to read cached pages. Think of a cached page as a snapshot of the page as it looked when Google indexed it. To appreciate this feature, consider all the reasons why that old snapshot might differ from what's available right now: A page could get new content, or a new address, or just disappear. So, if Google can't find a page after you click a link, try the cached page instead; the information may be old, but it could still be useful for you.

Google also makes available the same hand-selected and care-fully organized directory that AOL Search uses. With Google, you can search the directory by clicking the Browse link. Or, you can do a normal Web search. Any pages you find that just happen to be in the directory indicate the page's description and category; you can click the category link to view all the category's sites.

Search with a Human Face

The first generation of search engines indexed Web sites automatically, making the search process hit or miss, at best. The Open Directory Project, upon which AOL Search is based, replaced automatic indexing with human selection — directories built by people who care about a particular subject.

The biggest search services on the Internet — including AltaVista, Google, and Lycos — have adopted the Open Directory, whose goal is to provide "the most comprehensive directory of the Web by relying on a vast army of volunteer editors." Currently more than 20,000 editors contribute site reviews to Open Directory's countless categories. Editors exercise their judgment in choosing sites, placing them in one or more categories, and describing them in a few words. This human touch adds enormous value, setting the Open Directory apart from the mechanically compiled search engines.

The Open Directory has a deep hierarchy of sites. This depth serves the two purposes of providing meaningful categories for all selected sites and providing you, the user, with usefully focused categories that contain clusters of closely related pages. When you browse the directory, the at symbol (@) indicates a subcategory of sites; a plain link indicates a link to an actual site.

About.com begins with the human approach to searching and adds interactive features. This service consists of some 700 guides covering more than 35,000 subjects. Each guide is led by one or more subject matter experts, who assemble enthusiasts to help put together focused collections of Web sites, write lengthy articles, and provide all kinds of interactive opportunities, including chat. Unlike other search services, About.com is seeking to generate new content and build communities of people with a strong interest in certain subjects.

Click SafeSearch to filter out objectionable results.

For any good pages returned by your search, click Similar Pages to see more of the same.

Find It Online

In addition to the Open Directory Project catalog, Lycos owns the HotBot search engine (www.hotbot.com), which features useful filters for finding specific types of media used on the Web, such as JavaScript, RealAudio, MP3, Shockwave, and video. From www.hotbot.com, click Advanced Search.

Tip

Parents wary of adult content can click Lycos's Search Scrub to filter out unwanted images and music.

Cross-Reference

FTP (file transfer protocol) is the focus of Chapter 16, and MP3 is discussed in Chapters 6, 17, and 18.

Caution

If you're doing research, beware of the shopping links integrated throughout your search results. These options create many distractions that don't get you any closer to your goals.

Lycos

One of the Net's earliest general-purpose Web-search engines, Lycos, is now based primarily on the Open Directory Project, the same used by AOL Search. As with AOL Search, you can easily extend a Lycos directory search to a general search.

Lycos excels in supporting specialized searches. A sound-and-images search service is available from the Multimedia link on the opening page (see Figure 9-3), as is the outstanding FTP search tool (FTP Search) discussed in Chapter 15. When you use Lycos's Multimedia link, you can search through a million MP3 files and approximately 100 million files available through FTP, the Internet's trusty tool for copying files from one place to another. You can also search for image, video, and sound files. Lycos offers a set of special-purpose tools for playing these files.

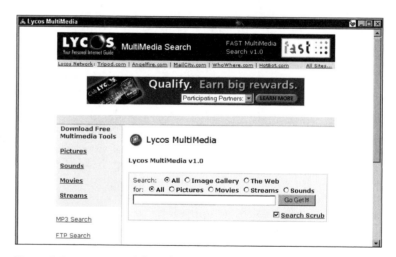

Figure 9-3. Lycos is a good choice for multimedia searches for things like MP3 music files, FTP files, images, sounds, and video.

Unfortunately, Lycos integrates shopping throughout its search areas, making it hard to focus on what you are seeking. Not that I'm biased, but AOL does a good job keeping Shop@AOL and AOL Search distinct, improving both in the process.

Northern Light

Northern Light (www.northernlight.com), shown in Figure 9-4, is highly respected among librarians, academics, and people who require reliable and up-to-date information. Although much of great value is free at Northern Light, you must pay a fee for some of the content retrieved by specialized searches. Currently you pay $1 to $4 for any article in its Special Collections, which consist of 20 million documents from approximately 250 print and electronic sources. In the USGOV area, you can find a Special Collection of over 6,700 publications.

Northern Light groups search results in folders that are arranged by data type (such as press release), source (the Web, for example), and language. This highly usable format gives you an overview of your results and allows you to focus on specific ones. On the left side of the page, a box lists the folders; the actual results display in the center of the page.

Among these free resources are Special Editions, which include links arranged and annotated by search professionals on topics of the day, such as autism and managed care. Useful, too, is the free version of USGOVSEARCH (www.usgovsearch.com), which offers powerful filtered searches: You can specify how recent your information must be, from what part of the government (executive branch, federal agency, and so on), where your search terms must appear on a page, and other criteria.

Tip

For free, you can subscribe to Northern Light's Search Alerts to receive e-mail notification when new sites or Special Collections become available on a specific subject.

Tip

Northern Light boasts a large index combined with a low number of dead links relative to other engines. Try a search from the opening page, using the Search For box.

Definition

A *meta-search service* can search for your topic on more than one search engine and supply you with a variety of results from a slew of directories. When you conduct a meta search, you're using just such a search site.

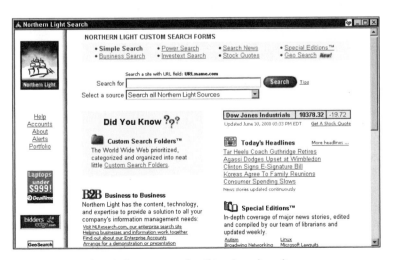

Figure 9-4. Northern Light: an engine for sifting through quality content.

Doing Many Searches at Once

Caution

Because meta-search sites have to send your questions to so many search engines, you're often required to keep your questions simple. The results do not appear quite as quickly as with other engines, and you get only a few results per search engine.

Find It Online

A handful of meta-search tools have survived many years, which is often a sign of quality on the Internet. In addition to Dogpile, you might want to try MetaCrawler (`www.metacrawler.com`) and CNET's SavvySearch (`savvy.search.com`).

With so many sites that search the Web, meta-search sites — sites that search *other* search engines — didn't take long to pop up. You type in some search terms, and the meta-search tool feeds your query to many search engines at the same time.

Meta-searchers have their uses, but they do have a few drawbacks. For one thing, these tools lack power features. Because they feed your queries to so many search services, they often require that you use simple queries. Meta searches can be a little slow compared with a single search on one of the underlying search engines. And on your results page, only a few returns are presented for each engine. Still, seeing how various services handle the same query can be enlightening and even funny. A meta-search service can be a way of identifying the best engine for your information needs.

A favorite meta-search tool for many is called Dogpile (`www.dogpile.com`), shown in Figure 9-5. You type in a query indicating what you want to find, choose what underlying engines to search, and Dogpile does its thing. Dogpile lets you search several standard Web search engines such as Google, along with major directories such as the Open Directory. You can also search for Usenet (newsgroup) postings, news articles, and FTP files. Plus, you can do media searches for MP3 songs and images. Custom Search lets you pick the engines you want, in the order you want them to be searched. Dogpile presents the results in a continuous list rather than in separate windows for each engine.

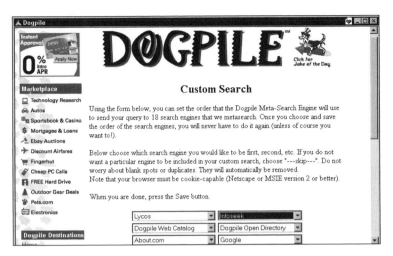

Figure 9-5. Dogpile presents an admirably simple view of a wide range of search tools.

Tips for Asking Good Questions

At the heart of every search is a query, whether you are searching a directory or an engine, a multimedia archive or one of Northern Light's collections. A query translates what you want to find out into a string of words that can be usefully processed by a computer. Your success with any search can depend on putting your query in just the right way. Here are some general guidelines for turning good questions into effective queries:

▶ **Be clear about what you want to know and whether the Web is the best place to start.** If you want to tap opinions and expertise (to get advice on buying a piano, for example), searching for specific newsgroups postings may make more sense than searching the Web, because in newsgroups you can ask people questions and then ask follow-up questions.

▶ **Think of specific words that convey what you want to find out.** Use all these different words in the same query, and put them in order from most important to least important.

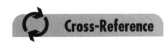

Cross-Reference

See Chapters 13 and 14 on mailing lists and newsgroups.

A *filter* is just a little box in which you check or otherwise select options to define exactly how your search terms are related to each other. AOL's Search Options box, described in Chapter 8, is one example.

Find It Online

Can't find what you need? The University of Leiden's Collection of Special Search Engines consists of a long and highly selective (but not particularly user-friendly) list, arranged by subject (www.leidenuniv.nl/ ub/biv/specials.htm). Often overlooked in the search world are directories and indexes that specialize in a locality or region. From About.com's websearch.about.com/ internet/websearch/, click Regional for links to these services. Northern Light, too, recently began offering regional searches.

▶ **Use a search tool's filters** to specify whether your words form a phrase ("London bridges falling down") and whether you will only accept pages containing specific words or phrases (or both).

▶ **Avoid empty words.** Many search engines ignore words like *the*, *and*, and *in* — even in phrases, which are otherwise considered to be strings of characters.

▶ **Check your spelling.** Some engines give you latitude if you misspell something; others take you at your word and give you just what you asked for. If your search turned up nothing useful, check your spelling!

▶ **Refine your query and run it again**. When you finally start to turn up valuable sites, use a Show More Like This link if it's available (as in AOL Search and Google). If your search didn't turn up anything at all or anything relevant, think of synonyms, additional words, or painfully specific words.

Special-Purpose Search Collections

Does *authoritative* sound dull? Think of it this way: Do you want your doctor making a decision based on literature that is not peer-reviewed? Or your lawyer engaging in speculation about your legal rights? Probably not. These are only the most obvious examples of instances in which only the best data will do. From elementary school through grad school, you need good, vetted information at every step. In business life, and parenting, and in any area that really matters to you, you need to trust what you get on the Net.

For searches requiring authoritative results, consider starting with specialized directories. Instead of mechanically harvested, blindly indexed pages, you receive material that experts select, which is often based on printed information. The best authoritative resources are not only compiled by experts, but also arranged in a way that suits both the audience and the subject matter.

The following pages profile three major, subject-organized directories of high-quality Internet resources: the Digital Librarian, the WWW Virtual Library, and the Argus

Clearinghouse. Considering these sites authoritative does not imply that the search services discussed earlier in this chapter are not authoritative. What sets these final sites apart is their specialized focus, academic orientation, and use of subject matter experts. Over the years these three resources have become indispensable to serious searchers.

Digital Librarian

Digital Librarian is the one-woman work of Margaret Vail Anderson, a librarian in Cortland, New York. With its 100 or so categories arranged into a conveniently compact interface, the Digital Librarian avoids the deeply layered scheme used by commercial directories. Instead of burrowing down five levels, you choose from the long list of librarian-vetted main categories. For each, you get a list of choice resources for that category. Each list is alphabetized, and almost every individual listing is sufficiently annotated to give you a sense of what you will find at the site when you click the link. Ms. Anderson uses a special icon to denote new resources as she adds them and keeps the site up to date. Go to www.digital-librarian.com.

The WWW Virtual Library (VLIB)

The Virtual Library (Figure 9-6) calls itself "the oldest catalog of the Web." The brainchild of Tim Berners-Lee, the creator of the World Wide Web, the VLIB is "run by a loose confederation of volunteers, who compile pages of key links for particular areas in which they are experts." Not the biggest index of the Web, the 300 or so virtual libraries, centrally cataloged and searchable at www.vlib.org, are widely recognized as some of the most reliable guides to subjects, particularly academic subjects.

The VLIB consists of both a browsable directory of libraries (shown in Figure 9-6) and a search tool for browsing across libraries (for example, do a search for *education*, and you'll uncover links to many individual libraries).

Tip

As with any information resource, make sure to find out who is behind a specialized resource, how current it is, and whether it is comprehensive. Specialized search sites used to be (and still are) a labor of love, often undertaken by experts. That's the origin of the Digital Librarian, the WWW Virtual Library, and Argus Clearinghouse.

Note

The Virtual Library can be found at www.vlib.org. The site is mirrored around the world. These mirrors, a term meaning identical site, make global access to the Virtual Library more feasible. Experts maintain the individual subject catalogs, which are housed on computers around the world. Individual libraries in the collection may not be available at all times.

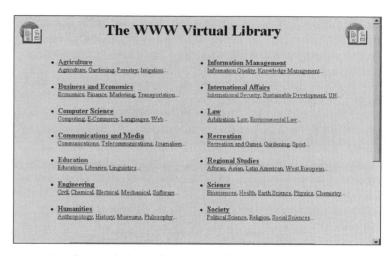

Figure 9-6. The Virtual Library: always open and worth your time.

Find It Online

This chapter focuses on resources of interest to adult researchers. For comparably reliable students' resources, start with the Internet Public Library, profiled in Chapter 4 (www.ipl.org). The IPL serves the needs of students through high school.

These libraries really are *virtual* — available only online. Each library has a virtual librarian who's responsible for the content, and you can readily find that person's e-mail address at the main VLIB site or on the catalogs to which the VLIB links. Virtual Library arranges resources by both content and type of resource and pulls together both scholarly and commercial information resources. A warning: Because hundreds of people maintain these virtual libraries, the design and up-to-dateness of the libraries vary.

Argus Clearinghouse: Librarians Rate the Net

Easier to navigate and more cleanly designed than the Virtual Library, the Argus Clearinghouse grew out of a collective project undertaken in the early 1990s by Lou Rosenfeld's information-science students at the University of Michigan (www.clearinghouse.net). Rosenfeld's design firm, Argus Associates, continues to maintain the site.

Like the Virtual Library, the Clearinghouse directory consists of guides to Internet resources about well-defined subjects, like disabilities or distance education. Unlike the Virtual Library, the Clearinghouse chooses only those resource guides

that meet its content and design standards. Therefore, users of
these guides have some assurance that the resources are well
chosen, described, and evaluated and that each guide is easy
to use.

Clearinghouse recognizes the very best guides with its
monthly Digital Librarian Award. Check the list of the award-
winners for the best guides. Seniorwomen.com, for example,
shown in Figure 9-7, won the award in late 1999; it features information and interactive resources for older women.

As with the Virtual Library, anyone can take part in the Argus
Clearinghouse and submit a guide to Internet resources on a
well-defined topic. However, Argus accepts fewer than 10 percent of the guides submitted to them, and each accepted
guide receives a rating before it's published in the
Clearinghouse. For you, as a searcher, this means that the
guides are top-drawer, selective guides to the reliable Internet
resources.

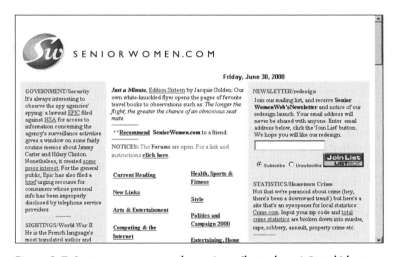

Figure 9-7. Seniorwomen.com recently won Argus Clearinghouse's Digital Librarian
Award.

Finding Authoritative Resources

This section looks at Health and Legal resources, two very practical areas where not having authoritative information — or at least not being well-informed — can be expensive. To be informed, you need access to experts and people with experience and pointers to the resources of leading organizations. Net resources on health and the law can also help you choose the lawyers and doctors who make the most sense given your needs and budget. Without the Net, choosing the right professionals can take luck and time. With this kind of information, you'll be able to ask the right questions.

Health: Specialized Resources

Most people have concerns about their health or the health of their kids, spouses, and parents. One of your first considerations should be to find information you can understand. Authoritative information you can't understand doesn't do a bit of good and may lead to misunderstandings with medical professionals. Fortunately, popular medical resources are cropping up on the Web, and many can be found on AOL itself.

AOL's Health Channel (AOL Keyword: **Health**) compiles reliable information about health, with resources such as the following:

> ▶ **Thrive Online.** The first priority for many is to stay fit. Thrive Online has a fitness planner, many calculators to help you burn calories, and recommended activities. Very readable, Thrive Online is nonetheless backed by medical professionals.

> ▶ **Mayo Clinics Conditions & Treatments.** When you or a loved one does get sick, you want the best information on care and prognosis. The Mayo Clinic's Conditions & Treatments service takes you to hundreds of Web pages, each devoted to a specific condition. For any condition, you can find solid information about the likely diagnosis and treatment. You'll also find links to related authoritative sites and community support resources, such as message boards.

> ▶ **HealthAtoZ** (www.healthatoz.com), includes forums about fitness and ailments. Each topic includes annotated and rated Web sites. Other core resources include

Find It Online

Start your health-related voyages at AOL's Health Channel, which guides you to the major specialized health resources. Click the Medical Resources & References link from the main Health window. For a searchable, highly selective, and very large collection of authoritative medical resources, start at the non-commercial Health On the Net Foundation (www.hon.ch/HONselect).

Reuters news stories and free access to Medline, the searchable guide to recent medical articles.

▶ **Drkoop.com** (www.drkoop.com), the Web enterprise founded by the former U.S. Surgeon General, features a directory of rated Web sites and a searchable database of detailed drug information in a question-and-answer format, including information about drug interactions. Start here, too, to learn about taking part in current clinical trials of as-yet unreleased medications. Drkoop.com includes forums on alternative medicine and mental health.

Law: Specialized Resources

Law, like medicine, is one of these areas of life where expertise is often well-rewarded and professional service can be unavoidable and expensive. You'll benefit from being an educated consumer of legal services.

Many consider FindLaw — a winner of Argus Clearinghouse's Digital Librarian Award — the best place to start looking for law information (www.findlaw.com). Because FindLaw has grown so big, so fast, it serves a broad range of users, including consumers, law students, businesses, lawyers, and paralegals of every specialty.

Consumers can locate guidelines for finding and interviewing a lawyer as well as formalizing an agreement. (To find a lawyer, look for the Lawyer Directory in Findlaw's Consumer section.) Included on FindLaw is an online copy of the Consumer's Resource Handbook, a comprehensive overview of your rights in the areas of credit, phone fraud, online shopping, and more.

If you own a small business, FindLaw gives you free information about employee benefits, intellectual property, credit and collections, unfair practices, and dealing with the government. Selected Web sites throw light on every aspect of forming, running, growing, and dissolving a business.

If you are a lawyer, a paralegal, or a legal librarian or are considering a career in law, turn to FindLaw to learn about law schools, connect with others, or get a more challenging job. Among hundreds of useful resources on FindLaw, you can find

Tip

Places like Drkoop.com feature online experts, but none tries to take the place of your own doctor. Use such sites to get information about disorders, find advice for staying well, and gather the information you need to both ask your doctors questions and understand what they tell you.

Tip

Medline, a longtime offering on AOL (AOL Keyword: **Medline**), is a searchable database of journal articles published in the last few years. The articles are usually for medical specialists. You cannot find the actual articles online, but on AOL you can order medical articles retrieved through Medline for a fee.

Find It Online

FindLaw seems to be everyone's favorite, but the Virtual Library provides guides to an even broader spectrum of legal resources on the Internet. The Argus Clearinghouse currently contains more than 70 law-related guides, with special guides on intellectual property, copyright law, Internet law, and so on.

Note

If you're not a lawyer and have no idea how a court case travels through the judicial system and, in some cases, up to the Supreme Court, you'll find basic information about the U.S. legal system at FindLaw. This information is a strong resource for middle- and high-school students.

Find It Online

Look for LIBWEB, a list of some 3,500 world libraries with searchable Web-based libraries, at sunsite. berkeley.edu/Libweb/.

▶ More than 100 years of Supreme Court decisions (searchable)

▶ The Merriam-Webster Dictionary of Law

▶ News pertaining to specific laws and trials

▶ Discussion forums where you can tap the expertise of the FindLaw community

From Libraries on the Web to Digital Libraries

The search for trustworthy information has traditionally led straight to the library stacks. Many researchers still automatically consider most Web sites less reliable than traditional sources, because no credible publisher has filtered them or taken responsibility for them. Also, copyright law is difficult enough to enforce, and the nature of the Web only adds to the uncertainty about the origins of any document.

Nothing, in fact, has done more for books than the Internet. Think of Amazon.com, for example. Or, consider the hundreds of libraries whose catalogs you can search over the Web. But the Net is more than a medium for supporting physical books; it has quickly become a place to publish books or make existing books available in digital form. Around the U.S., hundreds of libraries and museums are digitizing their collections to make them available to a larger and more dispersed audience. University libraries are leading huge projects to put millions of archival documents online and also to purchase electronic books and thus control their costs and storage requirements.

Library Catalogs on the Web

Even when you can't retrieve books and documents online, a Web service like LIBWEB can still make short work of library searches in your hometown or anywhere. You can't actually take out books yet, but you can:

▶ Create a bibliography for school or work.

▶ Find out what's current in any field.

▶ Find out who wrote what, when, and who published it.

▶ Find out which branch of your public library has a particular book and whether anyone has checked it out.

Searching a library's Web catalog is easier than searching the entire Web, because you're searching one place for a special kind of thing: a book. Therefore, the actual search can ask you for some standard features of a book, such as the author, title, or subject.

Digital Libraries

The first purely online publishing ventures on the Internet involved the re-publication of the textual versions of out-of-print, public domain books. Back in 1971, Project Gutenberg grew out of strange circumstances and a brainstorm by a gentleman named Michael Hart. Since 1971, the project's purpose has been to publish online versions of classic books in their original languages, including works by Herman Melville, Edith Wharton, Anton Chekhov, Agatha Christie, and Omar Khayyam. Mr. Hart has made more than 2,600 classics available and adds to them every month, with the help of volunteer transcribers and proofreaders. Many of these texts are finding their way into new formats suitable for use with a portable reading device or Palm-compatible handheld (see Chapter 18 for more about this new development).

With a focus on digitally publishing classical texts for students and scholars, Project Perseus at Tufts publishes the texts of Homer, Cicero, Plato, and other classical philosophers and playwrights (www.perseus.tufts.edu). Project Perseus (see Figure 9-8) aims to make the classics much more accessible by integrating maps, definitions, images, and commentaries into the texts. Available in the original classical languages and in English, these texts are searchable and annotated. Project Perseus uses hypertext to explain all the words and references that have confused students for centuries. With a resource like this, students don't have a good excuse any longer for not knowing what's going on in the classics!

Note

TechWeb's Technology News reports that the sales of electronically distributed books will become about 10 percent of the book market in the year 2005. Such books will be available via handheld computers (like today's Palms and PocketPCs) and over the Web. (Source: www.techweb.com, Technology News, June 1, 2000).

Cross-Reference

You can read the story of Project Gutenberg and find out how to volunteer for the ongoing project at promo.net/pg/.

Cross-Reference

Chapter 4 profiles the Encyclopedia Mythica, an ideal supplement to the original, heavily annotated texts available through Project Perseus.

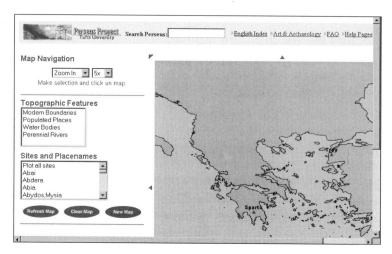

Figure 9-8. Homer's *Odyssey* comes alive when students can see where things happened, look up strange words, and get information about all those gods mentioned along the way.

Other libraries and archives aim to make older documents available in their original form, in order to preserve every bit of information available on an aging piece of paper and to enable more people to have the experience of combing through an archive. The University of Michigan's Making of America (MOA) digital archive, for example, currently holds more than 600,000 individually scanned pages of nineteenth-century American magazines and books. Access to original documents can bring the excitement of discovery to students and history buffs who otherwise lack access to archives. What a great way to grab the imagination of kids, and perhaps a few adults, who find the Civil War boring!

Find It Online

The Smithsonian Institution has created a long list of public libraries that are digitizing their rare holdings and making them available on the Web (`www.sil.si.edu/ SILPublications/ Online-Exhibitions`).

Major libraries like the Library of Congress are beginning to create digital versions of their holdings. Best known is the LOC's American Memory project (`memory.loc.gov`), a growing collection of more than 70 online exhibitions that depict daily life in American history. To assemble the collections, the LOC has digitized original sounds, motion pictures, photographs, and original documents to create the experience of a specific moment in the past.

Where to Go from Here

The Web's not much good if you can't find what you need.
This chapter provides some tips for doing just that by identifying the strengths of a few search engines and the value of con-
sulting a specialized service when you need deep, reliable, or
authoritative information.

▶ Chapter 8 guides you through AOL Search, a comprehensive, general-purpose search service. Make sure to
start your searches here, especially in the directory of
Web sites.

▶ For help finding mailing lists, see Chapter 14.

▶ For help finding newsgroup postings, see Chapter 15.

▶ For help finding files to download via FTP, an Internet
tool for downloading files, see Chapter 16.

Chapter 10
You've Got Mail: What to Do
with the E-mail You Receive

Chapter 11
Sending Mail

Chapter 12
Live Communication: From Instant Messages to
Internet Chats

Chapter 13
Joining Focused Communities: Mailing Lists

Chapter 14
Global Bulletin Boards: Newsgroups

Chapter 10

You've Got Mail: Handling the E-Mail You Receive

IN THIS CHAPTER

E-mail addresses and what you need to know about them

Reading and responding to AOL Mail

Downloading files attached to messages

Storing messages in your Filing Cabinet

Getting AOL Mail on the Web

Using AOL Mail on your PDA

What to do about unwanted e-mail

Electronic mail, or e-mail, or just plain mail directly supports everyday dealings between you and your colleagues, family, friends, and, well, anyone you have cause to communicate with. The most obvious advantages of electronic mail over paper letters are speed, cost, and convenience. An e-mail message gets to its destination in seconds, so that message meant for someone in Australia won't take significantly longer than a message meant for the guy next door. The two messages cost the same — practically nothing. As for convenience, you can send the same message to many people at the same time; you can search old mail for specific information (in seconds), and you can even *unsend* messages, at least your messages to other people on AOL, something you certainly can't do with old-fashioned letters.

This chapter looks at *getting* mail (which is easy) and managing messages (which AOL *makes* easy). The next chapter is all about sending messages, which is also fun because you can use signatures, smileys, embellishments, and wit to write messages that get the right kind of attention.

A Word about E-Mail Addresses

In order to receive mail, you must make sure that people know your e-mail address. To other AOL members, your e-mail address is just your screen name. If the person sending you a message is another AOL member, that person can just type your screen name into the Send To box in AOL's Write Mail window (shown in Figure 11-1 in the next chapter). Non-AOL members can also send you e-mail. They just have to add a bit of information to your screen name to make sure that you get the message: the *at* symbol, **@,** plus **aol.com**. See Figure 10-1.

Note

On AOL, your screen name is your e-mail address. All screen names set up under a master screen name (the screen name of the person paying the bills) receive their own mail and have their own password-protected mailboxes. Each AOL account can have as many as seven screen names.

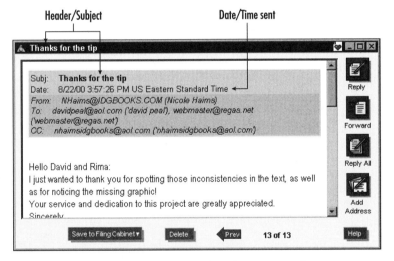

Header/Subject   Date/Time sent

Figure 10-1. This simple message was sent from the Internet, so the message includes @aol.com in the address.

You'll see e-mail addresses in many contexts and use them in many ways. An e-mail address identifies both a person and the organization, or computer *domain*, through which that person accesses the Internet. Take this made-up example: `milesdavis20000@aol.com`.

- ▶ milesdavis20000 is the person who sent the message — at any rate, it's the only way you can identify a real person when you're online.

- ▶ aol.com is the *domain* part of an e-mail address. It tells you, if you're interested, something about how the sender connects to the Internet (through AOL, in this case).

The parts of a domain proceed, roughly, from name of organization (AOL) to type of organization (COM): AOL is a company and interactive services provider (and much more, of course), and AOL is a *commercial* domain. Each part of a domain name is separated by a period (the famous dot). The most general part of the name, on the right, can have two levels, as in co.uk (a company in the United Kingdom) or ky.us (the State of Kentucky in the United States). Note that the major global domains — .edu, .com, .net, .mil, and .org — have three letters. National domains have two letters — .jp stands for Japan, .au for Australia, and .ru for Russia.

Table 10-1. *Common Domains and What They Mean*

Domain	Type of Organization	Example
.com	Commercial organization	well.com (The Well is a pioneer, San Francisco Bay Area access provider that Salon.com now owns.)
.edu	Educational organization in the U.S.	msu.edu (Michigan State University)
.mil	Branch of the U.S. military	js.pentagon.mil (the Pentagon's Joint Staff)
.net	A multipurpose domain (formerly network related)	fyi.net (a friend of mine's ISP in Pittsburgh)

Domain	Type of Organization	Example
.org	Non-profit organization in any country	pbs.org (Public Broadcasting Service in North America provides educational and entertainment television programming through local and national fund-raising

Finding Out Someone's E-Mail Address

How do you find e-mail addresses for people to whom you want to send e-mail?

- ▶ Ask them.
- ▶ Save e-mail from them.
- ▶ Use AOL Keyword: **People Directory**.
- ▶ Look them up in the e-mail finder at AOL Keyword: **AOL Search**, or use one of the other address-finding services available at AOL Keyword: **Mail Center**. Also try AOL Keyword **Email Finder**.

Getting E-Mail Help

E-mail seems so simple. Why would you ever need help? Because you can do so much with e-mail, from working with diverse types of attachments to taking part in mailing lists. Any time you use AOL's e-mail services, click Help for ideas and tips.

- ▶ While writing a message, click the Help button in the bottom right-hand corner for how-to procedures on approximately 50 basic tasks.
- ▶ AOL Keyword: **Mail Center**, shown in Figure 10-2, offers how-to help, useful links to mail-related destinations online, and direct access to AOL's mail tools and services.

Cross-Reference

Chapter 8 has a section on AOL Search's e-mail service.

10

You've Got Mail: Handling the E-Mail You Receive

Figure 10-2. Find out how many things you can do with simple electronic mail at AOL's Mail Center (AOL Keyword: **Mail Center**).

Doing Mail on AOL

The first thing millions of people do on AOL each day is read their mail. AOL's You've Got Mail icon and the famous voice telling you that "You've Got Mail" were already imprinted in many minds before Meg Ryan and Tom Hanks made a movie on electronic romance.

E-mail messages, like letters, are delivered in a mailbox. How do you get to your AOL mailbox? Here are three ways:

▶ Click the You've Got Mail icon on AOL's Welcome screen (see Figure 10-3).

▶ Click the Read icon on the AOL 6.0 toolbar.

▶ Use the keyboard shortcut Ctrl+R.

Your Online Mailbox appears onscreen (see Figure 10-4).

However you retrieve your mail from your Online Mailbox, up comes an electronic mailbox like the one shown in Figure 10-4.

If the You've Got Mail icon on the Welcome screen shows a raised flag, then you've got mail. You'll see the raised flag even if you have three-week old mail that you have "kept as new," explained later in this chapter.

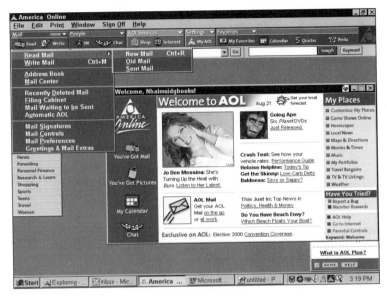

Figure 10-3. You can read your mail by clicking the You've Got Mail icon on the Welcome screen; clicking Read on the toolbar; using Ctrl+R; or by selecting Mail⇨ Read Mail⇨New Mail.

Messages more than 7 days old

Messages I've sent in the last 30 days

Click to sort

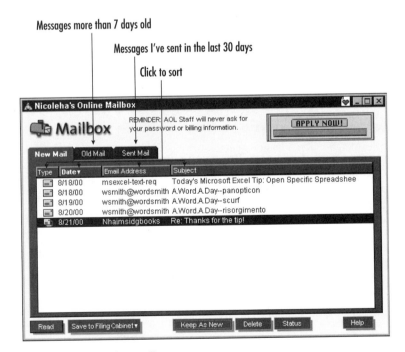

Figure 10-4. My Online Mailbox.

Definition

New mail consists of both messages you have never read and messages you have read but have decided to "keep as new," as explained later in this chapter.

10

You've Got Mail: Handling the E-Mail You Receive

Note

The New Mail list holds messages for up to 28 days, the Old Mail list for up to seven days. Both lists are being maintained on AOL's computers. After a message has been automatically removed from the New Mail list, it's gone forever.

Note

Messages stay in your Old Mail list for up to seven days. To adjust the number of days, choose Settings⇨Preferences⇨ Mail and click the up and down arrows to adjust the number of days you want your messages stored. You can also go to Mail⇨Mail Preferences

Your Online Mailbox has three tabs. Click a tab to see the three related (and similarly structured) mailboxes in your Online Mailbox: New Mail, Old Mail, and Sent Mail. Here's how they work:

▶ **New Mail:** This mailbox contains messages you have either not read or have decided to keep as new messages. Keeping a message is one way of temporarily saving that message in your New mailbox, perhaps as a reminder of something you need to do, or a response that is owed to the person who sent it to you. To keep a message as new, select it and click the Keep as New button. You can find out about saving messages permanently in "Using and Managing Your Filing Cabinet" later in this chapter.

▶ **Old Mail:** Here, you find the messages you have read but haven't kept as new. Messages stay here for only a few days — up to a week. Don't worry though. Any message you've read and neglected to keep as new is kept on your hard drive in your Personal Filing Cabinet. See "Using and Managing Your Filing Cabinet" later in this chapter to find out about setting these preferences.

▶ **Sent Mail:** This mailbox keeps copies of the messages you sent in the past 28 days.

Sizing Up Your Messages Before Reading Them

When you open your mailbox, you can see information about your messages. Each message is on its own line. By learning to size up messages before you read them, you can spot messages from friends, as well as unsolicited mail that you want to delete right away.

Your Online Mailbox categorizes mail into the following topics:

▶ **Type:** Indicates in picture form whether any files are attached to the e-mail and explains what type of file the attachment is (see Figure 10-5).

- If the picture in the far left of Online Mailbox looks like an envelope, you have a message with no file attachments.

- If you see what looks like a computer disk fastened to the back of the letter, a file is attached to the message. Using attachments is easy; how-to procedures are provided later in this chapter for handling attachments.

- If you see a letter icon with a check through it, you've already read the message. Unless you select this message and click the Keep as New button, the message is transferred from the New list to the Old list when you close the mailbox window.

- If you see a small square in the corner of the letter icon, the message contains an inserted picture. Only AOL members can insert and receive messages with pictures.

- A blue message icon signifies Official AOL Mail, like the message you receive when you join AOL. All important messages directly from AOL to you have this official indicator.

▶ **Date:** Indicates the date that your Online Mailbox received the message. Open the message to find out the exact time when the message was sent.

▶ **E-mail Address:** Indicates the sender's e-mail address. This information appears as a screen name or Internet e-mail address. Mailing lists that you receive may come from something called LISTSERV, a piece of software that automatically distributes mail to the tens or thousands of people on the list. See Chapter 13 for more about mailing lists. Long e-mail addresses are chopped off at about 16 characters.

▶ **Subject:** The information that takes up the most space is devoted to the message's subject, as typed in by the person who sent the message. Some subjects are generated by mailing-list software and have subjects like Finance - Internet Daily @ 10/10/2001.

In Figure 10-5, you see how all this information looks in your mailbox. With a little practice, you can tell at a glance, for any message, when you got it, who sent it, what it's about, and whether there is a file attached or inserted.

Feature

You can now sort your mail by any of the categories listed in your Online Mailbox. To sort by date (either beginning with the most recent or the oldest mail you've received), file type, sender, or subject, just click the appropriate column head.

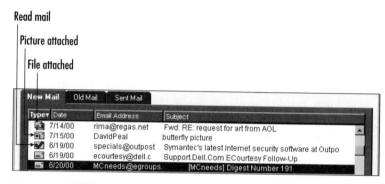

Figure 10-5. All the information available for every message.

Note

If you want to see a message that you've read and that no longer appears in your Online Mailbox, you can access the message online or offline in your Filing Cabinet. "Using and Managing Your Filing Cabinet" later in this chapter contains instructions for using this feature.

Note

You can also get to My Preferences by using AOL Keyword: **Preferences**. Then click Mail Preferences.

Reading Your Mail

To open a message, either double-click it in the mailbox or select the message and click the Read button at the bottom of your mailbox.

When you open any message in your mailbox, the first thing you see is the *message header,* which provides even more information than what you scanned before opening the message (and probably more than you want or need to know). You'll also see the names and addresses of other people who got the message (that is, who received a courtesy copy, or CC).

AOL's Mail Preferences (available at Mail⇨Mail Preferences⇨ Mail) enable you to make addresses appear as hyperlinks, so you can reply to an address by merely clicking it.

You're likely to receive e-mail that contains blue underlined *links,* also called *hyperlinks*. In a header, a link launches a Write Mail window in which you can write a message to the linked e-mail address. In the message body, a link takes you either to AOL content (if the link is in a channel e-mail newsletter, for example) or to the Web. For example, the Scout Report, a weekly review of new Internet sites mentioned in Chapter 13, links you directly to the sites reviewed in the report. Pass your mouse over a link to see the actual Web address (URL).

Managing Your Mail

The idea of managing your mail may sound complicated, but all that's involved is deciding what to do with messages that come your way. You can do any or all of the following to any message you receive:

▶ Reply to the person sending the message

▶ Reply to the sender *and* to all the other people who received the message

▶ Forward the message and any file attachment to someone else or several other people

▶ Move the message to your Filing Cabinet, where you now have the option of storing it in named folders

▶ Save the message as a text file for use in other programs, such as a word processor

▶ Delete the message

Replying to a Message

E-mail messages have a conversational feel; some people consider messages closer to talking than writing. Even if you lavish care on your messages, they can still form part of larger conversations with another person or a number of people, depending on how you reply to a message. To start or sustain a conversation, follow these simple steps:

1. With a message displayed, decide if you want to quote the original message, and what you want to reply to.

   • To quote part of the message, use your mouse to select the part of the text that you want to include in your reply, and click the Reply button.

   • If you'd rather not quote anything, leave all the text unselected. In this case, the only indication that you are replying lies in the Subject line, which will have *Re:* and the same Subject line that the sender of the original message used.

2. Decide who to reply to:

   • To reply to a message someone sent just to you, click the Reply button in the upper-right hand corner of the Read Mail window.

Feature

AOL mail you receive now supports HTML. This means that you can easily go back and forth between your Online Mailbox and the Net when you receive links to Web sites in your mail messages.

Caution

Unsolicited mail can contain links considered unsuitable for children. Use AOL Keyword: **Mail Controls** (Chapter 4) to restrict the ability of strangers to send mail to a child's mailbox. Report such mail to screen name TOSEmail1. Use AOL Keyword: **Notify AOL**.

Tip

When you read your mail, you can use your keyboard to simplify tasks. With a message open, the right and left arrow keys take you to the next and previous messages, respectively, and the Delete key does what you'd expect. After opening the first of your new messages, simply use the Delete and right arrow keys to work through your messages.

With a message displayed, you can add the sender's e-mail address or screen name to your Address Book. Just click the Add Address button, edit the Address Book entry for that person, and click OK. Chapter 11 has all the details.

To chat with a buddy who sent you mail, open the e-mail message and open your Buddy List (AOL Keyword: **Buddyview**). A list of Mail Contacts Online appears at the top of your Buddy List. If the person who sent the message *is* online, you'll see his or her screen name. Double-click it to send an instant message and have a live electronic conversation. See Chapter 3 for more about Buddy Lists and Chapter 12 for more about Mail Contacts Online.

Quoting means to include part of a message in your reply as context for your response.

- If you were one of many recipients of the message, as in an informal mailing list for your bowling team, click the Reply All button instead of Reply.

In either case, if you first selected some text, it appears to the right of a vertical blue bar in your Write Mail window, as shown in Figure 10-6.

3. Compose your message in any fashion you see fit. Some people use fancy formatting while others avoid it. The point to remember is that if any of the recipients of your message are not on AOL, they probably won't be able to see the formatting effects.

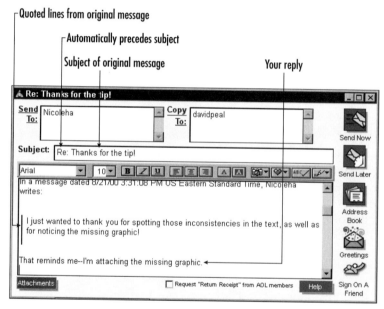

Figure 10-6. A quoted reply, with a follow-up message.

4. When you reply to a message, you usually want to leave the Subject line alone. Doing nothing means the original Subject line (preceded by *Re:*) is picked up automatically.

Keeping the *Re:* indicates that your message is a reply. In brackets or parentheses you can add a word or two indicating the content of your reply.

```
Re: Squash tomorrow AM? [you bet]
```

5. All done? Click Send Now.

Forwarding a Message

Forwarding a message means to pass the message on to someone who was neither a direct nor an indirect recipient. Unlike replying, you'll have to find the new recipient's address yourself or use the AOL Address Book. To forward a message, first display it and then:

1. Select nothing if you want to forward the entire message.

   Select part of the message to just highlight that part to someone else. The original message is also sent in its entirety.

2. Click Forward. Your new message picks up the original message's Subject line, preceded by *Fwd:* and a space. Edit the Subject line as you see fit. In the body of the message, you see nothing if you forward the entire message (yes, you read that right), or just a few words if that's all you want to forward. In either case, the entire message is forwarded.

3. Add some words of your own, if you wish, to provide context for the entire forwarded message or the message fragment. Click Send Now.

Saving a Message as a Text File

To save a message, display it and then:

1. Select File⇨Save As.
2. Give the message a name and find a folder in which to keep it. If the message has an embedded Web link, the message is saved as HTML.
3. Click Save.

   You can now retrieve the saved message at any time while on AOL by choosing File⇨Open and navigating to the place where you saved the message.

Printing Messages

Whether or not you have a message open, you can print it as long as it's selected in your AOL mailbox. To print from your mailbox, you must be online. From your Filing Cabinet, you can print at any time, online or off. Here's how:

Cross-Reference

The next chapter explains what Send Later is all about.

Note

You can't select discontinuous parts of a message.

Tip

Don't embarrass yourself by forwarding part of a long message and assuming that only the selected part will be sent.

Tip

Mailing lists often include rich information about the list's topic. Meaty messages can be saved as separate text files and dropped into a handy folder in your Filing Cabinet for quick reference. Chapter 12 is devoted to mailing lists.

10

You've Got Mail: Handling the E-Mail You Receive

Feature

AOL's new Print menu includes Print Central and Print Supplies, as well as Print. Print Central, a Web site created by HP, has ideas for projects you can carry out with an inkjet printer. Print Supplies takes you to an online store where you can buy equipment for your printer, including cartridges and special papers.

Tip

Once upon a time, If you deleted a message before you read it, the message was history. In AOL 6.0 (and 5.0), you can restore messages for a day or so after deleting them. From the AOL toolbar, select Mail⇨Recently Deleted Mail. From the list of deleted messages, select the one to retrieve and click the Keep as New button. Click Read first if you want to verify that you've found the right message. The next time you open your Online Mailbox, look for your salvaged messages around the original sending date.

1. Select the message (or make sure it's open).
2. Select Print⇨Print or use the keyboard shortcut, Control+P. Set any printer options if you want (number of copies, which page to print, and so on), and print the document.

Deleting Messages

To delete a message, display it in any of your mailboxes (New, Old, or Sent), and click Delete. You can shift-click to select many messages in a row and delete them all at once. Or, press the Control key as you click to select messages scattered all over the place. Deleting messages is a good way to prevent your mailbox from becoming unmanageable.

Got Files?

What's a *file attachment*? A file attachment is either a document, picture, or sound that is sent to you along with the message you received. It is called "attachment" because it is sent together with the e-mail, much like a regular letter with a check or a snapshot paper-clipped to it.

If a picture of the computer disk clipped to a letter appears under the Type heading in your mailbox, the e-mail contains both a message to read and a file to download from AOL to your computer. When you open a message with an attached file, the header shows you

▶ The name of the attached file, including the all-important file extension, which tells you what program you'll need to use the file.

▶ The size of the file.

▶ The approximate time to download the file (DL), given your connection type and modem speed. Figure 10-7 shows how this information appears.

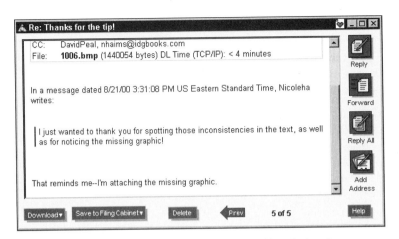

Figure 10-7. You've got a file to download. While most files take less than a minute to download, this file is 1,440,054 bytes and will take less than 4 minutes (< 4 minutes) to download (DL).

Downloading Attached Files

The longer you're on AOL the higher the likelihood that someone you know will send you a file attachment. What do you do when that day comes? AOL makes downloading attached files easy. Just follow these steps:

1. With the message displayed, click Download. From the drop-down menu that automatically comes up (new in AOL 6.0), choose Download Now.

   A standard AOL window comes up warning you about the dangers of downloading files from unknown sources. When you're done reading it, click Yes to continue the download.

   If you have downloaded the file before (which can happen for many reasons), a message asks whether you want to do so again. If you're unsure that you still have the file or ever saw it, use Download Manager to look for the file. Go to File⇨Download Manager, and click the Show Files Downloaded button. Look for the file using Ctrl+F.

   • If you have in fact downloaded the file, select it and click Locate to find out where it is and whether it is still available.

   • If you haven't downloaded the file, download it from the open message.

Tip

When you clean up your Online Mailbox and decide which messages to delete, sort your messages (click the mailbox header, such as Type or Subject) to identify messages you clearly don't want any longer.

10

You've Got Mail: Handling the E-Mail You Receive

Caution

Don't download files if you don't know who sent them. Become familiar with the virus information at AOL Keyword: **Virus**. Even DOC (Word) files can contain a Macro virus, which can cause significant havoc.

Tip

Keeping downloaded files in a convenient folder is the best way to avoid losing them. You can use Download Manager to change the default folder into which files are downloaded. From the Download Manager, click Download Preferences. At the bottom of the preferences window, look for a box in which you can specify a new default download folder.

Feature

After downloading a file, AOL 6.0 gives you the option of going directly to the folder where it was downloaded and highlights it. Double-click to use the file right away!

Cross-Reference

Which sound, image, or video player opens when you double-click a downloaded file? It depends entirely on file associations — what program opens with what file type. Chapter 15 discusses file associations in more detail.

2. Confirm where you want to save the file and what you want to call it.

3. Retrieve the file and use it as you wish.

Using Downloaded Files

Anything can be attached to a message: a picture (JPG or GIF), a word-processor document (DOC, TXT), a compressed file (several files packaged up in one file), software, or something else.

▶ Image and sound files are pretty easy to handle. Usually, AOL displays its built-in image viewer to display an image that you've downloaded. AOL displays a simple media player when you're down-loading various standard sound files.

▶ You can easily open DOC and TXT (text) files in a word processor. Text files can be opened from within AOL at File⇨Open.

▶ You'll frequently see zipped files attached to messages; these files are reduced in size and zipped up into a single file for speedy downloading. First download the file, as normal.

▶ WinZip can often handle oddball formats like MIM. (MIM is an old Internet standard for digitizing binary files in order to transmit them quickly as text over networks.) WinZip can also handle UU encoded files (binary files converted into text and used in newsgroups) and BinHex (Mac) files. Chapter 16 tells you how to get WinZip 8.

Using and Managing Your Filing Cabinet

Your Filing Cabinet is the storage space on your hard drive where all your messages can be automatically stored — the ones you've read, the ones you've sent, and the ones you've written but not yet sent — for as long as you want. You can even save messages in individual folders for convenient retrieval (see Figure 10-8). But first you have to set up your Filing Cabinet.

You can also set up your Filing Cabinet to keep track of downloaded files and the newsgroup postings you've downloaded using Automatic AOL, described in the next section. Your FC is always available, online or offline, at Mail⇨Filing Cabinet.

NEW   **Feature**

After you download a zipped file, AOL 6.0 can be set either to unzip it right away or to wait until you sign off. You can also delete zipped files after their files are extracted. To set these preferences, go to File⇨ ownload Manager and then click Download Preferences.

10

You've Got Mail: Handling
the E-Mail You Receive

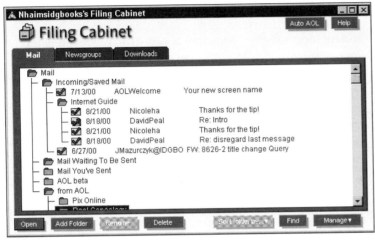

Figure 10-8. Your Filing Cabinet keeps all your messages, files, and postings on your hard drive.

Can You Have Too Many Filing Cabinets?

In a nutshell, yes. AOL keeps your new, saved, and sent mail for a month or so and makes the mail available through any copy of AOL you use with the same screen name. So, if you delete mail from your Online Mailbox, the mail disappears from every copy of AOL that you use. Your Filing Cabinet saves mail on the hard drive of the computer you used to log on to AOL, though, so you have as many Filing Cabinets as you have PCs. As a result, your trail of messages can easily spread across several Filing Cabinets, making it difficult to retrieve a specific message.

To get around the problem, you *could* copy your Filing Cabinet file from one copy of AOL to another. That file has the same name as your screen name, and it is located in your America Online 6.0/Organize folder. However, because

(Continued)

Note

If you log on to AOL as a guest your old mail isn't retrievable and you can't save mail to your Filing Cabinet.

Caution

Over several months, your Filing Cabinet can become bloated with copies of mailing list messages, online digests, or other messages that you've downloaded from newsgroups. A big FC can seriously increase the time your AOL software takes to open every day. To manage your FC, use your preferences to limit the FC's size and compact your FC from time to time. In your FC, choose Manage FC⇨Compact FC.

(Continued)

the AOL software has no way of merging two different file cabinets, you lose (overwrite) the Filing Cabinet in the AOL copy to which you copy the file. If you do copy your FC file, make sure to rename the file being copied over and consider that your different FCs are likely to diverge before long. Further, you cannot copy the read or deleted messages from a PDA, or any other device to a copy of AOL on a desktop PC.

The practical solution is to have a main copy of AOL and avoid deleting worthwhile mail on PDAs or other devices. Then, add messages manually to the Filing Cabinet on your main copy of AOL before AOL's host computer deletes them automatically.

▶ To save all your messages in your FC, you need to adjust your preferences (Settings⇨Preferences⇨Filing Cabinet). Figure 10-9 shows where you indicate your preference to keep mail in your FC. Make sure a check appears in the boxes, and click OK. You can also tell the AOL software how much space on your hard drive you want your FC to take up as well as how frequently your FC makes a back-up copy of itself.

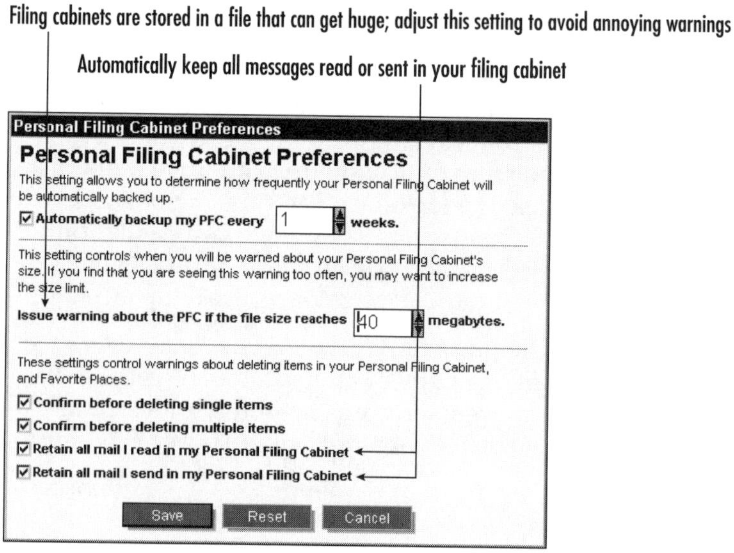

Filing cabinets are stored in a file that can get huge; adjust this setting to avoid annoying warnings

Automatically keep all messages read or sent in your filing cabinet

Personal Filing Cabinet Preferences

Personal Filing Cabinet Preferences

This setting allows you to determine how frequently your Personal Filing Cabinet will be automatically backed up.

☑ **Automatically backup my PFC every** `1` **weeks.**

This setting controls when you will be warned about your Personal Filing Cabinet's size. If you find that you are seeing this warning too often, you may want to increase the size limit.

Issue warning about the PFC if the file size reaches `40` **megabytes.**

These settings control warnings about deleting items in your Personal Filing Cabinet, and Favorite Places.

☑ **Confirm before deleting single items**
☑ **Confirm before deleting multiple items**
☑ **Retain all mail I read in my Personal Filing Cabinet** ◄
☑ **Retain all mail I send in my Personal Filing Cabinet** ◄

[Save]   [Reset]   [Cancel]

Figure 10-9. Your Filing Cabinet preferences.

When you read a message stored in your FC, it comes up in the same Read Mail window that you use for your daily mail. From this window, all the buttons work, so you can reply, delete, or forward a message or add the sender's address to your Address Book.

Feature

You can now create folders to hold messages from the same person, on the same subject, relating to the same project, and so on. Consider creating folders for family matters or for specific mailing lists. In your Filing Cabinet, open the folder and click Add Folder. Give the folder a name. You can drag the folder to a new position, or folder, and drag messages into it.

▶ To delete one or more messages, select them and click Delete. You can Shift-click or Ctrl-click to select groups of messages.

▶ To find a message tucked away in some obscure corner of your FC, open the folder (Incoming/Saved or Mail You've Sent), click Find, or press Ctrl+F. Bear in mind that Ctrl+F looks only through message headers. FC's Find button is slightly more complex: It gives you the ability to search the content of messages, as well as their headers. Searching content (message bodies) can be quite slow but retrieves information you specify.

▶ You can now create a subfolder in any Filing Cabinet folder and a subfolder within any subfolder. Then, sort your messages and drag messages into the folder.

▶ To sort a folder, simply select the folder and click the Sort Folder By button. Then, select how you want to sort the folders.

Feature

You can sort Filing Cabinet folders as well as your mailbox. Sorting folders helps you see all the messages from the same person or on the same subject.

Moving Messages to Your Filing Cabinet

To avoid having too many files in your FC (which happens when you store them automatically) and to make active use of the new folders feature, consider moving messages one at a time, manually, from your Online Mailbox to your FC. Saving messages manually keeps you from saving every mailing list digest and every piece of unsolicited e-mail, as happens when you have messages saved automatically in your FC.

To move an individual mail message to your FC, you can start in two places.

▶ From your Online Mailbox, you can select the messages you want to put in your FC. Then, click the Save To FC button at the bottom of the window and select an option.

▶ From inside a mail message, click the Save To FC button and make a choice.

In either case, the menu that appears when you click the Save To FC button is straightforward, offering these choices:

▶ **Mail.** Sends the message(s) to the top-level Mail folder of your Filing Cabinet. These extra special messages are visible at the same level as the major mail folders.

▶ **Incoming/Saved Mail.** Sends a selected or open message to the folder that contains the mail you receive.

▶ **Mail You've Sent.** Sends a selected or open message to the Mail You've Sent folder, which is designated for the messages you've sent.

▶ **Create Folder.** If you want to save selected mail in a new folder, choose this item. A small dialog box appears where you type the name of the new folder. In the future, you can save messages manually in your new folder.

Getting Your Mail Automatically

Automatic AOL lets you download e-mail messages, as well as message board and newsgroup postings, either on-demand or on a set schedule. If you do the downloading automatically, AOL automatically signs on for you, fetches messages, and signs off. You can find automatically retrieved messages in your Filing Cabinet, which is discussed in the previous section.

Here's how:

1. Choose Mail⇨Automatic AOL (Figure 10-10).

    Use the check boxes on the right side to tell AOL what to download. You can check as many as you like.

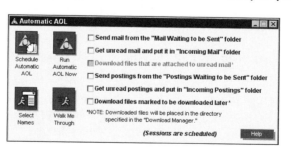

Figure 10-10. Tell AOL to retrieve all sorts of messages automatically for offline reading.

Tip

Saving manually provides you with useful long-term mail archives but requires daily vigilance. If you forget to save your sent or incoming messages, AOL automatically deletes them after a specified amount of time. Make sure to save your messages in the proper folder (Incoming/Saved versus Sent); otherwise, you'll be unable to retrieve them later.

Note

The Save To FC menu has separator lines. Any new folders you manually add to your FC appear between these lines in alphabetical order.

2. Indicate which screen names will receive the messages and files. Click the Select Names button and put a check by the screen name or names and the corresponding passwords, so AOL can sign on automatically.

3. Tell AOL when to download messages for the screen names selected in Step 2. Click the Schedule Automatic AOL button to open the scheduling window, where you:

   • Check Enable Scheduler.

   • Set the frequency for message pick-ups. You can have your mail downloaded from every half-hour to every day.

   • Specify the days when you want all this to happen: every day or specific days. You have less flexibility in setting a time when the downloading is to take place. Alas, this is specified for you down to the minute.

4. Close the Automatic AOL window to set your new schedule.

5. You can read your saved mail by opening your Filing Cabinet from Mail⇨Filing Cabinet.

If you don't like the idea of automatically signing on or you simply don't need the regular pick-ups, just run Automatic AOL whenever you need it. Select Mail⇨ Automatic AOL. From the Automatic AOL window, click the Run Automatic AOL Now button.

AOL Anywhere: New Ways To Do Mail

For the next few years, most people will continue doing AOL mail at a PC or laptop, signed onto AOL and hooked into a phone line and electrical outlet. New ways of doing mail point to a different future, in which e-mail is more convenient because it's available on smaller devices that require fewer cables and wires.

The AOL Anywhere service lets members have access to AOL whenever and wherever they have an Internet connection. You can now use high-speed connections, such as DSL, cable, or satellite, PDAs, such as Palms, as well as to get to AOL anytime, anywhere.

   ▶ AOL Mail on the Web gives you access to your AOL mail when you're using a browser but aren't signed on to AOL or even using the AOL software.

   ▶ AOL Mail for PDAs lets you get your AOL mail using handheld computers, such as a Palm or Pocket PC.

   ▶ A slew of newer mail-reading gadgets can't be documented here, because they're either brand new or still in development. As this book was being written, AOLTV launched; if you subscribe to this new service (described in Chapter 17), you can do your e-mail while watching *The Simpsons*. Wireless mail access (using a cell phone and wireless data Internet access) is just getting off the ground. A bevy of devices from Gateway will greatly simplify e-mail access around the house, making mail management easier and more fun than taking out the garbage.

AOL Mail on the Web

AOL Mail on the Web is just like the AOL Mail described so far in this chapter, with one difference: you don't need the AOL software. The only requirement is that the computer you're using have Netscape Navigator 3.02 or higher or Microsoft Internet Explorer (MSIE) 3.0 or higher. Any operating system will do: Windows NT/2000, Windows 95/98/ME, Mac OS 9/X, Unix, or even Linux. Here's what to do:

1. Using a computer, establish a network connection or Internet Service Provider connection.

2. Open the browser.

3. Go to aolmail.aol.com.

4. Type your screen name and password in the boxes provided. Doing so is safe — essentially, you're doing what you normally do when you log on to AOL — only you're doing it from the Web.

Figure 10-11 shows AOL Mail on the Web. Notice the similarities to your ordinary Online Mailbox. Everything in the New Mail, Old Mail, and Sent Mail tabs is identical to the mailbox you use in AOL.

Write a new message

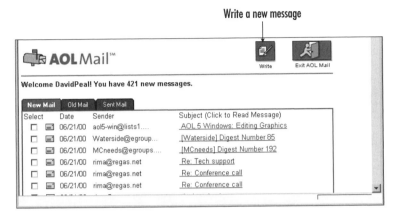

Figure 10-11. AOL Mail on the Web.

AOL Mail offers the features of regular AOL mail on the AOL service, but note some of the differences between mail on the AOL service and mail on the Web:

▶ AOL Mail on the Web may be slower than regular AOL mail because you're on the Web and subject to traffic jams, after all.

▶ Check boxes before each message give you the ability to select a group of messages that you want to Delete or Keep as New.

▶ New messages are linked (underlined and blue) and thus clickable: click once (instead of double-clicking, as in regular mail) to view a message. If a file is attached to a message, the file is also linked.

▶ With a message displayed, you can Reply and Forward, but you can't Send Later (for replies) or Download Later (for files).

▶ You can't yet quote selectively, but you can quote the entire original message by clicking the check box labeled Include Entire Original Text in Reply (right above the Reply button when you're reading a message).

▶ You can review an original message and selectively copy and paste (Ctrl+C and Ctrl+V). Use the Review Original Message button in the window where you're replying. You would do this to respond to specific portions of the original e-mail, point by point.

▶ Download Now, Close, Keep as New, and Delete are available at the top as well as bottom of the single Web page holding all your messages.

▶ Unlike AOL, everything on the Web takes place in a single browser window. You can, for example, use the Back button to return to the main New Mail list.

To write a new message, click the little Write button from the main AOL Mail window (see Figure 10-11). A window that looks like Figure 10–12 appears.

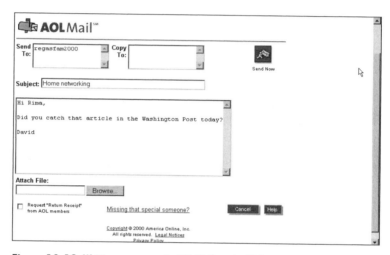

Figure 10-12. Writing a message in AOL Mail on the Web.

The message box is nearly identical in layout to AOL's Write Mail window, except you don't get Mail Extras, Send Later, your Address Book, and the formatting capabilities available for regular AOL Mail. You can, however, attach a file (if you have one on a floppy, say) and request a return receipt in a message to an AOL member.

To leave AOLMail, click the Exit AOL Mail button in the upper-right corner of the AOLMail window.

AOL Mail for Handhelds

AOL now lets you read, save, and send e-mail using the Palm handheld organizer, the world's most popular PDA (personal digital assistant), as well as Windows CE devices and Pocket PCs.

With this software and a portable modem, you can:

▶ Use your New, Old, and Sent mailboxes.
▶ Reply to and forward mail.
▶ Write and send messages, now or later.

Note

AOL Mail can be used with any Palm-compatible hand-held using PalmOS 3.0 or higher, including the HandSpring Visor. A version of AOL Mail is also available for handhelds based on Windows CE 2.1 or higher, including the new Pocket PC devices. PocketPC vendors include Hewlett-Packard, Casio, and Compaq.

▶ Use Automatic AOL.

▶ Keep a File Cabinet, similar to the Filing Cabinet you have for each copy of AOL on a PC. Unfortunately, File Cabinets are not currently synchronized with Filing Cabinets. Remember, however, that all messages in the New, Old, and Sent mailboxes are maintained on AOL's computers, hence available to PDAs and PCs. Delete a message from your mailboxes, however, and it won't be available any longer from any PC or PDA.

Using AOL Mail on a Palm Handheld

AOL Mail for the Palm (and compatibles) is as easy to use as AOL Mail on your desktop, and you'll find many familiar AOL elements on the tiny screen, including the look of the mailbox and the layout of individual messages.

To start AOL Mail on your Palm handheld, you first need to open your launcher by tapping on the House icon in the upper-left corner of the Palm's Graffitti writing area. If the file's been installed correctly, the familiar triangular AOL icon appears on the screen along with a group of other icons. Tap AOL Mail to run the application.

To sign on, you must have a modem for your Palm, and the modem must be plugged into a phone jack.

1. Open AOL Mail from the Palm desktop. AOL Mail is actually a series of mini applications available from the Sign On screen, including, currently, P Mailbox, File Cabinet, Instant Message, Buddy List, Write, and Auto AOL.

2. Tap the Sign On icon in the center of the AOL Mail display with your stylus.

   Notice that all your screen names have been downloaded to your Palm; these, too, are maintained on AOL's computers. Choose a screen name and enter the corresponding password. If you want to save the password so that you won't have to enter it again, tap the Store Password checkbox and enter your password.

   To edit your location (where you store your local access numbers), click Setup and follow the onscreen prompts.

Because you cannot import your PDA's File Cabinet into the Filing Cabinet on your main copy of AOL, you probably won't want to delete important messages from your Palm or PocketPC. Instead, read them on your desktop copy of AOL and save them in your Filing Cabinet.

This section is not comprehensive. It assumes you have already installed and set up AOL Mail on your Palm, using the procedures in Chapter 17 or at AOL Keyword: **PDA**, which is also the source for Macintosh and non-Palm procedures.

3. Tap the small Sign On button when you're ready to go. When you're signed on, the screen is identical, but Sign Off replaces Sign On.

After you're signed on, tap Mailbox. Your mail now downloads. Just as with your ordinary mail, you have three mailboxes: New, Old, and Sent, with identical meanings to those provided earlier in this chapter. To read a message, tap it and then tap Read. A scroll bar along the right lets you move up and down in the message. Tap gently to scroll.

Managing messages on a Palm means replying, forwarding, and deleting them, and moving them to your File Cabinet. When you reply, you get the standard Reply/Reply All choice. Clicking Save places a copy of any open (or selected) message in your Palm's File Cabinet, which resembles your PC's Filing Cabinet.

AOL Mail for the Palm's Write Mail window (available by tapping Write from the main Mail window after you sign on) is formatted like a memo pad, with To, CC, and Subject lines, plus dotted lines on which to write. Of course, you must be adept at using Graffiti (Palm's mode of writing) or have sufficient fine-motor control to use the onscreen keyboard in order to write either messages or Instant Messages. You can send e-mail now or later; go to the File Cabinet's Waiting tab to edit or send waiting messages.

You've Got Junk Mail

At home, I get so much junk mail on paper that I usually go through the day's mail at the garbage can, throwing away much more than I keep. That's an example of managing mail. Fortunately, you can stop junk e-mail on AOL easier than you can stop junk paper mail at home.

The swarms of unsolicited messages that find their way to subscribers' mailboxes plague every Internet Service Provider (ISP). Although AOL uses advanced technology and legal tactics to combat purveyors of unsolicited mail, you are likely to get unwanted mail from time to time. Such mail includes make-money-fast schemes, advertisements of adult Web sites, barely credible (when not laughable) business offers, and the occasional, incredibly annoying chain letter.

Note

With a Palm you can't download files, view inserted images, or embellish text. You can see your Buddy List (which is maintained on AOL's computers), but your screen name won't show up on others' Buddy Lists, so don't expect too many incoming instant messages.

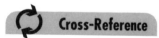
Cross-Reference

For more information about avoiding spam (unsolicited, bulk mail), see "Loathsome Lists and What to Do about Them" in Chapter 13.

Caution

AOL takes a dim view of members who abuse their accounts, the network's bandwidth, and everyone's time by sending unsolicited commercial e-mail. Such abuses can result in account termination.

Deleting unwanted messages without opening them is the best thing to do. Just in case you happen to open one of these messages:

- ▶ Forward any offensive message (as long as it has no file attached) to screen name: TOSEMail1.
- ▶ Forward e-mail with files attached to screen name: TOS Files.
- ▶ Forward unsolicited commercial e-mail to screen name: TOSspam.

Or, go to AOL Keyword: **Notify AOL** and follow the instructions for handling different sorts of online nuisance, and not just the mail-related ones.

Cross-Reference

Chapter 13, on mailing lists, concludes with a lengthier description of what to do about unwanted mail.

Where to Go from Here

E-mail can quickly become more of a daily essential than anything you do on the Internet. AOL already offers what many consider the easiest-to-use e-mail service in the business. AOL e-mail now comes to you in more ways, from desktop computers to AOLTV and wireless phones. With version 6.0, e-mail has improved in numerous ways, including sortable mailboxes, nameable Filing-Cabinet folders, and improved ways to handle file attachments.

- ▶ The next chapter looks at sending messages — styling them, using the new Address Book, following netiquette, adding signatures, and more.
- ▶ Chapter 13 is all about *mailing lists*, communities based on e-mail.
- ▶ E-mail is not going to replace the paper letter any time soon, so you'll be happy that you can now buy electronic postage stamps on the Internet. Go to AOL Keyword: **stamps.com** to find out how. These are digital stamps for your old-fashioned envelopes!

10

You've Got Mail: Handling the E-Mail You Receive

CHAPTER

11

SENDING MAIL

Chapter 11
Sending Mail

IN THIS CHAPTER

Determining to whom you want to send e-mail and what you want to say

Using your Address Book

Attaching a file

Formatting messages and inserting pictures

Signing off with a personal signature

Sending messages is an essential way of taking active part in the world of the Internet. In this chapter you'll find what you need to get started as quickly as possible. And I'll also show you the fun stuff — links, pictures, signatures, emoticons, and more.

Chapter 10 covers the easiest ways to send a message: replying to a message and forwarding to someone else, a message that someone sends you. To generate a message from scratch requires a shade more creativity, and is that much more fun to do.

To create a new message, start by clicking the toolbar's Write button. Up comes the Write Mail window, shown in Figure 11-1. Your basic message has three parts: the e-mail address or addresses of your recipient(s); the subject line, where you describe what's in the message; and the message itself.

Tip

You don't have to be signed on to AOL to write a message, only to send it. You can draft messages offline, and then click Send Later to store them. As soon as you're online, retrieve your message (Mail⇨Mail Waiting to be Sent) and send it.

Enter addresses of indirect recipients

Click to open Address Book

Enter topic of message

Enter addresses of direct recipients

Type message here

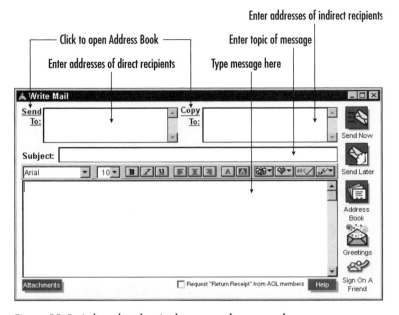

Figure 11-1. A clean slate: here's where you make your mark.

Who's the Message For?

Sending a message requires at least one piece of information — an e-mail address (though a message about nothing would not be much use, except on *Seinfeld,* of course). In the Send To box, enter an AOL screen name (without the *@aol.com* part). For friends not on AOL, a full Internet e-mail address is required (for example, friend@suchandsuch.com or mypal@thisandthat.net).

If you want to send your message to several people at once, you can easily do so. Whether the addresses are on AOL or the Internet, whether they're recipients (Send To) or indirect recipients (Copy To), simply separate their e-mail addresses by commas, or by pressing Enter. Don't worry if the addresses break in weird places. Maximizing your Write Mail window usually displays them properly. The following list breaks down the types of e-mail recipients that you can address in your messages:

▶ The direct recipient of your e-mail (the person whose e-mail address goes in the Send To box) is the person for whom your message is primarily intended (*John* in a *Dear John* letter, for example).

Feature

In the Send To box of a new e-mail message you can now start typing an address, and AOL 6.0 finishes it for you when it has enough letters to identify it uniquely as one of the addresses in your Address Book.

Cross-Reference

See "A Word about E-Mail Addresses" in Chapter 10 for the low-down about the specific components of an address.

Definition

When I say *direct reference,* I am referring to any people whose addresses go in the Send To box; these are the people you are writing the message to. In the Copy To box, type addresses of *indirect recipients,* people whom you want to see the message.

Caution

BCCs can be risky. If the direct recipient finds someone else was privy to an exchange, it can seem like a breach of confidentiality. BCCs do make sense in some circumstances, for instance when sending mail to a very large group of people. Having a gazillion names in the To: field isn't attractive or necessary, and you almost certainly do not want to share the address list with everyone on it.

Tip

You can also send BCCs to serveral people using this format: ((jd@mid.net, helen@io,net, kermit@ high.com)).

▶ A CC used to mean *carbon copy;* now it means *courtesy copy,* which is more accurate because sharing your e-mail with others is a courtesy and because one of the perks of e-mail is that it is paperless. The main recipient can see the screen names or e-mail addresses of anyone you CCd. To send someone a courtesy copy (CC) of your message (your boss, for example, if you're writing someone in another department or outside the company), place that person's e-mail address in the Copy To box. If you want to send a courtesy copy of the message to more than one person, make sure to separate the e-mail addresses with commas, or by pressing Enter after each address.

▶ A *BCC* is a blind courtesy copy, of which the main recipient is unaware. To send someone a blind courtesy copy (BCC) of your message, enclose each e-mail address in one or two sets of parentheses in the *Copy To* box (there is no special BCC box). For multiple BCCs, separate the enclosed addresses with commas, as in: (jd@mid.net), (helen@lo.net),(kermit@high.com). A good way to send mail to many recipients is to address the e-mail to yourself and BCC everyone else; the recipients won't be aware of each other's address or existence.

What's the Message About? (Subject Line)

You can give your mail the best possible chance of being read by letting the recipient know at a glance what the message is about. Using the Subject line, you describe what's in the message and can characterize the message's attitude as well. Refer to Figure 11-1.

Many people read the first paragraph or two of a message and then respond. Some people, like me, make the mistake of asking several questions in one message; as a rule much of my multi-subject messages never gets read. One subject per message can help ensure that the recipient doesn't overlook anything.

People get so much mail these days that unless your Subject line is clear, your recipients may delete it without bothering to open it. A short, punchy, communicative, and descriptive Subject line is likely to get positive attention.

Playing Nice: Mail Netiquette

In an e-mail message as in a phone call, you are communicating from a distance. In e-mail, however, you cannot hear the grain of someone's voice. E-mail is also much more drawn out — *asynchronous* is the formal term, meaning you can take as long as you want to respond to mail or not respond at all. Here are some suggestions to help you make the most of communicating by e-mail.

Keep Your Voice Down

Less evident than several years ago, some message writers still feel the need to shout by using ALL CAPITAL LETTERS. People who send out unsolicited commercial messages use this technique all the time. Net newcomers and people new to typing also frequently use Caps Lock. The attention their messages receive is usually negative. Most important, messages are difficult to read in all caps.

```
BE THE FIRST TO INVEST IN THIS SURE-FIRE
WINNER!!!
```

How do you emphasize certain words? In messages you send to someone on AOL, you can use italics, as I explain in "Embellishing Messages" later in this chapter. In messages sent over the Net, use asterisks on either side of the word (to get some *attention*) or underscores (to get some _attention_). The very best way to get attention and emphasize words is to write concisely, directly, and respectfully.

Avoid Needless Provocation

Messages to the Internet cannot be unsent, unlike messages sent to people on AOL (See "Unsending a Message" later in this chapter). That's a good reason to avoid sending any message you might later regret. Messages are easily misunderstood because there's no body language to clarify the context of a hastily typed-and-sent message. That's why it's easy to write hot-headed and intemperate messages. Don't even bother counting to ten. Click the Send Later button to give yourself a chance to calm down, as I explain in "Sending That Message on Its Way" later in this chapter. I'm not being a nag; it's just too easy to say something stupid by mail, even to a good friend.

Fight Fires When They Do Break Out

Brevity can help in the competition for the world's scarcest resource (other people's attention), but excessive brevity can easily sound clipped and insultingly to-the-point. It can therefore be a good idea to personalize your messages. Begin with the recipient's name on a separate line, for example.

Quote Pithily in Thy Replies

In responding to someone's message, you can save a recipient's time (multiplied by the number of recipients) if you quote only the most relevant parts of the message sent to you. In mailing lists in particular, no one wants to see the same message in its entirety over and over again. Just use your mouse to select the most pertinent words in the original and, only then, click Reply or Reply to All.

Signal Your Feelings

Words on paper can't convey intention and emotion the way a raised eyebrow or wrinkled nose can; that's what e-mail *emoticons* (also called *smileys*) are for. At AOL Keyword: **LOL Online**, you'll find lists of abbreviations to help you signal your feelings. Here are some common smileys:

:-(Frown

:-)   Smile

:P   Sticking-out tongue

Tilt your head to the left to see the effect.

Smileys include some common acronyms — shortcuts that signal emotions, clarify intentions, explain gaps in the communication, and provide a bit of shared meaning:

Btw   By the way

Lol   Laughing out loud

Ttyl   Talk to you later

Definition

Quoting means to select part of a message before clicking the Reply or Reply to All button. The selected part alone appears in your response, and can be used to frame and focus your specific response.

Tip

Show your surprise, tell a joke, wink knowingly. If you feel the need to express an emotion in e-mail, click the Greetings icon on the Write Mail window and click Smileys. (Or type AOL Keyword: **Smileys** to find a fitting piece of art.)

Rewrite Again and Again

The single most frequent reason why I unsend a message is that I discover a glaring and embarrassing typo. If you take the time to reread your messages before you click Send Now, you can spare yourself the consequences of hasty comments and silly misspellings. The more important the message, the greater the consequences of sending too hastily.

On AOL you can spell-check your message by clicking the little ABC button in the Write Mail toolbar (Figure 11-8). The spell checker compares each of your words to its own list of words. For each word it can't recognize, it provides a list of choices. You can tell the spell checker to add the unrecognized word to its list, learn the word because it is correctly spelled, or skip the word just this time or all the time. Sometimes, you'll want to replace your word with the spell checker's recommended word.

Talking Back

E-mail works best if it's two-way. Not answering mail from someone you know, and especially if a reply is reasonably expected, can be rude. You shouldn't, of course, answer unsolicited mail; it can even be against your interests (because doing so just confirms the validity of your mail address).

Just Say No to E-Mail

Some people don't like to write. Some hopelessly busy people don't answer their mail quickly, or at all. If your message matters and your recipient may not be the writing type, give the message in person or over the phone. If you're sending the same message to many people with whom you work, the overhead of everyone reading and responding to your message may be greater than the trouble it takes to walk door-to-door to get a response. A face to face *(F2F)* conversation can consist of more replies, counter-replies, and nuances of tone and body language in a minute than an e-mail exchange can accommodate in an hour. It's also a way to schmooze and offers the chance to put out fires before they become flames.

Make It Easy on Your Reader

Here are two tips to help recipients with the mechanics of reading your message.

▶ Add a blank line between paragraphs. This visual cue says that one discrete paragraph is done and another is coming up. The space gives people a chance to breathe.

▶ If you want to include items in list form, keep each item short. Use asterisks (*) for unnumbered lists (items that don't have a necessary sequence, as in a grocery list) and numbers (1, 2, 3...) for numbered lists (steps that have an order, as in a recipe or any procedure).

Sending Your Message on Its Way

Cross-Reference

You can also click Send Later if you have a reason for not sending your message right away (see the "When and How to Send Later" box).

Sending messages is not the hard part; it's knowing when to send — after you proof the addresses, reread the message, and added any finishing touches. Before you do send a message, there's one more thing you can do. If you are sending mail to AOL members, you can request a *return receipt* — a message that is automatically generated letting you know when a recipient opens your message. All you have to do is click the Return Receipt box at the bottom of the Write Mail window so that it has a check mark in it. Note that the return receipt merely registers a message being opened — not being read, or read in its entirety. Only when you send a message to AOL members can you get an automatic receipt.

After you have typed your recipient(s) screen names or e-mail addresses in the Send To box and Copy To boxes, given the message a subject, and written a message, click Send Now.

Sending Mail: Preferences

Three of your AOL Mail preferences (available at Settings⇨ Preferences⇨Mail or Mail⇨Mail Preferences) have to do with what happens *after* you send a message.

▶ **Confirm mail after it has been sent** causes a little box to pop up when a message has been successfully sent; click OK to close it. Having the box appear can be useful when you've sent a large file. The little confirmation message serves as reassurance that the file is on its way.

▶ **Close mail after it has been sent** automatically closes the mail window after the message is sent. You may prefer to de-select this preference and keep a message *open* after it's sent so that you can modify and re-send it to other people. For example, you can send the same message to ten people you want to invite to a party. For each guest, add a personal comment and change the name in the Send To box.

▶ **Confirm when mail is marked to send later** serves to remind you that the message *wasn't* sent but was marked for sending later and is still available in your Filing Cabinet (Mail⇨Mail Waiting to Be Sent). In the Filing Cabinet, you can edit messages online or offline, and then send the message when you are online.

When and How to Send Later

The genuinely useful Send Later button comes in handy on many occasions. For example, send a message later when the text of a message is particularly sensitive or has been written in the heat of the moment, to boss or employee, spouse or child, or friend. Draft the letter as usual, but instead of clicking Send Now, click Send Later to let it sit for a while — give yourself time to reflect or cool off, or to gather more information, or have dinner, or proofread it, or whatever.

Or use Send Later to send a message to a high-volume mailing list (see Chapter 13), so you can perfect your message before having others perfect it for you.

Just to make sure the message *still* doesn't inadvertently get sent, I often put a fake one or two letter screen name in the Send To box. Some people BCC themselves in all their messages just to have a record of what they send and to see it from a recipient's perspective. (Note that you can't actually send the message unless all e-mail addresses in the Send To box are valid. Because addresses must have three or more characters, a one or two letter address won't get sent.)

(Continued)

11

Sending Mail

(Continued)

You can edit your Send Later messages whether you're on-line or offline. They're maintained by selecting Mail⇨Mail Waiting to Be Sent, a folder within your Filing Cabinet, which I discuss more generally in Chapter 10. To receive an automatic reminder when you sign off AOL that there's a message waiting to be sent, use Mail preferences. You can also use the Send Later option if you only have one phone line and you don't want to tie it up while you read and write e-mail messages. Here's what you do:

1. Choose Mail⇨Automatic AOL.

2. Select your preferences, and click Run Automatic AOL now. If you choose to have e-mail downloaded, you can read and reply to the mail offline.

3. When you're ready to send responses and new messages, sign on and go to Mail⇨Mail Waiting to Be Sent. Open the message and click Send Now.

After the Message Is Out the Door

After you've sent that message, you can keep track of it in ways not possible with an old-fashioned paper letter.

Cross-Reference

Your Filing Cabinet and Sent mailbox are discussed in Chapter 10.

Tip

You can even check the status of *your* mail, in the New mailbox, to find out whether and when someone reads your message. Select the message and click Status.

▶ Rereading mail you've sent. Your Sent mailbox has all your recent e-mail messages for the last month or so (Mail⇨Read Mail⇨Sent Mail). In your Filing Cabinet (FC), you can maintain an archive extending back as far as you want.

▶ Notification of receipt of mail you've sent. Click the Return Receipt box at the bottom of your Write Mail window, and you can find out automatically whether any of your AOL recipients got your message.

▶ Status of mail you've sent. Here's something you can do in your Sent mailbox but not in your Filing Cabinet: Find out when your message was read (at least, when it was opened) by any of your recipients who are on AOL. In Sent Mail, right-click any message to someone on AOL and choose Status. You'll see a little window like the one in Figure 11-2 that provides the Subject line of your message in the title bar (after *Status of*), who read it, at what exact time.

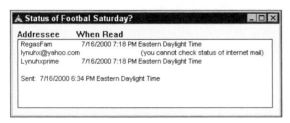

Figure 11-2. Mission accomplished: message has been opened by recipients on AOL.

Unsending a Message

Another thing you can't do with a real letter — change your mind after it's in the mailbox. By contrast, you can unsend and then re-send any message to someone on AOL as long as the message hasn't yet been opened. How do you find out if it's been opened? Select the message in Sent Mail, click Status, read the status, and close the window. If the message hasn't been read, select it, click Unsend, and click Yes to confirm that, yes indeed, you want to remove all traces of it.

Address Book

To really appreciate the Address Book, all you have to do is use it. The Address Book lets you keep a great deal of useful information about all your friends — their first and last names, their e-mail addresses, plus their postal addresses and all sorts of other information. Because the Address Book is available offline, you can use it for more than a handy source of e-mail addresses. See Figure 11-3.

Messages to the Internet can't be unsent. If you send an e-mail to several AOL members and just one Internet e-mail address, the message can't be unsent.

Your Address Book is always available, offline or online, at Mail⇨Address Book. While online, it is available to you from any computer on which you use your AOL account, because it is *synchronized* across all copies of AOL on different computers. Online or off, you can print any single contact or all of them by selecting contact(s) and clicking the Print button.

11

Sending Mail

Insert selected address into e-mail

Add new contact or mailing group

Change information of existing address

Figure 11-3. The AOL Address Book.

Tip

To have names appear next to each other in your Address Book, add the same couple of letters to each name. You may, for example, want all of your Chicago relatives' names to appear next to each other in your Address Book. Type in *Chi* before each first name. All names with *Chi* now appear grouped together with each name on a separate line in your Address Book.

Note

The AOL Address Book orders items by whatever name is in the First Name field. If you use only a first name, as you might for a sibling or friend or a one-named person (Madonna or 007), the person is ordered by first name. If you fill in both first and last names, the contact is ordered by last name.

Adding a Name to the Address Book

You have two ways to add a new address to your Address Book.

▶ Display a message and click the mail window's Add Address button to bring up Contact Details window of your Address Book. This window contains the information from the message header (Figure 11-4). You almost always have to edit this information and provide a proper first and last name, plus any notes or other information. The Address Book often plugs the e-mail address into the First Name field. Copying and pasting is simple — select the text with your mouse, right click, and select Copy; move to the place where you want the text to appear, right-click, and select Paste. In the Details section you can type in anything about the contact.

▶ The other way to add an address is to display the Address Book (always available from the Mail menu) and click the New Contact button, shown in Figure 11-3. You'll see a window like the one shown in Figure 11-4, only it'll be completely blank. Type in a first and last name, e-mail address, and anything else you want. Whether manual or automatic, you can update entries any time.

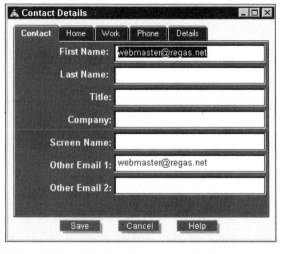

Figure 11-4. Clicking New Contact automatically creates a page like this in your Address Book. You can add detailed information, such as phone and fax numbers, Web addresses, birthdays, anniversaries, and other notes.

Though you use the Address Book for keeping street addresses, phone numbers, birthdays, and random notes, its primary purpose is to simplify access to your e-mail addresses when you're writing a message. Using the Address Book when writing a message can, in fact, save time and prevent errors. It also greatly simplifies the process of sending the same message to many people (creating simple lists is discussed in the next section). Here is how to quickly access the Address Book when you're composing an e-mail message:

1. Open the Write Mail window. Click Address Book. You can also click the Send To or Copy To hyperlinks (refer to Figure 11-1).

   The Address Book appears.

2. Select a name from the Address Book.

   You can select several names by pressing Shift or Control before clicking the names. If you then press Send To or Copy To *all* the selected names are copied into the Write Mail window (even if that window is not yet open). Double-clicking a selected contact does not add it to a message but brings up the contact window for that person, which you can then edit. You can edit contacts only one at a time.

Some people include detailed signatures. A *signature* is several lines of contact info, art, and wit often included at the end of a message. I often copy signatures and paste them into the Address Book (Details tab, in the free-form Notes section) to enter later in the correct tab. For more about signatures, see "Closing with a Signature" toward the end of this chapter.

Because the Address Book can be used for purposes other than e-mail, you need not type in an e-mail address, which is a requirement of earlier versions of the software.

Run your mouse across the Write Mail window and you may notice that the text that is next to the Send To and Copy To text entry boxes are clickable hyperlinks. Just click them to instantly open your Address Book. Note that if you choose to go ahead and begin typing the e-mail address of someone who's in your Address Book, the e-mail address automatically appears in the box.

11

Sending Mail

Tip

When writing e-mail, you may want to add the address last to avoid inadvertently sending a message before you're done.

Cross-Reference

I devote Chapter 13 to mailing lists, which on the Internet are managed by highly specialized server software. In Chapter 18, I discuss Groups@AOL, a new community feature that includes a built-in mailing list.

Caution

Remember to ask potential recipients if they want to be included in your group e-mail messages, especially if you intend to send them often. Although mailing lists among friends and family are not really spam, asking first is a courteous gesture. For more information about putting an end to unsolicited mass e-mail go to AOL Keyword: **Spam**. You can find information about avoiding unsolicited commercial e-mail, setting up your Parental Controls, and get insider tips on recognizing unwanted e-mail before you open it.

3. Click the Send To button to place the selected address(es) in the Send To box of the Write Mail window.

   Clicking the Copy To or Blind Copy button places addresses in the Copy To box.

4. Write your message and click Send Now or Send Later.

Creating a Group (Mailing List)

Over time real Address Books get filled with hard-to-read names, scratched-out notes, and names written along the sides of a page. The AOL Address Book is easy to edit. To change an address or add information or a picture, you can select an entry for an individual or a group (list) and click Edit or just double-click. To delete one or more entries, select and click Delete.

An e-mail group has two elements — a group name and a list of addresses of people belonging to the group.

1. With the Address Book open, click New Group to see the Manage Group window, shown in Figure 11-5.

2. Type in a name for the group — a single word or couple of words, such as Team Leaders or Bridge Club.

3. Type any AOL or Internet e-mail addresses you want to include in the group (Figure 11-5).

4. Add addresses directly from your Address Book or type an address not in your Address Book.

5. Click the Save button.

When you send group members a message, they can copy and paste the group's e-mail addresses and create a list in their own mail program. Or they can use the more cumbersome techique of using their Reply All button.

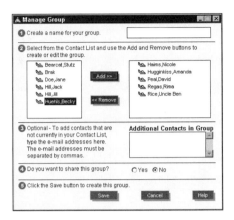

Figure 11-5. It's easy to create a simple mailing list with the AOL Address Book. Separate AOL and Internet addresses with a comma.

Attaching One or More Files

Everyone can find reasons to attach files. For instance, I attach files to submit chapters, share proposals, show work samples to potential clients, communicate with students in a course I teach, send my mother-in-law pictures of the kids, and so on.

To attach files:

1. Open the Write Mail window and click Attachments.
2. In the window that appears, click Attach. By default, a window appears that shows you all the files in your download file.
3. Scroll through the list of files until you find the file you want to attach. Then click the file and click Open. An Attachments window appears (see Figure 11-6).
4. Click Attach again if you want to attach additional files and repeat the steps. If you inadvertently add a file you don't want to send, select the file and click Detach.

Note

When you reply to a message that has a file attached, the reply doesn't include the originally attached file. When you forward a message that has a file attached, the file is forwarded along with the message.

11

Sending Mail

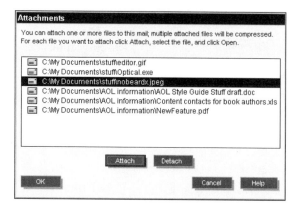

Figure 11-6. Include one or more files with your message.

Figure 11-6 shows several files to be attached to a message. When you attach more than one file, the files are combined into a single compressed file. Remember, also, to save and close a file before you attach it to an e-mail message.

When you send your message, it takes a bit longer than sending an ordinary file-free message because your file must be uploaded. Even before that, if you are sending several files, they're compressed and zipped first. A progress box tracks the upload.

Embellishing Messages

In your messages to other AOL members, you can add all sorts of effects, starting with styled text. You can:

▶ Style text

▶ Insert photos

▶ Include links to Web sites and AOL areas

▶ Add a colored or patterned background

▶ Include a personalized signature

▶ Create fancy stationery

▶ Use sounds, smilies. art, greetings, and banners

Emphasizing Text

You can create a default font that can be used in your mail and instant messages. Select Settings⇨Preferences⇨Font, Text & Graphics. Choose the following: type face, color, and size;

Note

Message fonts can be set only for your messages to AOL members. In both the Instant Message and Write Mail windows, you can override your default font by using the button bar above the message window.

default style (bold, italic, underline); or default background color. The sample text in the window gives you a preview of what your message will look like. Click OK when you like your choices. Reset restores AOL's choices.

While writing a message, you can override your default text by using the button bar just above the large message window. Here are some of the type variables you can play with using these convenient buttons:

▶ Type style (bold, italic, underline).

▶ Type size, color, and face. You may find more than 100 typefaces in the list, depending on the other programs you have installed. AOL itself does not come with any fonts, but it can use any of the fonts you have installed on your system.

▶ Background color. A background color for the entire message can create an effect to match your purposes, or it can enhance the legibility of your text given its size, font, and color.

To apply a text effect, open a Write Mail window (Ctrl+M or click Write on the toolbar). Type a message in the big box. Select the words you want to enhance and click the appropriate buttons, as shown in Figure 11-7.

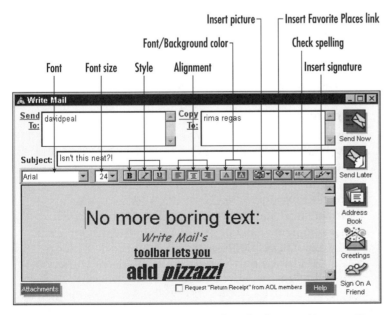

Figure 11-7. No more boring text: the Write Mail's toolbar lets you add groovy effects.

Right-click anywhere in the message body to see all your toolbar choices (change type size, style, color, and so on).

Adding Links, Text Files, and Images to Your Messages

Once simple, text-only affairs, e-mail messages can now carry non-text information such as links, images, and even HTML code — a Web page. With AOL, it's even easier to add the text itself. The following brief sections highlight these important additions to your e-mail repertoire. All these options except adding a link are available from the clickable Camera button that forms part of the Write Mail window's button bar.

Adding a Link to a Message

Adding a link to your messages lets your recipients click to visit the link to a Web page or AOL area. To link to an AOL area, recipients must be AOL members. To create a link in a message you are writing

> ▶ Use a Favorite Place. With nothing selected in the body of your message, click the heart button on the Write Mail toolbar. A list of your Favorite Places comes up; click a favorite to add a link to your message. The Favorite Place's name (what you see in your Favorite Places folder) appears as clickable text; the Favorite Place's Web address specifies where the reader goes when she clicks the text. You can view the Web address by moving your mouse over the link.

> ▶ Link to a site that's not a Favorite Place. With a Web site or AOL area open (but not maximized) and the Write Mail window open, select some text in the body of your message. Drag the heart in the upper-right hand corner of the Web site or AOL window on to the selected text. Doing so automatically creates a link to the Web site or AOL area.

> ▶ Create a link from scratch — if you know the URL (Web address). With a message open and without anything selected, you can right-click and select Insert Hyperlink. The Edit Hyperlink window, with two text boxes (Description and Internet Address), pops up. Provide both a description of the link (this is the text that recipients can click) and a URL (the destination where your recipients go when they click); click OK. Use the Launch button to make sure you've chosen the correct URL.

▶ Or select words in the message, right-click, and select Insert a Hyperlink. The Edit Hyperlink window appears, but this time with a single box, in which you enter the link's Internet address.

Inserting an Image

Attaching images to messages is a convenient way of sharing them with someone on the Internet. For your AOL recipients you can include any number of messages directly in messages. Use this technique to share any digital picture on your hard drive or to add visual flare (icons, logos, doo-dads, and so on) to your text messages. Inserting a picture is less obtrusive than attaching a picture, which requires the recipient to take several extra steps to view the image.

Where do you get digital pictures to enhance your messages?

▶ You can use a scanner to turn your prints into digital pictures. From your hard drive, the pictures will be available when you go to insert an image from the Write Mail window.

▶ You can use a digital camera to create digital pictures instead of paper ones, which you can then transfer to your computer with your camera's cable or removable memory card.

▶ You can use AOL's "You've Got Pictures" to get digital pictures without owning a scanner or a digital camera. With this service, you take your traditional film to the photo store. Your prints are scanned and then posted directly to AOL as digital pictures. To use a picture in AOL Mail, select and download it to your hard drive. "You've Got Pictures" includes a way of sending pictures to buddies, but it currently lacks the flexibility of AOL Mail.

To insert an image in a message:

1. Position the cursor at the point in your message where you want to put the picture.
2. From the Mail toolbar, click the Camera button and select Insert a Picture.
3. Find the picture and double-click.

   You can insert small images directly into text (even in a sentence). To align an inserted image, use the Write Mail button bar's right, center, and left align buttons,

Where do you get graphics files for backgrounds and similar uses? Check out AOL Keyword: **Web Art**. or **Mail Extras**.

Click the "You've Got Pictures" button on the AOL 6.0 Welcome screen for more details. For details, see my *Official AOL Guide to Pictures Online* (IDG Books Worldwide, 2000).

11

Sending Mail

which apply to the whole paragraph in which a picture is inserted (or the picture itself, if it's not part of a paragraph). If you insert a large image, you'll probably get a message asking you if you want to resize the picture to fit the message window. Choose Yes to automatically resize the picture and No to insert it full-size.

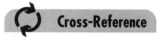

Cross-Reference

See Chapter 10 to find out more about how file attachments appear in your AOL Mail Box.

When you send an inserted image to people on AOL, they see a picture icon. When they double-click the message, a message pops up with a warning about opening unsolicited messages from unknown parties. As soon as this message is removed (with a click of the OK button), the image appears a little at a time until it's fully displayed. Double-clicking the picture opens the AOL Picture Gallery, and from there they can save or edit the picture.

Inserting a Background Picture

Web pages have gotten people used to background colors and pictures as a decorative touch. You can add backgrounds into your AOL messages, but they'll be viewable only by AOL members unless they are part of an HTML page. To use a digital picture as a background, click the Camera button, choose Background Picture, and select the image. To add a color, use the button bar's Background Color button, an A set against a blue background (Figure 11-7).

Tip

Use Insert Text File as an alternative to Send Later. You can write long text messages (using AOL's text writer at File⇨New, if you want). Keep perfecting your message until it's ready to go and then send it.

Inserting a Text File into a Message

Inserting a text file into the Write Mail window can save you from typing text again and again. It also gives you the chance to draft and edit as much as you want until the message is ready to send. In either case, after you finish, a copy of the original remains on your hard drive to use later or to review (the outgoing message will be in your Filing Cabinet, too). Text files must be just that: pure text (simple characters).

From the body of the Write Mail toolbar, you can click the little Camera button and select Insert Text File. Find your file and double-click to insert it.

Inserting HTML

New in AOL 6.0 is the ability to add formatting and links to your messages to non-AOL members. To do so, you must have a Web page (HTML file) on your hard drive containing the entire message, with any links and backgrounds. From the Mail Window's Camera button, select Insert an HTML File, select the page, and send the message. Note that many HTML effects, such as tables, frames, and forms, will not appear in your message.

Caffeinated Stationery

In your mail to AOL members, you can choose from a wide variety of mail gizmos, including sounds, photos, and banners. To do so, click Greetings from any Write Mail window. Click Greetings again to use American Greetings card designs and services. You can send a variety of free online cards to anyone on AOL or the Internet. Some of these cards include multimedia effects, such as animations and Java programs.

Closing with a Signature

Signatures are bits of text automatically added to the end of any or all your e-mail messages. With AOL 5.0 and 6.0, you can create several signatures and use any of them on any message, depending on occasion.

To create a signature

1. Click the last button on the far right of the Write Mail toolbar or select Mail⊅Mail Signatures. In either case, you'll see a window like the one shown in Figure 11-8. If you already have one or more signatures set up, this button shows a drop-down list of your previously created signatures. Or you can click Set up Signatures.

Note

These effects will not appear in your messages to people on the Internet. For them, use your own HTML files (see the previous section) or American Greetings' online cards. For much more information about creating attractive and fun AOL e-mail, see *Your Official America Online Tour Guide,* 7th edition, by David Marx and Jennifer Watson (IDG Books Worldwide, Inc.).

Tip

For signatures used on e-mail bound for the Internet, use unformatted text. For your messages to AOL members, you can format your signatures all you want. You can try your hand at ASCII art, like the squirrel shown in "Warning: Squirrels," later in this chapter.

Tip

Here's how to make a signature your default so that it is added to every message you send. From the Set up Signatures window (Figure 11-10), select a signature and click Default On/Off button. A red check appears before the signature.

11

Sending Mail

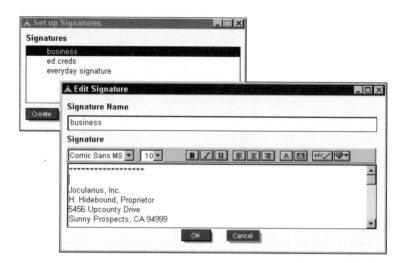

Figure 11-8. Create a signature to tell people about your latest achievements or share a joke or contact information.

2. Click the Create button. A signature has two elements: *the signature's name,* which you use to identify a particular signature (when you have several signatures), and *the actual signature,* consisting of text and optional formatting.

3. Give the signature a name and type in the actual text, with any effects you want. Note the toolbar with different fonts, type sizes, styles, and colors — even backgrounds (click the A set on a square blue field button) and links (click the heart button). Have fun with them, and click OK when you're done.

To edit an existing signature, go to the Set Up Signatures window, select an existing signature, and click Edit.

To add a signature to a message, open the Write Mail window. Type your message as usual. When done, click the Signature button and select a particular signature to use, which is automatically added. Send your message.

Warning: Squirrels

If this chapter were an e-mail message, I'd end it with a signature. Instead, I'm ending it with a whole collection of signatures to give you just a taste of how you can add personality to your own AOL e-mail.

Watch out for the squirrels!

```
                              .~~~.  ))
  (\__/)  .'      )  ))      Patrick Douglas
Crispen
 /o o  \/    .~
{o_,    \    {
crispen@netsquirrel.com
 / , , )     \
http://www.netsquirrel.com/
  `~ '-' \    } ))    AOL Instant Messenger:
Squirrel2K
 _(    (  )_.'
'---..{____}              Warning:
squirrels.
=-=-==
I am perfectly capable of learning from my
mistakes. I will surely learn a great deal
today.
=-=-==
QOTD: "Due to budget cuts, the light at the
end of the tunnel has been turned off."
  --anon.

Note: QOTD stands for quote of the day.


=-=-=-=-

It doesn't *take* all kinds, we just *have*
all kinds.


=-=-= -- =

Kindness is loving people more than they
deserve.
-Joseph Joubert, French
moralist and essayist (1754-1824)
```

Where to Go from Here

In this chapter, I wanted to show you how you can create e-mail to communicate with anyone in the world who has an Internet account, including the 25 million or so AOL members. Among other things, you learned to write an effective message, embellish a message, send a message, use your Address Book to keep more than addresses, and insert personality into your messages with smileys, links, pictures, signatures, and even Web pages. Two other chapters in this book focus on aspects of electronic mail:

▶ Chapter 10 has everything you need to know about receiving and managing mail as well as downloading and storing mail.

▶ Chapter 12 is devoted to my favorite topic: mailing lists, dynamic and enduring communities based on nothing more than electronic mail and some special software.

Chapter 12

Live Communication: From Instant Messages to Internet Chats

IN THIS CHAPTER

Messaging on AOL

Messaging on the Internet with AOL "Instant Messenger"ˢᵐ (AIM)

Sending and receiving messages with AIM

Exchanging files and images with AIM

Using AIM's news and stock tickers

With instant messages on AOL and the Internet, you get quick, easy, live communication that bypasses some of the time delays caused by playing phone tag and waiting for an e-mail reply. This chapter provides all you need to know about sending instant messages on AOL, and about the AOL Instant Messenger (AIM) service available for Internet users.

You will quickly see that instant messages are more than just a full-featured communications tool. AOL revolutionized real-time communications with instant messages, and AIM functions as an information hub, giving you ready access to your e-mail, stocks, and headlines if you're logged on to the Internet from work or school. Before talking about AIM, I want to introduce AOL's instant message feature, out of which AIM grew and through which you, as an AOL member, can communicate with friends who use AIM.

Communicating Live on AOL

AOL did more than any online company to make live electronic conversations fun and easy. Communicating *live* (or in *real time*) means communicating with someone else when you and the other person are in different places and when you're typing instead of talking. With other AOL members, you take part in one-to-one discussions using *instant messages* (IMs). Live communication involving more than two AOL members is called *chat*. You can find out more at AOL Keyword: **Chat** or AOL Keyword: **People Connection**, or click People on the AOL toolbar. For the full story, start with *Your Official America Online Tour Guide,* by David Marx and Jennifer Watson (IDG Books Worldwide Inc.)

On AOL you use one tool for IMs and another tool for chats. These tools could not be simpler to use. But suppose you want to talk to an Internet friend who doesn't use AOL. Or suppose you're using a computer without AOL installed. You can do all of the following:

- Have a one-to-one discussion with an Internet friend if that person is using AOL Instant Messenger.

- Chat with an Internet friend using AOL Instant Messenger. See "Creating and Joining AIM Chats," later in this chapter.

- Have discussions or chat with anyone on AOL or using AIM, even if you're on the road or using a computer without AOL installed. See "Using AIM When You're Away from Your PC," later in this chapter.

- Use AIM with your AOL/non-AOL communications, if you have an AOL Bring Your Own Access account.

Here are some things to keep in mind about live communication:

- Unlike e-mail, chat and instant messenging are fast-and-loose. You don't have to worry about grammar and spelling quite as much as you do with other forms of communication. Have fun.

- People who IM and chat speak a different language — which can be daunting. Abbreviations, emoticons, smileys, Buddy icons (that help give you and your pals a distinct personality), and cool downloadable sounds

12

Live Communication: From Instant
Messages to Internet Chats

are commonly used in live chats. To find out about setting up these preferences, click Setup in the Buddy List window, and then click IMs. To find out about setting up AOL's chat preferences, click Settings on the AOL toolbar and then click Chat.

• Because chat and instant messenging can be such a speedy way to communicate, and because real-time chat is so much like a real-world conversation, the friendships you create with AOL members (and Internet buddies) are likely to be as rewarding, surprising, fun, and creative. Watch out, however, about revealing too much personal information about yourself to a virtual stranger. Go to AOL Keyword: **Neighborhood Watch**.

Getting Started with Instant Messages

You can use instant messages (IMs) to carry on electronic discussions with any AOL acquaintance who is online at the same time. The communication is immediate, often informal, and can be much more fun (and productive) than e-mail or the telephone. Unlike chat rooms, which often lack a clear focus, one-to-one IMs have a way of getting right to the point (Your Internet buddies must use AIM to IM you.).

How do you find out whether a buddy or colleague of yours is online? When you sign on to AOL, a special *Buddy List* window pops up automatically (see Figure 12-1). Sometimes it takes a while to appear. If you don't see it, use AOL Keyword: **BuddyView** to bring it up right away. Your Buddy List lists any of your buddies who are currently online.

To send an instant message to any buddy currently online, simply double-click that person's name on your Buddy List, and the Instant Message window (see Figure 12-2) comes up with your buddy's screen name filled in. Type a message and click Send.

Definition

Instant messages (IMs) can be exchanged only among AOL members. They enable one-to-one conversations, whereas AOL chat rooms involve *group* conversations. The AOL Instant Messenger service (AIM) is free software that brings IM capabilities to anyone on the Internet. AIM supports both one-to-one and group conversations, facilitates communication between AOL members and Internet users, and packs a range of features such as file exchange, headlines, Web searching, e-mail access, and stock tickers. For both IMs and AIM, you need a screen name and password; AOL members can use the same screen name and password for both.

Tip

Your Buddy List can include the screen names of Internet friends friends who use AOL Instant Messenger and thus have *AIM* screen names. Chapter 3 shows you how to add buddies to your Buddy List.

Figure 12-1. The Buddy List window appears when you sign on to AOL. If you should ever close the window, use AOL Keyword: **BuddyView** to reopen it.

Note

AOL maintains your Buddy List on its computers, so you'll be aware of who's online no matter how you access AOL. Whether you sign on to AOL on your PC, or your Palm handheld computer, or someone else's PC, you'll have access to the same Buddy List.

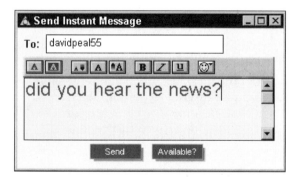

Figure 12-2. Composing IMs is like composing e-mail, except you don't have a subject line, and netiquette is not such a big deal.

When someone sends you an instant message for the first time, a message pops up on-screen, accompanied by a tinkling sound. You can either accept the message (click Yes), decline the message (click No), or click Questions to get more information. Usually, you want to accept messages from people you know and refuse them from people you don't.

After you accept a message (or send one), the IM window changes to display a two-way dialogue in one window and a typing window just below it. Everything you do while instant

Note

There's no spell checker when you use instant messages, but don't worry about niceties such as good spelling. People tend to be less fussy about spelling and grammar in IMs than in e-mail, making the medium much more like talking than writing.

12

Live Communication: From Instant Messages to Internet Chats

IMs are much closer to talking than writing. But even though they're more conversational than e-mail, they still lack body language and context and give rise to all sorts of misunderstandings. With IMs, you can address such misunderstandings on the spot.

If your buddy has created a profile at AOL Keyword: **People Directory**, you can read it by clicking the Get Profile button.

messaging involves either (1) typing into the *bottom part* of the window and (2) reading words and your friend's responses in the *top part* of the window.

Customizing Your IM Experience

Like the Write Mail window I describe in Chapter 11, the IM window has a formatting bar — the horizontal line of buttons just above the message window. Use these buttons to apply color to the text, create a colored background for the message, vary the type size, and use bold, underline, and italic.

You can include a live link to a Web site or other online area in three ways:

> ▶ On AOL, with the IM window displayed, open the Web page to which you want to link. Then drag the Favorite Places heart from that window into the open IM window. The name of the favorite place appears as the clickable part of the link.
>
> Or type some text first and then select it. Drag the heart icon to the selected text to make the selected words a clickable link to the displayed page.
>
> ▶ Type a message. Select a bit of text, right-click that text, and choose Insert a Hyperlink from the menu. Type in a Web address.
>
> ▶ Select nothing from the message. When you right-click the message and choose Insert a Hyperlink, you have to provide both text (that becomes the clickable part of the message) and a Web address, which is the link's destination.

Friends who receive your IMs can visit the linked site by clicking them.

Setting Your IM Privacy Preferences

Work to do? Tired of communicating with people you don't know? Totally exhausted from communicating with people you do know? You can take a break while online and receive IMs only from a few people or from no one at all. You have a number of options when it comes to limiting others' access to you via instant messages.

The easiest option to use is AOL 6.0's new Away message. When anyone tries to IM you, they'll see your Away message, saying something like "I'll be right back." To turn it on, follow these steps:

1. From the Buddy List main window, click Away Message.

2. In the Away Message box, choose either an existing message or click New to create your new message (providing, for example, an alternative way in which you can be reached). Each message has both a name (which appears in the Away Message box) and an actual message (which is displayed to anyone trying to IM you. Click OK.

3. Now, at the top of your Buddy List, you'll see, in color, a line that reads Away Message On.

4. To turn the message off, and be available for messages again, click the Away Notice on the Buddy List.

You can use your Privacy settings to set up more lasting controls on the people with whom you want to communicate. To screen your incoming messages, click the Setup button at the bottom of your Buddy List to display the Buddy List Setup window. Click the Preferences button to display the Privacy Preferences window (see Figure 12-3).

Feature

With AOL 6.0's new Away message, you can let people know exactly why you're unable to return their instant messages. You save yourself embarrassment in the process, and avoid having to sign off frequently, which can be a hassle with newer, broadband connections.

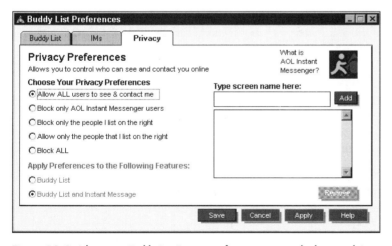

Figure 12-3. Adjust your Buddy List Privacy preferences to control other people's access to you.

On AOL, using your Buddy preferences, you can control who has access to you by IM. You can

12

Live Communication: From Instant Messages to Internet Chats

Note

Internet friends can use the AOL Instant Messenger service to talk to you. You'll see their messages in the AOL IM window, not in the AOL Instant Messenger window — even if you have AIM installed.

▶ Opt for complete privacy, so no one can send you an instant message

▶ Permit only AOL members to talk to you

▶ Let all Internet users of the AOL Instant Messenger service (AIM) send you messages

▶ Block specific screen names

Select one option; the choices are mutually exclusive.

To allow specific users to contact you or to block specific users from accessing you, follow these steps:

1. Choose the appropriate option on the left (Block Only... or Allow Only...).

2. Type in the AOL or AIM screen names in the Type Screen Name Here box.

3. Click Add.

4. Repeat the process to add as many users to your blacklist as you want.

Likewise, remove names by selecting them one at a time and clicking Remove.

Using the AOL Instant Messenger Service

Tip

New in AIM is the mail alert. A small window gives you direct access to AOL Mail on the Web (see Chapter 10 for more information). If you don't see the window, sign on to AIM and choose My AIM⇨My Alert Window. Click the linked e-mail address (it's your own address). You'll see an AOL Web site where you can sign on and read your e-mail.

The AIM service brings AOL-style chat to the Internet frontier. AIM can meet serious needs, such as communicating with business colleagues, providing quick facts, and exchanging documents. It's also a wonderful way to maintain friendships and take a break while you're working.

The balance of the chapter focuses on the AIM service. As an AOL member you can download, install, and use the free AIM software. Like AOL, AIM requires the use of screen names. You can use your AOL screen name on AIM. If you do, however, you will be communicating with non-AOL folks through AOL's IM window (refer to Figure 12-2). Only if you create a new AIM screen name (see the "Creating a New AIM Screen Name" sidebar) will you be able to use the AIM service to communicate with people on the Internet. The main AIM window is shown in Figure 12-4.

Among other benefits, AIM . . .

▶ Enables you to carry on both two-way electronic conversations and group chats. AOL's instant messages (refer to Figure 12-2) support only two-way conversations. Think of AIM as an Internet tool that combines IM and chat features, extends both sets of features, and enables AOL members and Internet users to carry on conversations, chats, and file/image exchanges.

▶ Costs nothing for both AOL members and anyone on the Internet.

▶ Comes in versions for Windows, Macintosh, and Unix.

▶ Is usable without the AIM software. See the "Using AIM When You're Away from Your PC" section later in this chapter, for the details.

▶ Provides a sophisticated and easy-to-maintain Buddy List of its own, which enables you to create profiles comparable to the profiles in the AOL People Directory.

▶ Can be embedded in your Web pages. Using the Web tools at AOL Hometown (1-2-3 Publish and Easy Designer), you can add a panel of buttons to even the simplest Web page. Visitors to the page can click a button to send you e-mail, create an AIM-style chat room, or communicate in other ways.

Downloading, Installing, and Running the AOL Instant Messenger Service

Here's how you can get The AOL Instant Messenger service for yourself for use with AOL or any Internet connection:

1. Start at www.aol.com/aim.

   Have a look at the features overview.

2. Click the Get It Now (or similar) button.

3. You're ready to provide a screen name and password.

   • If you're already an AOL member (which you probably are) and want to use your existing screen name and password, click the Already a Member link. On the next page, provide your screen name and zip code. Click Continue.

Find It Online

AIM features so many options that it's easy to lose sight of its simplicity. It's primarily a tool for exchanging instant messages; the interface differs from AOL's IM window, but they both do the same thing. If you ever need help using the AIM service or want to learn a new feature, choose Help⟶Help Topics from the main AIM window, shown in Figure 12-4.

Tip

If you have Netscape Navigator, which I discuss in Chapter 7, you already have the AOL Instant Messenger service. Select it from the Tools taskbar or by choosing Tasks⟶Instant Messenger. On Netscape, your Buddy List is contained in your Sidebar, and the message window differs slightly from the AIM window.

Tip

If you have ever registered and created a screen name at Netscape's Netcenter, AOL's My News, CompuServe 2000, or AOL Hometown, you can use this screen name as your AIM screen name.

Tip

With parallel sets of screen names on AOL and AIM, you can easily get them mixed up. Print out your registration messages, or write down your screen names and passwords and put them in a folder.

Cross-Reference

Chapter 15 outlines the general process of downloading from the Web.

Note

AIM sends you an e-mail message confirming your screen name and password. Your registration is not complete until you respond to that message with an *OK*, as explained in the message. When your registration is confirmed, the new screen name appears in a drop-down list of screen names available from the copy of AIM you just installed.

Tip

To use the AIM service while signed on to AOL, sign on to AIM using a different screen name from your AOL screen name.

- If you are not an AOL member (or if you are but don't want to use your existing AOL screen name), type in your AOL screen name, the password you want to use with that new screen name, and your e-mail address. Click Continue.

Now you're ready to get the AIM software.

4. Click the Windows or Macintosh button, depending on what computer you use.

5. Follow the online instructions and indicate where to store the program on your hard drive. Press Enter to start the download process.

6. When the download is finished, click Open File (or otherwise retrieve the downloaded file), and double-click the file to install it.

You'll be asked some standard installation questions — where to install the software, whether you accept the terms of use (say Yes), whether you want to sign on using your AIM screen name right away, and so forth.

When installation is complete, you'll be asked whether you want to create another screen name. See the "Creating a New AIM Screen Name" sidebar, later in this chapter.

7. After installation and registration, you can run AIM right away.

In the AIM window, check the Save Password box if you don't want to enter your password again.

8. One more thing. Your registration is not complete until you respond to the confirmation e-mail that shows up in your mailbox shortly after your register your new screen name!

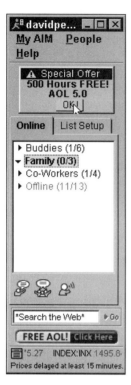

Figure 12-4. My AIM Buddy List already has a few entries. Click a folder (group) to see who's online right now. Online buddies are capable of receiving your messages.

Adding Buddies to Your Buddy List

For your buddies on the Internet to use AIM, they must first download the free software. You can make it easy for them, as follows. From AIM's main menu (Figure 12-5), choose People⟿ Sign On a Friend to invite your friends to use AIM. Enter the e-mail address of a friend and type a short message that personally describes AIM. Your friend receives an e-mail explaining how to get AIM.

AIM has its own Buddy List, which shows you which of your AIM buddies is signed on to AIM at the moment. Your first job is to to add buddies to your AIM Buddy List. Note that the AIM and AOL Buddy Lists differ, so even if you have a long AOL Buddy List, you have to reenter names in the AIM Buddy List list.

> ▶ You can add a buddy to your AIM Buddy List by clicking the List Setup tab (see Figure 12-5). Click the Add a Buddy button and type in the buddy's screen name.

Note

Your AOL Buddy List can include AIM buddies' screen names.

Note

You don't *have* to create groups, and you can enter groups and buddies in any order. That is, you don't have to create a group first and then add buddies to it.

12

▶ You can add a group of buddies from the office, from your high school class, or from your reading group to your AIM Buddy List. Just click the Add a Group button and give the new group a name. If your groups are already created and you're still using List Setup, you can drag a buddy into a group, or from one group to another. Or you can create new buddies within a group by opening the group and clicking the add buddy button.

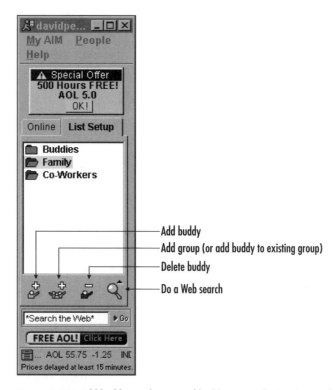

Figure 12-5. Add buddies and groups of buddies using the List Setup tab. AIM requires screen names, so you have to ask your Internet buddies for their AIM screen names.

Making New Buddies

With more than 64 million people using the AOL Instant Messenger service, there's a good chance you already have friends on AIM. There's an even better chance you'll find people who aren't friends but who share a personal interest or a career interest. Some of these people might even live in your community. How can you find them?

Use the Find a Buddy Wizard. From AIM's main menu, choose People⇨Find a Buddy Wizard. Select one of the three options for finding a buddy — by e-mail address, by name and address, or by a common interest.

To be *found* by others who are using the Buddy Wizard, set up a profile about yourself at My AIM⇨Edit Profile. In the profile, you can indicate whether and how you want others to find out about you. If you don't want others to be able to find you at random, simply don't fill out a profile.

A good way to find like-minded folk is to search for buddies by interest. Suppose you want to find AIM users who are expert gardeners. Here's how:

1. Choose People⇨Find a Buddy⇨By Common Interest⇨House and Gardening⇨Gardening. Click Next.

   Fellow gardeners who are registered AIM users and who allow strangers (you, in other words) to contact them are listed, along with any personal information that they have chosen to share in their AIM profile (first and last name, state, and so on).

2. You can now send an AIM message to any of these people, making sure to introduce yourself, avoid intrusions, and so on.

Helping Potential New Buddies Find You

Your AIM profile says who you are, whether you're available for chatting, and anything else you want to share. By creating a profile, you can help friends and family find you online. Make your profile available for searching, and others can then use the Find a Buddy Wizard to look for you by interest, name, or e-mail address.

To create a personal profile, or to edit it, choose My AIM⇨My Profile from the AIM main window. In the Create a Profile window (shown in Figure 12-6), follow these steps:

1. First, use the check box to indicate whether you want people to be able to search for you based on the information you enter. If you say yes, type in as much or as little information as you wish, and decide whether you want other users to be able to find you — not providing

them access can be compared to having an unlisted telephone number. Click Next.

2. Next, you are asked whether you want others to be able to chat with you if they find your name by doing a search. If you say yes, you then select several interests with which you want to be associated. Other AIM users will find your screen name by searching for people with those interests. Click Next.

3. You can then enter a brief personal description, formatted as you want. Click Finish.

You can edit this profile at any time by again choosing My AIM⇨My Profile from the Buddy List menu.

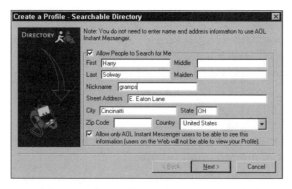

Figure 12-6. Edit your profile to reflect your personal information and your interests.

The downside to having a profile is that strangers also have access to this information unless you block all but a specific number of users (which can be self-defeating). Like your profile in the AOL People Directory, creating an AIM profile is voluntary and involves the same benefits and risks.

Sounds Like Fun

One of the most useful new features of AIM 4.0 is Buddy Alert, which is a sound that plays automatically when a buddy on your AIM Buddy List goes online and is available to receive messages from you. The audio cue might be the sound of a creaking door, for example, or a choir of angels. If you want to be automatically alerted by a buddy's signing on, follow these steps:

1. In the List Setup tab of the Buddy List (refer to Figure 12-5), find the buddy's screen name.

2. Right-click the screen name and select Alert Me when the buddy signs on to AIM.

3. Save the alert by clicking the Save This Alert check box. Click OK.

Sounds can be attached to other "events"—such as when you receive a message. Likewise, messages from buddies can be signalled by a sound (a ring or some other sound available on the Sounds tab).

Using the Sounds tab of the Edit Preferences window, you can customize AIM's sounds. Choose My AIM⇨Edit Options⇨ Edit Preferences and click the Sounds tab. For each of three events (getting a message, and buddies coming and going), you'll get a drop-down list of sounds from which to choose. Click Preview to hear the sound and then click OK when you're done making selections.

If you want to use your own sound file (and the Internet abounds with a zillion of them), make sure it's in the standard Windows (.wav) format and available on your hard drive. On the Sounds tab, with an event checked, click Browse to select that sound and to preview it. If it's the sound you want, click OK.

Protecting Your Privacy on AIM

AOL's Privacy preferences, discussed earlier in this chapter, apply to AIM messages arriving while you're on AOL, but do not apply to your use of the AIM software, regardless of whether you are signed on to AOL at the time. AIM's own Privacy controls enable you to prevent some, all, or no users from contacting you. You can also determine how much information other users can find out about you.

To set your AIM Privacy Preference, choose My AIM⇨Edit Options⇨Edit Preferences, and click the Privacy tab. Decide who can send you messages and what they can find out about you, and then click OK. You can change your choices at any time. They take effect right away.

To ensure some privacy for a brief period, use an *Away message*. It's similar to a "be right back" note tacked to the door of a local shop. You can design messages that say when you will be back, or provide other information (such as "send me e-mail, and I'll respond right away"). Your Away message will be sent automatically to anyone attempting to send you an AIM message while you're away. You create Away messages by using your AIM preferences: Choose My AIM⇨Edit Options⇨Edit Preferences, and then click the Away tab.

People in an office environment or at home can turn off all IM sounds by making sure all of the sound boxes are unchecked. Click OK to accept the change.

To temporarily prevent people from contacting you via IM, click Block All Users. When you wake up or finish your work, turn instant messages back on.

In AOL 6.0, you can now create an Away message for use with AOL instant messages.

12

Live Communication: From Instant Messages to Internet Chats

Tip

Your AOL and AIM Buddy Lists make life simpler, but you can still send an AOL or AIM message as long as you know the other person's screen name and that person is online at the time. The beauty of Buddy Lists is that they let you know who is online at the time.

Sending Messages with AIM

With your AIM Buddy List, you can see right away whether your buddies are online and signed on to AIM. To send any one of them a message, double-click the person's screen name. Even if you initiate an AIM session, if you're signed on to AOL using the same screen name, you receive messages in the IM window. Figure 12-7 shows the AIM messaging window.

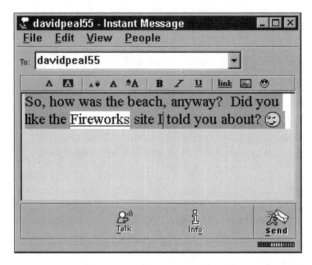

Figure 12-7. When you send a message such as this one from AIM, Internet recipients get the message in an AIM window; AOL recipients see it as an IM-type message.

You can copy and paste text in your AIM messages for other people to see and read. If you copy or type a Web address (or other URL) in your IM, it is automatically hyperlinked, and your recipient can click the link to visit the Web site.

Tip

When you type a smiley : -) AIM automatically turns the smiley into a proper, yellow, right side up cartoonish happy face. Many other smileys are available from the Smile button on the AIM message window. On AOL, using your IM preferences, you can now send graphical smileys in your messages to other AOL members.

Chatting with Your E-Mail Buddies

Chapter 10 shows all the ways you can respond to an e-mail message — except for the one way that doesn't involve e-mail. In AOL 6.0, whenever you open an e-mail message and your AOL Buddy List appears on-screen, the Buddy List window displays a new section indicating whether the message's sender and other recipients are currently online. This new section of the Buddy List, viewable only as long as a message is open, is called Mail Contacts Online.

The address of anyone online who *can't* receive AIM messages is surrounded by square brackets. Any buddy who can receive AIM messages appears without brackets. Bear in mind that your AIM buddies can be online yet not signed onto AIM. In this case, their names appear in square brackets, too.

Creating and Joining AIM Chats

The AIM service makes it easy for you to invite others to chat and to join chats yourself. To start up a chat, simply go to the Online tab and click the Send a Buddy Chat Invitation button at the bottom of your Buddy List window. Type in buddies' screen names and separate each name with a comma. After you click Send, you'll be taken to the chat window. Your invitees can click a button in the messages they receive if they wish to join you. Similarly, if you receive an invitation to a chat, you can click a button to take part.

Note

Mail Contacts Online displays only e-mail senders and any other recipients (for example, people CC'ed) who are also on your Buddy List.

Find It Online

AIM has brought AOL-style chat to the Net. At www.aol.com/community/chat/allchats.html you will find a directory of many noisy AIM chat rooms you can join.

Knock Knock. Who's There?

If you receive an AIM message from someone on the Internet while you're on AOL, you receive a message from AOL giving you the option of accepting or not accepting the message. If you know the person, click OK. If you're unsure click Questions. Up comes a "knock, knock" message, as AOL calls it, warning you about communicating with people you don't know.

Here's what AOL has to say on the matter (from AOL Keyword: **Notify AOL**):

```
Instant Message conversations with people
using AOL Instant Messenger are not subject
to AOL's Terms of Service. When you receive
an Instant Message note from an Instant
Messenger user, you will be asked if you want
to accept or ignore the message. To further
control who can send you Instant Message
notes, use the Buddy List feature's Privacy
Preferences. Go to AOL Keyword: Buddy, then
click Privacy Preferences.
```

For more on these preferences, see "Setting Your IM Privacy Preferences," earlier in this chapter.

Tip

You can use your Buddy List preferences to turn off the Mail Contacts Online feature. Here's how: From your Buddy List, click Setup. From Buddy List Setup, click Preferences. Uncheck the Show Me the Mail Contacts Online Group check box. Click Save.

Note

If you can't currently see your Buddy List, go to AOL Keyword: **BuddyView**.

12

After you are in the chat room, you type your comments in the blank message field in the center. Click Send to transmit your message to the rest of the chat room participants. Your messages appear, along with everyone else's, in the order you sent them.

Exchanging Files with AIM

Want to send your friend the latest digital baby picture or a Web page you are developing? Exchanging files with AIM offers real-time immediacy that e-mail and FTP lack.

Before starting, both you and your buddy must make sure your AIM Preference settings allow file exchange (choose My AIM⇨ Edit Options⇨Edit Preferences; use the File Transfer tab). These preferences (in the left-hand side of the File Transfer tab) let you define

> ▶ Who can send you files and where those files will be automatically stored on your hard drive
>
> ▶ Who can get files from you and from which directory on your hard drive

Here's how to do it:

1. Choose People⇨Send File to Buddy. In the Send File box, type in your buddy's screen name, and press Enter.
2. In the Send File To box, type in a few words describing the file, and then click Browse to find the file on your hard drive.
3. If you want, type a few words describing the file. Then send it off!

AIM takes file sharing a step further by letting people help themselves to your files. In the Preference window's Files tab, you can create a folder of files you want to make available to specific people or to anyone. Think of this as a type of personal FTP service. In a work project, others can help themselves to any of the files you choose to make available. Likewise, others can make a shared folder available to you. You can keep a record of who gets files and have AIM check files for viruses.

Changing Your Screen Name

AIM lets you change and format your AIM screen name. You may want to change screen names to suit your different roles

Make sure to have any received files automatically checked by antivirus software. Using the Virus Checker tab of your AIM preferences, you can require that all transferred files be automatically checked for viruses and indicate which antivirus program you want to do the checking. See AOL Keyword: **Virus** for general information and Chapter 16 for a profile of antivirus software.

(work and home) or to personalize access if several people in your house want to use AIM. To add a new screen name follow these steps:

1. Go to www.aol.com/aim. Click the Get It Now button. At the AIM Registration page, type in a new screen name and password, along with your e-mail address. Note that you may need to try a couple of screen names until you find an unused one.

2. After your new information is accepted, click the link that says Click Here To Add the Screen Name Shown Above, and the new screen name will be added to your existing AIM software.

Creating a New AIM Screen Name

As an AOL member, you will need to use an AIM screen name *other* than the AOL screen name you use when registering AIM. You may want to use AIM if you spend much of your time communicating with Internet friends or if you make active use of AIM's chat features, or if you need to exchange files and images with other AIM users. To create a new AIM screen name, you can do any of the following:

▶ When initially installing AIM, toward the end of the process, you'll be asked whether you want to create another screen name. To do so, click Yes and follow the on-screen prompts. With that new screen name, you'll be able to use AIM while using AOL. Instead of downloading the AIM software again from the Web, click the Click Here to Add the Screen Name Shown Above link.

▶ At the AIM Web page (www.aol.com/aim), click the Get It Now button and follow the instructions in the "Changing Your Screen Name" section.

▶ From the AIM Sign-On window (what you see when you open the program), select <New User> from the Screen Name box. In the new window, click Register a New Screen Name. You'll be taken back to the same registration page you originally used to set up your screen name and password. See "Downloading, Installing, and Running the AOL Instant Messenger Service," earlier in this chapter.

12

Live Communication: From Instant
Messages to Internet Chats

Soon after registering, you get an e-mail message (to the address you provided during registration) asking you to confirm your registration. Respond as indicated within the message.

Next time you use the AIM software, the new screen name will be available from the drop-down list. Enter the new password. If you want, check the two boxes to have AIM remember your password and sign you on with minimal fuss.

Formatting Your Screen Name

Why would you want to format an AIM screen name? Most people (teens in particular) format screen names in order to project a certain image — bold, serious, funky, whimsical, whatever. You can alter the appearance of your screen name so that it uses the capitalization and spacing you like—HoLLy HoX 2001, for example. Choose My AIM⇨Edit Options⇨Format Screen Name. Or, you can change your screen name's appearance to make it easier for others to follow your conversation when you're in a heated chat. Enter your screen name and change the capitalization, colors, and spacing. All that matters is that the characters appear in the same order as your original AIM screen name.

Using AIM When You're Away from Your PC

Note

AIM Express takes the place of Quick Buddy, which provided the same services and can still be used on older browsers.

What if you're on the road and can only manage a quick visit to the Net to check your mail and check in with your buddies? And what if you don't have AOL on that laptop or rental computer? AIM Express (shown in Figure 12-8) gives you access to AIM even if you don't happen to have AOL or AIM on the computer you're using. All you need is an Internet connection and recent browser that supports Java, as most browsers have done for several years.

To use AIM Express, you must have already registered with AIM. If you haven't already done so, as explained earlier in this chapter, follow these steps:

Figure 12-8. Use AIM Express when you don't have AIM but do have an Internet connection and an up-to-date browser.

1. Go to www.aol.com/aim/aimexpress.html.
2. Click Start.
3. Wait for the AIM Express software to start, which is created in Java, a kind of Web software that you don't have to store and install.
4. When the AIM Express window is available, sign on using any AIM screen name. If you're using AOL, choose a screen name other than your AOL one. AIM Express does not provide a drop-down menu showing all your screen names and doesn't allow you to save passwords.

   For any screen name, you can use the Buddy List for that screen name created on a copy of AIM.
5. To send a message to someone on your Buddy List, double-click the person's name. In the window that comes up, you can type and send messages, and take part in a conversation. You can send messages from AIM Express to Internet and AOL buddies who are using AIM.

The full range of AIM features (file and image sharing, sounds, wizards, and so on) is not available in AIM Express. Still, the software makes it very easy to have electronic conversations when you are away from your computer.

Using AIM's Stock and News Tickers

When you sign on to AIM, you may notice an additional window with scrolling headlines (see Figure 12-9). The News Ticker brings you the latest news, entertainment, business, and sports headlines refreshed every 30 minutes. To read any story, just click it. To see an easier-to-read list of stories in addition to the ticker, click the ticker's News button. The list of headlines displays best if you make it as wide as possible by clicking the right window border and dragging.

Note

Both the AOL Anywhere service and AIM draw from the same news sources. When you click a link of the AIM ticker, you're taken to a news story from AOL Anywhere.

Tip

Double-click any index or stock as it scrolls by, and you're taken to a Personal Finance Web Center page with up to the moment data on the stock's performance or the index's movement.

Note

AIM Express has no preferences. The preferences in this section apply to installed AIM software. For each screen name, you can create different preferences.

Figure 12-9. AIM's News Ticker makes it easier to keep up with breaking stories.

The news ticker's options can all be set in the AIM preferences window, also available from the ticker itself (see Figure 12-9). The News Ticker options let you choose the headline topics (you can deselect Entertainment, for example), the update frequency (from every 30 minutes to daily), and the ticker's speed. But you can't choose the source of the news.

The second flow of information you can receive on AIM provides customizable stock information. This data appears as a scrolling ticker, too, but within the main AIM window (refer to Figure 12-4). Using the Ticker tab of the AIM Preferences, click Edit Stocks to add individual companies' symbols as well as the major indexes to your stock tickers. The Stock Ticker options on the main Ticker Preferences page, again, are pretty straightforward, giving you control of how often the data gets refreshed and how fast the scroll moves.

Setting Your AIM Preferences

AIM preferences let you alter the look of your messages, the sounds that announce them, who can contact you, and all kinds of other things. Preferences always seem to look more complicated than they are; see Figure 12-10 to get an idea of the extent to which you can tweak AIM to suit your fancy. In fact, the individual preferences are quite simple— there's just so many of them. AIM's truly helpful Help system (choose File⇨Help⇨Help Topics) can show you how to set up all the other preferences not mentioned in this chapter.

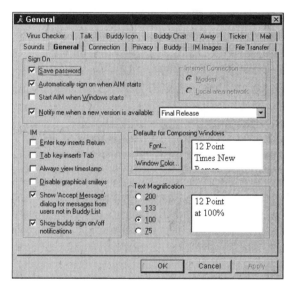

Figure 12-10. Edit your General preferences to make AIM work your way.

To edit any of your preferences, choose My AIM⇨Edit Options⇨Edit Preferences from the Buddy List menu. The Edit Preferences window appears (see Figure 12-10). Each of the tabs contains a set of related preferences. Click a tab to set the preferences. The most important preferences — relating to privacy, files, and sounds — are discussed earlier in this chapter, in the context of specific features.

12

Where to Go from Here

The AOL Instant Messenger service counts as one of AOL's most exciting contributions to the Internet. Just wait until it's available for Linux on Internet appliances you can carry around the house and take wherever you go! This genuinely flexible program, available to AOL members and Internet users alike, functions as a full-featured communications program and information hub. The AOL Instant Messenger service ties you to the Web and to e-mail, and it supports informal chats and serious business. It's always available, even when you are using a computer that doesn't have the AOL or AIM software.

▶ AOL also creates a communications program called ICQ, with an even wider array of features, for people who truly live online. You can read a brief characterization of ICQ in Chapter 16. At AOL Keyword: **ICQ** you can download the software.

▶ Instant messaging is coming to the world of personal digital assistants (PDAs, such as Palms and PocketPCs), as you can see in Chapter 18.

Chapter 13

Joining Focused Communities: Mailing Lists

IN THIS CHAPTER

What's a mailing list?

What's the difference between discussion lists and newsletters?

Finding mailing lists

Joining, taking part in, and leaving mailing lists

Lists worth knowing about

Creating your own mailing list

What you can do about unsolicited mail

Internet mailing lists take a great idea — electronic mail — and improve upon it. Many people consider lists the Net's most informative resource. They can plug you into groups of people who share a strong professional or personal concern.

A mailing list gives you a way to stay in close touch with a group of people who rarely, if ever, meet in the real world. Here's how a list works. Suppose you work for a company with many off-site workers scattered across several states. Or you belong to a PTA chapter that meets only once a month. A mailing list could keep subscribers informed about projects, events, and company news. Or it could plug subscribers into the day-to-day school issues that take place between those monthly meetings.

Lists serve countless purposes and vary enormously in *size* (number of people subscribed) and *volume* (number of messages sent per day). Some lists are interactive, meaning anyone can send a message that reaches everyone on the list. Some lists are passive, meaning subscribers receive a more-or-less regular message, or *newsletter,* from the person, organization, or business running the list. This chapter explores the range of lists available to you through AOL.

Mailing Lists and the Web

As more and more people have started using the Web, mailing lists have taken advantage of many aspects of Web technologies. As a result, lists have taken on a new vitality as part of the larger Internet strategy of organizations and companies. It's also become easier for individuals to start and manage lists, as well as to take part in them. Here's a list of some other mailing-list features:

- ▶ Lists have always been a good way to share news about Internet resources with a group of people who have the same interests. Because hyperlinks are supported in AOL 6.0, sharing discoveries is now a more immediate experience. An example is the AOL's Update newsletter, which brings site reviews to your mailbox each week. The reviews are linked, so you can visit the reviewed sites with just a click.

- ▶ Many lists now have searchable Web archives of list messages so that even non-subscribers can find messages to read on particular subjects. Non-subscribers can't send messages to the list, however. Searching such archives can help you decide whether list members are interested in the same things as you.

- ▶ Many lists become the nucleus of dedicated communities, which have real-world meetings and create Web sites that form tangible, or at least visual, community centers. Such sites also share their resources with others on the Internet.

 Definition

A *mailing list* is nothing more than a list of e-mail addresses managed by software on a centrally available Internet computer, or server. Only people on the list can send mail to other *subscribers* (list members), or receive messages from the list, or both.

 Definition

Subscribing to a list just means joining it. To join a list, you send a request to the *software* managing the list (this chapter shows you how). You don't pay anything and can quit at any time.

 Feature

Now that AOL 6.0 supports HTML (Web) mail, AOL members and Internet users can share links to Web sites of mutual interest.

 Tip

You can search over 150 lists on AOL's computers (listserv.aol.com/ archives/). "Finding Lists to Join," later in this chapter, discusses several other tools to help you find lists.

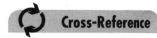

Cross-Reference

Groups@AOL, discussed in Chapter 18, support small communities on the Web. Formed around a shared Web site, Groups include their own mailing lists among many other communications tools.

▶ Increasingly, you can join mailing lists on Web sites, rather than through the cumbersome mail-based subscription methods of the recent past. On such sites, especially corporate ones like the one in Figure 13-1, all you have to do is fill in your e-mail address to subscribe automatically. Likewise, Web fill-in-the-blank forms let you set your preferences and unsubscribe from (leave) a list.

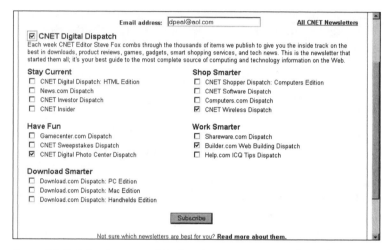

Figure 13-1. Subscribe to any of the four dozen or so CNET newsletters by providing your e-mail address, selecting a couple of lists, and clicking Subscribe.

▶ Many Web sites use mailing lists to keep in touch with their communities — the people who frequent them and share the same interests. Such lists are very easy to join (usually you only have to type in your e-mail address and press Enter), and they can help you stay informed about additions to the Web site.

▶ Finally, a new crop of companies such as Topica and eGroups make it possible for anyone to set up and manage a list on the Web. With such services, subscription requests can be managed and actual messages read on the Web. See "Creating Your Own Mailing List" later in this chapter.

Understanding the Difference between Discussion Lists and Newsletters

Web-based features have powerfully extended lists' popularity and usefulness. This section looks at the two major types of mailing lists:

▶ Interactive *discussion lists,* in which any subscriber can send messages to the entire group and respond to others' messages.

▶ Passive or at least non-interactive lists, sometimes called *newsletters,* which are sent from one person or organization to a list of subscribers.

Discussion Lists

Since the 1970s, people have started and joined lists to stay in touch with other people who share a professional or personal interest. Lists enable communication among a group of friends or colleagues, regardless of the number or location of the people.

E-mail has many advantages as a communication tool, and so, by extension, does the mailing list. Most important, you're under less pressure to respond than if you were having a face-to-face conversation or live electronic conversation (chat). When you get a message, you can respond at your own pace or choose not to respond. With mail and mailing lists, you can keep a record of these slow-motion electronic conversations and listen in to the conversations of the real and self-appointed experts.

Discussion lists differ in three important ways:

▶ How they're managed, or what software keeps them going. That's not your problem, it's the business of the list's "owner." However, the software does affect minor mechanical things like how you subscribe to a list and leave it.

Note

Newsletters at AOL are becoming more interactive. Look for Web-based newsletters soon.

Note

Not surprisingly, the first lists covered technical subjects. Telecomm Digest, which is still active, claims to be the first list (1975). You can find the list's digest and history, a rich resource dealing with the history of telecommunications technology, at hyperarchive. lcs.mit.edu/ telecom-archives/.

Note

The same software can be used to manage discussion lists and newsletters. Much of this chapter focuses on Listserv, the most popular of this software.

▶ How they're moderated. Moderation refers to the right of the list owner to screen list messages and keep out the offensive or off-topic ones. Substantive, useful, on-topic lists tend to be moderated in order to keep them focused. Good lists also thrive on trust and sociability, and don't like one person silencing members without a good reason.

▶ How much the content varies. Every discussion list has its own character: the daily traffic, the ratio of signal to noise (good stuff to garbage), and the general spirit of the group.

You can find discussion lists that cover every subject. For example, I receive a handful of education-related discussion lists. In these lists, teachers discuss how they use the Internet in their classrooms (WWWEDU) and distance educators relate how they adapt their teaching for students who are not in the classroom (DEOS-L). Because of the sheer volume of daily messages, I usually skim these lists and save the notable postings to read when I have more time. Later in this chapter, I give some tips for identifying the mailing lists that best address your interests.

Tip

To save any message to a file, open it and choose File⇨ Save As. Give the file a name and put it in a convenient folder on your hard drive. The message is saved as a text file, with a title and folder location of your choice.

Listiquette (Mailing List Netiquette)

Lurking on lists is okay. That is, feel free to listen to what others have to say without saying anything yourself. As in any community, such observation is often the best way to figure out how things are done and to learn about a list's subject. No rule says you ever have to take part — in fact, most lists expect that you participate only if you have something to say.

On the other hand, lists have their own cultural quirks, and lurking can help you respect them if you do eventually take part; on smaller groups or support groups, for example, not speaking can make you conspicuous. Introducing yourself to a smaller group through a mail message (in list-based support groups focused on a disease, for example) is fine. People in a very large group may be less interested in knowing about every new member. And they definitely don't appreciate responses such as "right on" or "me too!" because they don't add substantively to the discussion.

Avoid asking basic questions that can be answered through other resources.

When you reply to messages, make sure to *quote,* which means to provide some context by selecting relevant lines of a message before clicking Reply. Selective quoting is critical because the quoted material goes into the mailboxes of dozens or perhaps thousands of other people. Re-reading entire messages is annoying, when a word or two would have provided enough context for a person's comments.

Another bit of netiquette carries over from simple e-mail: Humor and irony can backfire easily in a semi-anonymous environment. Write clear subject lines and respect the diversity of your audience in your messages.

Many people like to know who is behind a mailing list message. AOL 5.0 and 6.0 let you create a signature, which is text that identifies you to the others. For Internet mailing lists, make sure to use plain (not formatted text) and provide enough background information to give an idea of where you are coming from. Chapter 11 shows how to create signatures and provides some examples.

Electronic Newsletters

A growing number of lists do *not* let you carry on discussions with the other subscribers. In fact, you usually can't even find out who those people are. These non-interactive lists work like newsletters, with the same message and same information going out from one person (or small team) to a large number of people. Here are some types of electronic newsletters that individuals or organizations create and send to anyone interested in their subject or service:

▶ AOL publishes many channel and forum newsletters, which you can join at AOL Keyword: **Newsletter.** Figure 13-2 shows a sampling of the newsletters AOL offers. Most AOL channels create weekly newsletters devoted to new AOL resources, new Internet resources, and relevant activities in the channel.

AOL's New Web-Based Newsletters

AOL 6.0 allows you to receive and read newsletters from your Online Mailbox in a new Web-like (or HTML) format that makes your reading experience more interactive. While AOL's earlier method of putting colors and links in pages worked only for AOL members, HTML-based mail messages are accessible to anyone — which means you can forward them to your Internet friends. Although your Internet friends may not be able to subscribe to all of the newsletters, Internet users will be able to subscribe to newsletters for some services, such as "You've Got Pictures" and AOL Hometown. The following figure shows you what the new Web format will look like.

If you're already using AOL 6.0, you won't have to create an Interest Profile, but if you use earlier AOL versions you may want to use both AOL Keyword: **Interest Profile** and AOL Keyword: **Newsletters**. If you have AOL 6.0 already, you automatically have access to the new AOL 6.0 format. Earlier versions of AOL do not support HTML mail.

Figure 13-2. Join any of AOL's mailing lists at AOL Keyword: **Newsletter**.

▶ Organizations that have a Web presence often offer mailing lists to keep members, donors, and other interested parties up to date. Such informational mailing lists can provide a key professional service while also promoting the organization's work. For example, I receive several mailing lists on learning disabilities, including the LD Online Newsletter, created by the leading Web site on the subject. At LD Online (www.ldonline.org) you can join the list by merely typing in your e-mail address.

▶ Some newsletters serve informational purposes, but the information is strictly commercial. For example, if you buy books, CDs, and software on the Web, almost all major producers and distributors make it easy for you to join a mailing list. The purpose of these lists is to bring special sales and offers to your attention. Joining such lists is optional, but you may not be aware of your options. Read the fine print when you make an online purchase!

▶ Some electronic newsletters have a strong personal point of view, and share editorials, essays, links, and perspectives. Created by individuals, they serve specialized audiences. One such list is David Strom's Web Informant, which you can join at www.strom.com/ awards. A networking guru and magazine columnist

Cross-Reference

The Dummies Daily (www.dummies.com) lets you subscribe to several dozen newsletters on numerous computing topics (and other topics in the popular For Dummies series). Among the newsletters you will find Computing Basics, Internet Search Tips, Web After Five, and Internet Tools & Techniques.

who writes clearly on a wide range of computing topics, Strom uses Web Informant to share useful insights into subjects such as home networking.

▶ Many newsletters want to offer you something new every day. For example, A Word A Day (AWAD) features daily words, based on themes that change every week or so. (Figure 13-3 shows a typical daily message.) Each day's word includes a definition, a quote, and a link to an audio file in which the word is pronounced. At AWAD's Web site, you can search archives of words as well as subscribe to and unsubscribe from the list. Using Liszt, as described later in this chapter, you can find lists that bring you recipes, Bible passages, jokes (clean or dirty, take your pick), or just about anything else. You can subscribe by merely typing your name and e-mail address into a form on the Web (www. wordsmith.org/awad/).

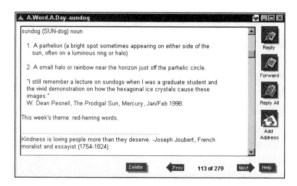

Figure 13-3. The popular A Word A Day mailing list.

▶ Several big news services and Web sites bring the day's news to your mailbox — before you see it on TV. Wired Daily is one such service, which you can customize to your interests (www.wired.com). Infobeat offers different types of daily business news (www. infobeat.com).

Subscribing to AOL Newsletters

AOL's list of forum and channel newsletters is impressive, with categories such as:

▶ AOL User and Computing Tips

▶ Entertainment

► Health and Fitness

► International and Travel

► Lifestyle

► Shopping on AOL

► Younger Set (Kids Only)

Within each category you can find a variety of individual newsletters. In the Lifestyle category alone you can find newsletters about books, parenting, and politics. Figure 13-2 shows individual newsletters (the A–Z listings, not the categories) available through AOL. Most AOL newsletters are weekly.

To join any AOL newsletter:

1. Type AOL Keyword: **Newsletters**.

2. A window appears displaying a variety of categories. Scroll through them and double-click your choice.

3. Choose from among the newsletters available and double-click one.

4. The window that appears allows you to look at archived newsletters and to view the list's current newsletter. Feel free to browse through past newsletters.

5. When you're ready to subscribe, click Subscribe. If you've changed your mind, click Cancel.

A Sampler of AOL Newsletters

Many AOL channels and areas use newsletters to keep AOL members informed about events, resources, and goings-on. Many of these newsletters have a strong point of view and give you a good sense of an AOL area's purpose, resources, and personality. Here is a sample of the newsletters you can find:

► The Kids Only newsletter uses large colorful text, with background colors and an easy-to-read typeface. Kids' poems and messages are often featured.

► The large, growing, and highly informative Computer Center Channel, which caters to the greenest newbie and the most seasoned Internaut, puts out a newsletter that conveys the breadth of the channel's offerings. A typical issue of the Weekly Byte tells you about forums, classes, new downloads, bargains, and contests. Live links take you directly to the forums and areas described.

▶ The Research & Learn Channel's newsletter, Know It All, takes a personal view of the channel's and Web's amazing reference resources. The newsletter's author, Dr. Dewey, compiles lots of info related to the week, the season, and Research & Learn Channel resources.

▶ The Hometown Page Journal (Figure 13-4 shows the newsletter's Web archive) supports AOL's Hometown Web site, where members and non-members can add their Web sites to a fast-growing community of pages. The newsletter looks at a single theme each week (for example Graphic Formats for the Web). It offers a slew of tips for improving your page layout, color use, and more. Especially useful are the links to related online HTML classes and to exemplary member pages.

Figure 13-4. Hometown Page Journal gives you tips for smart Web design and making the most of AOL Hometown's creative Web tools.

Finding Lists to Join

Searching for mailing lists, whether a discussion list or a newsletter, is different from searching for Web sites. You can't readily search the content of mailing lists the way you can search for words that appear on Web pages. Your only clues are the names of mailing lists. That's one reason why you don't have a hopeless profusion of search engines to choose from, as you do in the Web world (see Chapter 9). Instead, you have a few major search services:

► Liszt, a large list of lists with some nifty features.

► PAML, short for Publicly Accessibly Mailing Lists, a hand-created and well-organized directory of mailing lists, similar in structure to a Web directory.

► Listserv's Catalist, a searchable list of the 30,000-plus public Listserv lists, the Internet's most popular type of mailing list software, discussed in "Using Listserv Lists."

I also look at some of the lesser-known sources of information about mailing lists.

Liszt

Liszt (pronounced *list,* a friendly, gratuitous play on the name of the composer) is a searchable database of close to 100,000 mailing lists of all kinds. The number is impressive, but Liszt includes its share of chaff. Searching Liszt means asking Liszt to search its database for the *names* of mailing lists. In your searches, you type a few words and then ask Liszt to look for lists containing those words.

Notice that when you enter more than one word in the Liszt text box, you can specify whether to search for any of the words, all the words in any order, or all the words in the order you type them (that is, a *phrase*). When I typed **Labrador retriever** I didn't get any hits, but when I searched for **dog**, I turned up an entire Liszt Select category — 13 Liszt Select lists and 81 other mailing lists that have the word dog in their names, as shown in Figure 13-5.

Cross-Reference

Chapter 8 goes into the difference between indexes (which are automatically created by software) and directories (which consist of hand-picked resources).

Find It Online

On AOL, you can reach Liszt's Web site by going to AOL Keyword: **Liszt**. The full Web address is www.liszt.com.

Tip

While narrow queries help you ensure useful results in your Web searches, broader queries can help you with your list searches. Remember that Liszt looks only at the names of lists, not the lists' content. A broader search for lists often improves your results. For example, try typing **dog** instead of **Labrador retriever** to see lists that will allow you to discuss your Lab with other loving dog owners.

Tip

Consider starting your
searches for lists with AOL
Search. An AOL Search for
**mailing list Labrador
retriever** produces good
results. It's a way of retrieving
Web pages with mentions of,
or subscription information
about, Lab-related lists. On
AOL Search, see Chapter 8.

Liszt Select is a smallish browsable directory of lists recommended by Liszt users. These lists are arranged in categories
such as Nature and Religion.

Figure 13-5. Liszt, where you can search for specific mailing lists and browse a
directory of recommended lists.

To see results that Liszt retrieves, click an underlined list
name, as in Figure 13-5, and Liszt takes you to a page of information; scroll down for instructions to get information about
the list and instructions for joining it. For lists in the Select category, clicking the link takes you to a somewhat fuller description of what the list discusses, including a link to the list's
home page on the Web, if such a page exists.

Publicly Accessible Mailing Lists (PAML)

An annotated directory of mailing lists, usefully organized into
subjects, PAML goes back to the 1980s. Since 1992, Stephanie
da Silva has kept this Internet classic current, a good example
of Net voluntarism. Today it is available at `paml.net/`.
Browsing PAML's subjects and mailing-list names almost always turns up valuable lists. Here is another example of the
value that only people can add to the search process.
Typically, PAML provides more in-depth information and more
usable information than Liszt. However, PAML's group of lists,
which numbers 7,500, is less than a tenth the size of Liszt's.

Listserv

Listserv is a type of software used to manage a mailing list. Because Listserv has been around so long and can *scale* (or support) huge mailing lists, some of the Net's most popular mailing lists run on Listserv software. On L-Soft International, which currently owns the software, you can search for the world's 35,000 public Listserv lists (`www.lsoft.com/lists/LIST_Q.html`), and your results will include more information than either Liszt or PAML. You find out the size of a list and its official description. When possible, you can also link to a list's home page on the Web. You can find subscription information here as well, and links to a Listserv list's searchable archive.

Using Listserv Lists

As the world's most popular way of managing lists, Listserv hosts a huge number of newsletters and discussion lists, plus the widest available assortment of options.

In a sense, the software used to run a mailing list doesn't make much difference because strong communities can thrive on any kind of list: Listserv or Listproc or whatever. But the important details of joining, participating, and leaving a list differ in small but important ways.

Two other types of lists you may encounter include ListProc (`www.cren.net/listproc/`) and Majordomo (`www.greatcircle.com/majordomo/`). More and more, commercial listproviding services host lists. Such lists strive for simplicity from the perspective of both the list owner (so setting up and managing a list is easy) and the list user (so finding and joining a list is easy).

Every Listserv list, whether newsletter or discussion list, has two addresses, the *administrative* and the *list* address. Where do you find these addresses? Start at LSoft International's very useful Listserv Web site (`www.lsoft.com/lists/listref.html`). Here's what you need to know about these two addresses:

Note

Many people use the term *Listserv* as a generic word to refer to any mailing list. This usage is incorrect. Listserv is a trademarked name referring to a specific type of software created by L-Soft International, Inc. Other kinds of lists work differently.

Note

The following pages on Listserv lists also apply generally to lists – except for the specific commands used to join lists, set options, and leave lists.

▶ You use one address, sometimes called the *administrative address,* to join and leave the list and to set your preferences. Software usually handles the tasks assigned to this address automatically. Smaller lists and some moderated lists have a person who manually handles subscription requests. An administrative address looks like LISTSERV@MAELSTROM.STJOHNS.EDU.

▶ You use the other address, the *list address,* to send messages to the people on the list. A list address looks like OUR-KIDS@MAELSTROM.STJOHNS.EDU.

▶ Listserv commands and list-names are sometimes in all capital letters, but you don't have to follow that pattern. You can use lowercase letters for your addresses, commands, and messages to both administrative addresses and list addresses.

▶ Listserv (the software) doesn't care what's in your message's Subject line when you are writing to the administrative address, you can leave it blank.

Joining Lists (Listserv)

If you want to subscribe to a Listserv list from the Internet, you can send an e-mail message to the list's *administrative address* with a very specific command in the message's body, following these steps (see Figure 13-6 for the result):

1. Click the Write icon on the toolbar. A new Write Mail window appears.

2. In the Send To box, type **listserv@listserv.aol.com**. For your list, the address will differ, but administrative lists often begin with *listserv@.*

3. Leave the Subject box blank.

4. In the body of the e-mail, type the word subscribe and then the name of the list, such as **subscribe hpj2**. Instead of **hpj2**, for your list you would type in the name of the mailing list you want to join.

   What is this list? An AOL newsletter! All AOL newsletters are managed by Listserv. Instead of using AOL Keyword: **Newsletter**, you can send a message directly to the administrative address.

5. Click Send Now.

Find It Online

A comprehensive Listserv help guide is available on AOL at listserv.aol.com.

Note

After you have subscribed to a list, you may receive random administrative messages that ask you to confirm your continued interest in the list or to verify that your e-mail address is still active. You can usually renew your interest with a simple reply to the messages, but you can ignore messages checking your address, as well as the occasional message to test some new piece of software.

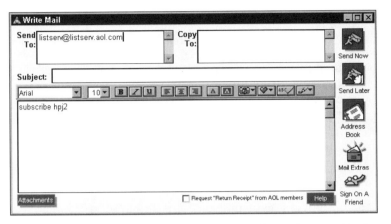

Figure 13-6. Subscribing to a Listserv list requires a simple e-mail message like this one, which subscribes you to AOL's Hometown Press Journal (about AOL Hometown).

Soon after subscribing, you receive an e-mail acknowledging your request. In some cases, you receive a Welcome message almost immediately. Save this message. In fact, it's a good idea to save all your Welcome messages in a safe place. Or, print them out and keep them in a real folder. The Welcome message tells you how to take part in the list, how to get a list of commands for the list, and how to unsubscribe.

Tip

The easiest way to subscribe to a list is to use AOL Keyword: **Newsletters.**

Amazing Listserv Statistics

Public Listserv mailing lists now number more than 30,000, which represents about a fifth of all Listservs. The rest are private lists used within companies and other organizations.

▶ Public Listserv lists are maintained in more than 50 countries, but only the U.S. and Canada each have more that 1,000 lists, with the U.S. having 25,000 lists.

▶ More than 280 public Listserv lists have at least 10,000 subscribers. Among these popular lists, which are available to anyone in the Internet community, are AOL-hosted lists such as Tourbus, NetGuide, Antagonist, Online Investor, and Moms Online. To see all the lists AOL sponsors, use AOL Keyword: **Listserv** or go to listserv.aol.com.

Tip

Always use a brief, precise Subject line to clarify your new topic. Your message will reach many people, and you want them to know what's in the message.

Sending Messages (Listserv)

After you join a Listserv-type discussion list, messages from the list start coming into your AOL Online Mailbox. The number of messages per day depends entirely on the list.

If you want to participate by responding to another *message*, you're taking part in a *thread*, as in the *thread of an argument* or a *common thread*. Each response or reply to a posting continues the thread until another topic takes its place. You can start a topic of your own by sending an e-mail message to the *list* address — *not* the administative address.

Most lists reject commercial postings and unsolicited mail. For example, a list for English teachers is not the place for textbook salespeople to make an unsolicited pitch for their new titles. Spamming a list, or sending unsolicited commercial messages without any relation to the list's purpose, is not smart and is likely to have some negative consequences, like getting you kicked off the list, which is always the list owner's prerogative.

Responding to the List or to an Individual

Suppose that you feel strongly about a message sent to a discussion list, or that you know the sender, or you have a strong response that is unrelated to the list's topic. Should you respond to the whole list or just to the person who sent the message? Here are some considerations to make when you're trying to decide how to respond:

▶ Does the posting make you think of something personal that you want to share just with the sender of the message? If a message asks for specific information that you happen to know, consider responding directly to the person asking, not to the whole group.

▶ If a posting inspires a personal comment or aside, don't send it to the group. Likewise, if you know the sender and have a personal or allusive response, write that person directly.

▶ If you're replying to an individual, beware of that Reply button in the Write Mail window. Clicking Reply usually picks up the list's address as the recipient of your message, not the author of the message you're responding to.

Making the List Work Your Way (Listserv)

Listserv lists, whether discussion or newsletters, offer a wide range of options for users to tailor how and when they receive messages. People rarely use many of these options, probably (I suspect) because the options' usefulness aren't obvious or because few know they exist. Such preferences can be helpful. You set them by sending specific commands to any list's administrative address. For a summary of available commands for a list, send a message to the administrative address (for example, `listserv@listserv.aol.com`) with the single word *help* in the message's body.

Note

Any message sent to automatic-list software such as Listserv has commands in the body of the message. Each command must appear on a separate line and must be spelled correctly.

Digests: A Message a Day

Of all the Listserv commands, many people find digests the most useful. A *digest* packages all messages for the day into a single message. Getting all your messages at once is easier than reading a dozen messages interspersed throughout your day's e-mail, unless you take active part in the list. For a lurker, a digest provides a perfect overview of what's happening on a list. On AOL, digests are often sent as e-mail attachments. Digests packaged as attached files have specific file names. To use attachments, you must download them and read them in a word processor or a text editor such as AOL's, available at File⇨ Open. See Chapter 10 for more about working with attachments.

To find information in a message containing a digest:

▶ The Subject headers for the day's messages are listed at the top of the digest, so you can find interesting threads easily. The following figure shows an example of a digest.

▶ On AOL you can search for specific words in a long digest by pressing Ctrl+F and doing a search.

One drawback of digests is that you can't click the Reply button and respond to the people on the list or even to the individual whose message you are reading. Instead, you must manually identify the list address or an individual poster's e-mail address and then copy and paste it into a new message.

(Continued)

Tip

For comprehensive Listserv commands, send a message to a Listserv administrative address with the command *info refcard* in the body of the message.

(Continued)

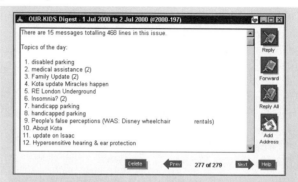

An alternative to digests, available to subscribers and non-subscribers, is a list's searchable Web archive, if one exists. One benefit of Listserv is that archiving is handled automatically. The archives of many Listserv lists can be searched at (`www.lsoft.com/lists/list_q.html`).

Caution

If you ever cancel your AOL account, first make sure to unsubscribe to all the mailing lists you've subscribed to. If you don't unsubscribe, the messages the list sends to your account bounce back to AOL, creating unwanted mail and extra work for the list administrator.

Note

Other types of list software have procedures that are similar in form while differing in the specific commands. Listproc and Majordomo lists, for example, use the *unsubscribe* command, for example, instead of signoff. For every list you join, make sure to save the Welcome message, which includes information about leaving. Many newsletters include unsubscription information with every message.

Leaving a List (Listserv)

You can leave a mailing list for many reasons. You don't like it; it's taking too much time; it's not what you thought it would be. When you're ready to leave the list (unsubscribe), send a message to the list's administrative address. In the message body, include the word *signoff* followed by the name of the specific list. For example, if you want to leave the TOURBUS list, type **signoff tourbus**.

Creating Your Own Mailing List

Taking part in a few good lists can inspire you to create your own list for a Girl Scout troop, extended family, neighborhood, business, or other group. Without much difficulty, you can use

your own mailing list. You have a fairly simple choice, depending on the size of your list and your plans for it. AOL's Address Book can support small and stable lists; Web-based commercial lists can support larger and more anonymous lists where management and security issues can be critical. Here are some mailing-list resources to consider:

▶ Use the AOL Address Book. To create your own mailing list, click the New Group button in your Address Book (available from the Mail menu). In the Manage Group window, give your list a name. Then select names for the list, either from the names (and e-mail addresses) currently in your Address Book or from e-mail addresses you have not yet added to your Address Book. Indicate whether you want to share the list with a group you are creating, and click Save when you're done. The Address Book doesn't care whether the people you include are on AOL, as long as you provide full addresses (with domains) for Internet contacts. When you're done, the list's name appears in the alphabetical list of contacts in your Address Book. Use the list name to send one message to everyone on the list.

▶ For a much greater range of features, you can use the services of a company that does much of the work for you. One such company, Topica (www.topica.com), which owns the Liszt search site, lets anyone set up a mailing list for free. (See Figure 13-7.) You can transfer existing lists to Topica and create new lists by just filling in a Web form with your name and address, the list's name and address, a description, and the associated Web site. Potential subscribers can find the list in the Topica directory, subscribe to it by filling in a simple form, and take part using e-mail.

Caution

Of the ways of creating a group, using an Address Book is the only one that puts the ability to add names in your hands. Before creating such a list, consider telling people what you are trying to do and find out whether they want to join.

Tip

Groups@AOL gives you the tools to create communities of people on AOL and the Net with a strong shared interest. Sharing an Address Book group allows you to make a list of contacts available to everyone in a Group. Chapter 18 introduces Groups@AOL.

Find It Online

Topica lists can be created and managed at www.topica.com. You can also search and read lists there. eGroups (www.egroups.com) is another popular list provider.

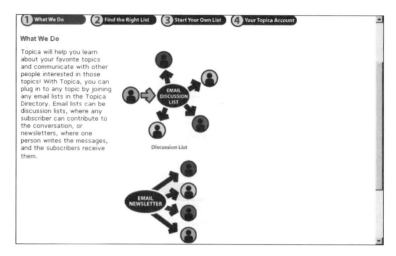

Figure 13-7. You can create and manage a mailing list from Topica.

Newsletters to Help You Keep up with the Net

In choosing a company to host your list, look beyond the price (especially if a company's services are free!) to see whether the list provider can guarantee security, offer technical support, and allow your list to grow. At the very least, the list should be easy for you to maintain and for the user to read.

Increasingly, you can join and read Listserv (and other) newsletters entirely on the Web.

Not surprisingly, the Net provides the best resources for keeping up *with* the Internet. Mailing lists in particular can let you know about Internet resources relating to the subjects that interest you, as well as larger trends in the Internet world. From the lists I read, I learn about many Web sites each day.

An authoritative place to start is the Scout Report. Created by a team at the University of Wisconsin, the Scout Report is a weekly e-mail newsletter containing information about and links to new, high-quality Internet resources. Subscribing ensures that you won't miss an issue, but you can always see the current isssue (and every previous, archived issue) on the Web at scout.cs.wisc.edu/report/sr. Figure 13-8 shows part of the Web version of the Scout Report.

In addition to the classic Scout Report, the Scout Project folks have created a KIDS Report and three specialized reports. You can read, join, and search them all at scout.cs.wisc.edu/.

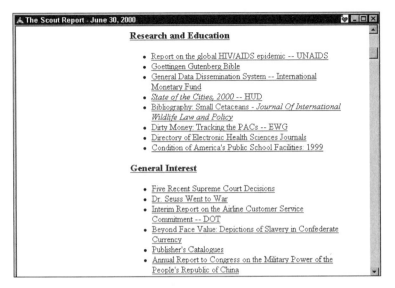

Figure 13-8. The Scout Report reviews some of the highest-quality new Internet resources every week. This figure shows the report's Web edition.

The monthly Search Engine Watch analyzes new features of individual engines and new trends in the frenetic search industry. Searching is fun and essential, and this newsletter is a good way to stay informed about it. To subscribe, just go to `searchenginewatch.com/sereport/` and fill in the form.

Bob Rankin and Patrick Crispen's Internet Tourbus, hosted on AOL's Listserv computers, brings you an inside look into a special Internet topic every few days. Topics range from useful ("sending a fax over the Internet") to fun (a recent newsletter on "LEGOS and crayons"). Recently, the newsletter's authors discussed one of the hostile viruses making its way through the Internet as an e-mail attachment, and made useful recommendations for minimizing the threats from viruses in general. The popular list has its own Web site, where you can both read back issues and subscribe (`www.tourbus.com`).

Another Net-related list stands out for its novel use of multimedia. David Lawrence's Online Today, delivered each morning, contains a RealAudio file attachment. Download the day's file and then, in Windows 95/98, choose Start⇨Documents. Opening the file launches your AOL Media Player, which is included with AOL 6.0. You hear David's radio broadcast, which provides a human-interest view of Net industry news,

Tip

If you receive the HTML version of a list as an e-mail message, save the entire message as a file with the HTML extension. When you open the message (File⇨Open), it appears within a browser, where you click the links.

new resources, trend-setting online happenings, and the like. Each file weighs in at more than 500K, so downloading and storing the files can be burdensome. Alternatively, you can play current and archived issues online at David's site. To get more information, access the archive, and subscribe, start at his Web site, shown in Figure 13-9 (www.personalnetcast.com).

Note

AOL provides the following advice in its Mail Center: "Anything that includes the word 'free' or 'hot,' or has the phrase 'cash cow' or 'make money fast' [in its Subject line], is probably not from someone you know. Likewise, most of your friends have enough netiquette to know better than to type in all caps, and they probably don't end all of their sentences in exclamation points."

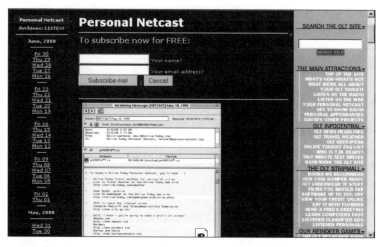

Figure 13-9. David Lawrence's Online Today list comes to your mailbox as a daily audio file with the day's Net gossip, company news, and more.

Note

Strictly speaking, unsolicited commercial bulk mail has nothing to do with *mailing lists*. But you receive such stuff precisely because someone has added your address without your consent to a list of addresses. Grasping the voluntary quality of true lists, whether discussion lists or newsletters, gives you a good sense of what a mailing list is all about.

Loathsome Lists and What to Do about Them

Simple ideas like the mailing list invariably attract deceptive and annoying people who see the potential for exploiting the idea for their own purposes. People who send unsolicited messages promising instant wealth (or at least rapid hair replenishment) compile or buy e-mail lists and send out messages without the recipients' approval. Some such *spam* is toxic, as in the case of some AOL members who have received e-mail messages with links to adult Web sites. At AOL Keyword: **Notify AOL** you can report such messages.

What do you do when people treat your mailbox as their garbage can?

▶ Whenever you see a message from someone whose address you don't recognize or whose subject line contains a pitch or a teaser, consider simply deleting the message right away. Opening such messages sometimes triggers a return receipt (message automatically sent to the person originating the message) and thus verifies the existence of your e-mail address for other spammers and list vendors.

▶ Often, you find hyperlinks (clickable words or phrases that link to Internet Web sites) in your e-mail messages. Beware of hyperlinks in e-mail messages from people you do not know! Spammers often use hyperlinks to direct you to Web sites that look like official AOL or pages, but are not. The e-mails and Web pages may claim that you've won a prize or encourage you to sign up for testing of a new product or service. Avoid clicking hyperlinks sent to you by strangers.

▶ Were you unsure enough about a message's origins to open it anyway? Here's AOL's advice: "To play it safe, you can display the destination of the hyperlinks before you click them. Simply position the cursor over the hyperlink. The destination (Web address) appears in a small box. Links to Web pages show the Web address or URL. Links to areas on AOL say *On AOL Only*. Displaying the destination before clicking a hyperlink is helpful if you're not sure if you should follow the link."

AOL has fought the worst spammers using technology, education, and the court system. When you do open an offensive unsolicited message, play your part by forwarding the message to AOL using AOL Keyword: **Notify AOL**. Unsolicited messages coming from AOL violate AOL's Terms of Service (Keyword: **TOS**) and can get spammers kicked off AOL. Don't hesitate to report them.

Use Mail Controls, as explained in Chapter 3. Spam e-mail addresses are often faked but you can often decode the domains from which they are sent (AOL Keyword: **Learn Domains** explains how). Remember that the domain in an address is the part that goes after the at (@) sign. In the Mail Controls area, click the button that says Block E-Mail from Selected AOL Members, Internet Domains, and Addresses. Enter the domain from which the spam came in the box in the upper right, and click Add, repeating as necessary. Save your additions when you are done.

Tip

Spam messages are phony, and can usually be easily identified as such. Sometimes, the senders cloak their purpose not in friendliness and come-ons, but in official-sounding requests for you to download something, send some money somewhere, or do something harmful like provide your password. At AOL's Mail Center, you can read about particular scams and find out what to do about them. Remember that no one from AOL will ever ask for your password.

Note

AOL takes legal and technical measures against anyone who (among other things) sends bulk e-mail to AOL members, uses fake addresses, and harvests addresses for the purpose of spamming. You can read its Unsolicited Bulk E-mail Policy at www.aol.com/info/ bulkemail.html.

Where to Go from Here

The word *community* is used just about everywhere on the Internet, yet mailing lists and newletters have been quietly and successfully supporting close communities for more than two decades now. This chapter looked at the concept of the list, explained the mechanics of joining and taking part, provided a small sampler of good lists, and suggested ways to find lists and newsletters of interest to you. You even found out how to create a list of your own.

▶ All you need to take part in mailing lists is e-mail. Chapters 10 and 11 provide thorough reviews of the mechanics of reading and sending mail.

▶ While a person usually runs mailing lists, newsgroups are more like public bulletin boards in which anyone can take part. The wilder world of newsgroups is the subject of Chapter 14.

▶ Groups@AOL is a new community feature for AOL and Internet users, and each Group has a mailing list managed using AOL 6.0's Address Book. For more on Groups, see Chapter 18.

CHAPTER

14

GLOBAL BULLETIN BOARDS:
NEWSGROUPS

Chapter 14

Global Bulletin Boards: Newsgroups

IN THIS CHAPTER

Understanding newsgroup organization

Finding newsgroups

Finding newsgroup postings

Some good newsgroups

Reading and posting newsgroup messages

Getting newsgroups to work the way you want

Tapping FAQs: Where they keep knowledge on the Net

N ewsgroups provide a central place for sharing information. They are open to anyone in the world with news-reading software. Because newsgroups (also called *bulletin boards*) can be archived and their collective wisdom condensed, they serve as human knowledge bases. You can turn to them for answers to hard questions on just about any subject. On AOL, you have immediate access to tens of thousands of newsgroups, and news-reading software is right at your fingertips. Read on to find out what newsgroups are about and how you can take part in them.

Newsgroups: The Untamed Frontier

With so many great mailing lists out there, why does anyone pay attention to newsgroups? The answer is complex. The upshot is that the two discussion forums complement each other, and using both of them is worth your time. Before you turn to mailing lists or newsgroups for information, keep these points in mind:

▶ **Mailing lists are more personal.** With a mailing list, you have to go to the trouble of joining. Then, messages (lots of them) come to your own mailbox. The membership on lists tends to be smaller as well as more personal, and list members often come to know each other.

▶ **Newsgroups are more public.** Newsgroups are meant for easy access, and you can flit in and out of them as often as you want. For example, you can read and respond to a posting at `soc.culture.afghanistan` today and never return again. Some newsgroups, however, develop devoted followers who come to know and respect each other.

Newsgroups have many benefits, and AOL helps you find the real treasure buried in them — the diverse perspectives and expert advice on countless subjects. AOL also helps you and your family avoid off-topic newsgroup postings. Parental Controls ward off the folks who send unsolicited commercial messages and lewd advertisements to as many newsgroups as possible. In addition to Parental Controls, AOL's junk filters weed out the nuisance posts. (See Chapter 4 for more about using Parental Controls to keep kids from seeing the trash that makes it through the filters.)

Newsgroups on AOL

Take your pick of two easy ways to get to newsgroups on AOL; both take you to the Newsgroups window, shown in Figure 14-1.

▶ AOL Keyword: **Newsgroups**
▶ AOL Services⇨Internet⇨Newsgroups

Tip

You can take part in both newsgroups and mailing lists on a particular topic, just so that you don't miss any valuable information.

Note

No one controls Usenet, the old-fashioned term for the system of computers and communities that make up the world of newsgroups. Users alone are responsible for respecting the system and its users. While mailing-list administrators moderate and guide mailing lists to some extent, most newsgroups have no effective mechanism for focusing the discussion and preventing conflicts or spamming. That's why netiquette matters more in newsgroups than in other environments. See "Playing Nice," toward the end of this chapter, for the guidelines.

Cross-Reference

Chapter 4 shows how to use Parental Controls to prevent access to all newsgroups, to specific newsgroups, and to newsgroup postings with files attached.

14

Global Bulletin Boards: Newsgroups

Definition

A *posting* is another word for a message. A *newsgroup* contains postings about a specific subject. An *off-topic posting* has nothing to do with a newsgroup's subject.

Tip

If you're new to all this, use NetHelp and the other help resources in the list box (see Figure 14-1).

Tip

You can now search for specific postings on any AOL message board. At AOL Keyword: **AOL Search**, scroll to the bottom of the page and click Message Boards.

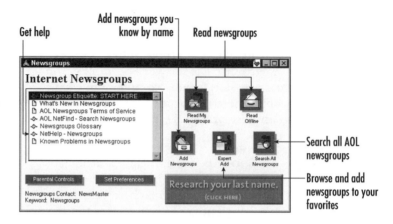

Figure 14-1. Start at AOL's Newsgroups window to find newsgroups, set your newsgroup preferences, and set Parental Controls.

Net Newsgroups and AOL Message Boards: What's the Diff?

If a subject is timely, controversial, popular, or just interesting, AOL probably has a message board for it. Some AOL boards include the MTV message boards (use AOL Keyword: **MTVmessageboards**), Grandstand Message Boards (in the Sports channel), and the Teens Message Boards (AOL Keyword: **AOLTeens**). The following figure shows boards from AOL's Teens Channel.

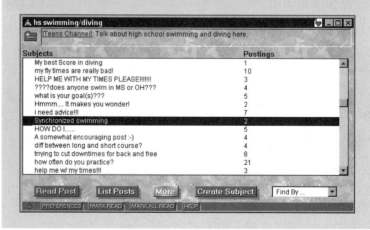

What's the difference between newsgroups on the Net and message boards on AOL? In structure, not much. As time goes by, AOL's boards have come to look and work more like the Net's newsgroups. The audience size, breadth of subjects, and depth of postings are quite similar. You can read AOL's message boards offline, just like newsgroups, and both let you mark messages as read and unread to simplify reading.

The real differences lie in organization and content. Newsgroups, as you can read in the next section, have a top-down structure. Their content is, well, uncensored (hence the need for Parental Controls). AOL's message boards are attached to AOL areas, so no overall organizational scheme exists. AOL's Terms of Service make AOL's boards family-friendlier than newsgroups.

You set your message-board preferences in much the same way you do for newsgroups. When you click the Preferences button on any message board, you get a window that allows you to create custom signatures and filter out messages from certain people and on certain subjects. Newsgroup preferences, discussed later, give you the same capabilities but offer much finer-grained controls, through the use of Parental Controls and controls that apply to individual newsgroups.

How Newsgroups are Organized

Think of newsgroups as a set of boxes within boxes, with subjects containing topics, and topics containing newsgroups, and newsgroups containing messages.

▶ A newsgroup is like a box containing messages. *Newsgroups* are the places where you read and post messages about a narrowly defined area of interest.

▶ Every newsgroup is stored in a box called a *topic*.

▶ Each topic is contained in an even larger box called a *category*.

For example, the rec category contains recreational topics on everything from autos to woodworking. Each topic consists of many individual newsgroups. Bigger topics even have subtopics, which then contain the newsgroups. You can find the actual human postings — the part that interests you — in a newsgroup. Figure 14-2 shows part of the list of rec topics, with a specific newsgroup in that topic highlighted.

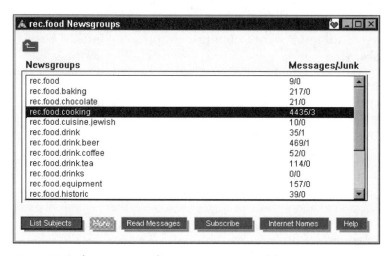

Figure 14-2. The rec category, the rec.food topic, and the rec.food. cooking newsgroup.

Tip

At AOL Keyword: **Newsgroups**, click Add Newsgroups to see which categories AOL carries and the topics, subtopics, and individual newsgroups available for every category.

Note

In earlier editions of this book, *hierarchies* referred to categories and *articles* referred to messages. In this chapter, I'll use categories, topics, newsgroups, and messages (or postings). Messages that are replies to other messages form *threads*. An asterisk (*), as in comp.dcom.*, refers to all the newsgroups in a topic. Newsgroup names are lowercase.

Newsgroup names look like e-mail addresses (explained in Chapter 10), but they are quite different. A newsgroup like rec.food.cooking consists of elements that are separated by dots. The elements proceed from the general to the specific, from the rec category, to the rec.food topic, to the rec.food.cooking newsgroup. The element to the far left is always a category; the element to the far right is the newsgroup; everything in between is a topic (and sometimes a subtopic).

You can find the oldest core newsgroups in the so-called Big Seven categories: comp, misc, news, rec, sci, soc, and talk. Humanities, a newer category, is often included among these big, somewhat formal categories.

The easy-to-set-up alternative newsgroups have surpassed the Big Seven in numbers and popularity. *Alternative* refers to non-Big Seven newsgroups in general and to the alt category in particular. In other words, alt is a disparate, messy category that includes some newsgroups on topics that aren't very alternative. For example, you can find newsgroups on theology here, as well as newsgroups on numerology. You also find mainstream alternative newsgroups (non-Big Seven) devoted to geographical locations, universities, professions, and other less-general areas of interest. Alt newsgroups are still publicly available to anyone in the world who has newsgroup access and whose ISP carries those particular categories.

Here is an overview of some common top-level categories (the part that appears at the beginning of a newsgroup name):

▶ **aol.** AOL's own newsgroup category, for AOL-related newsgroups. The newsgroups in this category tend to meet the general needs of AOL members in specific parts of the U.S.

▶ **alt.** Alt is bigger than some of the traditional categories — rec, soc, and so on — because starting an alt newsgroup involves less fuss than starting one in the traditional categories.

  • Alt does contain many valuable newsgroups, but you have to look for them. For example, in the `alt.support.*` category you can take part in `alt.support.alzheimers`. Postings here often provide good information and vital support for both patients and caregivers.

  • Celebrity watchers will enjoy the `alt.fan.*` newsgroups. Stanley Kubrick fans may want to spend time listening to the banter in `alt.movies.kubrick`.

  • Two interesting hobby newsgroups include `alt.true-crime`, in which both current and past crimes are discussed, and the hugely popular `alt.folklore.urban`, in which participants keep track of the strange obsessions, myths, and stories that haunt city minds.

▶ **bit.** Based on the old BITNET network, which housed the Net's early mailing lists, bit consists of the newsgroup versions of serious mailing lists. For example, `bit.listserv.lawsch-l` contains postings from the LAWSCH-L mailing list and `bit.listserv.autism` carries messages from the AUTISM-L mailing list.

▶ **biz.** Want to get rich fast? The biz category offers a place for some business, or at least some inexpensive advertising. For the most part, blatant profit-making attempts are discouraged elsewhere. In the appropriate biz newsgroup, these efforts can be welcome and won't shock anyone. Whether people notice them is another question. The `biz.marketplace.*` category is particularly busy.

▶ **comp.** As you might expect, this category is devoted to computers, software, programming, and related topics.

- Computer novices can find much value in this category. If you want to learn more about using HTML, for example, turn to the newsgroup `comp.infosystems.www.authoring.html`.

- If you want to learn more about using Windows, check out `comp.windows.misc`.

- Particularly informative are the data communications (dcom) newsgroups (`comp.dcom.*`).

▶ **misc.** Includes newsgroups that don't readily fit easily elsewhere, or in only one category. You can read about parenting in `misc.kids` and about immigration in `misc.immigration.usa`. Get educational information from the `misc.education` newsgroups. The best way to see what is available in this category is to browse (from AOL Keyword: **Newsgroups**, click Add Newsgroup, and double click the misc category).

▶ **news.** Look here for USENET news, not political news. For example, you can find answers to a lot of your questions about newsgroups in the group `news.answers`, one of the most popular. Read about proposed new groups in `news.groups`. Want real news? Check AOL's News Channel.

▶ **rec.** Recreational subjects. For example, look in the `rec.travel.*` subcategory for general discussions about traveling and in `rec.travel.air` for grousing, cheap tickets, and tips for solving airline disputes. The `rec.sports.*` category offers newsgroups for numerous sports.

▶ **sci.** Devoted to newsgroups with a strong scientific orientation. The participants tend to be well-informed, and many are pursuing advanced degrees. Interested amateurs have a strong place, also. Some newsgroups in the sci category include `sci.astro.amateur`, `sci.physics`, `sci.environment`, and `sci.lang`. The latter group focuses on linguistics.

▶ **soc.** Embraces newsgroups that focus on big social issues or big personal issues, like relationships. Some of the groups include `soc.support.pregnancy.loss`, a moderated group for parents who have suffered early bereavement, and `soc.couples.intercultural`, for couples dealing with intercultural issues. One volatile category tends to be the `soc.culture.*` topic, which is home to many ethnic feuds. If you're studying another country or traveling abroad, ask a question in `soc.culture.*` to get inside info and perhaps meet someone who lives where you are going.

▶ **talk.** Provides a forum for the discussion of divisive issues, usually relating to public policy. You can spot the potential for controversy in the newsgroups' names: `talk.politics.guns`, `talk.politics.mideast`, and `talk.origins` (for evolutionists and creationists). The people who take part in such newsgroups tend to like amateur boxing.

▶ **regional categories.** Newsgroups within a regional category begin with their own category name and can focus on all issues particular to that region, if the traffic is heavy enough. Often, the individual newsgroups are practically empty. Local Web sites and destinations such as Digital City (on AOL) are replacing these newsgroups.

- Regional categories for state newsgroups use the two letter postal abbreviation, such as `ca.*` (for California) or `co.*` (for Colorado). The prefix for cities or other regions may be three characters or longer, such as `atl.*` (for Atlanta), `triangle.*` (for the Research Triangle area in North Carolina), and so on.

- In many regional categories, you can likely find a newsgroup in which job ads are posted that for the area. For example, if you are in California, check out the newsgroup `ca.jobs`. If you want a newsgroup that is even more geographically specialized, check out `la.jobs` or `sacramento.jobs`, to name just a few.

14

Global Bulletin Boards: Newsgroups

Definition

As with mailing lists, a *subscription* to a newsgroup merely simplifies the process of taking part in the newsgroup, but you don't have to take part if you subscribe. In AOL, subscribing means adding a newsgroup to a list called Read My Newsgroups. Adding a newsgroup to this list (subscribing) gives you quick access to your favorite newsgroup. You must add a newsgroup to this list if you want to use Automatic AOL to download postings from that newsgroup.

Tip

To remove a newsgroup from your list, select it and click the Remove button.

Adding Newsgroups to Your Favorites

Read My Newsgroups contains your favorite newsgroups — the ones you want to read regularly. You can easily change what's in the list as your needs change. For example, you may use newsgroups as a temporary resource of information about a financial, medical, or other problem, or you may be looking for specific information about an upcoming trip or event. Including a newsgroup in Read My Newsgroups also allows you to keep track of which messages you've read in any newsgroup, so you won't have to re-read messages.

To add groups to Read My Newsgroups, you use either the Add Newsgroups button or the Expert Add button in the main Newsgroup window.

> ▶ Use the Expert Add button if you know the full name of the newsgroup you want to add (for example, `rec.pets.cats`). Clicking Expert Add at AOL Keyword: **Newsgroups** saves a few steps but makes sense only if you know a newsgroup's full name and don't want to know what else is available in the same topic. Make sure to get the name exactly right!

> ▶ Use the Add Newsgroups button to browse categories and view an interesting newsgroup before subscribing to it.

> Say you want to subscribe to a newsgroup about cooking but aren't aware of what's out there. After clicking Add Newsgroups at AOL Keyword: **Newsgroups**, double-click rec (the category where hobby topics are kept) and then `rec.food` (topics about food). Select a newsgroup and click the Subscribe button. In Figure 14-3, `rec.food.cooking` has been added to Read My Newsgroups. Repeat the process for any other groups you want to read regularly.

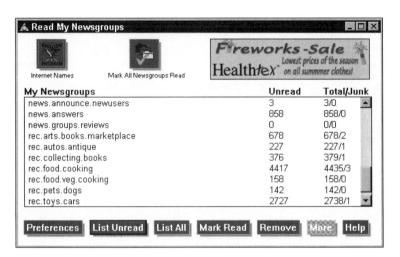

Figure 14-3. Read My Newsgroups contains the newsgroups to which you subscribe.

Searching for *Newsgroups* on AOL

Burrowing through levels and levels of topics and subtopics
can leave you empty-handed. To search for newsgroups containing certain words or parts of words in their names, click
the Search All Newsgroups button in the Newsgroups window to display the Search All Newsgroups window. Use this
window to search for newsgroups (by name), not postings (by
content). For content searching, see the next section.

Suppose you want to find newsgroups about cars (that is,
newsgroups with *cars* in their name). Type **cars** in the box at
the top of the Search All Newsgroups window, and click the
List Articles button. You see a list of newsgroups containing
articles on the subject, as in Figure 14-4.

Double-click the newsgroup you want to read. In a new window, you have a choice. You can either list a newsgroup's articles or subscribe to the newsgroup (add it to Read My
Newsgroups). Actually, clicking either List or Subscribe has the
same immediate effect: Either one allows you to read the
newsgroup. The difference is that, when you subscribe, the
newsgroup goes into Read My Newsgroups, and from there,
you can quickly retrieve the newsgroup for future reading.

Tip

You can add either individual
messages or entire news-
groups to your Favorite
Places folder just by clicking
the heart in the respective
windows' upper right-hand
corners. You might do this to
create a Favorite Places
folder devoted to a very specific topic and put all sorts of
content — e-mail messages,
newsgroups, Web sites, and
so on — into the folder.

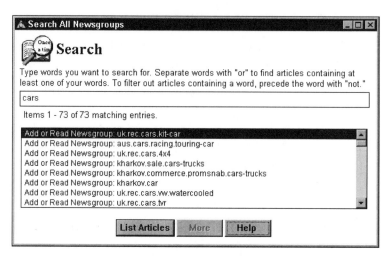

Figure 14-4. Many of the newsgroups about cars are in regional categories, such as those created for the UK and the Ukrainian city of Kharkov.

Searching for Newsgroup *Postings* on Deja

Deja (formerly DejaNews) is available on the Web at www.deja.com.

Deja searches are not subject to AOL's Parental Controls. Children who are underage could use Deja to access inappropriate newsgroup postings. See Chapter 4 to find ways your whole family can surf the Net safely.

The free Deja Web site archives newsgroup postings from 1995 to the present. With Deja, you can quickly unearth postings about highly specific subjects scattered across newsgroups you may not have considered using in your search. I've successfully used Deja to find topics ranging from buying used pianos to repairing the Microsoft Windows registry (the software that keeps track of software installed on your system).

In recent years, Deja has developed into a product-research tool as well as a newsgroup searcher. The following instructions for searching newsgroups (called *discussions* by Deja) may differ slightly from what you find when you conduct your own search. Deja remains the best newsgroup searcher, however, so be patient! To use Deja to browse or search newsgroups

1. Go to the Deja Web site at www.deja.com, and then click Search Discussions (see Figure 14-5). The direct Web address for Search Discussions is www.deja.com/usenet.

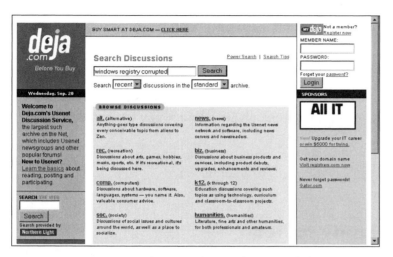

Figure 14-5. Use Deja to search across newsgroups for postings dealing with a specific topic (Search box). You can also browse newsgroups (Browse section).

2. To search for postings on a specific subject, use the search box (refer to Figure 14-4). You can review search results by posting date or alphabetically by subject, forum (newsgroup), or by the person posting. You can also refine your search and restrict it to just one of the newsgroups with relevant postings.

   To browse categories and individual newsgroups, as you would on AOL (Add Newsgroup), use the Browse Discussion sections.

In Figure 14-5, you can see the results of a search for *windows registry corrupted*. When I did the search, more than 400 other people had recently posted messages about the subject to various newsgroups. If you're posting a question, you can increase the chances that you'll get a response by choosing the newsgroups with the most postings.

Use Deja's Power Search to refine your queries, specify the language in which you want to read, tap the full Deja newsgroups archive, or restrict your search to specific newsgroups, posters, or dates. For advice on buying pianos, for example, you may want to look at one of the more heavily trafficked newsgroups, such as `rec.music.makers.piano`.

Tip

Whether you're browsing or searching, use Deja to find the exact names of newsgroups for use with AOL's Expert Add feature. Go to AOL Keyword: **Newsgroups** and click Expert Add. Type the name of the newsgroup in the Internet Name field to add it to your Read My Newsgroups list.

14

Global Bulletin Boards: Newsgroups

Deja lets you browse newsgroups once you've pinpointed specific postings, and you can read about Deja's additional newsgroup features when you visit the site. Here's a sampler of what you can do:

- ▶ Follow the next and previous messages in the thread.
- ▶ E-mail the person who wrote a message and view that person's posting history.
- ▶ Read the newsgroup postings online.
- ▶ Sort messages in different ways.

Ready to Read

Definition

On AOL, a newsgroup subject is the same as a discussion thread. A thread con-sists of two or more messages with the same subject line. A one-message subject is, well, just a message.

From AOL Keyword: **Newsgroups**, click Read My Newsgroups to see the newsgroups to which you have sub-scribed. Double-click the newsgroup you want to read. The newsgroup comes up in its own window (like the one in Figure 14-6), with all the subjects displayed.

Double-click to select the subject you want to read about. Subjects consist of several postings about the same thing (they have the same subject line). To read the messages with this subject, click Read. The first message with that subject appears in the window.

To jump to a specific message in a subject, simply click List in-stead of Read. The authors of posts with that subject appear in the window. Double-click the specific message you want to read. To proceed to the next message within a subject (same thread), click the Message --> button. To proceed to the next subject, click the Subject --> button. Likewise, you can read previous messages within the subject as well as previous sub-jects by clicking the left-pointing arrows, as shown in Figure 14-7.

A thread of related messages   Click to see all the headers for a list

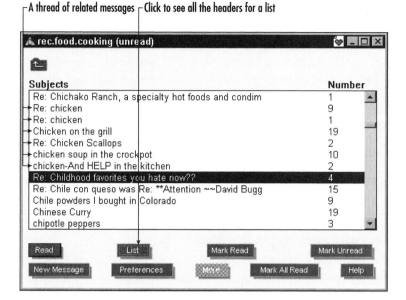

Figure 14-6. You can see a list of subjects in the newsgroup window.

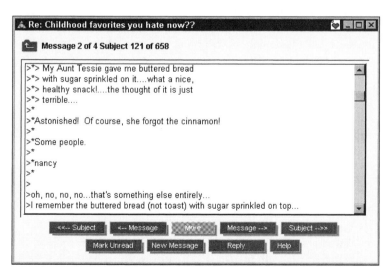

Figure 14-7. The second message from one of the subjects shown in Figure 14-6.

Marking Messages as Unread or Read

When you open a message in a newsgroup, whether it's on AOL or Deja or elsewhere, it is automatically marked as read (meaning you at least opened it up). If you want to see the message again, next time you visit the newsgroup, click the Mark Unread button. Marking postings unread can be compared to keeping e-mails "as new," as described in Chapter 10. It's a way of ensuring access in the near future.

If you don't want to see any old messages in a newsgroup, just subsequent messages, then select the newsgroup in the Read My Newsgroups window (click once) and click the Mark Read button.

Saving Newsgroup Messages

If you want to print a message you're reading choose Print⇨Print from the AOL menu bar.

You can save a newsgroup message for future reference by displaying it and choosing File⇨Save. Give the message a name and put it into a folder. Postings are saved as text, so you can later view them in AOL's text editor (File⇨Open) or any word processor. As always on the Net, be mindful of copyright laws and common courtesy. You can't redistribute a great posting or borrow large parts of it just because you like it. Ask the poster's permission. If you haven't done so already, familiarize yourself with the information at AOL Keyword: **Copyright**.

Sending Messages

You can post a newsgroup message of your own in two ways:

▶ The easy way is to reply to someone else's message, which is just like replying to a mail message.

▶ Or, you can start your own subject by asking a question, making a comment, or sharing a recipe or opinion — whatever is appropriate in the newsgroup.

However you take part, bear in mind the Netiquette guidelines outlined in "Playing Nice."

Replying to a Newsgroup Message

To reply to a message you are reading, click Reply. The Post Response window appears, with the original message in the Original Message Text box at the left. See Figure 14-8.

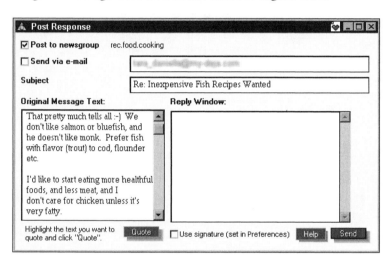

Figure 14-8. Replying to someone else's message is easy in a newsgroup.

You can, if you wish, send your reply only to the sender of the original posting, as a mail message (click in the Send Via E-Mail box). Or you can send the message to the entire newsgroup, as a newsgroup posting (click in the Post to Newsgroup box). Or, check both boxes. Proceed by highlighting, in the Original Message Text box, the portion of the post to which you are responding. When you have selected the text that you want to include, click Quote. The quoted text appears in the Reply Window box on the right, serving as context for your replies. Now, type your response.

If you want to include your signature in your post, click in the Use Signature box. You can find instructions for creating a signature later in "Setting Newsgroup Preferences." All done? Click Send.

Composing a New Message

Click the New Message button in the newsgroup window if you want to post a message with a new subject. Of course, your message can grow out of earlier discussions in the newsgroup or revive themes of common interest. Figure 14-9

Definition

A *signature* generally contains your name and any other information you want to provide and goes at the end of your messages.

shows the Post New Message window. Type the subject in the Subject box, and type your message in the Message box. If you want to include your signature in the post, click in the Use Signature box. Click Send when you're done.

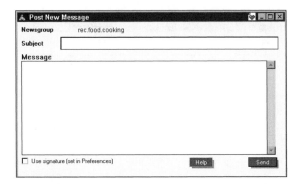

Figure 14-9. Start a new message in the Post New Message window. If others reply, then you've started a thread. Congratulations!

Deleting Your Posts

Oops. When you post something you wish you hadn't, you can sometimes delete the message before anyone catches your blunder. You have no guarantees, of course. Your message may have made its way from AOL to the Internet's countless newsgroup servers (computers). If the message is still on AOL's computers, chances are that you can still delete your message. Here's how: Click Read My Newsgroups and select the newsgroup to which you posted your message. Open your message, and click Delete.

Playing Nice

Getting along in newsgroups is not much different from getting along with your neighbors — in a very big city. Unfortunately, newsgroups are even more anonymous than the biggest city. In the absence of other people's sighs, smiles, smirks, grins, and countless cues, the full meaning of any message can be unclear. That's why adhering to some common-sense guidelines helps, a few of which follow.

Online, common sense serves as the best guide. If you were attending your first meeting about a topic, you probably wouldn't shout out a question to the expert at the microphone or ask a simple question of an expert when you know you could get the answer on your own. On newsgroups, too, you may want to listen and read for a while in order to figure out what behavior is appropriate.

Another way to get up to speed is to read the FAQ, the frequently asked questions document created by many newsgroups to distill the group's point of view and collected wisdom. See "FAQs: Essential Reading."

Flaming Hurts

To *flame* someone is to lash out verbally; it's an old, obnoxious Internet hobby inflicted self-righteously by people who think they know better or who like to humiliate others, or both. Flaming is generally discouraged in newsgroups, with the exception of newsgroups like `alt.flame`. AOL's message boards are prone to the same excesses but usually have explicit rules regarding flaming. If you aren't sure whether the message you are going to send is a flame, save it as a text file and look at it tomorrow, or ask someone else to look at it.

You don't have to curtail your style completely on newsgroups, just use the same degree of discretion you would if you were speaking to an audience of thousands. That is, after all, what you are potentially doing in newsgroups.

Lurk Before Posting

Before you post anything to a particular newsgroup, read and hold back for a while in order to figure out what is appropriate. Many newsgroups are populated by long-time members and have cliques. Members accept you more easily if you lurk and understand the group dynamic before posting at a newsgroup for the first time. Many newsgroups and mailing lists, in particular, have distinctive cultures, and some are more inhospitable to newcomers than others.

Note

Unlike e-mail, newsgroups can't be sent later. You've got to do your proofreading on the spot. If you want to wait before you send something, create your posting as a text file and proof it once or twice before sending it.

Definition

In the Newsgroup Glossary, available from the list box at AOL Keyword: **Newsgroups**, a *troll* is defined as "A purposely stupid, inflammatory, or downright wrong article (closely related to *flamebait*). Its purpose is to get people mad and make them look stupid and gullible."

Definition

Spamming means sending an unsolicited commercial posting to newsgroups whose scope is clearly unrelated to the product or service being peddled, whether it's hair tonic, penny stocks, or a miracle diet.

Find It Online

To read the FAQs for the newsgroups listed, go to AOL Keyword: **FTP** and then click the Go To FTP button. In the Favorite Sites list, double-click on `rtfm.mit.edu:/pub`. The FAQs cited in this section are in the usenet-by-hierarchy folder.

Post Appropriately

I don't like to nag, but here are some don'ts to consider:

▶ Don't post chain letters, get-rich schemes, multilevel marketing plans (even if you are convinced of their worth), or anything clearly unrelated to the newsgroup.

▶ Don't cross-post, which means to send the same posting to many newsgroups.

▶ Don't spam! AOL is very clear about the consequences of sending unsolicited commercial messages. You can read AOL's Unsolicited Mail policy in the Community Guidelines available at AOL Keyword: **TOS**.

▶ Don't post questions for which the answer is readily available elsewhere, such as in an encyclopedia or the newsgroup's FAQ. Later in this chapter I provide a section on FAQs, with places where you can find FAQs for many newsgroups.

▶ Don't quote an entire message if you're responding to a single message. Quoting excessively wastes space and time.

A Few Good Newsgroups

You can find newsgroups for just about any taste or topic. The posters who participate in the ones shown here tend to have long-standing bonds and a strong sense of community. These newsgroups serve as examples. Take the time to find newsgroups that focus on your own interests.

`alt.folklore.urban.` Based on the work of folklorist Jan Brunvand, who coined the term *urban legends*. Designed for (and as a parody of) the gullible, this acerbic newsgroup may turn you into a confirmed skeptic. Posters note the re-emergence of old tales, and pick apart new ones. This old newsgroup has created a series of spin-off Web sites, including `www.urbanlegends.com` and `www.snopes.com` (for newsgroup FAQs and background information). The newsgroup's no smiley rule has caused grief to some newbies. The guideline regarding lurking-before-posting applies here.

misc.kids.moderated. This newsgroup serves parents or anyone seeking information or advice about children. The moderation is lightly wielded but effective, and the postings tend to be substantive and on-topic The postings about creative baby gifts in Figure 14-10 are an example of what you can find here. Be sure to check out the other misc.kids groups and their FAQs for the collective wisdom of this experienced crowd.

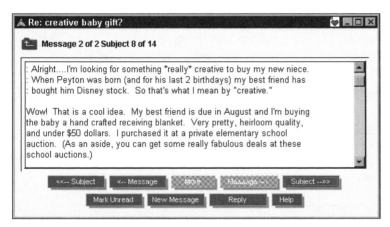

Figure 14-10. Ideas for creative baby gifts from misc.kids.moderated.

rec.arts.books.childrens. This group is for people who love children's literature, as well as for those seeking to find the best books for kids. The enthusiasm of the participants is contagious. Lively discussions routinely flare up around the latest Harry Potter book and the casting for the movie(s). On Harry Potter, also check out alt.fan.harry-potter. (The alt category is the place for fan newsgroups.)

rec.food.*. This family of topics contains many useful newsgroups for cooks and gourmets.

rec.pets.dogs. You, too, can join the online community of dog lovers. Hundreds of FAQs discuss things like breeding dogs, traveling with them, and caring for them. Currently, you can find seven, more specialized newsgroups on this topic, including rec.pets.dogs.behavior and rec.pets. dogs.health.

Setting Newsgroup Preferences

Global Newsgroup Preferences affect every newsgroup you read on AOL. They govern such things as how newsgroups appear, whether a signature is added to all your messages, and the removal of irrelevant postings.

On AOL, you can set finer-grained preferences for each newsgroup in the Read My Newsgroups list. For example, if certain subjects in rec.creative-cooking simply don't interest you, use the Set Preferences button to filter them out. This section reviews global and newsgroup-specific preferences.

Setting Global Newsgroup Preferences

At AOL Keyword: **Newsgroups**, click the Set Preferences button to display the Global Newsgroup Preferences window, shown in Figure 14-11. The window has three tabs: Viewing, Posting, and Filtering. Click a tab to see a different set of preferences.

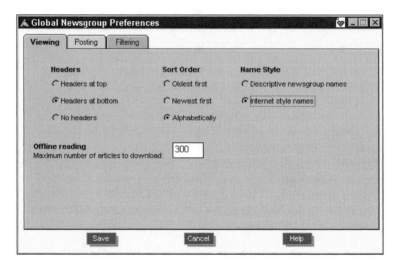

Figure 14-11. Control how you want to view your newsgroup messages in the Global Newsgroup Preferences window.

Newsgroup-Viewing Preferences (Viewing Tab)

Click the Viewing tab to control how the messages appear.

> ▶ **Headers.** Headers provide more documentation than most mortals need about a posting's circuitous path

from a message-writer to your PC. If you aren't deeply interested in network routing, you can choose to banish headers to the bottom of the message or to make them go away altogether.

▶ **Sort Order.** You can view postings with the oldest posting first, or the newest. Starting with the newest first can help you get up-to-date quickly, while starting with the oldest lets you follow discussions as they develop. If you choose to view postings alphabetically, you can scan through the subjects and quickly identify threads that interest you.

▶ **Name Style.** If you have used other Internet providers besides AOL, you are likely used to Internet-style (actually, Usenet-style) newsgroup names. This is the naming scheme that is introduced above, with categories, topics, and newsgroup names (for example `rec.food. cooking`). AOL applies its own Descriptive names to many newsgroups, such as food, cooking, cookbooks, and recipes. If you don't feel comfortable with dots and terse naming-systems, use the descriptive style names.

▶ **Offline reading.** Use this box to limit the number of messages downloaded when you use Automatic AOL, as described in "Using Automatic AOL for Your Newsgroups."

Posting Preferences (Posting Tab)

Click the Posting tab to set posting preferences. These preferences relate to how you want others to identify you when you post. Do you want to use your real name? Do you want people to know your e-mail address? Or, do you want to provide some personal information about yourself, using a signature?

▶ **Using Your Real Name.** If you want to be identified by your real name in parentheses after your e-mail address, which is included with your postings, enter your name in the box. You can also use a nickname or choose to provide no personal information. Use your judgment, and weigh the risks and benefits of using your real name.

▶ **Junk Block.** Senders of unsolicited e-mail, or *spammers,* are always looking for new e-mail addresses. One way to help deter spammers from finding yours is to add a Junk Block to your e-mail address. For example, if

Tip

Because descriptive names aren't available for all newsgroups (and they're not available outside of AOL, for example on Deja), no one will know what newsgroup you mean when you use a Descriptive name. Becoming comfortable with the Internet style comes in handy!

14

Global Bulletin Boards: Newsgroups

Definition

A *signature* consists of the contact info, quotes, URLs, and other tidbits that you can append automatically to your message. On AOL you can have signatures appended automatically to mail messages (see Chapter 11) and to newsgroup postings.

Caution

AOL does not control newsgroups and therefore cannot control the content of specific postings. Instead, AOL gives you the tools to avoid what you dislike.

Cross-Reference

A domain is the part of an e-mail address after the at symbol (@). See Chapter 10 for the lowdown.

someone with the screen name `PineFirForest` puts *applepie* in his Junk Block, his posting address appears as `PineFirForest@aol.comapplepie`. Any attempts to e-mail that address would be unsuccessful. Enter whatever word you like. The drawback is that legit readers who want to e-mail you may have a more difficult time, because they won't be able to use the Reply-To feature without editing the Junk Block address.

▶ **Using a Signature.** You can use a signature to express your personality, tell a joke, display your insight, provide business contact information, or all the above. You type a signature in the lower box. A signature block is shown in the box. Note that people who don't use AOL may not see any color, size, or type effects — stick with simple text.

Filtering Out Garbage (Filtering Tab)

Online garbage consists of any message, delivered by e-mail or newsgroups, that you didn't ask for; you may find it lewd, offensive, or obnoxious. You may even question the message's legality. That's why using newsgroup filters is a good idea — these fillters are a great supplement the newsgroup Parental Controls described in Chapter 4.

Your Filtering preferences let you block messages that contain a particular word or words in the subject line. You can also block messages from particular people and messages from particular domains. (In message boards, all the messages are within the AOL domain.) Here are the different ways to filter postings:

▶ If you want to filter out all messages containing a particular word in the subject, select Subject Contains from the Select Filter Type drop-down list. Enter the word in the Enter New Filter box and click the Add Filter button. Add as many filtering words as you want.

▶ If you want to avoid all posts from the poster who is sending unsolicited messages, select Author Is from the Select Filter Type drop-down list and enter the appropriate e-mail information.

▶ If you notice that a particular domain seems to produce many unwanted postings, select Domain Is and type in the name of the offending domain.

Here's a more benign use of filters: If you're an avid cook but you don't like vegetarian food, just block messages containing *tofu* or whatever you would not like to see in your `rec.food` newsgroup.

Setting Preferences for an Individual Newsgroup

You can refine your newsgroup-reading experience by setting preferences for individual newsgroups. The Preferences window, shown in Figure 14-12, is available in two places:

▶ At AOL Keyword: **Newsgroups**, click Read My Newsgroups. Select a newsgroup, and then click the Preferences button.

▶ Open any newsgroup in Read My Newsgroups and click Preferences.

A glance at Figure 14-12 indicates how you can loosen or tighten the application of global controls to specific newsgroups. The checkboxes allow you to determine which messages are downloaded during an Automatic AOL session. You can choose to see messages up to 30 days old and enable offline reading of messages fetched with Automatic AOL. Apply filters and block messages from certain people and domains the same way you do for your global preferences. See "Newsgroup-Viewing Preferences (Viewing Tab)."

Filtering messages that contain words such as the following can reduce the trash: adult, ADULT, 18, 18+, FREE, free, teen, porn,!!, !!!. People who send this stuff try to get attention by using all capital letters and several exclamation marks. The Filtering preferences don't restrict their rights to send such messages but do give you the ability to avoid them.

You can always change your global preferences. The Remove Filter and Clear Filter List buttons at the bottom of the Filtering tab let you remove or clear your filters.

AOL has its own newsgroup category — called *aol*, of course. The `aol.newsgroups.help` newsgroup is home to FAQs on subjects like participating in newsgroups, handling files, and using your Filing Cabinet.

14

Global Bulletin Boards: Newsgroups

---

misc.kids.moderated (group preferences)

Note: These preferences only affect the newsgroup you are currently reading. You must set these preferences for each newsgroup individually.

☐ Hide binary files.

☐ Enable offline reading for this newsgroup

☐ Don't show me messages longer than [500 ▼] characters

Show messages no more than [14] days old. (Max 30 days)

Note: Filters shown here are for this group only, and are in addition to filters specified in your Global Preferences.

Current filters:

Select filter type: [Subject Contains ▼]

Enter new filter: [   ]

[Add Filter]   [Remove Filter]   [Clear Filter List]

[Save]   [Cancel]

Figure 14-12. Setting preferences for an individual newsgroup.

Places to Get FAQs

You can find archives of newsgroup FAQs at several places:

▶ At AOL Keyword: **FTP**, click the Go To FTP button and then double-click `rtfm.mit.edu:/pub` in the Favorite Sites list. Browse by group to see a long list of all newsgroups; browse by hierarchy (the old-fashioned term for category) to see just the big categories. Explore downward from category to topic to newsgroup FAQ.

▶ At AOL Keyword: **Newsgroups**, use Expert Add to browse `news.answers` for a huge crop of current FAQs. This newsgroup is the traditional home of FAQs and the place where updates are posted.

▶ On the Web, the Internet FAQ Consortium (`www.faqs.org`) maintains an outstanding searchable archive of newsgroup FAQs. If you're technically inclined, you can appreciate the collections of Internet standards documents.

FAQs were invented in the context of newsgroups, but people have created countless FAQs for Web sites as well, to answer recurring questions about the sites and their subject matter. Many big Web-based stores have their own FAQs about products, transactions, and customer service. You need to use AOL Search to find Web FAQs about specific subjects — just add the word FAQ to your query when you do a Web search on a topic of interest. For example, a search for *Labrador retriever FAQ* turned up numerous FAQs on Labs right on the Web.

FAQs: Essential Reading

Find It Online

AOL Keyword: **Computing FAQs** provides access to rich informational FAQs developed on AOL, for AOL members.

FAQ is short for *Frequently Asked Questions*. A FAQ includes answers to those questions. Some people pronounce it F-A-Q and others say *fak*. The Internet FAQ Consortium (`www.faqs.org`) currently archives 3,300 FAQs, and you can find countless unarchived FAQs on the World Wide Web.

The Internet is a here-and-now kind of place, with no long-term memory. Thousands of thoughtful people have contributed to FAQs on thousands topics, which allow newcomers to access knowledge gained over time. Most of these repositories are voluntarily created and maintained.

A newsgroup's FAQ can be a better place to look for answers than the actual newsgroup. Perhaps you know a high-school student who wants to post a question at `sci.math` about the status of Fermat's Last Theorem. The `sci.math` FAQ may answer the question and save the kid from potential ridicule.

Messages with Files

Sometimes newsgroup messages contain multimedia files — music in MP3 format, pictures, or short movies, for example. Before people insert these files into messages, the multimedia files are scrambled into a text document that's unreadable to people but that (as text) can move easily around the Internet. You must unscramble such files before you can view or play them. AOL's newsgroups use a feature called FileGrabber that automatically unscrambles these files.

When a file is attached to a newsgroup posting and you attempt to open the message, you see a message giving you a choice: Download File or Download Message? Click Download File, and you are prompted to save the file on your computer. If you don't want to accept the default folder, change it and then click Save. As the file downloads, a progress indicator tells you how much has been downloaded. Most MIDI and JPG files download quickly, because of their small file size. Video and MP3 files take more time unless you have AOL Plus, a cable modem, or other type of high-speed access as discussed in Chapter 17.

Once a MIDI file has been downloaded, it plays within AOL immediately. A graphic shows up automatically in a new window.

Note

Unlike an e-mail message, you will not know before opening a newsgroup posting whether it has a file attached. All you have to go on is the subject line.

Caution

When downloading any file from the Internet, make sure you have state-of-the-art antivirus software from a recognized vendor such as McAfee or Norton.

14

Global Bulletin Boards: Newsgroups

Using Automatic AOL for Your Newsgroups

Downloading newsgroup messages one at a time, particularly if you subscribe to even a few high-volume newsgroups, can eat up much of your time online. Why not read those postings offline? Using Automatic AOL, you can carry out this task automatically while you're doing something else. Later, at your leisure, you can browse the postings in your Filing Cabinet without having to sign on. They'll be in the Newsgroups folder under Incoming/Saved Postings.

The following process seems complex but is quite simple. Remember that all you are doing is telling AOL what you want to download (or upload), for what screen name, and when. At Mail⇨Automatic AOL, you can be walked through the entire process, with the help of clear on-screen instructions. To download postings into your Filing Cabinet:

1. Add any newsgroups you want to read offline to Read My Newsgroups. See "Adding Newsgroups to Your Favorites."

2. Go to AOL Keyword: **Newsgroups**, and click Read Offline. The Choose Newsgroups window appears, with the names of all the newsgroups that you subscribe to. Click Add All if you want to read all these newsgroups offline, or select specific newsgroups and click Add to include newsgroups one by one. Likewise, clicking Remove All removes all your offline choices, and clicking Remove applies to a single, selected newsgroup.

3. Choose Mail⇨Automatic AOL.

4. Put a check by one or both of the options relating to newsgroups:

   • Send Postings from the Postings Waiting to be Sent Folder: These postings are the newsgroup messages you wrote offline either as new messages or in response to other messages.

   • Get Unread Postings and Put in "Incoming Postings" Folder: This choice retrieves messages from the

Note

The first time you use Automatic AOL you're automatically walked through the process of setting up your Automatic AOL preferences and settings.

newsgroup for offline reading. This is the one you're probably interested in.

5. Click Select Names. Select one or more screen names whose postings are to be uploaded or downloaded, and type in the password for them, so that the sign-on process can be automated. Click OK.

6. Click Schedule Automatic AOL, and indicate when you want postings sent or retrieved. Probably you want postings retrieved regularly but sent only when you have something to send. Make sure to put a check in the Enable Scheduler box. Click OK when you've figured out the schedule.

7. Close the Automatic AOL window when you're done. Make sure your computer is turned on and the AOL software is open during the time when you have scheduled automatic uploading and downloading.

Message Boards on the Web

Like everything else, newsgroups and AOL message boards have been migrating to the Web. Boards add a valuable interactive dimension to the largely static Web in that they give people a chance to linger at a site, read and reflect upon other postings, respond to them, and get to know other people who like the same Web site. By restricting Web-based boards to those people who care about the subject, Web boards tend to be on-topic, while spam and cross-posting are next to impossible.

How do you find Web boards? Start with ForumOne, which does for Web bulletin boards what Liszt does for mailing lists and Deja does for newsgroups (www.forumone.com). You can browse for, and search, more than 300,000 topical Web forums for postings about specific subjects. ForumOne includes a useful listing of mega-forums, the ones with the largest audiences and often the liveliest communities. The advantage in numbers is the diversity and dynamics. Some of the largest boards, currently, are Café Utne (www.utne.com/cafe), Salon (tabletalk.salon.com), and Time (www.time.com/

Tip

ForumOne (www.forumone.com) offers a good solution to the disparate organization and naming practices of the world's Web boards. You can search for subjects of interest. I did a search for *digital cameras,* and at the time of my search retrieved 20 focused Web boards on this topic. The Web is a dynamic place where additional items can be added everyday or several times a day.

Tip

Make sure you write down your registration passwords on a piece of paper and keep them with all the other passwords you've been collecting.

time/community/). Many much smaller Web conferencing systems, like Howard Rheingold's Brainstorms, support dynamic boards based on the activity of several hundred people.

More and more AOL message boards are starting to crop up on the Web. YouthTech, for example, shown in Figure 14-13, offers a focal point for the geekier segment of AOL's teen community. Many Web boards, like this one, let you see many messages at the same time, so you can scroll up and down for the context of any particular message. With newsgroups and AOL message boards, you can often wind up with window clutter.

Because completely different people and organizations create and run Web boards, the interfaces (how they look and work) and organizational structures of Web boards differ. The lack of uniformity, along with the larger newsgroups' registration requirements, can be annoying. Fortunately, however, everything's in normal language, not the newsgroup-speak of rec, comp, and alt.

Category: Youth Tech Community	Topics	Posts	Last Post	Moderator
This N That	20	196	07-05-2000 12:17 PM	YTCC Funktion
Almost Anything Goes	155	1416	07-05-2000 12:37 PM	YTCC Funktion
Meet the Community	55	241	06-19-2000 07:21 PM	YTCC Funktion
July Birthdays	2	3	07-04-2000 11:44 PM	YTCC Funktion
MUSIC	20	69	07-05-2000 08:56 AM	YTCC Funktion
Love & Friendships	13	75	07-02-2000 05:02 PM	YTCC Funktion
Signature Lines - Quotes	14	42	07-03-2000 01:59 PM	YTCC Funktion
Youth Tech Suggestions	15	56	06-30-2000 10:30 PM	YTCC Funktion
Techie Pals	320	890	07-05-2000 06:43 PM	YTCC Funktion
Poetry Corner	51	138	07-03-2000 06:05 PM	YTCC Funktion
Board Games!	7	30	06-07-2000 09:52 PM	YTCC Funktion

Figure 14-13. YouthTech's Web boards (AOL Keyword: **YT**) contain topics and posts just like newsgroups.

Where to Go from Here

Chapter 14 concludes Part III, covering the myriad ways of communicating on the Internet. AOL gives you the tools you need, including e-mail, mailing lists, chat, instant messages, newsgroups, and message boards on AOL and the Web. Don't worry about figuring out all of them. Instead, pick them one at a time as you see the need and remember that you can always find help at AOL Keyword: **Help**, or from the Help icon.

▶ For the complete story of AOL's message boards, with many examples, see *Your Official America Online Tour Guide* by Dave Marx and Jennifer Watson (IDG Books Worldwide, Inc.).

▶ For a list of newsgroup categories, go to `http://www.magma.ca/~leisen/mlnh/`.

▶ To create your own community with a Web-based bulletin board, read about Groups@AOL, a new community-building tool described in Chapter 18.

P A R T

IV

EXTENDING YOUR INTERNET
CONNECTION

Chapter 15
From the Internet to You: Downloading Software

Chapter 16
Internet Tools that Extend Your Reach

Chapter 17
Internet Everywhere: New Ways to Access AOL

Chapter 18
Did You Know You Can . . . on AOL?

Chapter 15

From the Internet to You: Downloading Software

IN THIS CHAPTER

Downloading software from the Web

Using AOL's Download Manager

Downloading software using FTP

Transferring files using FTP on AOL

Understanding file types

Searching for files

Everything your computer does requires files. A file has a name (like letter.doc or butterfly.jpg) and takes up space on your hard drive or other disk. A file has information that you need, and it comes in a format you can use (butter.jpg is a picture). Files also have information that your computer needs to do its work, in a format that makes sense only to a computer (ms09.dll). Most software consists of a set of files that does something for you on your own computer, like write a letter (a word processor). AOL itself is made up of a big file (aol.exe) and lots of little files that give you the ability to do things on *other* computers.

As usual, the Internet provides many ways to do something —
in this case, to get files. The Web and FTP (*file transfer
protocol*) are the leading methods of getting software from
the Internet today, and sometimes when you use the Web to
get software, you're really using FTP behind the scenes. The
importance of FTP lies in its specialization. Its sole function is
to move files from one computer to another. With FTP, you can
upload files as well, which is indispensable when you build
Web pages. On AOL, you have no fewer than four ways of using FTP, which I discuss in this chapter. Downloading software
and files with the Web and FTP can add tremendous value to
your Internet experience on AOL.

In Chapter 10, you can read
about attaching files to e-mail
messages; Chapter 14 dis-
cusses decoding the multimedia files included in
newsgroup messages.

Getting Software from the Web

Downloading software from the Web has become pretty
much point-and-click. In this section, I discuss how to download software from the Web to your computer. Profiled in
Chapter 16, Winamp delivers high-quality music based on
the MP3 format. Software such as Winamp can turn your
computer and AOL connection into a new kind of round-the-
clock radio. But remember that the AOL media pops up by
default to meet all your multimedia needs.

If you ever forget where
you've downloaded that new
software, look on the Start
Menu⇨Documents list after
the download completes.

To download Winamp, follow these steps. You'll quickly learn
that in downloading *any* software from the Web, you follow a
similar sequence, although some of the details vary.

1. Go to the Web page from which you want to download
   the software; in this case www.winamp.com. Or, use
   AOL Keyword: **Winamp.**

   How do you know where to *start* when you want to
   download software? You can search a download site
   like Tucows (profiled in Chapter 15), which has well-
   organized links to thousands of programs around the
   world (in this case, you would search for *winamp*). Or,
   start with the company that makes the software; often
   a company bears the name of its leading software package or at least has a site devoted to its leading software
   products. Finally, do a search for the program using
   AOL Search.

   The Winamp home page appears, as shown in
   Figure 15-1.

AOL's media player automatically loads when you click a
media file, such as an MP3.
It's so simple you don't even
have to think about down-
loading the software.

15

From the Internet to You:
Downloading Software

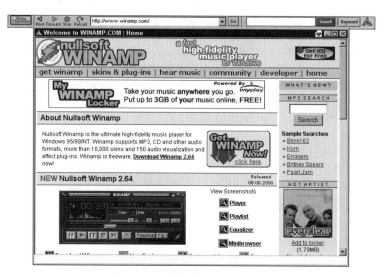

Figure 15-1. Winamp's home page; click the Download link to get the software.

2. Look for a download link, and click it.

   Sometimes the link is on the opening page, and sometimes you have to dig a bit (for starters, look for a Products link). You can also do a site search if one is available.

3. In the page that appears (see Figure 15-2), read any information about software versions. Print out installation instructions, if any are available.

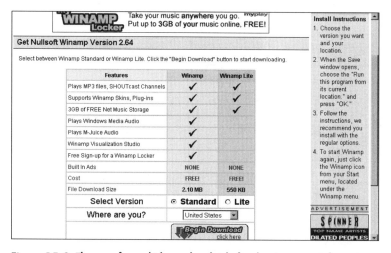

Figure 15-2. The page from which you download often has important information. Read it carefully.

4. Look for a button or link that reads Download Now or Begin Download button, and click it. After a moment or two, the box shown in Figure 15-3 appears, asking you whether you want to save the file (the default choice) or open the file upon download. As a rule, you want to keep the default choice and save what you're downloading. Click OK.

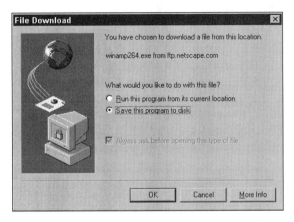

Figure 15-3. This standard Windows box asks you whether you want to download and open software or download and save it.

5. In the standard Save As box, shown in Figure 15-4, navigate to the place on your hard drive where you want to save the software. You want to use the file's name as is, so don't change it. Click OK to download the file and save it in the place you indicated.

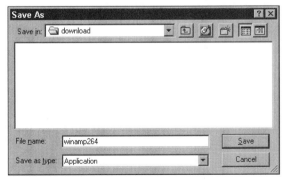

Figure 15-4. Tell Windows where to save your file.

When you download a file from an AOL software library, a newsgroup, or from AOL Mail, you'll hear, "File's done," upon completion of the download. When downloading over the Web, you won't hear that voice, so you need to check the standard Windows Download box from time to time (available by pressing Alt+Tab until the box appears).

Note

Sometimes downloaded software arrives in the ZIP format, meaning the file must first be decompressed.

Feature

AOL 6.0 automatically decompresses files immediately, so you can use them right away. In previous versions, you could either decompress them manually at AOL Keyword: **Download Manager** or wait for AOL to decompress them automatically when you downloaded.

Depending on your connection type and speed, the download can take seconds or minutes. While it takes place, you can do something else, such as check the download's progress at the File Download box.

6. When the download completes, a box like the one in Figure 15-5 appears.

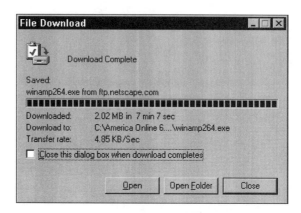

Figure 15-5. To retrieve the file just downloaded, click Open Folder.

To find the file you just downloaded, click Open Folder. The folder you selected in Step 4 comes up, with the downloaded file selected.

7. To install your new software, double-click the selected file and follow the online instructions.

Installation differs from program to program. More and more programs use a standard program called InstallShield, which makes the process practically identical no matter which program you install. With or without InstallShield, the process is automatic (the software installs itself, asking you for information whenever necessary). You'll be asked the following questions:

▶ Do you accept the software's licensing agreement? Click Yes.

▶ Where do you want to install the program? Make sure to choose both a folder where similar (or all) programs are installed and a drive with enough room.

▶ Do you want to do a typical or custom installation? Choose typical.

▶ Into which Program Folder do you want to install the various files? Accept the default.

After your new software installs, you usually have the options of reading about what's new in the program, registering it, and using it right away. Make a choice. Sometimes, however, you have to restart your computer first.

Getting Software from AOL

You can download thousands of files and programs directly from AOL's software libraries, as well as via newsgroups and FTP. The Download Manager (AOL Keyword: **Download Manager**) keeps track of files downloaded from AOL, including files downloaded from e-mail.

Download Manager keeps track of where you downloaded those files in the first place, lets you select a specific folder into which everything downloads by default, and also gives you the tools to decompress files if they're compressed.

To decompress a file using Download Manager:

1. From AOL Keyword: **Download Manager**, click the Show Files Downloaded button to bring up the Files You've Downloaded window.
2. Select the file you want to decompress, and click the Decompress button.

To decompress files automatically upon sign off when you download or delete the compressed files, click Download Preferences and uncheck those preferences.

Getting Software and Other Files Using FTP on AOL

FTP makes available more than 100 million files for download. FTP also gives you the most convenient way to upload files, including Web pages, in order to make Web sites viewable by anyone. How do you find what you're seeking among the 100 million? See "Finding FTP Files" later in this chapter.

Cross-Reference

AOL has a built-in program that decompresses files for you. Chapter 16 profiles a software utility called WinZip, which you can use to create your own compressed files and manage the ones you've downloaded.

Definition

A *compressed* file often consists of more than one file processed by special software such as WinZip. This software not only packages up the files, but also reduces their size (as measured in kilobytes). Chapter 16 profiles WinZip.

Note

Once decompressed and installed, programs take up much more hard-drive space than you may expect from the size of the downloaded file.

Definition

Downloading means copying files from a publicly accessible computer to your own computer; *uploading* means copying them from your computer to a central place, where others can use them.

FTP stands for the Internet's *file transfer protocol.* Think of FTP as a tool for downloading software and other files — games, Internet software, MP3 files, and documents of every type — for your own use from across the Internet. FTP also lets you *upload* files — making them available for others (such as when you build a Web site). Before the advent of the Web, FTP was *the* way of moving files from one place to another on the Internet, and it remains very popular when you download files from software vendors and big shareware archives like Tucows.

Through AOL, you have a choice of four ways to connect to FTP:

- ▶ Through the AOL Web browser, for browsing and downloading
- ▶ AOL Keyword: **My FTP Space**, for uploading files to and managing them on AOL's computers
- ▶ AOL Keyword: **FTP**, for browsing and downloading *any* public FTP sites or other FTP sites to which you have access
- ▶ Using a third-party application such as WS_FTP for uploading, managing, and downloading on any computer to which you have access

The AOL Browser

Getting access to an FTP site on the Internet is like using your own hard drive. Both your hard drive and an FTP site consist of folders containing either files or *more* folders. They're both places to store files.

As Chapter 6 explains, your AOL browser works like an all-purpose tool, giving you access to e-mail and FTP, as well as Web browsing. Downloading a file from an FTP site while using a browser couldn't be easier. First, you type the site's address into the AOL Address box. Usually an address has the form rtfm.mit.edu, ftp.netscape.com, or ftp.aol.com. Type in **ftp://** before the address to tell the browser you want to use an FTP site.

Figure 15-6 shows the University of Kansas FTP site, which contains good articles on the early history of the Internet. The figure shows three different folders at this site. Notice the different types of files available at this site. *HTML files*, for example, are Web pages, viewable as such (within your AOL browser) if you click them. The files marked with a little question mark are just text files; click to read them on-screen.

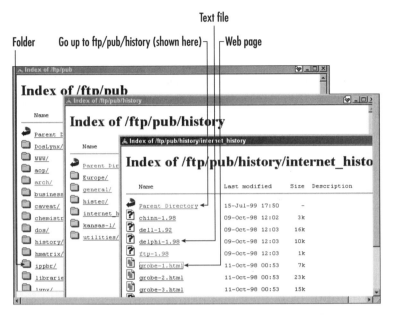

Text file

Folder   Go up to ftp/pub/history (shown here)   Web page

Figure 15-6. The University of Kansas FTP site, an excellent resource on the early Internet. (The text-based Web browser, *Lynx*, was invented at this university.)

As with newsgroups, nothing on FTP is quite as instantaneous on the Web. Sometimes you will need to wait. Another minor drawback: While adequate for using public FTP sites and downloading files from them, you can't use the browser to upload files, nor can you use it with FTP sites that are password-protected, where you need to enter a log-in and username.

AOL Keyword: My FTP Space

My FTP Space has been around since 1995, when AOL started giving every member 2MB of space on AOL's computers. As members started using that space to store Web pages and AOL started offering a full range of Web-publishing services, AOL began offering much more than 2MB of space, but the FTP uploading process has changed little over the years.

Why use My FTP Space? Most people use it for storing Web pages, and when you build a page on AOL Hometown, the files are automatically saved in your FTP space. My FTP Space refers to the many Internet computers collectively known as `hometown.aol.com`. Here, you make your Web pages (and other files) available for others to use.

Note

Using an FTP site opens a connection that is usually limited in duration. Many sites, too, place a limit on the number of visitors who can be admitted at the same time. That's why you may not be able to access an FTP site right away. Try again later.

Note

Every screen name automatically has 2MB of online storage space at Keyword: **My FTP Space**. Any screen name that publishes (makes publicly available) a Web page at AOL Hometown receives an additional 2MB of space, and any screen name publishing all My FTP Space Web pages on AOL Hometown receives a total of 12MB. Chapter 18 provides a brief introduction to AOL Hometown.

15

From the Internet to You:
Downloading Software

Find It Online

AOL Keyword: **My FTP Space** takes you to your own space on AOL's computers for storing and sharing files.

Figure 15-7 shows what you see at AOL Keyword: **My FTP Space**. You may see some other AOL windows before you get there, so be prepared to wait a few moments.

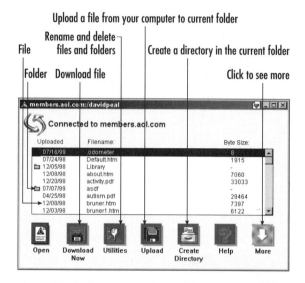

Upload a file from your computer to current folder

Rename and delete
File   files and folders   Create a directory in the current folder

Folder   Download file   Click to see more

Figure 15-7. Welcome to my personal FTP space. Your folder will show different files and folders.

Note

With easy Web tools such as 1-2-3 Publish and Easy Designer, more and more of the uploading and downloading now takes place behind the scenes. The fancier your site, however, and the more control you want, the more you'll want direct access to My FTP Space in order to manage your growing family of files.

The uses for My FTP Space extend well beyond Web publishing. You can use My FTP Space to make files available to friends or coworkers. For example, you can upload word-processed documents or PDF reports — anything that fits within the 2MB limit. In revising this book, I used a colleague's FTP server to exchange chapters.

Uploading a File to My FTP Space

To upload a file to My FTP Space, follow these steps. If you have many files to upload, you'll have to upload them one at a time using the following steps, because for now you can't upload several at a time:

1. Go to AOL Keyword: **My FTP Space**.

A list of files and folders in My FTP Space eventually appears. Your file list will be different from anyone else's — this is *your* area, accessible only to your screen name.

2. Click Upload.

   The Remote Filename box appears.

3. Provide the name ("remote file name") that you want for the file on My FTP Space.

   Yes, before selecting a file to upload, you provide the name by which you want that file to be known *after* it uploads. Usually, you want to use the same name as the file on your hard drive. Sometimes, however, as in Figure 15-8, your own naming scheme may require some tweaking to make your files readily recognizable by others.

   Notice that *Binary* is selected on the window below the "pile" of screens. This setting helps FTP recognize *all* file types, including simple text.

4. Click Continue.

5. Click Select File.

6. In the file selection dialog box, find your file on your hard drive, and double-click it.

7. Click Send.

   A little box that looks like a thermometer tracks the progress of your file transfer. Next time you visit My FTP Space, your file will be there.

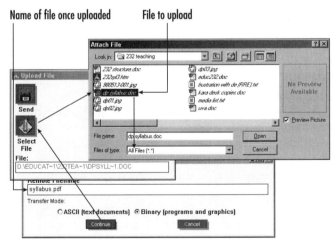

Name of file once uploaded   File to upload

Figure 15-8. Select a file from your hard drive and send it.

15

From the Internet to You:
Downloading Software

If you do change filenames, delete files, and move things around, make sure to change the links in your Web pages that refer to those files!

If you're making a Web site, make sure to store files in folders corresponding to the way they are linked to each other on the site. In other words, when creating a Web page and defining a directory path to a linked-to page, that path corresponds to how the folders are ultimately related to each other on the FTP site.

If you want to make files available to others, you must create a /pub directory in the top level (opening FTP windows). If you want people to share files with you, you must create an /incoming directory.

Managing My FTP Space

Any computer storage space, such as your hard drive, your Favorite Places folder, or My FTP Space, can quickly get overgrown with many files having, even to you, unrecognizable names and forgotten purposes. When you need a specific file for a new purpose, where you can find it is not always clear.

On My FTP Space, housekeeping requires a good organizational scheme. *Good* means that it works for you, that you can find files when you need them, and that filenames correspond to how you think of the content. The following chores can help you keep track of your files:

▶ **To delete a file or folder:** Highlight the file, and choose Utilities⇨Delete. You can remove only one file at a time. Note that you cannot delete a folder until all of its files have been removed; when the files are removed, highlight the folder and delete it as you would delete a file.

▶ **To create a new directory:** Click the Create Directory button, as shown previously in Figure 15-7, and type in the directory name in the Remote Directory Name box. Click Continue to create another, or close the box (clicking the X in the upper-right corner) when you're done. Using forward slashes (/), you can create a subdirectory, such as /pub/work.

▶ **To change the name of a file or folder:** Select the file or folder, and choose Utilities⇨Rename. In the New Name box, type in the full new name, including all the folders and subfolders, separated by forward slashes.

▶ **To move a file or folder:** Moving a file or folder (within your FTP space) means changing its name from one reflecting its old location to one reflecting its new location. That is, you move a file by simply changing the directory path to the file — the path from the top level of the site, or root, through the folders and subfolders in which the file is contained. You first select the file or folder and choose Utilities⇨Rename. You then provide a different path to the file. For example, /charlieparker2000/README could be moved "down" a level by changing it to /charlieparker2000/ pub/README. You can also change the filename in the process, moving the file to a different directory and changing its name.

AOL's Built-in FTP Program

My FTP Space gives you access to FTP — but only *your* FTP space on AOL. To access other FTP sites, especially those that are password-protected, you need to use AOL Keyword: **FTP** (see Figure 15-9).

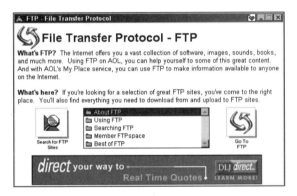

Figure 15-9. At AOL Keyword: **FTP**, AOL gives you essential FTP features, including the ability to browse and download.

Downloading a File at AOL Keyword: FTP

To download a file, you must first identify the site's exact address (for example, ftp.aol.com). Knowing the whole directory path, with full filename and extension, is best. Figure 15-10 shows one of AOL's Favorite Sites (MIT's rtfm.mit.edu/pub), available at AOL Keyword: **FTP**. This site contains FAQ documents for hundreds of newsgroups. See "Finding FTP Files" later in this chapter for more information about finding complete file information.

A good way to think of My FTP Space and AOL Keyword: **FTP** is that they form a whole, with My FTP Space providing uploading services and FTP providing downloading services.

Read the FAQs about AOL Keyword: **FTP** in Chapter 14.

Viruses are small programs that can mess up your computer. They get into your system as part of downloaded files. You can trust that files downloaded directly from AOL's software libraries will be virus-free, but there's no guarantee regarding FTP files. Be safe. Do a virus check and stay informed at AOL Keyword: **Virus**. Chapter 16 profiles an antivirus program.

15

From the Internet to You: Downloading Software

Place folder in Favorite Places, for direct access later (Favorites⇨Favorite Places)

Download selected files

Folders   Downloadable files   Folder names

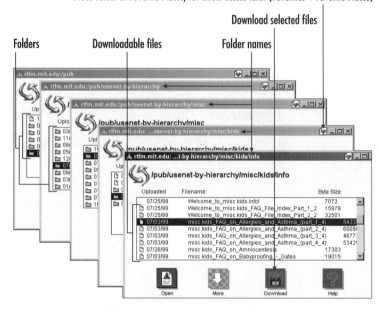

Tip

You can add FTP sites such as `rtfm.mit.edu` to your Favorite Places folder by clicking the heart in the upper-right corner of the FTP window. See Chapter 3 for more about the subject.

Tip

If you're used to tooling around the Web, you'll have to throttle back to enjoy FTP. Many sites have logins and passwords. The good news is that logging in to the most popular sites (called *anonymous FTP* sites) is automatic. Such sites permit *public* access, at least to the top-level's `/pub` folder. Why is it called *anonymous*? Your login name is "anonymous," and your username is your e-mail address (for example, milesdavis2000@aol.com). A non-anonymous site requires a login and password. If you want access to a non-anonymous FTP site, you need a password and login. For this information, just ask the person who told you about the file you're trying to retrieve.

Figure 15-10. From folders to files. Browsing from MIT's `rtfm.mit.edu/pub` to the FAQs available for the `misc.kids` newsgroups.

Here's how to download a file using FTP on AOL:

1. At AOL Keyword: **FTP**, click Go To FTP.
2. At the Anonymous FTP window, click Other Site.
3. In the Other Site box, type in the address of the FTP site. For Anonymous FTP Sites, leave the Ask for Login Name and Password box unchecked. Click Connect.

    The site comes up. If it doesn't, it's busy — try again later. If it's a non-anonymous FTP site, you'll be prompted to enter a password and login.

4. With a file displayed and selected, you can either download it (click Download Now) or, if it's a text file, view it online without downloading it (choose Open⇨View File Now). If you want to download, you'll be prompted to use the directory specified by AOL's Download Manager. Note that no Download Later option exists. Usually, you'll want to download and run the file right away.

Using Third-party FTP Programs

Several third-party FTP programs give you additional features not available in either AOL's browser or built-in FTP program. For example, programs like WS_FTP provide a visual display that shows your hard drive's folders on one side and the Internet (FTP) computer's folders on the other, so that uploading and downloading involves no more than dragging files from one panel of the window to the other! Or, if you are building a Web site with more than two or three pages, you can upload and download many files at the same time.

Understanding File Types

Why do you need to bother with file types? Usually, you don't, but when downloading a multimedia sound or music file, you often need to know how to use the file — what software can play it, or display it, or otherwise use it. Windows 95/98 makes many assumptions about what programs run what files. As you acquire more software, however, you may want to change Windows's assumptions so you can use your favorite programs. You find out how to do so in "Telling Windows How to Handle File Formats."

File types are usually (but not always) identified by a three-letter suffix, or *file extension*, tacked onto a filename. A file's extension can tell you its type (video, sound, Web, and so on), its platform (Mac, Windows, or both), and what kind of program you need in order to use it.

The following sections review the most common file types and extensions.

General Files

A file with a general file extension has a name similar to the following: purchase.htm. This file would probably depict a Web page that can be used in a browser or HTML editor on Mac or Windows. Here is a list of other general file extensions and what they depict:

▶ **HTM, HTML:** A page of HTML code — in other words, a Web page. You can use any browser and can view the file on any platform.

Tip

If you know the directory in which you can find the file, enter it, too. Include the filename, and you can go directly to the file and download it!

Cross-Reference

Chapter 16 profiles WS_FTP, a full-featured commercial product whose shareware version is available from Keyword: **Publishing Tools** (click Shareware).

15

From the Internet to You:
Downloading Software

Definition

Filenames have two parts. The first part is provided by a person and often describes the file's content; this part comes before the period, as in *census*.pdf. And then there's the file *extension* provided by software, indicating the file type, which comes after the period (census.*pdf*). The file extension provides the information about a file's format, platform, and the software required to use it.

▶ **TXT:** A text file, usable on any platform, with any text editor, word processor, or similar program. *Text* just refers to simple letters, punctuation marks, and numerals — no formatting or fancy symbols.

▶ **ZIP:** A compressed PC file, requiring AOL or a program like WinZip to decompress and use it. The corresponding Macintosh file formats are SIT and SEAHQX.

Graphics Files

A file with a graphics extension might look like Tip.gif. This filename represents an image file that can be used on a Web page or in any graphics program on Mac or Windows. The following list provides additional common graphic file extensions and information:

▶ **GIF:** Short for Graphic Interchange Format. GIFs were popularized by CompuServe (now part of AOL) in the 1980s. GIF was a well-known format at the time the World Wide Web was created, and most images on the Web are in either this multiplatform format or JPG. Any browser and graphics program on any platform can display GIFs, on any platform. This format is used for images with simple shapes and only 256 colors.

▶ **JPG:** The JPG or JPEG (Joint Photographic Experts Group) format displays millions of colors, and hence is used for detailed images and digital pictures. They're compressed, hence thus small. Along with GIFs, they're the most popular format on the Web, and can be viewed with any browser or graphics program on any platform.

▶ **ART:** ART files are unique to AOL. By default, AOL's built-in browser converts image files in other formats to ART; often, when you download or save a Web graphic, it will have an ART extension.

Sound Files

▶ **WAV:** The Windows format for sound recordings that attempt to faithfully record the original sound. If you're using a PC, many sounds you record will be saved in this format.

Tip

On AOL, choose File➪Open Picture Finder to view and edit GIFs and JPGs, as well as BMPs (Windows bitmapped graphics) and ARTs (an AOL file format you can use to compress other file formats you download from the Web).

Feature

You can play most sounds with the AOL 6.0's new multimedia player, discussed in Chapter 6.

▶ **MP3:** Books have been written about MP3, and companies founded to capitalize on its enormous popularity. The sound recording system originally developed for MPEG movies (see *MPG*, in the next section). AOL's media player can handle MP3 files, as can the Winamp, and Spinner, (and many other) players, a few of which I discuss in Chapter 16.

▶ **MID or MIDI:** MIDI stands for Musical Instrument Digital Interface. Unlike WAV files, which are similar to recordings, MIDI files contain simulated sounds.

Video Files

Each of the following file formats work in AOL 6's new multimedia player.

▶ **AVI:** The standard Windows video format.

▶ **MOV:** Short for movie, the format used by Apple Computer's popular QuickTime video system. With the right plug-in, Windows machines can play QuickTime movies, too. The latest version of QuickTime is available for Windows as well as Mac, and supports many types of multimedia files.

▶ **MPG or MPEG:** Moving Pictures Experts Group. A very efficient and popular method of compressing video clips.

Handling File Formats in Windows

In Microsoft Windows 95/98, you can tell Windows what to do with different file types — that is, which program to open when you want to use a specific file. If you like Winamp, for example, you can double-click an MP3 file called raga01.mp3 and have the music play in Winamp. Or, you can have MPG video files play in AOL instead of the Windows media player. Changing your associations lets you use the software of your choice.

This useful procedure seems difficult because of the cluttered Windows 95/98 dialog boxes and the unhelpfully terse language. These few steps can, however, go a long way to customizing Windows to suit your style. *Associating* a file with a program is the first step to making the file (and the program) useful after you download it.

This example changes the way MPG video files are configured on my system so that, when opened, such files automatically play in AOL instead of the Windows media player. To set up your system the same way, follow these steps:

1. While using Windows 95/98, choose Start Menu⇨ Settings⇨Folder Options and click the File Types tab.

   A window like the one shown in Figure 15-11 appears.

2. In the list of Registered file types in the Folder Options window, select a file type. In this case, select Movie File. Browse the whole list if you don't find what you're seeking.

   In the File Type Details box at the bottom of the Folder Options window, the following information appears for the selected file type:

   - **File extension(s):** The part of the filename after the period. In other words, you're telling Windows what to do when you try to open a file ending in JPG, GIF, or some other format.

   - **Content type:** This is also known as MIME type (for example, text/plain). Don't worry about it; you can leave the MIME type blank.

   - **Opens with:** This important option indicates which program launches when you try to use any MPG video file.

3. Click Edit to open the Edit File Type box.

   In the Actions box in the lower part of this window:

   - Double-click Open to bring up the Editing Action box. In this box you specify that you want the file to *open* in AOL.

   - Now, double-click Play and, likewise, specify that you want the file to play in AOL.

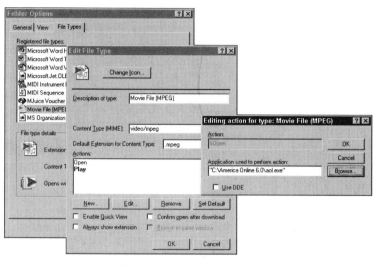

Figure 15-11. Use the Folder Options dialog box to edit file types.

For both Open and Play, you need to click Browse to find the program with which you want to associate the file type. Double-click the program when you find it.

4. Click OK to close the Editing Action box.

5. Click Close OK to close the Edit File Type box.

6. Test the new association by looking for an appropriate file (by using Start Menu⇨Find⇨Files or Folders, searching for *.MPG in your system, and double-clicking an MPG file.

The program specified in Step 3 opens automatically. If it doesn't, return to the list of file types in Step 2 and make sure you have chosen the correct file.

Finding FTP Files

Downloading FTP files requires that you know the following:

▶ The FTP site where the file can be found

▶ The file's location (folder) on the FTP site

How do you find out this information? One way is through FTP Search.

Find It Online

Want to learn about Archie? At AOL Keyword: **FTP**, double-click the list box item Searching FTP. AOL's search tool lets you search a list of FTP sites and folders, and also provides instructions for using an actual Archie server via e-mail.

Why Searching FTP is a Pain

On the Web, you can search for information about penguins, Mao, baseball, or anything else. With FTP, however, you can only search for filenames, and a file's name does not always say much about its content. Just as no standard ways exist for searching for images (what do you search for, after all?), no widely accepted ways exist for indexing the highly diverse content found in FTP files. Some have only text, some pictures, some software, and so on.

Think of an FTP site as something like your hard drive (and think of how difficult it can be to lose things on your own computer!). FTP is *not* organized like the more intuitive World Wide Web, with its contextual links from one piece of information to another related piece of information. Further, browsing FTP sites doesn't make sense: Where do you start? How do you interpret filenames? You need to zero in on the file you want.

It used to be that you needed a special search tool called Archie to search for FTP files. You had to use e-mail or Telnet to get in touch with Archie, a distributed database of files available by anonymous FTP. However reached, Archie was usually painfully slow over a modem, if available at all. Archie often made no sense unless you knew exactly what you wanted in the first place. Now you can do your own, more intuitive searches on the Web, but even so, some of the built-in difficulties of FTP can make finding the right file hard.

Find It Online

FTP Search is part of the Lycos complex of Web sites. The Norwegian developers of FTP Search have created a Web search engine (www.alltheweb.com).

FTP Search, available through the Web, was developed by a Norwegian company called Fast Search and Transfer, which is creating other tools for finding and transferring images, videos, and other types of complex data. You can use their FTP search engine at ftpsearch.lycos.com/. Figure 15-12 shows FTP Search.

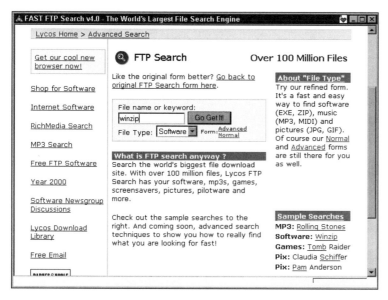

Figure 15-12. FTP Search simplifies your FTP searches.

In using FTP Search, you provide two pieces of information: a *filename* or keyword and the *file type* (software, MP3 sound file, a ZIP file, and so on). Type in the filename or keyword and select the file type from a drop-down File Type list.

A keyword can be one or more words describing what you're looking for, but in my experience the keywords must be simple and similar to the actual file (or folder) names. Your choices of file types are either generic (sound) or specific (AU, MIDI, WAV, and MP3). Some people want MP3 for the quality, but if you're trying to document the sound of a whale, format doesn't count as much. (Try a search for **whale** and **sounds** to see what's available!)

Figure 15-13 shows a result of the FTP search shown in Figure 15-12.

Tip

FTP Search is fast, but making your search query retrieve the files you want can take several refinements.

15

From the Internet to You: Downloading Software

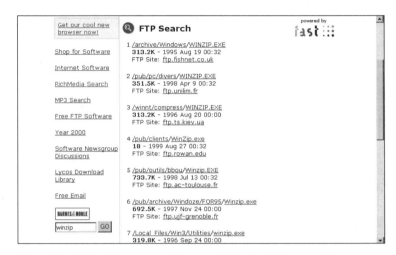

Figure 15-13. Link from here to FTP sites and individual folders and files.

Each entry in Figure 15-13 has several clickable pieces of information:

▶ **The FTP site itself:** Click to browse the entire site (or at least the /pub directory).

▶ **The folder containing the file you seek:** Click to see what other, similar files can be found there.

▶ **The file itself:** Click to hear, play, see, or download it.

You'll recognize individual files by their sizes and file extensions.

If you have experience with Archie, click the Advanced link, shown in Figure 15-12. A benefit of this Web-based form for accessing Archie is the use of drop-down menus and extensive help for each field. You can use the form to search for files from certain domains (such as EDU) and of certain dates (for example, the last year); you can also search for *part* of a filename (called a *substring*). The more information you have about the file you're seeking, the better your chances of retrieving it.

Where to Go from Here

FTP once counted as an essential Internet tool, right up there with newsgroups and electronic mail. Nowadays, it's the Web that gets all the attention and is the subject of all the over-heated new business magazines. Even so, FTP remains the Net's workhorse for storing and sharing files of all kinds. And the fact is that all those boring files (software in particular) can make your online experience much more exciting.

► For more about file types, and the way they're sup-ported by (played in) the AOL browser, see Chapter 6.

► Chapter 16 looks at the fun side of downloading: get-ting software. I discuss selected downloadable programs.

► I just touched on the "other" part of FTP — uploading — in this chapter. Ed Willett explores the topic in depth in *Creating Cool Web Pages*, 2nd edition, also published by IDG Books Worldwide and available at AOL Keyword: **AOL Store** (click Books).

Chapter 16

Internet Tools that Extend Your Reach

IN THIS CHAPTER

Discovering reasons to use Internet software with AOL

Choosing the right Internet software

Finding software

Using Internet software with AOL

Software profiled in this chapter: Aladdin, Bobby, ICQ, NetNanny, NetTerm, Real Jukebox, Spinner, Winamp, WinZip, WS_FTP

Internet software and Internet-related software give you the opportunity to add new capabilities to your AOL Internet connection. WS_FTP, for example, gives you features that supplement and extend what you can do at AOL Keyword: **FTP**. NetNanny, a filtering program, can help keep kids safe in cyberspace.

Why would you want more software? One reason is personal *style*. Additional software can give you the tools you simply *prefer*. Some people prefer Navigator 6.0, for example, while others prefer Microsoft Internet Explorer. (See Chapter 7 for more on Netscape 6 as an alternative browser.)

Another reason for using Internet software is personal *need*. Additional software can help meet specific needs such as playing MP3 files or designing accessible Web sites. If you need this function or that feature, you can usually find suitable and often free Net software. This chapter introduces a few of these programs and also shows you where to find just about any Internet software for any preference or need.

Software for the Asking

Freeware means what it says — software with no financial outlay on your part. The installation may be complicated and the learning curve steep, and you may want to buy documentation or a fuller-featured version of the software, but the freeware itself won't cost a nickel. Freeware products are often every bit as good as expensive commercial alternatives. A great browser such as Netscape Navigator is an example of freeware, as are the leading music and video players such as Winamp, which I discuss later in this chapter.

Shareware means what it says, too — the *author* (programmer) wants to make it broadly available by giving it away, but often under certain conditions. The most important condition, customarily, is that you can use the software free during a trial period (30 days, for example), after which you pay a nominal charge to use it. Sometimes restricted use is enforced by the software itself; you can't use it after a certain number of days (NetNanny works this way). Sometimes, continued use works on the honor system; you'll be prompted to register without being forced to do so.

Software makers realize the importance of creating a big community of happy users who can spread the word about their wonderful programs. Also, on the Net, there's a strong tradition of "giving back," of creating and freely distributing software for the sake of the community. Making software is expensive, however, and the commercial instinct is now every bit as strong on the Net as the community spirit.

Tip

If you like the shareware you're using, consider paying the usually nominal fee to register it. In return, you often get documentation and other forms of support, additional features, and notification of new versions. At the least, you avoid having the software become unusable after the evaluation period is over. Some shareware lacks key features unless you register and pay the shareware fee.

16

Internet Tools that
Extend Your Reach

To identify the best products in specific niches, start your product research at ZDNet (www.zdnet.com) or AOL Keyword: **CNET**.

How do you tell one software version from another? In addition to the version number, usually included in the product's name (for example, Netscape Navigator 4.72), look for a *build* number (within a version number), which indicates changes to the software that are too minor to warrant a new version number. *Beta* software is prerelease software, which may be incomplete or unstable. Support is usually not provided for beta. Some products (like the AOL Instant Messenger service) make betas broadly available. Some products (like ICQ) are terminally alpha or beta, because, with their many components, change is constant.

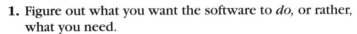

Choosing the Right Software

How do you get the best piece of shareware or freeware for your preferences and needs?

Follow these steps to figure out the best software to get:

1. Figure out what you want the software to *do,* or rather, what you need.

   Does AOL already offer what you want? Is the required functionality so important to you that you will pay for support and documentation?

2. Figure out whether you need every feature under the sun, or just the basic ones.

   At the big download sites described in the next section, you'll find toolkits that do many things at the same time, such as manage both FTP and Telnet, or e-mail and newsgroups, or bundle together Internet utilities of interest to advanced users.

3. Get the appropriate version for your operating system.

   If you have Windows 95/98, look for something called *32-bit* software, because it's faster and often has more features. If you're reluctant to pay for software whose utility is unknown to you, look for special deals offering older versions of good shareware as freeware. If you're outfitting older machines (as in a school), don't assume the latest software is the best. Newer software sprouts new features while often offering little improvement in basic functionality. On the other hand, newer versions tend to perform better, and sport a brighter interface with fewer bugs.

   Look at the various rating systems out there to see what experts and users consider best — ZDNet, Stroud, CNET, and Tucows have rating systems. (You can read about all of these resources in the next section.) Also look (as in ZDNet) for *number* of downloads. A high number of downloads can indicate software that users consider better or cooler. Make sure the high number of downloads is not a mere reflection of how old the software is, however (that is, the longer a software is available to download, the more often it will have been downloaded).

4. If you'll be downloading many programs, or a few large programs, wait until the end of the day, so that you won't encounter as much traffic or run the risk of getting disconnected during a long download time.

Finding Internet Software . . . on AOL

AOL Keyword: **Shareware** takes you to AOL's Download Center, which gives you access to many shareware programs, including Internet tools. The Shareware section of the Download Center is divided into folders such as Internet Tools and Web Publishing. Open a folder for a list of both programs and the files to use with those programs (for example, players for WAV files, plus Star Wars sounds in WAV format). The Download Center includes a list of the "best" shareware by topic. A search function gives you the ability to search across shareware categories, a feature that recognizes the fact that much shareware is multi-faceted and multi-purpose.

Finding Internet Software

Here are four well-regarded collections of shareware and freeware. At these sites, you can find the major applications discussed in this chapter (for others, use the vendors' site, such as www.netnanny.com for the NetNanny program). These sites all make finding Internet applications easy. They all have reliable performance, and they rate and review software.

▶ **Stroud's Consummate Winsock Applications** (cws.internet.com): In addition to outstanding shareware listings, this site, now more than five years old, includes updates to major commercial software such as Windows Media Player, MS Office, the MSIE and Netscape browsers, and the Norton and McAfee virus-scanning programs.

▶ **Tucows** (www.tucows.com): This gigantic site has a large network of *mirrors* — alternate sites that contain the same information as the main site, but in a location closer to a large number of users. This means that you can usually find a download site geographically close to you. Figure 16-1 suggests the depth of Tucows

Tip

When you have a choice, use a download site close to you. Why? When downloading, you're usually working with dedicated, network-intensive FTP connection. Minimizing distance between you and the FTP server can minimize the use of network resources. In other words, it's the polite thing to do. Tucows gives you such a choice, and big companies like Netscape and Microsoft often give you a choice of the site from which to download.

Find It Online

These four sites are extremely popular, for good reason — archive size, software quality, download time, rating systems, and organizational clarity. CNET and ZDNet recently announced a merger of their online empires. Who knows what will become of their respective file fiefdoms. A smaller, personal favorite of mine is Dave Central (www.davecentral.com), which is easier to navigate than the giant sites, and includes perceptive software reviews.

Cross-Reference

Downloading and installing software has become easier (see Chapter 15 for the steps involved). After your computer does its thing, you're ready to go. Usually, you have the option of using the newly installed software right away, so downloading and installing software can lead directly to actually using it. Try downloading a program just to see how the process works.

holdings. Tucows offers Mac, Linux, Palm, BeOS, and Java software, as well as the Windows 98/Millennium Edition/2000/NT software you expect. In case you're wondering, Tucows stands for "The Ultimate Collection of Winsock Software."

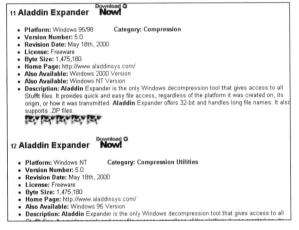

Figure 16-1. Tucows has a clear, readable organization and offers ratings and reviews. Here's a review of software mentioned later in this chapter. Note the cute and coveted five-cow Tucows rating.

> ▶ **ZDNet** (www.zdnet.com): This site features reviewed software, with recommendations and related content from Ziff-Davis's large family of online and print magazines.

> ▶ **CNET:** This organization has more than one site from which to download software, but start with Shareware.com (www.shareware.com), which boasts a collection of 250,000 downloadable files.

Awesome Internet Software

Here's a worthy but highly selective group of useful Internet software packages, both shareware and freeware, all readily available from one of the big archives (Tucows, and so on) or directly from the software's maker. For every piece of software, read the fine print. More important: have fun. With AOL and software like this, you can take your Internet connection as far as you want to go.

Compressing and Decompressing Mac and Windows Files: Aladdin Expander and WinZip

You can't work with the compressed files you get from e-mail or download from software archives without a program for *decompressing* them. WinZip, shown in Figure 16-2, specializes in ZIP files, the popular PC format; such files end in the file extension ZIP. Aladdin can handle both ZIP files and many other types as well. Depending on how your file associations are set up, double-clicking ZIP files brings up WinZip or Aladdin. Why two programs you ask? Because one of the programs may not be able to handle an odd-ball file type, while the other program can.

The advantage of Aladdin Expander: It's no-strings-attached freeware that can work with files zipped up on a Mac or Unix computer and distributed for broad use (this is the Net, after all). Expander works on the classic Macintosh principle of drag and drop. Just drop a compressed file onto the Aladdin Expander icon on your desktop and voilà — the individual files are extracted and placed for you in their own folder.

The advantage of WinZip: It's pretty much Windows only, but it offers a ton of features for both unzipping files and making them — indispensable when you're trying to get many files on one disk.

Note

File associations, in Windows, determine what program opens when you open a file of a specific type (such as DOC, JPG, or HTML). Chapter 15 discusses the specifics. You can associate ZIP files to open with feature-rich programs like Aladdin or WinZip.

Feature

Since AOL 5.0, selecting more than one file to send by e-mail automatically creates a ZIP file.

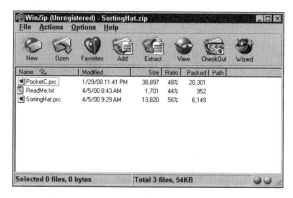

Figure 16-2. WinZip, the perennially indispensable PC file utility.

Bobby is the only program in this chapter available as Java — software that runs, in theory, on any operating system. Other types of software are available in this flexible format (for example, Tucows has a Java Telnet application).

The full set of Web-usability guidelines is available at `www.w3.org/WAI/`. The Bobby software was created by the Center for Applied Special Technology in Peabody, Massachusetts. CAST is a nonprofit organization that designs learning materials for students with special needs (`www.cast.org/bobby`).

Content available through ICQ is unfiltered, open, and "not for use by children under 13."

Whence the name ICQ? "I seek you." Get it?

Making Accessible Web Sites: Bobby

This free software, Bobby, was developed to enforce an important new set of usability guidelines drawn up by the W3 Consortium, which helps set (and occasionally enforce) Web standards. The Consortium estimates that 10–20 percent of the population has a visual, cognitive, or other disability that makes the "universal" Web at least partly inaccessible to them. Nonetheless, disabilities can be readily accommodated through appropriate Web design, which the W3C specifies in its guidelines. Video and audio clips, for example, should have text captions for the benefit of people who cannot hear or see the multimedia effects.

Bobby was created for Web developers concerned about making pages that are usable — that is, can be easily *perceived*, understood, and navigated — by the broadest possible audience. Bobby gives Web developers the chance to analyze their pages' usability both *before* publishing them and *after*. Using Bobby is simple: Give it the name of a local Web file (on your hard drive) or an actual Web address to analyze, and it creates a report showing whether or not the W3C's guidelines are met, providing suggestions for any problems it uncovers. And it *will* uncover problems.

Communications Software on Steroids: ICQ

What began as simple messaging software from a small Israeli company has blossomed into the Net's newest tool for communicating with other people. Frighteningly comprehensive, too. This free software is available at `www.icq.com`.

When you open ICQ, you start at the small window shown in Figure 16-3. This window has two modes: simple and advanced, which differ primarily in the range of features they make available. Many features, like buddy lists, will be familiar to users of the AOL Instant Messenger service. Others, like the Web pages that function primarily as communication boards, take some getting used to. The best advice I can give is to explore and learn ICQ with a friend who is online at the same time you are. How do you find such a person? Random chat can be a good way to meet a friendly soul on ICQ. Just click Chat with a Friend on ICQ's Advanced Mode main window (shown in Figure 16-3).

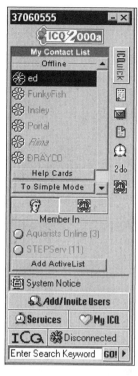

Figure 16-3. The main ICQ window can be minimized into the taskbar so it's out of the way. When you get a message, the icon flashes in the Windows system tray at the bottom of your screen.

Here are a few of ICQ's many features:

▶ ICQ comes with messaging, videoconferencing, and e-mail capabilities, plus an archive for all your messages.

▶ If you have telephony software such as Internet Phone, plus a headset (microphone and headphones), you can use ICQ to have telephone conversations over the Net. ICQ includes an online directory of ICQ users who have telephony software.

▶ If you misplaced your Palm organizer, ICQ includes a datebook, reminder service, handy note-jotting feature, and To Do list.

▶ To find and keep track of your contacts, ICQ offers directories, searchable in many ways, plus a personal address book. The ICQ people *want* you to meet people online.

Tip

As with all software, you'll quickly figure out the ICQ functions you want to use — like messaging or keeping a To Do list. You don't need and won't want to do everything possible on ICQ. Fortunately, help is available on the main ICQ window by choosing ICQ⇨Help and choosing from the drop-down list. On the Web, the ICQ rescue squad can always be found at www.icq.com/ icq123/. This software is so complex you may want a book. Yep, there's a Dummies title on the subject: *ICQ For Dummies*, by Peter Weverka (IDG Books Worldwide, Inc.).

16

Internet Tools that Extend Your Reach

▶ ICQ's community tools let you join chat rooms with a truly global audience, and create Web pages with dedicated chat rooms and message boards.

Avoiding Viruses: McAfee and Norton

Although wandering the Internet is *not* like walking a dark street in the bad part of town, there are immoral folk called *crackers* who do want to cause damage, whether for the technical challenge, the sociopathic urge, or something in between. (Crackers differ from *hackers*, the priestly elite of the digital world, who see technical challenges even where none exist.) One recent big scare was the I_LOVE_YOU Outlook worm that disabled several million computers. For general information about viruses, go to AOL Keyword: **Virus**, shown in Figure 16-4.

The best way to avoid contracting a virus is to limit the places from which you download new software. AOL's file libraries, big software vendors like Microsoft, and the big download sites profiled earlier in this chapter can all be considered as safe as anything online.

A virus is a small program that can attach itself to any kind of file except for pure-text (TXT) files. Viruses are designed to damage files, even wipe out hard drives. They can be difficult to detect until they have done their damage. If you do much downloading from the Internet (as opposed to downloading from AOL's file libraries), you would be wise to protect your system with antivirus software. Such programs use virus definitions that identify viruses; after they identify a virus, they seek to render it harmless.

For more information about McAfee visit AOL Keyword: McAfee or their Web site at www.mcafee.com. You can reach Norton on the Web at www.norton.com. Both programs are excellent, so if you buy a computer with one or the other already installed, you can't go far wrong.

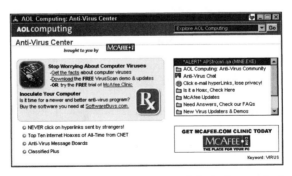

Figure 16-4. AOL's Anti-Virus Center includes both general information, breaking news about specific viruses, and links to vendors' sites.

To protect yourself from viruses, you need to purchase a software package such as McAfee or Norton AntiVirus. Both programs check incoming files for viruses automatically and let you scan your system on demand if something seems fishy.

Because viruses are always being updated, virus definitions are updated regularly as well, and you cannot update your list of virus defintions and software too frequently. Both programs let you update your software online on a schedule or whenever you want; just follow the on-screen instructions.

Keeping Kids Safe: NetNanny

Statisticians have shown that the *proportion* of raunchy Web sites to all Web sites is trivial. Parents and teachers still have cause for concern, however, because kids are curious and the open Internet mirrors the world top to bottom, raunchy to rarefied.

AOL has its own, integrated browser, based on Microsoft Internet Explorer (MSIE), as you can read in Chapter 6. The stand-alone browsers you can use *with* AOL, such as Netscape Navigator and the full-blown version of Microsoft Internet Explorer (available on your Windows desktop), do *not* support AOL's Parental Controls. For these occasions, Web "filtering software" such as NetNanny (www.netnanny.com) can give parents and teachers some peace of mind that kids will not stray too far from family-sanctioned sites. Figure 16-5 shows the shareware version of this popular program, which lacks a few features of the full, commercial version; the evaluation period lasts 30 days. You can find the software at www.netnanny.com.

Tip

Many parents these days work closely with their kids so that they learn to evaluate materials by themselves, identify and respond to situations in which they are uncomfortable, and become familiar with online destinations that everyone can agree are fun, safe, and challenging. I devote Chapter 4 to the issues of family-friendly Internet use.

Cross-Reference

Chapter 4 goes into the details relating to AOL's Parental Controls.

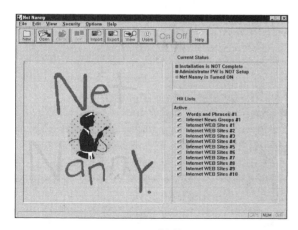

Figure 16-5. NetNanny's powerful filtering program can keep kids out of trouble by keeping trouble away from kids.

NetNanny works by scanning downloaded messages, file-names, Web addresses, newsgroup names, and other words streaming into your house from the Internet. The software is able to detect any words or phrases deemed unacceptable, as defined in a list of words and phrases that parents can add to and edit. When NetNanny encounters an apparently objection-able word, it can respond in several ways: making a warning sound, shutting down the program, or unobtrusively logging the activity for parents to view later. The program is password-protected to prevent access by kids. The administrator (grown up) can set up NetNanny to turn on automatically when the computer is turned on.

Logging on to Remote Computers: NetTerm

Telnet is an old-fashioned Internet protocol and set of related tools for using databases, searchable library catalogs, and other resources. When using Telnet, you're actually logged onto a distant Internet computer and directly using its processing power to perform tasks on that computer.

The Telnet experience differs from the Web experience. It's a world of text, not pictures, as you can see in Figure 16-6. Because it's a world of characters, the keyboard is king and the mouse has little to say. In fact, when you sign onto many Telnet sites, you're asked what keyboard you're using (VT100 or VT102 usually works fine). With Telnet you're using some-one else's computer, in a sense, so you usually need a login name. Most Telnet resources are public, however, so the login is either provided on the opening screen or not required at all.

On AOL, you can do your telnetting through the AOL browser using Microsoft Telnet, a small program included with Windows 95/98. If you have to do some serious telnetting for work, you may want to use a program with more features and greater ease of use, such as NetTerm. It presents text attrac-tively, allowing you to alter font, size, color, and background color. It allows you to set up new addresses and access them easily in the built-in directory. NetTerm doubles as a dialer when you're using a BBS or similar phone-based system. NetTerm also lets you print screens and save sessions to text files for later review.

Note

Telnet resources are dwin-dling in number, as data-bases and other Telnet applications migrate to the Web. You can still find many libraries, government offices, and other public and acade-mic organizations with Telnet sites. I provide this informa-tion to show you how to use these resources on AOL when you come across them.

Tip

A Telnet address is like any Internet address, except it be-gins with *telnet://*. On the AOL browser, you can visit a Telnet site by simply typing **telnet://** and its address into the AOL Address box. You'll almost always need a user-name and password.

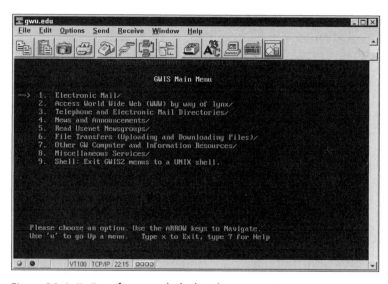

Figure 16-6. NetTerm, feature-packed Telnet shareware.

Software for Playing and Making MP3s

MP3 music files represent an entirely new way of producing, distributing, and listening to music. In quality, MP3 blows right past the older, popular formats like WAV and RealAudio. MP3s achieve sound quality close to that of an audio CD despite the fact that they compress music to less than one fifth the size of the original files. Special software players for your PC and Mac can play MP3 files, and these players let you build your own playlists. You can also use the downloaded files away from the computer, using new portable hardware devices. Recorders even let you create your own MP3 files.

Making Music Files: Real JukeBox and MusicMatch

How do you *make* MP3s? Using free software such as MusicMatch or Real Jukebox, ripping involves nothing more than copying tracks of music from an audio CD to your PC as MP3 files. MusicMatch is available at Tucows, Real Jukebox at www.realjukebox.com. Both come in commercial versions packing additional features.

With Real Jukebox, all you do is insert an audio CD into your CD-ROM drive, select the tracks you wish to copy, and click the Record button. The CD tracks are individually copied and saved in your hard drive's My Music directory (or whatever folder you specify). With both Real Jukebox and MusicMatch, I strongly suggest spending some time looking through online

Find It Online

Check out Hytelnet (www.lights.com/ hytelnet), an older directory of libraries with catalogs that you can search by Telnet. Many former Telnettable libraries now reside on the Web (see Chapter 9).

Definition

Streaming means that you can hear these MP3 files right after they start to download.

Find It Online

CNET's huge Music Center (music.cnet.com) has a section devoted to creating music, including tutorials for encoding MP3s and creating CDs.

16

Internet Tools that Extend Your Reach

Definition

Rip is not some sort of violent ritual, but refers to copying a track of music from an audio CD-ROM. *Burn* sounds just as menacing but simply means copying music to a record-able CD. Many new PCs include CD-R and CD-RW drives for making your own CDs.

Tip

Because of their quality and portability, MP3 files are worth listening to even when you're not on the Web, not online, and not even at your computer. Many MP3 gadgets let you transfer your downloaded MP3 files and play them anywhere. With such players, you can listen to music when the radio sig-nals are weak. Or, listen to CD-quality music put together from different online sources and CDs, in any order. At AOL Keyword: **Shop@AOL**, you can purchase any of sev-eral MP3 players to enjoy while working, jogging, cooking, working outside, or in the car getting bored with the limited choice and tired programming.

help so that you will understand recording preferences and the mechanics of making and playing playlists.

MusicMatch gives you great flexibility in recording CD tracks into MP3 of various quality grades, from FM quality through near-CD to CD quality. Make sure you record in a format such as MP3 that other players can read. To do so, use the Options➪Recorder to set your preferences (make sure to record in digital mode and to choose a sufficiently high audio quality). The process is simple:

1. Insert a CD.

   The CD's tracks display in the Recorder.

2. Select the tracks to record (I've selected just all tracks by clicking All).

   When the recording has completed, you can play the recorded files as follows:

   - Use the Player's Lib button to view the library.
   - Click the Music Library's Add button to add music to the library.
   - Click and drag songs from the library to playlist.

3. In the Player, select a song in the playlist to play it.

To play the track recorded, click the Lib button to display the Music Library if it's not already displayed. In the Music Library, double-click the track to transfer it to the player and play it.

Figure 16-7. MusicMatch records and plays MP3.

An MP3 file will eat up roughly one megabyte of hard drive space for a minute of play time. If you purchased a new computer in the last 12 months, it's possible that you have a 10 gigabyte hard disk or even larger. Five gigabytes is sufficient to store nearly 100 CDs. Or, if you have a writable CD, you should be able to store 5–10 hour-long CDs on a CD-R disk, which you can then take wherever you want without having to schlep around all those CDs.

Playing Music Files: Spinner and Winamp

Music can also come to you over the Internet in a streaming format and is perfect for radio-like services such as Spinner.com, shown in Figure 16-8. Spinner is an Internet audio-streaming application that plays the 140-plus custom programmed music channels. Spinner works very much like a conventional radio station — you choose a style of music that fits your mood and a continuous stream of music comes your way. You can also get information on your favorite artists, purchase CD's and read music news and reviews.

The Spinner service does not let you play individual MP3 files. You can find versions of Spinner on AOL as AOL Plus Radio and on ICQ as ICQ Radio.

Figure 16-8. Better than having the radio on: Spinner Plus (available at www.spinner.com).

A *playlist* is simply a list of MP3 songs you like, in the order you like them.

MusicMatch has three sections: a player, which includes a playlist; a library, where you pick and choose files for your playlist; and a recorder, where you select tracks and create MP3 files for your library. You can close the parts individually, as in Figure 16-7, which doesn't show the library.

Using Spinner, click Artist Information to learn about the performers and composers whose work you hear and like online. Spinner can be a good way to acquire new tastes, refine old ones, and learn about new artists.

Net traffic jams can impair smooth reception, causing stuttering or stopping and starting of the audio streamer. Explore a broadband connection—see Chapter 17.

16

Internet Tools that Extend Your Reach

Winamp, a very popular player also owned by AOL and available at AOL Keyword: **Winamp**, offers a broader range of capabilities than Spinner, but it also serves different purposes. It's more like high-quality stereo equipment (the kind where you don't understand what all the dials do) than a perfectly functional table radio (like Spinner). Unlike Spinner, Winamp plays MP3s from any Web site you like and can also play your audio CDs. With Winamp open, put in a CD and click Winamp's Play button, the right-pointing triangle. If another program comes up to play the CD, close it. If the CD isn't available, click the playlist's ADD button, select Add Dir, and find and double-click the drive with the CD.

Tip

The Winamp playlist lets you add MP3 music from anywhere on your computer to a single list, then play the music in any order. Click Add to get started.

Cross-Reference

At sites like Audiofind, you can find out about rising artists in your favorite musical genres (www. audiofind.com). For more tips about where to find music for Winamp, check out Chapter 18.

Note that Winamp (shown in Figure 16-9) has three parts:

▶ **Winamp player:** The player has the basic controls (Start, Stop, Pause, Eject, and so on) for the music currently being played.

▶ **Winamp equalizer:** The equalizer has fancy audio settings, which are very handy if you have any idea what they do (and I don't) and have an audio system that can do them justice. You can close this part of the software or keep it open and impress friends.

▶ **Winamp playlist:** The playlist shows what's playing, and the list of songs of which it is part. Figure 16-9 shows only one song, from a Shoutcast.com radio station.

Only the player *must* be displayed to use Winamp. You can close the equalizer or playlist by clicking the close button (the X in the upper-right corner). To restore the playlist or equalizer, click the PL or EQ button on the player.

Ready to listen to music with Winamp? A megasite like MP3.COM will have just about anything, of course. For music that focuses in depth on a specific genre, start with a venue like the Ultimate Band List (www.ubl.com). Shoutcast.com, a favorite of mine (www.shoutcast.com), links you to many sites that focus on this or that kind of music — reggae, klezmer, fusion jazz, disco, '80s, and so on.

Figure 16-9. The popular (and free) Winamp MP3 player, shown in one of the more popular *skins*, which you can choose to change the player's look.

Downloading and Uploading Files: WS_FTP

Sharing files on the Internet — and creating Web sites in particular — requires some familiarity with a program like WS_FTP, because you'll eventually need to do some heavy-duty *uploading* of all those HTML files you keep tweaking. From any FTP site to which you have access, you can also *download* one or more files directly to your hard drive. For both uploading and downloading, WS_FTP provides point-and-click controls. The clear design gives you parallel views of your hard drive and of the remote FTP site, as you can see in Figure 16-10. Just select a file and click a button to upload from your hard drive to the FTP site, or download from the FTP site to your hard drive. You can move many files at once by simply selecting more than one file to upload or download.

Cross-Reference

You use FTP to move files back and forth between computers on the Internet. Chapter 15 provides a thorough overview of FTP.

16

Internet Tools that
Extend Your Reach

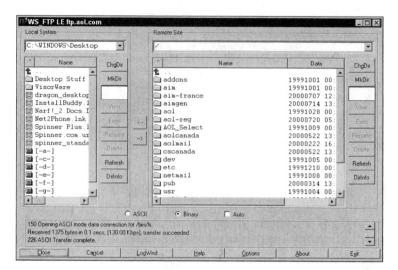

Figure 16-10. WS_FTP, the easiest way to use FTP sites. To log on to an FTP site, you need to create a session profile like the one shown.

Where to Go from Here

This chapter introduces some of the useful and fun Internet software you can use with AOL to expand and enrich your Internet experience. These programs let you play music, create Web sites, keep your kids safe, download countless files, and avoid file viruses. The sample is small and very selective; hundreds of programs are available at sites like those mentioned in this chapter. Two other chapters in this book touch on similar issues:

▶ For everything you need to know about downloading and using files from AOL and the Web, see Chapter 15.

▶ For suggestions about what you can *do* with the Internet resources at your disposal on and through AOL, see Chapter 18.

Chapter 17

Internet Everywhere:
New Ways to Access AOL

IN THIS CHAPTER

Modem limitations, high-speed solutions

High-speed access from your phone line: AOL Plus

High-speed access from cable wires

"AOL Anywhere"sm: wireless phones, PDAs, TVs

Getting online used to require the purchase of a modem for your computer so that you could use the telephone lines to dial into some distant computer. Modems work by taking *digital* computer data (lots of 1's and 0's) and changing it into an *analog* signal (composed of waves) that can be sent along telephone wires to another computer, which converts it back into data. The problem is, modems can send data no faster than permitted using the narrow part of the telephone wire devoted to telephone communications. Modems can only transmit data so fast, and no faster.

In the last few years, Internet technology has improved substantially, allowing broader, more complex methods to speed up your connection. This chapter gives an overview of

▶ High-speed options for accessing AOL and the Internet from your home PC

▶ Alternative methods to get online for the times when you're not near a computer

AOL now offers a family of new ways to access AOL and the Internet. Not only are these alternatives faster than modem-based connections, they are also much more convenient. They bring AOL to a variety of new venues, including your television, wireless phone, and portable digital assistant (PDA).

Introducing High-Speed Internet Access

"Downloading Web pages with narrowband technology has been likened to sucking Jell-o through a straw," say the authors of a *McKinsey Quarterly* article, "The Last Mile to the Internet." "Broadband technologies, on the other hand, promise to deliver crisp text, video and sound as quickly as if the user were watching television."

With high-speed solutions like AOL Plus, discussed in this chapter, you don't have to deal with noisy dial-up modems, busy signals, slow downloads, or conflicts with household members who need to use the phone or fax when you're on-line. You can just open AOL and sign on whenever you want to.

The new high-speed technologies enable a new crop of services so that you can:

▶ Have real-time conversations online by talking, not typing. As a result, you can engage in teleconferencing so realistic you'll forget the *tele* part. Conferencing will make possible collaborative projects between schools and effective teamwork in business among workers at different locations and at home.

▶ Download large software files from the Internet in seconds instead of minutes. The software profile in Chapter 16 can now be yours much more quickly.

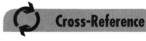
Cross-Reference

For more on what you can do with high-speed AOL access, see Chapter 18.

▶ Immerse yourself in an online art gallery or a huge database of images like the Fine Arts Museums of San Francisco's ImageBase (available at `www.thinker.org`).

▶ Take part in lifetime education at your pace when you need it on the subjects you want to learn about. For a directory of distance education programs, start at Peterson's directory of programs and courses at `www.lifelonglearning.com`.

▶ Use your computer as a radio, with a selection of radio stations around the world instead of around the neighboring counties. Chapter 18 has the details for how to play music online.

Essential Definitions

This section gives you a basic idea of what all this new technology means. You don't necessarily have to know how your Internet connection works, but you may find it useful to understand the terminology. Here's the least you need to know:

▶ *Bandwidth* refers to the data-carrying capacity of a network, as measured in bits per second. It's a fancy way of referring to how fast a network is. Geeks measure speed in bits. A *bit* is the smallest unit measurement given to computer data, and the speed of data transfer is usually measured in *bps*, bits per second. In human terms, speed is relative to what you need to do and how you are used to doing it. If a file took ten minutes to download with a modem and takes under a minute with broadband, that's fast.

▶ *Broadband* is another word for *high-speed* and usually refers to Internet access. Broadband Internet access can be delivered in many ways: over phone lines, cable wires, and even through the air. Today, however, broadband comes in two major flavors: cable and DSL.

  • *Cable* technology brings the high data-carrying capacity of coaxial cable (the same wiring used to bring you cable TV) to your computer as well. See "Cable: The Familiar Broadband Alternative" in this chapter.

- *DSL* (digital subscriber line) technologies pack as much as 99 percent more capacity into existing phone lines by using the part of the bandwidth *not* used in voice communication. *AOL Plus* is AOL's complete DSL solution. See "Awesome DSL" in this chapter.

▶ *Downstream* refers to the speed of data transfer from the Internet to your computer, as when you are *downloading* a big Web page. *Upstream* measures how fast your messages and files travel from your PC to the Internet, as when you are *uploading* pages to a Web server or sending someone an e-mail message. With broadband connections, downstream rates are much faster than upstream rates.

Note

Satellite and wireless transmissions are just emerging as broadband options. Each broadband connection method works differently and has varying degrees of costs, benefits, and availability. I'll have more to say about these issues in this chapter.

Awesome DSL

Digital subscriber lines (DSL) use existing copper telephone lines, the kind probably coming into your home, to connect you to the Internet. In the following sections, I give you all the information you need to understand how DSL works and what benefits and costs you can expect. You can find out more about how AOL supports DSL at AOL Keyword: **AOL Plus**.

As an AOL Plus user, I can speak firsthand of its benefits:

▶ AOL Plus lets you share a single phone line between data communications (AOL and the Internet) and voice communication (phone, fax, and analog modem). Thus, you can use the phone (voice) and the Internet (data) at the same time while experiencing the Net at a much faster speed than you did via your old fashioned modem.

▶ With AOL Plus, in contrast to cable, the line by which you connect to the Internet is *your* line, not a shared line, which is especially important if you need to transmit sensitive business data.

Note

ISDN, an older technology from the phone companies, also combines voice and data, but it's expensive, complex to install, and doesn't achieve the speed of DSL.

▶ With AOL Plus, connecting to AOL becomes almost as simple as turning on the light. Like cable, your Internet connection is always on, so you don't have to put up with busy signals.

▶ Most importantly, with AOL Plus, a whole new world of video and multimedia opens up to you. As it expands broadband options, AOL is adding new content throughout the service. As you move through AOL while connected by AOL Plus, a tall box (shown in Figure 17-1) in the lower right-hand corner of the AOL window alerts you to special content optimized for a broadband connection.

AOL Plus tower

Figure 17-1. In the Kids Only channel, for example, look for multimedia features like this kid-driven circus from Mamamedia.com. The AOL tower highlights such content as you move from area to area throughout AOL.

Getting AOL Plus

Ordering AOL Plus requires no more than a visit to AOL Keyword: **AOL Plus**. You're asked to provide information about your geographical location; the rest is pretty much automatic. Because demand for the service is so high, you may have to wait several weeks between the time you order AOL Plus and the time your service begins. As soon as you receive AOL Plus, your days of waiting for the Internet will be over.

Note

AOL offers AOL Plus through your regional Bell operating company (Bell Atlantic, SBC, etc.). The phone company is responsible for many of the physical aspects of your connection, while AOL is responsible for customer and technical service, which I have found to be prompt and reliable. When you order AOL Plus from AOL, the phone company will get in touch with you and do a test to see whether you have DSL-ready phone lines. Your subsequent contact with the phone company is limited.

If AOL Plus is available in your area (which depends on many factors), two things happen within a week or two of your switch-on date, the date when you can actually use your new service:

▶ Someone from your phone company arrives at your home to examine the wiring going into your house. This person installs a box on the outside of your house as a plug for the high-speed copper wire and assesses the distance to and DSL-readiness of your *central office*. If the technician finds problems in wiring *within* the house you may have to pay the phone company for materials and labor.

▶ You receive a box with the AOL Plus equipment you need for your new connection, including:

• A DSL modem

• A cable from the modem to your PC

• Several filters to screen out the data traffic from the telephones, computers, and fax lines sharing the DSL line

Installing AOL Plus

Installing the equipment is painfree. Simply follow the instructions in the brochure that comes with your box of equipment. I found the steps easy to follow, and setup took under 20 minutes, with the longest amount of time spent waiting for Windows 98 to restart!

Setup involves several steps:

1. Put filters on the phone lines of every other phone, computer (with analog modem), or fax sharing the same phone number as your DSL line. A filter removes data traffic from your voice line, which otherwise interrupts the signal.

   To install a filter, remove the existing modem or fax cable from the phone jack in the wall, and put the filter into the phone jack in its place. Then, plug the modem or fax line into the filter. This filter screens out the high-speed data coming in over DSL and delivers only the voice portion of the signal.

Definition

The *central office* is the point at which local residences and businesses are joined to equipment that enables both local and long-distance calling.

Note

Unlike traditional analog modems, a DSL modem doesn't convert digital into analog (voice) signals. The DSL modem takes data from your computer and encodes it for transmission over the unused parts of the phone line. It's a data line, end to end, but shares the copper phone wire with voice communications (phone, fax, old-fashioned modem).

To use AOL Plus, you must have a *USB port*, a special kind of plug on the back of your computer, increasingly used for printers, scanners, and other hardware devices. The AOL Plus modem plugs right into your computer's USB port. You can also install an internal modem, following the instructions included in your AOL Plus package. While earlier DSL connections required high-speed network cards in your PC, AOL Plus uses your existing USB port, so you don't need a network card.

In the future, your DSL (AOL Plus) connection will always be running in the background, even when you're not on AOL. In fact, the connection is live from the time you turn on your PC for the day until the time you turn it off.

2. Plug in your DSL modem. You'll want to set it up next to your computer because of the short cable. It needs to be attached to three different places. A USB cable attaches to the back of your computer. An electrical cord goes into the wall. A phone cable (the same kind used by your older modems) goes into the phone jack. That's it.

3. Install two pieces of software on your PC, using the CDs that come with your AOL Plus package. Both CDs have complete on-screen instructions:

   • First, install the DSL connection software, called Speed Stream, which makes it possible for AOL to communicate with the high-speed DSL connection.

   • Second, install a special version of the AOL software, optimized to take advantage of high-speed access but otherwise identical to the software you use now. When you install AOL, you have to go through the process of copying or moving your personal files and telling AOL whether you want to create a new account or use an existing one.

4. When you're done, you'll be prompted to restart Windows. Do so. Sign on to AOL and follow any on-screen instructions to complete the process.

There's an old Internet acronym, YMMV, which stands for *Your mileage may vary.* DSL's speed is subject to constraints on the Internet itself, where popular Web sites, for example, can be very slow. Like an amusement park, the Net's biggest attractions often have the longest lines. Another limitation: Data speed varies with the length of copper wire over which it must travel from your house to the "central office," where copper feeds into the networks that take your phone calls and data across town and around the world. In addition, the phone companies are not always able to offer the fastest speeds possible.

Securing Your AOL Plus Connection

Networks are inherently risky; you have access to people, but they have access to you, too. You can minimize the risk in several ways. When you have a live DSL connection, you have access to the Internet only when you're signed on to AOL using the DSL connection. This fact in itself reduces your security risk. Further, you can set your PC's network preferences to prevent anyone or any computer from accessing any file on your computer. Follow these steps:

1. From the Start menu, choose Settings⇨Control Panels.
2. Double-click the Network control panel.
3. On the Configuration tab, click File and Print Sharing. Make sure that neither of the check boxes is checked. Click OK twice to shut both open boxes.

Beyond that, you can purchase what is known as firewall software from companies like NetIce (www.netice.com, makers of BlackIce), Norton (www.norton.com), and McAffee (www.mcaffee.com). You may consider purchasing that extra level of protection to protect your work or other sensitive information. At AOL Keyword: **Shop@AOL**, you can find the software you need.

Cable: The Familiar Broadband Alternative

More than 65 million Americans have cable TV, and a growing number of cable companies also offer Internet access services. So, if you have cable service and your cable company offers Internet service, you should be able to connect to the Internet over your cable TV wires. After you're connected to the Net, you can then sign on to AOL and enjoy high-speed access to AOL's content and the Internet.

The requirements for cable modem Net access include

- ▶ Typically, a subscription to cable TV.
- ▶ In addition, a subscription to your local cable Internet access company.
- ▶ A USB plug on the back of your computer.
- ▶ A cable modem, a piece of hardware that connects your PC to the high-speed cabling ordinarily used for cable TV transmission. The cable modem plugs into both the cable outlet on the wall and your computer. Unlike your standard dial-up modem, you may not have a choice when you purchase a cable modem, just as you may not have a vast array of cable companies to choose from in the first place; your cable company can tell you which cable modems you must use.

Tip

AOL can detect a live Internet connection (such as a DSL or cable connection) and prompt you to sign on to AOL. Right-click the AOL icon in the Windows system tray (at the bottom of your desktop). Select Auto Start Options, and click by Automatically Start AOL.

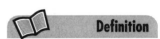

Definition

Designed originally to keep company Web servers secure from hackers, firewalls are now available to keep home computers secure from unwanted probes by hackers and others. Firewalls often work by screening out data packets from certain Internet addresses.

To find out whether your cable provider offers Internet services, you can check out the chart at `www.catv.org/frame/cmsa_state.html`. If your cable provider does offer Internet services, you must set up a TCP/IP Location, as explained in Chapter 3, and run AOL "over" the cable Internet connection. AOL Keyword: **Cable** (Connecting to AOL via Cable Modem) has the details. If you plan to use AOL exclusively over a cable connection, you may want to consider a Bring Your Own Access plan, explained at AOL Keyword: **Billing**.

In every case, talk with your cable ISP about what you need, what it costs, who installs it, and what kind of data-transmission rate you can expect.

Cable's Benefits

Why would you want to access AOL using cable?

> ▶ **Convenience.** If you have cable TV and your provider offers Internet access, you're most of the way to cable-based AOL access already.

The Data Packet that Couldn't

For a variety of reasons, data rarely travels as fast as it could, so even a 56K modem rarely moves data at 56K. Cable wires are often shared in a network with hundreds of families, and such sharing can create a local traffic slow-down. In addition, data zooming to your cable operator's gateway to the Internet often crawls along the Internet at a slower rate. *In any network, the slowest link sets the pace for the rest of the network.* That said, after you get a taste of cable or DSL, you won't want to go back to analog modems, even if your connection is not exactly instantaneous.

> ▶ **Speed.** As with DSL, the speed you experience on cable far surpasses that available by modem, but it necessarily lags behind technical possibilities. In other words, you have to "settle" for a data transfer rate of only 500Kbps, which is still ten times faster than what the best of standard modems deliver. You'll notice the difference when you read your mail (and have a lot of saved messages), download a file, or browse graphics-rich Web sites.
>
> ▶ **Freeing up the phone line.** If you live in a home with a single phone line and find yourself constantly jostling for use of the phone, fax, or Internet connection, you will appreciate an important feature of the cable modem: It runs over a different network from the telephone. And, with a piece of equipment called a *splitter*, the same cabling can be used to both connect your PC and bring cable programming to your TV.

Cable's downside? Cable is often criticized for putting your connection on a shared line with (potentially) hundreds of other neighbors who connect at the same point of the larger cable network. If everyone on the block uses a cable connection, performance can slip. Also, your data passes through the local stretch of the network in an unencrypted form, meaning that a network-savvy snoop can detect and monitor its contents (*hacked* is the informal term). If you do any business-related work at home, you may not want to entrust the protection of any mission-critical data to your cable company! Seek the opinion of a networking or business consultant if you have concerns here.

Signing on to AOL with Your Cable Connection

After you connect to your cable Internet provider, you sign on to AOL:

1. From the Sign On Screen, click Set Up.
2. Click Add Location to create a new location for use with an ISP or LAN. Add a custom (TCP/IP) connection.
3. Sign on to AOL using this new location.

AOL's High-Speed Satellite Access

A satellite-based connection to AOL meets the needs of people

▶ who already have satellite TV because of the choice of channels and the picture quality
▶ who have access to neither cable nor AOL Plus (people not near a large metropolitan area, for example)

Together with Hughes Electronics Corp., AOL is planning to offer AOL Plus Powered by DirecPC, which brings you high-speed access to the full AOL service over a computer.

To use DirecPC, you need a satellite dish and mount for your roof, and you need a satellite modem that attaches to a USB port on your Windows 98 computer. An internal modem is available for people with a free PCI slot. Satellite dishes and

Note

With cable, you can't use Internet and phone on the same line, as you can with DSL. Another benefit of DSL: You can use two computers on the same phone line — if one person uses regular modem access and the other person uses DSL, for example. This capability takes advantage of AOL 6.0's support of multiple screen names on the same account being signed on at the same time.

Find It Online

You will also find procedures at AOL Keyword: **Cable**.

Note

AOL Plus Powered by DirecPC was being tested and readied for general availability as this book was going into production.

A PC using the DirecPC service can receive data at about 400Kbps. It sends data, however, at about the speed of a regular 56K modem. Two-way satellite connections are in development, but in the meantime, data transmission with a satellite connection, as with cable and DSL connections, is lopsided. Downloading is a lot faster than uploading.

Satellites work by sending data over the super-high-speed radio beams transmitted by the satellites that remain at a relatively fixed position over a given region of the earth. You must have a satellite dish to use DirecPC, and the satellite must have a clear line of sight to the south. A DirecTV set-top box is currently being used to deliver AOLTV, discussed later in this chapter.

modems come in several varieties, depending on whether you want Internet-only access or Internet access plus DirecTV's digital TV programming. The satellite dish handles your incoming data transmissions.

For your outgoing messages, you need an old-fashioned analog modem and phone jack plus a subscription to an Internet service provider.

As with cable modems, satellite modems can detect more than one kind of signal. In both cases, your data is riding the same path taken by TV signals (satellite TV in one case, cable in the other). If you're a fan of cable or satellite TV, you may have already gone most of the way to choosing a type of broadband AOL access. The next section goes into more detail about choosing a type of broadband.

Choosing the Right High-Speed Connection

So, you want broadband. Which type of broadband should you get?

The first point to make is that you're unlikely to notice a speed difference between the major broadband options. Cable, DSL, and satellite:

- ▶ deliver comparable speeds.
- ▶ can achieve downstream data rates that far surpass what you're used to with a dial-up connection and modem. (*Downstream* means from the Net to you, as when you download a Web page.)

You may have to make your decision based on the options available in your area. For example, the availability of cable and AOL Plus varies from region to region. Cable Internet service is still not available even in many suburbs — even those that are saturated with cable TV — and is even less prevalent in smaller cities and rural areas. If you don't have cable to begin with, you'll have to factor in a monthly cable TV subscription into your calculations, plus the cost of cable Internet access.

Because availability varies so widely, AOL is working to offer as many solutions as possible. In fact, AOL is working with the regional telephone companies to provide low-cost DSL connections (mine, from Bell Atlantic, currently costs about $20 a month in addition to AOL's monthly fee) and is also trying to persuade the cable companies to broaden Internet access. At the same time, AOL has launched several satellite initiatives with big companies like Hughes Electronic. Its wireless initiatives are even more aggressive, as you'll see in the next pages.

My advice is that you start with what you have. If AOL Plus is offered in your area (go to AOL Keyword: **AOL Plus** to find out), it's a solution that offers many advantages. If you have cable and your provider also offers cable Internet access, all you need is to subscribe to the cable Internet service and purchase a cable modem and related equipment. Finally, if you either don't have access to cable Internet service or your phone company doesn't offer DSL yet, consider AOL Plus Powered by DirecPC, which, because it's satellite based, should be available just about everywhere, especially in the places where cable and AOL Plus cannot yet be found.

AOL Anywhere: Through the Air and on TV

AOL offers much more than fast access to existing computers; it's beginning to offer a range of ways to access AOL *without* computers. AOL is about great content, after all, not desktop computers. The AOL Anywhere service consists of different initiatives for different needs. In each of the following areas, AOL adds an interactive dimension to a fairly static medium. Each of the following AOL technologies is discussed in the next few pages:

- ▶ **Handheld computers, also known as personal digital assistants (PDAs),** such as the Palm, can now give you access to your AOL mail and instant messages. All you need is a PDA, a modem, and access to a phone jack. Few PDAs are wireless, but that is changing.

- ▶ **Wireless cell phones** are starting to deliver a wide range of AOL content and services. All you need is a wireless phone and subscription to a wireless service (as well as AOL), and you can use e-mail, messaging, and Web content without wires, from anywhere! For now,

If you're not sure which high-speed connection is right for you, start with what you already have — figure out what is available in your area and what kind of services you already receive (such as cable TV) that would reduce the cost of any necessary equipment you might need.

Product and service offerings are likely to become richer and more affordable in the near future. AOL Keyword: **Anywhere** is a good place to start. AOL Keyword: **Press** can give you an idea of AOL's plans in this hot area.

Cross-Reference

For more information about using AOL Mail with Palms and PocketPCs, see Chapter 10.

Find It Online

The highly informative PDA Forum (AOL Keyword: **PDA**) provides message boards and PDA-related Web links. The forum has its own weekly e-mail newsletter, Pocket Press, to which you can subscribe at AOL Keyword: **Newsletter**. If you have a PDA, try downloading some of the thousands of books available in this forum!

Tip

AOL Keyword: **Shop@AOL** carries all major PDAs.

Note

To use AOL Mail on a PDA currently requires a modem and phone jack. In other words, you'll need to purchase a modem for your PDA ($100–$200), and you can use AOL Mail only when you have access to a phone jack. Eventually, wireless devices will be more common and affordable.

wireless seems to make the most sense for business travelers and for people in larger metropolitan areas, but over time you can expect to see all sorts of popular uses for wireless, such as instant messaging and ready access to essential Web services like Digital Cities, MapQuest, and Moviefone.

▶ **AOLTV** is for folks who simply want a livelier and more interactive TV experience. Leave it to AOL to improve on TV.

Installing and Using AOL Mail with PDAs

You can currently get your AOL mail and do instant messaging with both major PDA types:

▶ Palm-compatible devices (Palm and Handspring PDAs, and the forthcoming Sony devices). PDAs based on the Palm operating system are more popular and currently less expensive than PocketPCs. If you buy a Palm, make sure to buy a modem, too. The wireless option (no cords and analog modems) is available on the Palm V (via the OmniSky modem and service) and Palm VII. Figure 17-2 shows a Palm PDA.

▶ PocketPC devices (HP, Casio, Compaq, and others). The PocketPCs are the latest incarnation of the Microsoft Windows CE operating system, a scaled-down version of Windows that includes miniature versions of familiar programs like Microsoft Word. The new PocketPCs also play music, include a high-quality text reader, and display color — multimedia features not yet available on Palm-compatible PDAs.

The pleasure of using AOL Mail on a PDA results from sheer convenience. AOL is always as close as your shirt-pocket or purse-sized PDA. You'll also come to appreciate the simplicity and elegance of devices like the Palm. They were meant to be easy to use, and they currently do a much better job of supporting simple functions than any beefy desktop computer or svelte but clumsy laptop. AOL Mail for PDAs comes in especially handy if you'll be in a hotel room or away for short trips.

Figure 17-2. Major PDAs like this Palm are available at AOL Keyword: **Shop Direct**.

Currently, AOL Mail for PDAs works through a PDA's phone wire, and thus requires access to a phone jack. Some PDAs, however, offer wireless service, such as the Palm VII and the Palm V (with the OmniSky modem and wireless service), and AOL Mail software was being tested for the Palm VIII. As I completed this book, Handspring was developing a wireless module. In the future, expect to see more devices offering wireless Internet connections with small text-based Web browsers and wireless networks extending beyond the big cities.

AOL Mail provides access to your AOL e-mail through your Palm and PocketPC and older Windows CE organizers. The software is free, but if you're on an hourly usage plan, you get billed for time using AOL Mail on your PDA.

Using AOL Mail on a Palm requires the following:

▶ A handheld running the Palm-compatible operating system (version 3.0 or higher), with at least version 3.0 of the Palm operating system and at least 425K of RAM.

▶ A snap-on Palm modem or Handspring modem-module.

Palm's built-in infrared connection, TCP support, and cell modems are not fully supported. AOL Mail for the Palm is available for the Macintosh, as well as the PC; platform-specific instructions and the latest list of supported devices are available at AOL Keyword: **Anywhere**.

Net traffic jams can impair smooth reception, causing stuttering or starting and stopping of the audio streamer. Explore a broadband connection — See Chapter 18.

For more information, go to AOL Keyword: **Anywhere**. Choose Palm or Windows CE/PocketPC.

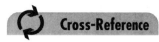

Cross-Reference

Chapter 10 has instructions for using AOL Mail on a Palm-compatible handheld.

Note

If you're getting used to broadband speeds, you will need to throttle back and get used to speeds of 14.4 or 33Kbps, especially when you need to display a long list of messages in your mailbox.

Note

AOL Mail for both Palm and PocketPC/Windows CE organizers supports the core e-mail functions of writing, sending, reading, and deleting e-mail messages. Currently *not* supported are fancier functions such as embedding graphics, creating backgrounds, checking e-mail status (whether a message has been read by an AOL recipient), inserting links, and attaching files.

To install AOL Mail on a Palm:

1. Download the free AOL Mail software (contained in a small file called `aolmail.prc`) to your PC from AOL Keyword: **Anywhere**.

2. Transfer the file to your Palm and install it during your next HotSync session. All you do is put your PDA in its cradle and press the HotSync button; any uninstalled Palm programs get transferred to and installed in your PDA. See your handheld's instructions for the details.

   AOL Mail will then be available by tapping your Palm's Application icon on the PDA's opening menu.

3. To use e-mail, attach your modem, plug it into a phone jack, start the AOL application on your PDA, and tap Sign On. Online, you can read, write, send, and delete e-mail messages.

Using AOL Mail on a Windows CE organizer requires the following:

▶ Windows CE version 2.11. For a list of both Windows CE devices and newer PocketPC devices, check AOL Keyword: **PDA**.

▶ 200K of storage memory and 1.1MB of program memory.

▶ For any of these Windows CE/Pocket PC devices, you also need a clip-on modem, TCP/IP connection, or add-on PCMIA card. Network (Ethernet) cards work as well, as long as they're PCMIA-compatible or CompactFlash-compatible, depending on the standard your organizer supports.

To install AOL Mail on Windows CE/Pocket PC devices:

1. Download the free software (`AOLWinCE.exe`) from AOL Keyword: **Anywhere.**

2. Make sure your handheld is connected to your computer, and then run the software on your PC, following the on-screen directions to install AOL Mail on your PDA.

   For the new PocketPCs, the procedure is similar to that for Windows CE devices, except you run an installer on your PC and follow the instructions.

   You're now ready to read, write, send, and delete messages.

AOL Around the House

AOL and Gateway Computers recently announced a series of Internet "appliances" designed for the easiest and fastest access to indispensable AOL tools, such as e-mail and the Web. These appliances are designed to be unobtrusive, portable, and available wherever needed, especially around the house. The planned devices — Web Pad, countertop appliance, and desktop appliance — fill in the missing links in the chain between PDAs and cell phones, on the one hand, and desktop computers, on the other.

▶ The mobile Web Pad will come without a keyboard but with a touchscreen instead. You use features by gently touching parts of a membrane screen instead of moving a mouse or typing at a keyboard. You can take the wireless Web Pad anywhere in the house. The Web Pad will be able to communicate with a small computer called a base station to send and receive e-mail and Web pages.

▶ Like AOLTV, described shortly, the planned countertop appliance will come with a wireless keyboard.

▶ The desktop appliance will have a more traditional keyboard, mouse, and screen, plus familiar ways of accessing content but will cost less and take up less space than a desktop computer.

Underlying these cool new gadgets are the Linux operating system and the Gecko (mini-Netscape) browser. Linux supports faster and sleeker applications, on all types of hardware, while the Gecko browser will allow Web access on a wide range of portable and handheld devices.

Using AOL Mail for Wireless Phones

Many people see a brilliant future in wireless communications. What is wireless? It refers to the ability of a phone or PDA to exchange data with the Internet without an analog modem (which needs a cable and phone jack). Phones are offering the service already, and PDAs will be catching up as wireless modems become less expensive and wireless networks become more extensive and affordable. What's special about wireless? It untethers you from the desktop and its tangle of plugs and cords. You can work and play anywhere.

 Find It Online

AOL Keyword: **Mobile** has more information about current wireless service and will be the source where you can learn about future wireless services as they become available.

Wireless works by sending data over radio waves rather than over physical cables. The entire network is not wireless; ultimately the information you need is sitting on a computer somewhere, and it must travel over high-speed physical networks, as well as radio waves. What counts is that the network link between your device and the physical network *is* wireless, which untangles your online experience.

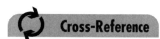

Cross-Reference

The kind of services eventually available by wireless can already be used on desktop computers. I discuss My AOL in Chapter 3, and MovieFone and Digital Cities in Chapter 5.

While this book was being completed, AOL announced the availability of its first wireless service, which you can use if you subscribe to the Sprint PCS's Internet-ready wireless service. The Sprint phone is shown in Figure 17-3. AOL members who also subscribe to the Sprint PCS Wireless Web (AOL Keyword: **Mobile**) service have access to e-mail, stock quotes, and customized content from My AOL, including news and weather. Sprint PCS subscribers who aren't AOL members still have instant access to AOL's location-based Web services:

▶ MapQuest (AOL Keyword: **Mapquest**) provides driving directions and traffic updates.
▶ Moviefone (AOL Keyword: **Moviefone**) brings you movie times, ticketing services, and other movie-related services (see Chapter 5).

Tip

An *Internet appliance* is a gadget that does one or two things well and simply. AOL's new Mobile Communicator offers e-mail and messaging services in the form of a sleek, handheld, wireless device. It costs less than a Palm (much less than a PocketPC), and a monthly subscription to the e-mail-only service costs less than your monthly AOL fee.

Figure 17-3. Read your AOL Mail and browse the Web using Sprint's Wireless Web service.

AOL in the Living Room: AOLTV

AOL recently launched AOLTV in order to extend the world of interactive services to anyone who doesn't have or want a home computer. The only equipment required to use the new service is a set-top box, which you can purchase online at AOL Keyword: **AOLTV** and at selected retailers whose names you can find at the same keyword. AOLTV costs about $15 a month in addition to members' monthly AOL charge, or about $25 a month for current non-members.

AOLTV offers a set of AOL's online services chosen to complement what you see on TV. For starters, the Programming Guide gives you detailed TV program listings for your area. You can save your favorite shows in a special Favorite Places folder. You can do your e-mail, take part in instant messaging, and join chats after your favorite shows. You'll even enjoy your AOL Buddy List, so you and your friends can watch games together, anywhere you all happen to be.

In addition to all these services, AOLTV watchers will experience Web browsing and entirely new interactive TV content created by media companies like Oxygen Media, Rolling Stone.com, Launch.com, Sesame Workshop, SoapCity, and Better Homes and Gardens. Family members can even view and share digital pictures using AOL's new "You've Got Pictures" service. You can view Web sites in a window within the TV screen, so that you can do several things at once. See Figure 17-4.

Among the equipment you receive with AOLTV is a wireless keyboard, which gives you control of all interactive features and lets you write your mail and chat messages. By the way, you can make the messaging windows as large as the whole screen, so you can easily see your messages while sitting halfway across the room. A wireless remote gives you control of both TV and VCR functions.

Note

A second variety of AOLTV is currently under development for people who subscribe to DirecTV, the digital TV service delivered by satellite (www.directv.com).

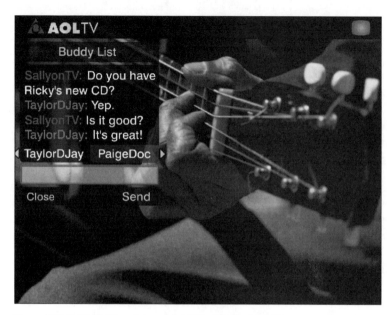

Figure 17-4. Watch TV and chat with AOL buddies with AOLTV.

Where to Go from Here

In the year since the previous edition of this book, AOL Plus and AOL Anywhere have become tangible. AOL Plus can now be ordered with a click of a button, and setup is a breeze. Equally dramatic, AOL Anywhere brings AOL and the Net to where you are, rather than requiring you to plant yourself in front of some big desktop computer to read your e-mail. The days of having to do things on the computer's terms may be coming slowly to an end.

▶ The next chapter profiles some of the music and video content made possible by AOL Plus and other types of broadband.

▶ The following keywords take you to focused information on AOL's high-speed and Anywhere offerings: **AOL Plus**, **Anywhere**, **PDA**, **Mobile**, and **Cable**.

▶ AOL Keyword: **CNET** has detailed information and product reviews on every aspect of wireless and broadband computing.

▶ To buy new equipment, start at AOL Keywords: **Shop Direct** and **Shop@AOL**.

Chapter 18

Did You Know You Can . . . on AOL?

IN THIS CHAPTER

Watching movies

Listening to music

Creating digital pictures

Reading books

Reading and writing e-mail away from AOL

Sending a fax

Using the phone over the Internet

Making payments

Creating Web pages: AOL Hometown

Creating a community: Groups@AOL

This chapter explores a few of the new activities possible on AOL and the Internet. No, I am not talking about buying CDs or gathering information for a trip to the mountains — real-world pleasures supported by online tools and services. Consider:

▶ Activities such as watching movies, using a phone and fax, staying in touch, listening to music, and reading a book can now be initiated and completed entirely online. New media are *not* replacing books, letters, radio, and the silver screen but *are* opening possibilities for how, when, and with whom you take part in your favorite activities, and what it all costs.

▶ More activity, less passivity. New AOL tools are taking the Net experience beyond the passive process of retrieving other people's information. The AOL tools profiled in this chapter make it possible to create your own digital pictures, your own graphical Web pages, even your own full-featured online communities.

Watching Movies

Movies and radio can actively engage the mind and senses in ways that the entertainment world understands all too well. Because film is a tried-and-true form of entertainment in the real world, your options are sometimes limited by what the industry can profitably produce. On the Internet, you're much less restricted — you can find films (called *video*, on the Net) at any time, in a variety of formats, and the sky's the limit when it comes to the creativity and subject-matter of the content. Still, even though video has been on the Internet for several years, the experience has been, well, pretty poor over 56K modems, having about as much appeal as watching spaghetti boil, mostly because of slow download rates.

Big changes are under way. Prices for high-speed Internet connections are coming down. At the same time, *player* technology (the technology that enables you to view movies online) has improved so much that you can now enjoy larger and sharper pictures even with older modems.

Check out the following sites for movies you can enjoy on the Internet.

▶ The About.com network (`about.com`) includes a guide to Movies Online (part of the World/Independent Film channel, `worldfilm.about.com/msub-online.htm`). This minidirectory takes you to many Net movie sites.

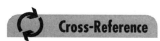

Cross-Reference

Chapter 17 has the details about AOL Plus and AOL's high-speed Internet services.

Note

Online movies tend to come in common formats such as RealVideo and QuickTime, which play automatically in the AOL 6.0 media player, as well as in common, free players such as RealPlayer, QuickTime, and the Windows Media Player. AOL embeds its media player in its interface for a much smoother experience, so you can focus your attention on the browser and not on the browser *and* the player.

▶ AFIonline (www.afionline.org) comes to you from the Maryland-based American Film Institute, which provides a broad range of educational programs for filmmakers. Visit the American Film Institute's CAFTS Movie Theater at www.afionline.org/cafts/cafts.home.html to see the impressive clips from students in AFI's Center for Advanced Film and Television Studies.

▶ Edgy AtomFilms (www.atomfilms.com), shown in Figure 18-1, features independent films, many playful, some artsy, most irreverent, and a few not fit for family viewing. You can now view films on a PocketPC (the latest Windows CE handhelds) thanks to a player available at this site. You will have to register before being able to view any clips. The process is quick and immediate. You have to register, a common experience at many new sites that offer original content and valuable services.

Figure 18-1. AtomFilms, a major destination for independent film buffs.

▶ The Independent Film Channel Broadband Theatre (broadband.thoughtbubble.com/ifc/cah/theater/main.html) is another valuable forum for the new talent that normally can't squeeze through Hollywood's barriers.

▶ Like Television (www.liketelevision.com) includes a diverse selection of old TV shows and full-length movies, as well as an eclectic mix of other media. Included are full-length movies like Roman Polanski's *Knife in the Water* (but make sure to brush up on your Polish first). The kids can tune into old Mickey Mouse cartoons and Beverly Hillbillies reruns.

▶ MTV Online (start at AOL Keyword: **MTV Online**) lets you hear and watch music videos, and then talk about the music using AOL chat and message boards.

▶ RealGuide.com (www.realguide.com), from the creators of the RealPlayer (see Chapters 6 and 16), provides listings of popular RealVideo movies, including movie trailers, news headlines, and music videos. Scores of TV channels' Web sites, by the way, include new clips. BBC Online is a notable example.

▶ The online dimension of the music magazine, RollingStone.com (AOL Keyword: **Rollingstone**), includes Video on Demand, with music videos of current superstars. Just click the Videos link when you visit the site.

▶ SonicNet (AOL Keyword: **Sonicnet**), now a part of the MTV Network Online, also offers music videos of all genres, including jazz and classical. Look for the All Videos link on the main page.

▶ Vidnet (www.vidnet.com) has music, sport, and style videos, as well as movie trailers.

Listening to Your Favorite Music at All Hours

Perhaps you remember, back in the late '80s, when cable companies were trying to get everyone to buy into digital audio over cable — 60-plus channels — one for jazz, another for soft jazz, yet others for bebop and big band! The All Weather Report, all the time! That was then. The Internet now offers more choice, more attitude, and many more types of musical offering, for free.

You have a choice of two major kinds of online radio, which vary in their source and music format:

 Cross-Reference

A place to start to find a radio station (whether rebroadcast or created for the online audience) is www.realguide.com, with more than one thousand radio stations to choose from. RealAudio broadcasts require RealPlayer, which is free and is included with AOL; MP3 broadcasts can be played through Winamp as well as through the AOL 6 media player.

Find It Online

Online radio does more than entertain. It is now finding practical uses throughout the business world. The Online Broadcast Network includes several invaluable services for the investment community. Vcall (www.vcall.com) airs live reports from Wall Street, including the quarterly earnings announcements of large and small companies via RealAudio. Reports are archived, enabling you to play them later. Another Investor Broadcast Network service, Radio Wall Street (www.radiowallstreet. com) features interviews and analyses, as well as earnings calls. Both online services offer message boards and other interactive features.

Find It Online

The Spinner Plus player, profiled in Chapter 16, lets you play any of almost 100 channels of music throughout the day. The music is available in the MP3 format.

▶ Hundreds of national radio stations rebroadcast their signal over the Internet so that anyone in the world (as opposed to anyone within 50 miles) can listen to their playlists using (for the most part) RealAudio. The sound quality can be good even on a modem, but it positively sings on a high-speed connection.

▶ In addition, hundreds of *online-only* radio stations broadcast *their* playlists 24 hours a day using streaming MP3 (which, like RealAudio, plays continuously). MP3's quality is consistently higher than RealAudio's (see Chapter 16 for more on MP3). Unlike traditional radio, the Internet variety offers greater variety of programming and is less subject to advertising and other forces that can often shape programming. Net radio has fewer ads and less talk.

On the wilder side, try ShoutCast (www.shoutcast.com), developed by the creators of Winamp. Anyone with gumption and spare time can get the ShoutCast server and broadcast their own radio station. Though the number changes daily, the last time I looked more than 1,200 servers were online, as shown in Figure 18-2.

Figure 18-2. ShoutCast, the place to find hundreds of Net-only radio stations playing streaming MP3 (CD-quality) sound.

Creating Digital Pictures

The engaging pleasures of the Web, such as online films and round-the-clock radio, are still fairly passive entertainments. With digital pictures, the experience becomes more active and creative; you can add to the Net as well as, well, just enjoying it.

What can you do with digital pictures?

▶ Make a T-shirt

▶ Print your own tote bags (or lunch bags)

▶ Create a family tree

▶ Assemble an inventory of household valuables

▶ Make your own greeting cards and invitations

▶ Use graphics software to remove red-eye or paint a moustache on your ex's photo

▶ Customize your business cards

▶ Make baseball cards for a Little League team

▶ Personalize a mouse pad or coffee cup

▶ Put an illustrated family or community newsletter on the Web

▶ Make your own photographic prints

The place to start is AOL's "You've Got Pictures" service, available at AOL Keyword: **You've Got Pictures**. The service provides the simplest way to turn your paper (traditional) snapshots into digital pictures that you can share, edit, and incorporate into projects at home and work, on the refrigerator, or on the Web.

Here's how it all works. You don't need any new hardware or software to use "You've Got Pictures"; you don't even need a digital camera. Instead, with your old-fashioned film camera (it doesn't matter whether it's a point-and-shoot or a Leica), you shoot a roll of film as you've always done. When the roll is done, take it to a participating photo retailer for processing. AOL works with this network of nearly 40,000 retailers in the PhotoNet network to make getting digital pictures convenient for you.

 Cross-Reference

See the author's *Official America Online Guide to Pictures Online* (IDG Books Worldwide, Inc.).

Find It Online

AOL 6.0's new Print Center (from the Print menu) has dozens of ideas for using digital pictures. You need a printer, of course, but you can find quality color inkjets for under $200 at AOL Keyword: **Shop@AOL**.

 Find It Online

At AOL Keyword: **You've Got Pictures**, **Pictures**, or **YGP**, you can find a short tutorial reviewing how the service works. If you have ever taken a roll of film to the drugstore to get developed, you can get digital pictures — and your digital pictures will probably be available online before your prints are ready!

Note

When you have a partici-
pating processor develop
your film, not only do you get
regular prints, but you also
get digital photos, posted
online at AOL Keyword:
You've Got Pictures. Getting
digital pictures is as easy as
reading your e-mail, and
much easier than going to
the drugstore.

When you drop off your film, you still have the option of receiving paper prints. After all, who doesn't enjoy the visceral
pleasure of passing around snapshots? Figure 18-3 illustrates
how much wider the distribution of digital images can be versus that of regular photographs. Now, you can also receive, for
a small fee, a set of digital pictures posted directly to your AOL
account. When you sign onto AOL, you hear a voice saying,
"You've Got Pictures!" — just like the "You've Got Mail" message of AOL and movie fame.

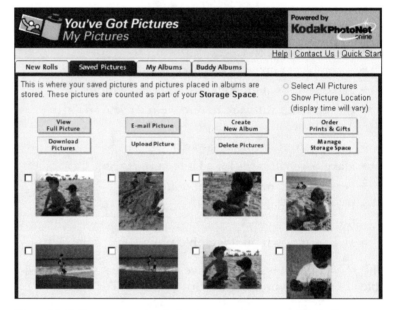

Figure 18-3. Here are some beach shots in my storage space at "You've Got
Pictures." Notice all the features available by merely selecting pictures and clicking a
button.

Tip

At AOL Keyword: **Photo
Developer**, you can quickly
and easily find the name
and address of the closest
PhotoNet developer. Plus, you
get names and addresses of
mail-order photo developers.

Now that you have your pictures, you need to either move
them from temporary storage into permenant storage or
delete them. AOL stores pictures in the temporary storage area
for only 30 days. AOL gives you room to store 50 pictures per
screen name. With seven screen names per account, that adds
up to 350 images per account. After you move your newly
received pictures over to your screen name space, they
remain there as long as you are an AOL member.

With your pictures online (as part of either your new rolls or
your permanently stored pictures), you can

▶ Order prints and photo gifts, place your pictures on teddy bears, mouse pads, coffee mugs, and more.

▶ Download *all* your digital pictures to your own computer, where you can edit them in any of a dozen major graphics programs such as MGI PhotoSuite III. On your computer, you can also use your pictures in your Web pages.

▶ Share them with others online, one at a time using the "You've Got Pictures" built-in e-mail program. Or, you can share several pictures at the same time by creating what are known as *buddy albums* of related pictures for your friends and family.

You can also upload pictures to "You've Got Pictures" to share them just as you can share the pictures you receive from your PhotoNet developer. You'll appreciate uploading if you already have digital pictures on your PC. For example, if you

▶ Have a digital camera, you can take digital pictures, import them to your PC by cable or card, and upload them directly to "You've Got Pictures." Digital cameras can open a new world of convenience and flexibility in your photography.

▶ Have a scanner, you can turn any photographic print into a digital file and, just as with a digital camera, upload it to "You've Got Pictures."

Find It Online

AOL frequently has good deals on scanners and digital cameras. Start at AOL Keyword: **Shop Direct**.

18

Did You Know You Can . . . on AOL?

Reading Books

Like radio, movies, and now photographs, books have become more accessible, more affordable, and packed with more capabilities thanks to electronic production and distribution. Using a handheld, Web plug-in, or Windows software to leaf through a book, for example, you can

▶ Search for specific words.

▶ Look up words in a built-in dictionary.

▶ Annotate text (more useful than writing in the margin!).

▶ Make bookmarks that won't ever fall out.

You can't take a digital book to bed or read it on the bus, you say? Not true. PDAs such as the Palm and the new PocketPCs

Note

The electronic book, or *eBook*, is so new that the choice of books to read is still limited, and display standards are still emerging.

offer features that can make an eBook easier to read for some people than paper books. Plus, a single handheld device can hold "all the books that fit" — in memory, that is.

Time Warner Trade Publishing recently announced an online publishing venture called iPublish (www.ipublish.com), which will eventually bring you electronic versions of traditional books, plus books written for the new medium. Imagine the ability of sampling a chapter before buying a book, discovering new authors before they're discovered for you, and reading about subjects previously neglected by the publishing establishment. The iPublish service will have an entire channel devoted to new works. The opportunity could benefit groups that have had a difficult time getting distributed or finding a niche. In addition to new publishing opportunities, look for new publishing formats, such as the publication of books and articles too specialized for general publishers or too short for the tastes of booksellers.

Here are three notable examples of new publishing ventures, available right now:

▶ Mightywords, with significant support by Barnes & Noble, makes technical and other publications available in PDF (Adobe's Portable Document Format, discussed in Chapter 6). A small fee applies to most publications downloaded. The use of PDF enables authors to create highly formatted and attractive documents, unlike the still pretty plain eBooks.

▶ Barnes & Noble both gives away and sells eBooks, which you can read either on the computer with the Glassbook reader or on a special gadget called Rocket eBook from NuvoMedia (www.nuvomedia.com). Other readers include the SoftBook (www.softbrook.com).

▶ PeanutPress, a division of a major electronic-publishing distributor (NetLibrary), provides software for reading eBooks on Palm organizers, plus hundreds of books to download and read. NetLibrary (www.netlibrary.com) has its own large selection of eBooks for reading on the PC.

Find It Online

Here are three large sources of free eBooks on the Web: MemoWare (www.memoware.com), NetLibrary (www.netlibrary.com), and CyberRead (www.cyberread.com). Barnes & Noble (AOL Keyword: BN) now has a whole new section devoted to eBooks. Downloaded books require special software readers, just as music requires a player. Such readers include Glassbook for PCs (www.glassbook.com), NetLibrary's reader, and the PeanutReader for the Palm (www.peanutpress.com).

Reading Your E-Mail Anywhere

Writing about AOL used to mean writing about the AOL service: what you could see and do when you opened the AOL software and signed on. Now, AOL is cropping up everywhere, and in the case of e-mail, you no longer need to be signed on to the AOL 6.0 or earlier software to read your e-mail, nor do you have to be sitting in front of a computer or even *have* a computer. You can find the details in Chapters 10 and 17; here's an overview of your e-mail options:

▶ AOL Mail on the Web gives you all the familiar e-mail features (reading, writing, replying, and forwarding). Formatting text, inserting pictures, and attaching files still require that you use a PC.

▶ While using AOL Instant Messenger (see Chapter 12), you can use the new Mail Alert window to get your AOL mail on the Web. Make sure this AIM feature is turned on by choosing MyAIM⇨Mail Alert Window.

▶ You can use handheld computers and Personal Digital Assistants (PDAs). Chapter 17 includes instructions for *installing* AOL Mail for handhelds, and Chapter 10 includes instructions for reading and writing mail using a Palm or Palm-compatible computer. In the future, look for expanded modem-based services plus wireless services that bring AOL mail and messaging to all Palms and PocketPCs.

▶ "Smart" wireless cell phones offer AOL mail now, but the number of supported phones will grow by the time the next version of AOL is released. Integrated into wireless services, such as Sprint's PCS Wireless Web, are AOL's information-rich resources such as MovieFone, Digital Cities, and MapQuest. While mail is available only to AOL members, the information services are available to all subscribers of the wireless services.

▶ AOLTV is the first of a series of home-focused and consumer-friendly alternatives to reading your mail on a large desktop computer (see Chapter 17). With a set-top box and the monthly AOLTV service, you can check e-mail, chat, and browse the Web while curled up on the couch with a wireless keyboard. TV and online are no longer enemies or even choices; they're deeply complementary sources of entertainment and connection.

Find It Online

With AOL Mail on the Web, you can do your mail from any computer, even if it doesn't have the AOL software. With just a browser and Internet connection, simply go to aolmail. aol.com.

Note

AOL Instant Messenger does not require the AOL software. It can run on any networked connection as a standalone Internet application (requiring a TCP/IP connection), you can use it on the Web (where it's called AIM Express, a newer version of Quick Buddy), and it now works on PDAs, as well.

18

Did You Know You Can . . . on AOL?

▶ The pathbreaking Gateway-AOL Internet Appliances point to a future of small and easy-to-use gadgets that bring the Net to you. As equipment and software cease to get in the way, a new channel opens between you and your friends.

▶ Mobile Communicator, another newcomer in AOL's garden of gadgets, is a wireless mail-only appliance that can be used out of the house. At under $200, it's more affordable than even the least expensive desktop computers.

Sending a Fax over the Internet

Even at $150, a fax machine is not cheap, and it's certainly not portable. Many Web services now make sending and receiving faxes over the Internet possible without cumbersome and costly equipment.

Need to send or receive an occasional fax? You can sign up for a free account at eFax (www.efax.com). Faxes you receive through eFax are e-mailed to you, and you can view them in eFax's miniviewer. The catch (pretty common on the Internet these days) is that you get these little ads in the miniviewer. Want to send faxes? A small fee gives you a local number and the ability to send faxes through the eFax service. The fee also entitles you to receive faxes as editable text, store faxes online, distribute faxes to your friends or customers, and get an alert of a fax's arrival on your wireless messaging device.

Using the Phone

Calling someone on the Internet can cut local and especially international costs and can reduce the need for a second phone line. On the downside, sound quality is not up to the phone companies' standards.

"Voice over IP" is the geeky way of saying that you can now place and receive phone calls over the Internet instead of through the expensive, dedicated connections of the phone companies. The cost savings can be considerable, especially for long-distance calls, but for now, the quality of Internet phone calls has some catching up to do. The tools are here right now, however, and broadband service such as AOL Plus can improve the experience.

Receiving Voice Mail over the Net

If you can't add a second phone line or don't have broadband access, then you probably won't be able to take a (real) phone call while you're connected to the Internet. A lot of people needlessly minimize their online time to avoid such problems. Online voice mail can fix that.

Onebox.com (`www.onebox.com`) rolls up a bundle of new services. With a Onebox number, you can receive both phone messages and faxes *online*. Anyone with a microphone and the proper software can send you a spoken e-mail message to you, as well. Recipients of *your* voice or fax messages can retrieve them at a Web address they receive by e-mail from Onebox.

This ad-supported service is free, or you can pony up a small monthly fee for premium service. Premium service buys you a customizable voice-mail system, your own number, an online address book, and the ability to get e-mail *read* to you over the phone by Onebox's computer. This is a real boon for cell-phone users.

Using the Net to Talk on the Phone

One of the promises of the Internet has always been to reduce the costs of and obstacles to simple human communication. One case in point is using Net services to reduce your costly telephone charges.

Today, several products deliver phone service at rates that can be realized only on the Net. First, the requirements: You need some software to emulate a phone on your PC, so you can dial numbers and place calls. To talk, you need a microphone, and to hear, you need headphones. You can get both a microphone and headphones if you buy an inexpensive headset.

Vocaltec's Internet Phone (soon to be superseded by the TrulyGlobal Internet Phone) is typical of the Internet phone services you can find (`www.vocaltec.com/iptelephony/iptel.htm`). You can send calls from a real phone to someone else's Internet Phone software, from your phone software to someone else's real phone, and from your PC to a friend's — if you both have the software.

You'll get more from Internet Phone Services with high-speed access. See Chapter 17 for the details.

This field bustles with activity and thus choices. Netscape 6.0 (Chapter 7) includes software from Net2Phone (`www.net2phone.com/net2phone/`).

ICQ (profiled in Chapter 16) has an Internet Telephony Center where you can download telephony programs, learn to use them, and find a directory of ICQ members with whom you can communicate by Internet phone software. The Web address is `www.icq.com/telephony/telephony.html`. You can also reach the center from the main ICQ window: Click Services and choose Phone⇨ICQ Phone Center.

Making Payments Online

Suppose you had dinner with some friends the other night and were the only one who had cash or credit card. Now your friends can pay you back without the bother of wiring you the money or your making a trip to the bank. Even checks can be cumbersome through the mail, and they also require a trip to the bank.

A new company called PayPal — the first of many such services, including a forthcoming service from Citigroup — simplifies the process of transferring money from one person to another. The service is free for consumers. You handle the entire process of exchanging money by e-mail, and now you can also use your PDA or wireless phone.

If you have a PayPal account, everyone in your dinner group could go home and use your account to send you their portion of the check. You would be notified immediately of the payment. After two to four days, you could move the funds to your bank account. Using PayPal is no more risky than using your bank or a wire service like Western Union.

PayPal is only the intermediary who either brings the money to you or gets it to the person at the other end of the transaction. It is backed by several powerful banking and Internet companies. Make sure to review the information on their Web site regarding protection for certain types of purchases.

Services like PayPal make it easy to

> ▶ Send a college student some extra funds.
> ▶ Pay for something you purchased at an online auction.
> ▶ Pay contract workers.
> ▶ Pay schools, online communities, and actual community organizations for membership and other fees.
> ▶ Contribute to charitable organizations.

Creating Web Pages: AOL Hometown

AOL Hometown (AOL Keyword: **Hometown**) provides a home on the World Wide Web for AOL members and nonmembers alike. Here's what you can do in this sprawling cyberopolis:

▶ **Create Web pages:** At AOL Hometown, you can use two free tools for making your own Web pages: 1-2-3 Publish (super easy) and Easy Designer (super flexible).

▶ **Publish your pages where others can find them:** Anyone can make any number of Web pages available on AOL Hometown. To make pages available simply means to save your pages at AOL Hometown, where they can be searched for and viewed by anyone with Web access. Uploading is handled automatically when you use 1-2-3 Publish and Easy Designer.

▶ **Store your Web pages and other files online:** AOL Hometown furnishes *anyone* with enough storage space to hold up to 12MB worth of digital pictures, Web pages, and anything else you want to make available to others. This storage space comes in handy for sharing non-Web documents, such as word-processed documents, spreadsheets, and reports for school and work.

▶ **Learn the secrets of Web design:** AOL Hometown provides resources for learning the ropes of page-building, whether you're new to HTML (the simple computer language used to build Web pages) or want to acquire more knowledge. Start at AOL Keyword: **Web Tutorial** or AOL Keyword: **Web Page**.

AOL's two Web tools take a different approach:

▶ 1-2-3 Publish is the fastest way to get yourself a page and publish it quickly at AOL Hometown. Choose a template, plug in your digital pictures, links, and text, put in some links, and you're done.

▶ Easy Designer lets you go beyond 1-2-3 Publish. You can add text and pictures wherever you want, at whatever location on your page, and in whatever way you want to format and link them.

On AOL, you get several free storage places: AOL Hometown (up to 12MB per screen name), Groups@AOL (up to 8MB per Group; see the next section), and "You've Got Pictures" (up to 50 permanently stored pictures per screen name, plus virtually unlimited temporary storage for new rolls of film).

If you start with 1-2-3 Publish, it is easy to continue editing the same page with Easy Designer, which offers more flexibility. Neither 1-2-3 Publish nor Easy Designer works with HTML pages created by non-AOL tools.

In addition to AOL's tools, you can use *any* Web page editor and manually upload the Web (HTML) pages to a special online area (AOL Keyword: **MyFTPSpace**) from which they can be added to AOL Hometown's communities and made searchable.

Take a little closer look at Easy Designer (AOL Keyword: **Easy Designer**). You can begin with a blank page. Or you can start with a template on a specific theme and choose from several sophisticated layout and color schemes. Figure 18-4 shows an Easy Designer template.

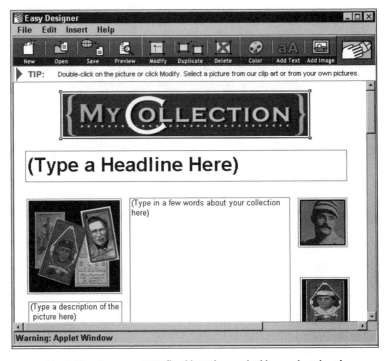

Figure 18-4. Easy Designer, AOL's flexible Web-page building tool, makes the process as simple as possible, from designing the page to sharing it on the Web.

To use either Easy Designer or 1-2-3 Publish, you don't need to know any HTML, the langauge used to create Web pages from scratch. If you do know some HTML, you can insert some code, then move it around on the page. I have used this trick to create tables for displaying information in rows and columns.

In Easy Designer, you're basically playing with text and pictures. Every block of text or individual picture goes in its own box, where you can edit, link, resize, format, and relocate it anywhere on the page.

▶ Text windows can take any shape — tall for columns or flat for headlines. You use the Text Editor to style, align, and link your words, just as in a word processor.

▶ The image window enables you to use any image on your hard drive or, instead, draw on AOL's library of thousands of images. You can drag around, resize, and link pictures.

When you're done with Easy Designer, click Save, and you'll be prompted to publish your page at AOL Hometown. After it's there, anyone can search for it and view it.

All pages you create with either 1-2-3 Publish or Easy Designer are automatically stored online on AOL's computers in a special FTP area reserved for your use only. You have direct access to this storage space (AOL Keyword: **My FTP Space**), and you can use this space to store other documents. Or, if you use your own Web-page editor, such as Macromedia Dreamweaver, you can upload the pages and graphics to your AOL storage space. Even easier, use any Microsoft Office application and save your documents as HTML (as a Web page) and then upload them to My FTP Space. PowerPoint slideshows and complex Word and Publisher designs become instant yet sophisticated Web pages. Because these Microsoft applications generate so many files for every Web page they create, you might want to use a special FTP program such as WS_FTP, profiled in Chapter 16, which lets you upload many files at the same time.

Creating a Community: Groups@AOL

A community-building tool is arguably the most effective when used in conjunction with other such tools and when it gives the community control of its own purpose and content. That is exactly what Groups@AOL are all about. Groups@AOL (AOL Keyword: **Groups**) provides a wired home on the Web for the close-knit communities in your life, no matter how far apart everyone lives.

Think of a *Group* as a circle of family, friends, or perhaps business associates, people in your profession, or maybe even total strangers who share an interest with you and who come together in a central online meeting place. Members can share ideas, information, and digital pictures with others in the Group. A Group can be an extension of a real-world group of people who already know each other and have a lot to share. Such groups include:

▶ Extended families

▶ Boy Scout and Girl Scout troops

▶ Students of all levels and ages

▶ Photo enthusiasts and other hobbyists

Tip

Each AOL screen name is automatically allotted 2MB of storage space for Web pages and other documents. Every screen name that adds *all* of its pages to AOL Hometown receives a total of 12MB of storage space. So if all 7 screen names register all their pages at AOL Hometown, you can have and use a total of 84MB of storage space per account. Pages on one screen name can be linked to another screen names' pages, creating the potential for a very large site with plenty of images. To register all the pages for a screen name, sign on with that screen name; go to AOL Keyword: **Hometown**; click Create Pages; select Add All and follow the on-screen instructions.

Cross-Reference

Look for Edward Willett's book, *Your Official America Online Guide to Creating Cool Web Pages,* 3rd Edition (IDG Books Worldwide, Inc.), which has everything you need to know about AOL Hometown and My FTP Space.

FTP is discussed in Chapter 15; your FTP space is hard-drive space on AOL's computers to which you can upload pages and from which others can download files, including HTML files (Web pages).

Groups@AOL is open to anyone, AOL member or not. Although only AOL members can *start* a Group, anyone with access to the Internet can be invited to join.

Every Group you create automatically includes a Group mailing list, flexible chat tools based on AOL Instant Messenger, and a Group bulletin board where members can post messages for other members to see and respond to. Group members can also create lists of favorite restaurants, movies, books, Web sites, and more, providing, if they choose, a rating and Web address for each. Creating and maintaining such lists can provide a tangible group focal point and good way of generating new things to share (see Figure 18-5), such as books, movies, jokes, and so on.

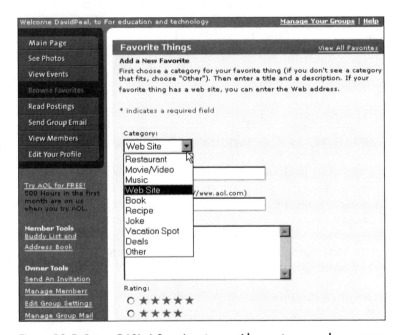

Figure 18-5. Groups@AOL: A Group's main page (the opening page when someone visits the Group).

Each Group has 8MB (megabytes) of storage space for its images.

Any member of your Group can upload pictures to the Group's photo collections, where the pictures become instantly available to other Group members.

What's unique about Groups@AOL is that the group's founder — the person who starts the group — has control over membership. In fact, Groups don't really exist until the founder sends invitations to people to join it and those people join it. The other side of the coin is more sensitive. Founders can remove participants for any reason but can make any participant a co-owner to share the responsibility of inviting people and kicking them out.

Groups are nicely integrated with other AOL features. Group chat takes advantage of AOL Instant Messenger (see Chapter 12), and Group members can add shared events (for example, scheduled AIM chats) to each others' calendar (Chapter 3).

Where to Go from Here

Anywhere, of course. Which is exactly why you need a haven to which you can return when the Net's limitless distractions and choices begin to overwhelm you. With AOL as your online home, you can begin to take control of your own online adventures:

▶ Use AOL's channels and AOL Search to find new places to go and things to do on the Internet.

▶ Use Favorite Places to keep track of your favorite communities, destinations, and activities.

▶ Use e-mail, mailing lists, newsgroups, instant messages, and AOL Instant Messenger to stay in touch; then use your Address Book and Buddy Lists to keep track of your friends, acquaintances, and others.

▶ Whenever you have a question about using a tool, AOL Help is always available, online or offline, from the AOL Help menu.

 Note

Groups@AOL is different from Internet Relay Chat (IRC) on the Net in several ways. For one thing, Group founders control who is invited to join, lowering the noise level and reducing the off-topic distractions you may find using IRC; anyone can join an IRC channel, at least a public one. Moreover, unlike IRC channels, Groups are permanent and visual (not text-only), and Groups support mail, a mailing list, and a bulletin board, in addition to text-based chat.

18

Did You Know You Can . . . on AOL?

Index

Symbols & Numbers

@ (*at*) symbol, 213, 311
/ (forward slashes), creating subdirectories, 358
1-2-3 Publish, 423, 424
32-bit software, 374
700 Great Sites for Kids, 77

A

About.com, 198, 411
access controls. *See* Parental Controls
access numbers, automatically dialing, 70
Accessibility dialog box, 144, 145
account controls, 48
acronyms, 91–92
acronyms, in e-mail messages, 244
activity log, 29
Add a Buddy button, 273
Add Address button, 222
Add Location window, 68
Add to Favorites command, 139, 140
AddALL Web site, 115
Address bar, Netscape 6, 163
Address Book
    accessing, 221
    adding names to, 250–252
    customizing, 64
    definition, 47
    groups, 252
    identifying e-mail recipients, 241
    sharing, 307
    sorting, 249
    synchronized, 17, 249
Address box
    in AOL's browser, 134
    Netscape 6, 163
administrative address, 301, 302
Adobe Acrobat Writer, 149
adult-oriented newsgroups, 83

Advanced Search option, AOL Search, 180
AFIonline Web site, 412
After School Web site, 95
age brackets
    Kids Only, 83
    screen names, 79–80
AIM (AOL Instant Messenger). *See also* instant
        messages (IMs); screen names
    accessing, 164
    advantages, 270–271
    Buddy List and, 62, 161
    chats, 279
    exchanging files with, 280
    features, 271, 419
    guidelines, 265–266
    Help system, 285
    installing, 271–273
    news sources, 284
    News Ticker, 284
    passwords, 281
    personal information, 64
    Privacy Preferences, 277
    screen names, 271, 280–282
    sending messages with, 278–282
    Sign On window, 281
    Stock Ticker, 284
    Virus Checker tab, 280
AIM Express, 282–283, 419
AIM Message window, 278
Aladdin Expander, 377
alpha software, 374
alt newsgroup category, 319
AltaVista
    Family Filter, 87, 189
    Open Directory and, 175
    translation services, 189
alternative newsgroups, 318–319
alt.folklore.urban newsgroup, 332
American Association of School
        Administrators, 86
American Film Institute, 14, 412

American Memory Project, Library of Congress, 94, 206
animation, 148
anonymous FTP sites, 360–361
antivirus software, 339, 380
Anywhere keyword, 401, 403, 404
AOL 6.0. *See also* **AOL Plus**
  accessing
    cable Internet connection, 397–399
    DSL (Digital Subscriber Line), 393–397
    over a network, 67–69
    satellite-based connection, 399–400
  account information, 65–67, 164
  ART files, 362
  customization features, 47–48
  ease of use, 2–3, 26
  Help menu, 151
  help resources, 36–38, 42–43, 72
  HTML support, 289
  improvements, 1–3
  Internet tools, 14–15
  keywords, 31–32
  menus, 32–34
  Mobile Communicator, 406
  new features, 15–18
  newsgroups, 315–317, 323–324
  newsletters, 296–298
  profile, creating, 185
  safety policies, 79
  Search directory, 172
  stored resources, 64, 66
  Terms of Service, 76, 317
  Web browser, 75
AOL Anywhere. *See also* **AOL Plus**
  accessing, 70
  accessing e-mail, 231–236
  customizing, 48–51
  definition, 16, 47, 231
  features, 401–402
  for handhelds, 234–236
  news sources, 284
AOL browser
  accessing, 36, 75
  accessing FTP sites, 354–355
  customizing, 140–145

  interface, 126–133
  navigating with, 133–140
  visiting Telnet sites, 382
AOL Guarantee keyword, 116
AOL Hometown, 131, 355, 423–425
AOL Instant Messenger. *See also* **e-mail**
AOL Mail, 419. *See also* **AOL Anywhere; AOL Plus; AOLTV; cable Internet connection; DirectPC; DSL; e-mail; satellite-based connection**
AOL NetHelp, 37
aol newsgroup category, 319, 337
AOL Plus. *See also* **AOL Anywhere; DSL**
  advantages, 391
  benefits, 393–394
  definition, 16
  DSL connection, 396–397
  features, 3
  getting, 394–395
  installing, 395–397
  "Voice over IP" service, 420
AOL Plus Radio, 385
AOL Search, 20, 172–182, 215. *See also* **online searching; search engines**
AOL Search keyword, 6, 135, 316
AOL Services button, 35
AOL Store keyword, 369
AOL White Pages, 182–183
AOL Yellow Pages, 182–183
AOL@School
  definition, 14, 75
  features, 85–86
AOL@School keyword, 75
AOLTeens keyword, 316
AOLTV, 14, 400, 407, 419. *See also* **DirectPC**
AOLTV keyword, 407
applets, 131
appointments. *See* **My Calendar**
Archie server, 365, 366
archives
  FTP, 82, 365
  investment reports, 414
  of mailing lists, 306
Argus Clearinghouse, 200–201, 204
arrow keys, managing e-mail, 221

ART files, 362
ASCII files, 84, 259, 261
Ask Jeeves, 175
at (@) symbol, 213, 311
Atomfilms, 14
AU sound files, 147, 150
auctions online, 120–121
audio CDs, playing, 117
audio files. *See* sound files
authoritative resources, 198, 202–204
Auto Start Options, 397
Automatic AOL window, 34, 231, 340–341
automatic indexing, 193
Autos Channel, 107–109
AutoWeb.com Web site, 108
AVI video format, 149, 363
AWAD (A Word A Day) mailing list, 296

B

Back button, in AOL's browser, 136, 138
background color, for e-mail messages, 255
background picture, in e-mail messages, 258
bandwidth, definition, 392
Banking keyword, 106
Barnes & Noble, 116, 418
Bartleby's Web site, 92
Bartlett's Familiar Quotations, 92–93
Basics keyword, 37, 39–40
BCC (blind courtesy copy), 242
Berners-Lee, Tim, 15, 125, 136, 199
BestBookBuys Web site, 115
beta software, 374
Better Homes and Gardens Home Improvement Encyclopedia, 118
Billing keyword, 67, 68, 398
binary files
    converted into text, 226
    definition, 84
    uploading, 357
BinHex (Mac) files, 226
bit newsgroup category, 319
biz newsgroup category, 320
blocking
    downloads, 82, 84
    e-mail, 82

instant messages, 277
junk mail, 335–336
newsgroups, 83, 84
Blue Squirrel Web site, 87
BMP (bitmap) files, 362
Bobby software, 378
Book Shop keyword, 30
Bookmark⇨Add Current Page command, 165
bookmarks
    definition, 158, 160
    managing, 166–167
    Netscape 6, 165–168
Bookmarks menu, Netscape 6, 159
Bookmarks⇨Manage Bookmarks command, 166
books
    buying online, 116
    ebooks, 417–418
    at Internet Public Library, 96–97
Boolean operators, 179, 181
Boston University Web site, 190
Brainstorms message board, 342
Bring Your Own Access billing plan, 68
Britannica Internet Guide, 89
broadband
    connections, 385
    content, 3
    data transmission speed considerations, 404
    definition, 392
    types of, 400–401
browser. *See* Web browser
browser window, Netscape 6, 157
browsing, compared to searching, 172
buddy albums, 417
Buddy Alert, 276–277
Buddy List. *See also* AIM (AOL Instant Messenger); e-mail; instant messages (IMs); screen names
    adding buddies to, 273–274
    AIM and, 62, 161
    contents, 267
    customizing, 61–63
    definition, 47
    finding new buddies, 274–275
    Mail Contacts Online, 278, 279
    personal profile, 275–276
    Privacy Preferences, 268–270
    viewing, 236

Buddy List sidebar, Netscape 6, 160–161
Buddy Wizard, 275
BuddyView keyword, 62, 222, 266–270, 279
bulk mail, 310
bulletin boards. *See* newsgroups
burning CDs, 384
business addresses, finding, 183
buttons, in AOL's browser, 136
buttons, on toolbar, 2
BYOA (Bring Your Own Access) account, 164, 398

C

cable Internet connection, 67, 392–393, 397–399
cache
   clearing, 29
   managing, 141–143
Café Utne message board, 341
CAFTS Movie Theater Web site, 412
calendar. *See* My Calendar; Netscape Calendar
Calendar keyword, 51
Camera button, 258
capital letters, in screen names, 65
car shopping. *See* Auto Channel
Careers & Work Channel, 111
CAST (Center for Applied Special Technology), 378
CC (courtesy copy), 242
CDNOW keyword, 117
CDNow store, 117
CDs
   buying online, 117
   creating, 383, 384
central office, DSL, 395
Change keyword, 67
Channels menu
   AOL 6.0
      features, 30, 32, 104
      Kids Only, 75
      My Places and, 60
      navigation, 103
   Netscape 6, 164
Chat keyword, 265
chat rooms
   AIM, 279
   Parental Control settings, 80

Chat with a Friend option, ICQ, 378
Check Encyclopedias option, AOL Search, 178
CIA World Factbook, 94–95
classes online, 39–40
ClassifiedPlus keyword, 109
Clear Filter List button, 337
CN.com sidebar, Netscape 6, 160
CNET
   consumer guides, 43
   features, 151
   megasite, 115
   Music Center, 383
   SavvySearch, 196
   shareware, 374, 375, 376
College keyword, 96
Colors button, Internet Options dialog box, 143
colors, for e-mail messages, 254–255
Columbia Encyclopedia, 88–89
Columbia House, 117
communication resources, 27
communications controls, 48
Communities keyword, 21
community information, 2
comp newsgroup category, 320
compressed files, 353, 377
Computer Center Channel, 32, 43, 115, 297–298
computer equipment, online resources, 32, 114–115
Computing Communities keyword, 37, 40–41
Computing FAQs keyword, 338
Computing keyword, 151
confidential information, 116
Configuration tab, 397
connectivity services, 3
Consumer's Resource Handbook, 203
content, customizing in My Sidebar, Netscape 6, 162–163
content type, 49, 103, 364
Copy command, 140
Copy Shortcut command, 140
Copyright keyword, 139, 141
countertop appliance, 405
crackers, 380
Create Directory button, 358
Create Shortcut command, 139
Create Shortcut tab, 70

Create Your Reminder tab, 61
credit card transactions, 116
Ctrl+ (window size), 33, 55
Ctrl+] (go back a page), 159
Ctrl+C (copy), 233
Ctrl+D (add a bookmark), 165
Ctrl+F (Find), 33, 58, 225, 305
Ctrl+K (Keyword window), 32
Ctrl+M (Write Mail window), 255
Ctrl+P (print), 224
Ctrl+R (read mail), 216, 217
Ctrl+V (adding to My Calendar), 53
Ctrl+V (paste), 233
Ctrl-click technique, 58
CultureFinder keyword, 118
Custom Controls area, Parental Controls, 80–85
Customer Service keyword, 37
Customize Sidebar dialog box, 162–163
customizing
    AOL Anywhere, 48–51
    AOL's browser, 140–145
    contact information, 61–64
    Favorite Places, 54–61
    instant messages (IMs), 268
    Internet connection, 67–71
    My Calendar, 51–53
    My Places, 60–61
    My Sidebar, Netscape 6, 161–163
    Stock Ticker, 284
CyberRead Web site, 418

D

Daily tab, 61
data transmission speed considerations, 390, 393, 400, 404
data zooming, 398
date, sorting e-mail messages by, 219
Dave Central, finding software, 375
DC keyword, 109, 110
Debt Reduction Planner, 105
Decision Maker guides, 115, 119
decompressing files, 377
default font, overriding, 254
Default On/Off button, 259

Deja Web site, newsgroup postings, 324–326
Delete key
    managing e-mail, 221
    removing bookmarks, 166
desktop appliance, 405
Destinations keyword, 119
dictionaries
    accessing, 33
    legal, 204
    resources, 91–94
digests, of mailing lists, 305–306
digital cameras, 417
digital certificate, 116
Digital Cities
    AOL and, 184
    classified ads, 108
    features, 2, 14
    searching for contractors, 118
Digital City keyword, 108, 109, 110
digital images
    adding to online storage space, 30
    capturing, 33
    creating, 415–417
    downloading, 225–226
    in e-mail messages, 257–258
    finding online, 190
    managing, 33
    on Web pages, 128–129
Digital Librarian, 199, 201
digital libraries, 205–206
direct recipients, of e-mail messages, 241
DirectPC, 3, 399, 400. *See also* AOLTV
discussion lists, 291–293
disk space, 142, 143
Dogpile, 175, 196
domain
    definition, 132
    example, 82, 213
    filters and, 336
    types of, 214–215
Download Center, 375
Download Manager, 225–226
Download Manager keyword, 352
downloading
    AOL Instant Messenger service, 271–273
    data transmission speed considerations, 400
    definition, 354

Continued

downloading *(continued)*
digital images, 417
e-mail messages, 230–231
file attachments, 225–226
files, 82, 359–361, 387–388
FTP files, 365–368
with Netscape Navigator, 155
newsgroup files, 339
newsgroup postings, 322
QuickTime player, 150
shareware, 375
software, 353–361
Web pages, 137
Winamp software, 349–353
downstream data transfer, 393, 400
driving directions, 184
DrKoop.com Web site, 203
DSL (Digital Subscriber Line)
accessing AOL, 68
with AOL Plus, 91
definition, 393
technology, 393–397
Dummies Daily newsletters, 296

E

Easy Designer, 132, 423–425
Ebay keyword, 120
eBay Web site, 107, 120
ebooks, 417–418
Edgy AtomFilms Web site, 412
Edit File Type box, 364
Edit Hyperlink window, 256
Edit menu
AOL 6.0, 33
Netscape 6, 158
Edit⊅Capture Pictures command, 33
Edit⊅Dictionary command, 33
Edit⊅Find command, 33
Edit⊅Preferences command, 167
Edit⊅Search command, 166
Edit⊅Thesaurus command, 33
education-related discussion lists, 292
education-related newsgroups, 320
eGroups Web site, 307
electronic book publishing, 13, 205

electronic newsletters
definition, 291
for Internet information, 308–310
Packet Press, 402
reading, 42
Web-based, 293–298
***Elements of Style*, 92**
e-mail. *See also* **Address Book; AIM (AOL Instant Messenger); AOL Anywhere; Filing Cabinet; ICQ; instant messages (IMs); mailing lists; newsgroups; Online Mailbox; Parental Controls; screen names**
accessing, 34, 402–405, 406
addresses
finding, 183, 215
hiding, 183
sorting messages by, 219
Archie server and, 365
automatic reminders, 61
enhanced features, 1–2, 17
exchanging money by, 421
help resources, 215–216
mail servers, 164
messages
AOL tool, 36
with attached files, 224–226, 253–254
composing, 222
deleting, 229
downloading, 230–231
embellishing, 254–259
finding, 33
forwarding, 223
header, 220
HTML links in, 27, 220, 259, 311
links in, 256–257
moving to Filing Cabinet, 229–230
new, 216–218
printing, 223–224
reading, 220, 419–420
replying to, 221–222
restoring, 224
return receipt, 246
saving, 223, 230
signatures, 251, 259–261, 329, 336
sorting, 218–220
specifying recipients, 241–242
stationery, 259

subject line, 219, 222, 242
titles, 59
unsending, 245, 249
unsolicited, 75–76, 229–230, 236–237, 310–311
Netiquette, 243–246
Parental Controls, 81
preferences, 246–247
reading electronic newsletters, 42
receiving news pages, 50–51
Web interface, 126, 232–234
E-Mail Finder keyword, 182, 183
emoticons, 244
employment agencies, 110
Encyclopedia Britannica, 89
Encyclopedia Mythica Web site, 89–90, 205
encyclopedias, 88–91
error messages, troubleshooting, 134
Etymology Of First Names dictionary, 94
evaluating Web sites, 181–182
Event Directory tab, 52
events. *See* **My Calendar**
Expert Add button, 322

F

Family Education Network, 86, 90
Family Filter, in AltaVista, 87, 189
Family PC's Kids'Safety & Parental Safety
**   Clearinghouse, 79**
family-oriented Web sites, 77–79
FAQs (Frequently Asked Questions), for
**   newsgroups, 337, 338**
Fast Search and Transfer, 366
Favorite Places
adding newsgroups to, 322–323
adding window to, 33
customizing, 54–61
definition, 47
synchronizing, 64
types of, 34
Favorites button, 35
Favorites menu, 56, 57
Favorites⇨Favorite Places command, 54–61
faxes, sending over the Internet, 420
FC. *See* **Filing Cabinet**
Fedstats Web site, 95–96

fetching files, from the cache, 142
file associations, in Windows, 377
file attachments, with e-mail messages, 224–226
File menu
AOL 6.0, 33
Netscape 6, 158
File Transfer tab, 280
file types, 361
File⇨Download Manager command, 225, 227
File⇨Edit Page, Netscape 6, 159
File⇨Help⇨Help Topics command, 285
File⇨New command, 258
File⇨New Separator command, 167
File⇨New⇨New Folder command, 166
File⇨Open command
in AOL, 223, 226
in Netscape 6, 158
File⇨Open Picture Finder keyword, 362
File⇨Save As command, 292
File⇨Voice Recognition command, 144
FileGrabber feature, 339
filenames, 361
files
downloading, 359–361
moving, 358–359
sharing, 387–388
Filing Cabinet
adding folders to, 229
copying, 227
definition, 226
features, 223
moving messages to, 229–230
preferences, 228
reading, 220
size, 228
storing e-mail, 17
Filtering tab, for newsgroups, 336–337
filters
in DSL technology, 395
for meta-search services, 198
NetNanny software, 372
for newsgroups, 336–337
for search engines, 87, 189, 193, 194
financial planning, 105–111
Find a Buddy Wizard, 275
FindLaw Web site, 203, 204
firewalls, 397
FirstGov Web site, 95

flamebait, 331
flames, 331
folders, moving, 358–359
Fonts button, Internet Options dialog box, 143
fonts, for e-mail messages, 254–255
Food keyword, 119
forms, on Web pages, 130
ForumOne message board, 341, 342
Forward button, in AOL's browser, 136, 138
forward slashes (/), creating subdirectories, 358
forwarding e-mail messages, 223
Fowler's *King's English*, 92
frames, on Web pages, 130
freeware
   Aladdin Expander, 377
   choosing, 374–375
Frommer's Destination Guides, 119
FTP (File Transfer Protocol)
   accessing, 354–355
   advantages, 349
   archives, 82
   definition, 127
   downloading files, 365–368
   finding files, 366
   Lycos options, 189, 194
   storage space for Web pages, 426
   third-party software, 361
   uploading Web pages, 355–358
FTP keyword, 36, 332, 338, 354, 359, 359–361,
      365, 372
FTP Search, in Lycos, 366–367
fun Web sites, 111–121

G

Gardenworks.com Web site, 118
Gateway-AOL Internet Appliances, 420
Get Help Now keyword, 37, 115
Get Profile button, 268
GetNetWise Web site, 78
GIF (Graphic Interchange Format) files, 362
Glassbook for PCs Web site, 418
global community, 22
global digital library, 18
global newsgroup preferences, 334–337

Go button, 28, 41
Go menu, Netscape 6, 159
Google
   features, 191–193
   I'm Feeling Lucky button, in searches, 192
   Open Directory and, 175
   SafeSearch, 87, 193
   Similar Pages option, 193
Gopher, 37
Government Guide Web site, 95
graphics. *See also* digital images
   file extensions, 362
   formats, 149–150
   in newsgroup messages, 339
   on Web pages, 128–129
Gray's Anatomy, 92
Groups keyword, 425
Groups@AOL
   definition, 18, 252, 290, 312, 343
   features, 27, 423, 425–427
guest sign-ons, e-mail options, 228

H

hackers, 380, 397
handheld organizer
   accessing AOL Mail, 234–236
   AOL Anywhere and, 401
handheld PCs, 419
hardware setup, viewing, 29
headers, in newsgroup postings, 334–335
Health Channel, 202
Health keyword, 32, 202
HealthAtoZ Web site, 202–203
Help Community keyword, 41, 115
Help Desk keyword, 40
Help keyword, 38, 343
Help menu
   AOL 6.0, 72, 151
   Netscape 6, 159, 168
help resources, 36–38, 42–43, 285
helper application, 130–131
Hide Channels button, 30
hiding e-mail addresses, 183
high-speed Internet access, 3, 391–392, 400–401
high-speed satellite access, 399–400

history trail, 141
home banking, 106
home page
    changing, 167
    definition, 158
    Web browser, 168
Hometown keyword, 425
Hometown Page Journal, 298
homework helper Web sites, 86
Homework Help keyword, 85
Hot Keys, 60
HotBot
    Lycos and, 194
    Open Directory and, 175
House & Home Channel, 118
House keyword, 118
househunting online, 109–110
HouseNet Web site, 118
HTML (HyperText Markup Language)
    definition, 125, 132
    documents, 127
    editing, 159
    file extensions, 361
    links in e-mail messages, 27, 220, 259, 311
    links supported, 144
    mailing lists and, 309
    online classes, 40, 298
    viewing, 158
    Web mail, 289
hubs, 191
humor sites, 20
hyperlinks. *See* links
Hytelnet, 383

I

icons
    adding to toolbar, 66
    Mail, 164
    Netscape 6 shortcut, 156
    with Netscape 6 sidebars, 162
    picture, 258
    Sign On, 235
    in this book, 7
    You've Got Mail, 216

ICQ keyword, 286
ICQ Radio, 385
ICQ software, 378–380, 421
Ifilm, 14
Ignore Colors Specified on Web Pages option, 144
Incoming/Saved Postings, in the Newsgroups folder, 340
Independent Film Channel Broadband Theatre, 412
indexed Web sites, 193
indexing, automatic, 193
indirect recipients, of e-mail messages, 241
InfoPlease.com Web site, 87, 88, 90–91
Insert Text File option, 258
instant messages (IMs)
    customizing, 268
    definition, 266
    guidelines, 265–266
    overriding default font, 254
    restricting, 79
    sending, 222, 266–270
Instant Message window, 63
Instant Messenger. *See* AOL Instant Messenger
interactivity, on Web pages, 130
Interest Profile keyword, 42, 294
International search, in AltaVista, 190
Internet. *See also* FTP; search engines; Telnet; World Wide Web
    accessing, 28
    AOL and, 14–15, 18, 70
    customizing your connection, 67–71
    definition, 19, 125
    destinations, 20
    development, 21–22
    electronic newsletters, 308–310
    finding software, 375–376
    firewalls, 397
    high-speed access, 3, 391–392
    phone services, 421
    recent developments, 13
    safety sites, 78–79
    tools with AOL 6.0, 14–15, 18, 20–21, 35–36
    traffic jams, 385, 403
    usage statistics, 19
    voice mail, 421
    "Voice over IP" service, 420
Internet appliance, 405, 406, 420

Internet computer (server), 132
Internet Connection, 35
Internet Extras, 35
Internet FAQ Consortium, 338
Internet keyword, 35
Internet Options dialog box, 142, 145
Internet Properties dialog box, 142, 143
Internet Pros keyword, 37
Internet Public Library, 88, 90, 96–97
Internet Tourbus, 309
investment reports, 414
iPublish Web site, 418
IRC (Internet Relay Chat), 427
ISDN, compared to DSL, 393
ISP (Internet Service Provider), accessing
        AOL, 67

J

Java programming language, 131–132
JavaScript language, 131, 132
job information online, 110–111
JPEG (Joing Photographic Experts Group), 362
JPG format, 339, 362
junk mail, 236, 335–336
Junk Mail keyword, 81

K

Kathy Shrock's Guide for Educators Web site, 77
Keep as New button, 224
Kelley Blue Book, 108
keyboard shortcuts
    Ctrl+ (window size), 33, 55
    Ctrl+[(go forward a page), 159
    Ctrl+] (go back a page), 159
    Ctrl+C (copy), 233
    Ctrl+D (add a bookmark), 165
    Ctrl+F (Find), 33, 58, 225, 305
    Ctrl+K (Keyword window), 32
    Ctrl+M (Write Mail window), 255
    Ctrl+P (print), 224
    Ctrl+R (read mail), 216, 217
    Ctrl+V (adding to My Calendar), 53
    Ctrl+V (paste), 233

Keyword keyword, 6, 31
Kids Only Help, 38
Kids Only newsletter, 297
Kids Only option, 79
Kids Pager keyword, 76
KIDS Report, 308–309
Kids Search keyword, 87, 98
"knock knock" message, 279
Know It All newsletter, 298
KO Help keyword, 38

L

LAN (local area network), accessing AOL, 67
Language Options link, in Google, 192
Language Settings, AltaVista, 190
Launch button, 256
Learn Domains keyword, 311
Learn2 keyword, 115
learning, with multimedia technologies, 13
legal information resources, 203–204
libraries, 204–206
Library of Congress, 94, 206
LIBWEB Web site, 204
Like Television Web site, 413
links
    clicking on, 103
    definition, 15, 31, 129
    in e-mail messages, 220, 256–257
    types of, 144
    in Web pages, 358
list address, 301, 302
List Articles button, 323
List Setup tab, 273
ListProc software, 301, 306
Listserv software
    definition, 219
    features, 301–308
    managing discussion lists and newsletters, 291
Liszt keyword, 299
Liszt mailing lists, 299–300
local access numbers, 47
Local Guide Channel, 118
locations
    considerations, 69–70
    creating, 47
    definition, 68

LOL Online keyword, 244
Look at Message Boards option, AOL Search, 178
Look at Newsgroup Postings option, AOL Search, 178
L-Soft International, 301
lurking
    in mailing lists, 292–293
    in newsgroups, 331
Lycos
    features, 194
    FTP Search, 366–367
    non-Web search options, 189
    Open Directory and, 175
    Search Scrub, 87, 194

M

Macro virus, 225
Macromedia's Shockwave, 148
magazines, at Internet Public Library, 96–97
Mail button, 34
Mail Center, 38, 311
Mail Center keyword, 215, 216
Mail Contacts Online, 278, 279
Mail Controls keyword, 221
Mail Controls window, 81–82, 311
Mail Extras keyword, 257
Mail icon, 164
mail servers, 164
Mail⇨Address Book command, 249
Mail⇨Automatic AOL command, 230, 231, 248, 340
Mail⇨Filing Cabinet command, 227, 231
Mail⇨Mail Preferences⇨Mail command, 220
Mail⇨Mail Preferences command, 246–247
Mail⇨Mail Waiting to be Sent command, 240, 247–248
Mail⇨Read Mail⇨New Mail command, 217
Mail⇨Read Mail⇨Sent Mail command, 248
Mail⇨Recently Deleted Mail command, 224
mailing lists
    archives, 306
    creating, 307–308
    definition, 288–289
    features, 289–291
    finding, 299–301
    info refcard command, 305

Majordomo software, 301, 306
Making of America (MOA) digital archive, 206
Manage FC⇨Compact FC command, 228
MapQuest, 2, 184, 406
MapQuest keyword, 184, 406
Mark Unread button, 328
master account holder, 79
Mature Teen option, Parental Controls, 80
maximized windows, 33
Mayo Clinics Conditions & Treatments, 202
McAfee antivirus software, 380–381
Media Player
    features, 117, 146, 349
    launching, 309
    playing sound files, 147, 362, 411, 413
Media search, in AltaVista, 190
Medical Resources & References links, Health Channel, 202
Medline keyword, 203
Member Directory. *See* People Directory
Member Services keyword, 38
Members Helping Members, 38, 41
MemoWare Web site, 418
menus, improvements, 32–34
message boards, 40, 316–317, 341–342
messages. *See* e-mail
MetaCrawler, 196
meta-search services, 195, 196–198. *See also* search engines
MHM keyword, 38, 41
Microsoft Internet Explorer 5.5 browser, 36
Microsoft Office applications, 127
Microsoft products, accessibility features, 144
Microsoft Windows
    CE operating system, 234–235, 402, 403, 404
    decompressing files, 377
    Media Player, 147, 363–365
MID file extension, 363
MIDI sound files, 147, 149, 150, 339, 363
Mightywords, 418
MIM format, 226, 364
Mirriam-Webster Dictionary of Law, 204
misc newsgroup category, 320
misc.kids.moderated newsgroup, 333
Mobile Communicator, 420
Mobile keyword, 405, 406

modems
alternative to, 67, 392–393, 397–399
cable, 398
data transmission speed considerations, 390
DSL, 395
file attachments and, 224
limitations, 131
with Palm handheld organizer, 235
for Palm handheld organizers, 403
for PDAs, 402
satellite, 399
wireless, 405
mortgage lenders online, 109–110
MOV video format, 363
MovieFone
AOL and, 184
features, 2, 14, 52, 117–118, 406
Moviefone keyword, 406
movies, resources, 411–413
Mozilla project, 168
MP3 music files. *See also* **Media Player**
creating, 147
file extension, 363
finding, 194
messages with, 339
playing, 146, 349, 384, 413, 414
MP3.com Web site, 386
MPEG (Moving Pictures Experts Group), 363
MPG video format, 149, 363
MSIE (Microsoft Internet Explorer), 126, 137, 232
MTV Online, 413
MTV Online keyword, 413
MTVmessageboards keyword, 316
multimedia
definition, 13, 127
Lycos options, 189, 194
in newsgroup messages, 339
in Online Today newsletter, 309–310
plug-ins, 146–150
tools, 349
music. *See also* **sound files**
in newsgroup messages, 339
resources, 413–414
Music Library, 384
MusicMatch, 383–385
My Account Manager keyword, 106
**My AIM⇨Edit Options⇨Edit Preferences
command, 277, 280, 285**

**My AIM⇨Edit Options⇨Format Screen Name
command, 281**
My AIM⇨Edit Profile command, 275
My AIM⇨My Alert Window command, 270
My AIM⇨My Profile command, 275, 276
My AOL. *See* **AOL Anywhere**
My AOL keyword, 61
My Calendar
accessing, 70
customizing, 51–53
definition, 18, 47
features, 2, 30
My FTP Space, 354, 355, 356, 358–359, 423, 425
My News service. *See* **AOL Anywhere**
My Places, 60, 60–61
My Preferences, 220
My Profile button, 49
My Sidebar, Netscape 6, 157, 159–163
mythology resources, 89–90

N

Names keyword, 65
naming scheme, for newsgroup categories, 335
National Aquarium in Baltimore Web site, 77
**National Center for Missing and Exploited
Children, 79**
National Education Association, 86
National School Board Association, 86
National Weather Service, 94
navigation buttons, 27–28
Neighborhood Watch keyword, 76, 78
The Net. *See* **Internet**
NetHelp, 316
NetHelp keyword, 37, 41
netiquette, 243–246, 310, 328, 330–332
NetLibrary Web site, 418
NetNanny software, 87, 372, 381–382
Netscape 6
AOL Instant Messenger, 271
installing, 155–156
interface, 156–157
menu bar, 158–159
status bar, 164
taskbar, 157, 164
Web browsing, 162–163
Netscape Calendar. *See* **AOL Anywhere**

Netscape Composer, 158
Netscape keyword, 17, 155
Netscape Navigator
  accessing, 232
  AOL Instant Messenger, 271
  features, 155
NetTerm software, 382
networking, 67–69
New Contact button, 250
New Mail list, 218, 248
New Message button, 329
New Place button, 60
New Search option, AOL Search, 178
news newsgroup category, 320
news page, AOL Anywhere, 48–51
News Profiles keyword, 50
newsgroups
  accessing, 36, 38, 126–127
  adding to Favorites, 322–323
  on AOL, 315–317, 323–324
  categories, 317–321, 343
  compared to message boards, 316–317
  definition, 14
  examples, 332–333
  features, 315
  messages
    downloading, 340–341
    with files, 339
    reading, 326–328
    replying to, 329
    saving, 328
    searching for postings on Deja, 324–326
    sending, 328–330
  preferences, 83–84, 334–338
  registration requirements, 342
Newsgroups keyword, 36, 83, 315, 318, 320, 322, 325, 326, 331, 334, 337, 338, 340
newsletters. *See* electronic newsletters
Newsletters keyword, 42, 293, 294, 295, 297, 303, 402
newspapers, at Internet Public Library, 96–97
non-streaming video, 130–131
Northern Light, 195, 198
Norton Anti-Virus, 380–381
Notify AOL keyword, 63, 75, 76, 221, 237, 279, 310, 311

O

Office of Personnel Management, 111
Official time Web site, 94
offline help, 42–43
offline reading, 335
off-topic posting, 316
Old Mail list, 218
1-2-3 Publish, 423, 424
Onebox.com Web site, 421
online activity log, 29, 141
online auctions, 120–121
Online Broadcast Network, 414
online classes, 39–40, 115, 298
Online Classrooms keyword, 115
Online Mailbox. *See also* e-mail
  categories, 218–220
  features, 216–218
  messages from Listserv lists, 304
online safety
  AOL tools, 75
  tips, 76
  Web sites, 77–79
Online Safety Web site, 78
online searching. *See also* search engines
  authoritative resources, 198, 202–204
  challenges, 171
  compared to browsing, 172
  family-oriented, 86–88
  libraries, 204–206
  research, 97, 111
  sample queries, 175–177
  specialized searches, 171
  with special-purpose search collections, 198–204
  Web-only interface, 27
Online Timer, 18, 84–85
Online Today newsletter, 309–310
online voice mail, 421
online-only radio stations, 414
Open Directory project, 174, 175, 193, 194
Open Link command, 140
Open Link in New Window command, 140
organization tools, 48
Organize folder, 227–228
Original Message Text box, 329

P

Palm handheld organizer
accessing AOL Mail, 234–235, 402–405
ICQ and, 379
PeanutReader, 418
PAML (Publicly Accessible Mailing Lists), 300
Parental Controls
accessing, 31, 77–78
definition, 18, 75
Web filters and, 381
Parental Controls keyword, 75, 77, 80, 84
Password command, 66
passwords
account controls, 48
AIM, 281
for anonymous FTP sites, 360
for family members, 78, 79
guidelines for selecting, 66
for message boards, 342
online safety considerations, 75
for screen names, 65–66
Telnet, 382
Paste command, 139
PayPal.com Web site, 107, 120, 421
PDA keyword, 235, 402, 404
PDA (personal digital assistant), 16, 234–235,
401, 417–418, 419
PDF (Portable Document Format), 149, 418
PeanutReader, 418
People button, 35
People Connection keyword, 265
People Directory, 63, 183, 184
People Directory keyword, 183, 184, 185,
215, 268
People⇨Find a Buddy Wizard, 275
People⇨Send File to Buddy command, 280
Personal Choice toolbar, Netscape 6, 158, 165
Personal Finance Channel, 105
Personal Toolbar folder, Netscape 6, 165
Personalize window, 49
Personalogic keyword, 108, 119
Phone⇨ICQ Phone Center command, 421
Photo Developer keyword, 416
photographs, 30, 33. *See also* **digital images;**
graphics; You've Got Pictures
PhotoNet network, 415
phrase, in searches, 180

PICT (Mac graphics) files, 149
Picture Finder, 33
Picture Gallery, 33
picture icon, 258
pictures. *See* **digital images**
Pictures keyword, 120
player technology, 411–413
playlist, of MP3 songs, 385
plug-ins, 146–150
plus (+) key, 55
Pocket PCs, 234–235, 402–405, 404, 419
Pocket Press newsletter, 402
POP3 mail server, address, 164
Population Reference Bureau Web site, 95
Post Response window, 329
Post to Newsgroup box, 329
posting, definition, 316
Posting tab, for newsgroups, 335–336
Power Operators, AOL Search, 180–182
Power Search, on Deja Web site, 325
Preferences keyword, 47, 71, 141, 220
Preferences window
Netscape 6, 167
Newsgroups, 337
Presidents on the Net, 90–91
Press keyword, 401
Print button, 249
Print Center, 415
Print Central Web site, 224
Print command, 139
Print menu, 224
Print Target command, 140
Print⇨Print command, 224, 328
Printing Center, 18
printing e-mail messages, 223–224
Privacy Preferences, 63, 269
product reviews, 115
Programs⇨Netscape 6⇨Netscape 6
command, 156
Project Gutenberg, 205
Project Perseus, 205
Properties command, 139
Properties option, Internet Explorer, 142
proprietary service, 26
protocol, 132
public access, to anonymous FTP sites, 360–361
public libraries, rare holdings, 206
publishing revolution, 13
Publishing Tools keyword, 361

Q

Quick Buddy. *See* AIM Express
Quick Check, 2
Quick Checkout, 113
Quick Checkout keyword, 114
Quicken.com Financial Health Checkup, 106
QuickTime player, 149–150, 363, 411. *See also*
        RealAudio
quotation marks, in search queries, 181
quoting, in replies to e-mail messages, 221, 222,
        233, 244

R

radio stations, rebroadcasts, 414
Radio Wall Street, 414
radio, with AOL Plus, 16
Read button, 36
Read Mail window, 221–222
Read My Newsgroups list, 322, 323, 326–328, 337
Real JukeBox, 383–385
RealAudio, 117, 147, 309, 413, 414
RealGuide.com Web site, 413
RealJukebox, 147
RealNetworks, 147
RealPlayer, 117, 146, 413
RealVideo, 411
rec newsgroup category, 320
rec.arts.books.childrens newsgroup, 333
rec.food.* newsgroup, 333
rec.pets.dogs newsgroup, 333
Refdesk.com Web site, 88, 98
reference resources, 88–97
refining online searches, 177–182, 198
Refresh command, 139
regional categories, of newsgroups, 321
regional searches, 198
registration requirements, for newsgroups, 342
relevancy ranking, for online searches, 177
Reload button, in AOL's browser, 137
Reminder keyword, 61, 113–114
Remote Directory Name box, 358
Remove Filter button, 337
Reply button, Read mail window, 221–222
Research & Learn Channel, 298

residential addresses, finding, 183
responding
    to messages from Listserv lists, 304
    to newsgroups, 329
return receipt, 246, 248
Review Original Message button, 233
Rheingold, Howard, 342
Right-click a link command, 140
right-clicking
    graphics on Web pages, 140
    text on Web pages, 138
ripping CDs, 384
Roget's II: Thesaurus, 92
Rollingstone keyword, 413
Run Automatic AOL Now button, 231

S

Safe Kids Web site, 79
Safe Surfing Web site, 78
SafeSearch, in Google, 87
Safeteens.com Web site, 79
satellite transmissions, 393
satellite-based connection, 399–400
Save As dialog box, 140
Save Background As command, 138
Save Picture As command, 140
Save Target As command, 140
Save To FC button, 230
saving
    e-mail messages, 223
    newsgroup messages, 328
SavvySearch, 196
scanner, controlling, 33
schedule. *See* My Calendar
Schedule Automatic AOL button, 231
sci newsgroup category, 320–321
Scout Report, 308–309
screen names. *See also* Buddy List; instant
        messages (IMs)
    AIM, 62, 271, 280–282
    assigning to age brackets, 79
    download controls, 82
    DSL and, 399
    for family members, 78
    Favorite Places for, 59
    finding, 63

Continued

screen names *(continued)*
guidelines for selecting, 65–66
news profiles for, 50
online storage space and, 355
switching, 33, 34
Screen Names keyword, 78
screen resolution, changing, 66
Search Alerts, Northern Light, 195
Search All Newsgroups window, 323
Search Discussions, at Deja Web site, 324–326
search engines. *See also* **meta-search services;**
online searching
AltaVista, 87, 175, 190–191
compared to Web directories, 172
definition, 172
Dogpile, 175
filters, 87, 189, 193, 194
Google, 87, 175, 191–193
HotBot, 175
Lycos, 87, 175, 189, 194
Northern Light, 195
search results, 176–177
translation services, 189
Search Engine Watch, 171, 189, 309
Search for AOL Access Numbers window, 70
Search keyword, 20, 105, 174, 180
Search menu, Netscape 6, 159
Search Options page, AOL Search, 179–180
Search Scrub, in Lycos, 87, 194
Search sidebar, Netscape 6, 160
searching. *See* **online searching**
Searchopolis Web site, 87
security issues. *See also* **AOL@School; Parental**
Controls; passwords
account controls, 48
AIM passwords, 281
anti-virus software, 339, 380
cable Internet connection, 398–399
DSL connection, 396, 397
NetNanny software, 381–382
newsgroups, 335–336
Privacy Preferences, 63, 268–270, 277
shopping online, 116
third-party software, 163
Select All command, 138
Send a Buddy Chat Invitation button, 279
Send Later option, 245, 247–248, 258
Send To box, 241

Send To FC menu, 230
Sent Mail list, 218, 248
separators, for bookmarks, 167
server, 132
Set as Wallpaper command, 140
Set Up Signatures window, 260
Setting⇨Preferences, 34, 47
Settings button, 35
Settings dialog box, 142–143
Settings menu, 47–48, 77, 113
Settings⇨Control Panels command, 397
Settings⇨Preferences command, 66, 71, 134
Settings⇨Preferences⇨Font, Text & Graphics
command, 254–255
Settings⇨Preferences⇨Mail command, 218,
246–247
Settings⇨Preferences⇨Passwords command, 66
Setup button, 68
700 Great Sites for Kids, 77
shareware
choosing, 374–375
registering, 373
Shareware keyword, 375
Shift-Click technique, 58
Shockwave, 148
Shop Direct keyword, 403, 417
Shop@AOL, 2, 13, 112–117
Shop@AOL keyword, 384, 402, 415
Shop@Netscape, 164
Shopping Assistant, 113–114
Shopping keyword, 13, 112, 114
ShoutCast Web site, 414
Shoutcast.com Web site, 386
Show Files Downloaded button, 225
Sigh Off⇨Switch Screen Names command, 34
Sign Off menu, 33
Sign On icon, 235
Sign On window, 66, 399
signatures, e-mail, 251, 259–261, 329, 336
signoff command, 306
Similar Pages option, Google, 193
Site Seeing on the Internet, 79
small business resources, 203
Smart Download program, 156
"smart" wireless cell phones, 419
Smile button, 278
smileys, 244

Smithsonian Institution, list of public libraries, 206
SMPT mail server, address, 164
soc newsgroup category, 321
software
creating CDs, 383–385
downloading, 349–353
finding, 375–376
freeware, 373–375
shareware, 373–375
software libraries, 82
Sonicnet, 184, 413
Sort Folder By button, 229
sorting
e-mail, 17
newsgroup postings, 335
sound files
downloading, 225–226
file extensions, 362–363
online resources, 190
playing, 147
Spam keyword, 252
spamming, 304, 311, 332
Special Collections, Northern Light, 195
specialized searches, 171, 198–204
Speed keyword, 13
Spinner service, 385–386, 414
splitter, for cable Internet connection, 398
Sprint PCS Wireless Web, 406
square brackets, indicating people not using AIM, 278–279
stamps.com keyword, 237
Start Menu⇨Settings⇨Folder Options command, 364
Start Menu, viewing hardware setup, 29
Start⇨Documents command, 309
statistical data, 94–96
status bar
in AOL's browser, 137–138
Netscape 6, 164
Status tab, online activity log, 29, 141
Stocks sidebar, Netscape 6, 161
Stop button, in AOL's browser, 136
Store Password checkbox, 235
stored resources, 142, 143
streaming sound, 147, 383
streaming video, 149

Stroud's Consummate Winsock Applications, 374, 375
Studyweb.com Web site, 86
subdirectories, creating, 358
subfolders, in Filing Cabinet, 229
subject line, e-mail
messages from Listserv lists, 304
Re: in, 222
sorting messages by, 219
subscribing
to mailing lists, 289, 302–303
to newsgroups, 322
switching screen names, 33, 34
synchronized address books, 17

T

tabbed interface, 160
tables, on Web pages, 130
talk newsgroup category, 321
taskbar, Netscape 6, 157, 164
Tasks menu, Netscape 6, 159
Tasks⇨Instant Messenger command, 271
Tasks⇨Mail command, 164
TechWeb's Technology News, 205
Teens Channel, 316
Telecomm Digest, 291
telephony software, 379, 421
Telnet, resources, 382
Temporary Internet files. *See* cache
Terms of Service, 76, 317
text files
definition, 84
in e-mail messages, 258
file extensions, 362
text in e-mail messages, embellishing, 254–255
thesaurus, accessing, 33
third-party Internet software, 15, 361
threads, in newsgroups, 326
Thrive Online, 202
Time Warner Trade Publishing, 418
timer, restricting kids' online access, 84
Today in History, Library of Congress, 94
toolbar
AOL 6.0
Favorite Places folder, 56
icons, adding, 66

improvements, 2, 28, 34, 112
Netscape 6, 156, 158
Topica, creating mailing lists, 307–308
TOS keyword, 76, 311
Tower Records, 117
tracking Web activity, 141
translating Web pages, 158, 189
Travel keyword, 119
troll, 331
troubleshooting, error messages, 134
TrulyGlobal Internet Phone, 421
Tucows
MusicMatch, 383
shareware, 374, 375
type size, for e-mail messages, 255
typefaces, for e-mail messages, 255

U

Ultimate Band List, 386
University of Kansas FTP site, 354–355
University of Leiden, Collection of Special
    Search Engines, 198
University of Michigan
Argus Clearinghouse, 200
Making of America (MOA) digital archive, 206
University of Wisconsin, Scout Report, 308–309
unsending e-mail messages, 245, 249
Unsolicited Bulk E-Mail Policy, 311
unsubscribe command, 306
unzipping files, 227, 377
uploading
data transmission speed considerations, 400
files, 120, 387–388
Web pages, 355–358
upstream data transfer, 393
urban legends, 332
URL (Universal Resource Locator)
copying to the Clipboard, 140
definition, 30
Web addresses, 103, 132
U.S. government agencies, 95–96
U.S. weather, 94
usability, 3, 378
USAJobs Web site, 111
USB port, 396, 399
used car information, 108

username, Telnet, 382
USGOVSEARCH Web site, 195
Utilities tab, 29
Utilities⇨Delete command, 358
Utilities⇨Rename command, 358
UU encoded files, 226

V

Vcall Web site, 414
version numbers, 29
video files
file extensions, 363
formats, 149–150
online resources, 190
on Web pages, 130
videoconferencing, 379
Vidnet Web site, 413
View Health Web sites option, AOL Search, 178
View Kids Only sites option, AOL Search, 178
View menu, Netscape 6, 158
View Personal Home Pages option, AOL Search,
    178
View Source command, 139
View Source option in Web browser, 127
View⇨Sidebar command, 159
View⇨Translate command, Netscape 6, 158
Viewing tab, for newsgroups, 334–335
Virus Checker tab, AIM, 280
Virus keyword, 75, 225, 280, 359, 380
viruses, avoiding, 380–381
Visual Help keyword, 38, 39
VLIB (WWW Virtual Library), 199–200, 204
Vocaltec's Internet Phone, 421
voice mail, 421
"Voice over IP" service, 420
voice recognition, 144

W

W3 Consortium, 144, 378
Wall Street reports, 414
WAV sound files, 147, 150, 362
weather forecasts, 94
Web. *See* **World Wide Web**

Web addresses. *See* URL (Universal Resource Locator)
Web Art keyword, 257
Web Boards, 341–342. *See also* message boards
Web browser. *See also* AOL browser; Netscape 6
    cache, 29
    definition, 125–126
    home page, 168
    online safety considerations, 87
    preferences, 48
Web controls, setting in Parental Controls, 82–83
Web directory, 172
Web of Online Dictionaries, 93–94
Web Pad, 405
Web pages. *See also* URL (Universal Resource Locator)
    accessing, 104
    creating, 127, 423–425
    design considerations, 129, 131
    editing, 158
    elements, 127–133
    file extensions, 361
    filetype extensions for, 132
    linking, 358
    storage space for, 425
    translating, 189
    translation, 158
    uploading, 355–358
Web Search option, AOL Search, 178
Web server, 393, 397
Web sites. *See also* specific names of Web sites
    family-oriented, 77–79
    linking to from Windows desktop, 70
Web-based newsletters, 291, 294
WebWhacker software, 87
Welcome Screen
    improvements, 2, 30–31
    links on, 103
    My Places selections, 61
    Parental Controls, 77
    You've Got Mail icon, 216
    You've Got Pictures, 30, 257
Whatis.com Web site, 91
What's Related sidebar, Netscape 6, 160
White Pages keyword, 183
wildcards, in search queries, 181–182
Winamp software, 349, 386, 413, 414

Window menu, 33
Window⇨Add Top Window, 33
Window⇨Add Top Window to Favorite Places, 55
Windows CE devices, 234–235, 402, 403, 404
WinZip utility, 226, 353, 377
wireless cell phones, 401–402, 405–406, 419
wireless transmissions, 393
Workplace keyword, 111
world libraries, 204
World Wide Web. *See also* search engines; Web browser
    accessing, 171
    AOL presence, expanded, 2
    conferencing systems, 342
    definition, 125
    development, 15, 125
    downloading software, 349–353
    FAQs, 338–339
    message boards, 341–342
    navigation, 103
    reference resources, 88–97
    usability guidelines, 378
    Web addresses, 6
    Web filters, 381
    Web-based newsletters, 291, 294
Write button, 36
Write Mail window, 213, 255, 260
WS_FTP software, 387–388
WWW Consortium, 144, 378
WWW Virtual library (VLIB), 199–200, 204

X

XML (Extensible Markup Language), 91

Y

Yellow Pages keyword, 183
Young Teen option, Parental Controls, 80
Your Town service, 109
YouthTech message board, 342
You've Got Mail icon, 216
"You've Got Pictures"
    downloading digital images, 257
    reference guide, 30

storing digital images, 415
You've Got Pictures keyword, 128, 415, 416
YT keyword, 342

Z

ZDNet Web site, 374, 375, 376
zipped files, 227, 362

Shop With Confidence At AOL Shop Direct!

1. Guaranteed Security

Millions of customers have shopped online safely with AOL and you can too! AOL uses advanced encryption technology to help insure the security, accuracy, and privacy of your AOL Shop Direct transaction. AOL protects you against liability for fraudulent charges if reported promptly to your credit card provider.

2. Guaranteed Satisfaction

AOL Buyers search the marketplace for today's best-quality products, and, with the purchasing power of our 20 million customers, AOL Shop Direct can bring them to you at terrific values. YOUR SATISFACTION IS GUARANTEED BY AOL Shop Direct. If you are not satisfied with your purchase, for any reason, return it within 30 days of receipt for a full refund, including original shipping and handling. How many other online companies offer that?

3. Guaranteed Service

We make every effort to provide a quick, trouble-free transaction and prompt delivery of your purchase. However, should you have a question or problem, you are entitled to quick and courteous assistance. Call us toll-free at 1-888-299-0329.

AMERICA
Online.
So easy to use,
no wonder it's #1

It's easy to get your photos online - just upload your pictures from a digital camera or scanner and discover all the fun things you can do with them! Send pictures to friends and family through email, create greeting cards, school projects, invitations, calendars - you can even order personalized gifts with your photos on t-shirts, mugs and other items at the online "You've Got Pictures" store.

America Online's

PhotoCam plus

LCD DIGITAL CAMERA

Download Your Pictures Directly To Your PC!

PhotoCam Plus is a high-quality yet affordable digital camera that allows you to create,edit, share and send photos to friends and family. It comes with an easy to follow manual and custom editing software.

America Online's Guide to

Pictures Online

Learn How Easy It Is To Enjoy Your Pictures Online!

This easy to follow guide shows your how to get your pictures online and share them with family and friends. Loaded with expert advice on everything from taking better pictures to selecting the right hardware, it walks you through AOL's "You've Got Pictures" service and explains just how easy it is to view, share and use your photos once you have them online.

America Online's

Digital Imaging Made Easy™

Explore The Many Things You Can Do Online With Your Pictures!

Learn about digital imaging in minutes with easy-to-follow multimedia videos. This CD shows you how to upload your pictures from a digital camera or scanner, edit your photos and share them online in email, web pages, and albums. Discover how easy it is to receive, view and personalize your photos online with AOL's "You've Got Pictures" service.

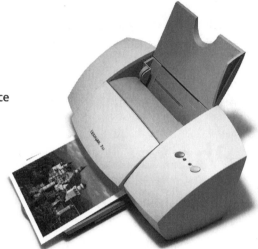

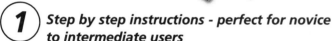